بسم الله الرحمن الرحيم

A SUFI STUDY *of* ḤADITH

الله نور السموات والأرض

A SUFI STUDY *of* ḤADITH

Ḥaqīqat al-Ṭarīqa min al-Sunna al-'Anīqa

MAWLĀNĀ ASHRAF ʿALĪ THĀNAWĪ

Translated by

Shaykh Yusuf Talal Delorenzo

TURATH PUBLISHING

ISBN: 978-1-906949-04-4

Published by:
Turath Publishing
79 Mitcham Road +44 (20) 8767 3666
London SW19 9PD www.turath.co.uk

Author	Mawlānā Ashraf ʿAlī Thānawī
Translation	Shaykh Yusuf Talal Delorenzo
Editor	Yusuf Arvasi
Referencing	Usman Madani, Deoband (India)
Trans. references	Ibrahim Amin
General editor	Yahya Batha
Proofreading	Muhammad Ansa, Uthman Ibrahim-Morrison
Indexing	Uthman Ibrahim-Morrison

British Library Cataloguing in Publication Data
Thānawī, Ashraf ʿAlī
Ṣūfī Study of Ḥadīth: *Ḥaqīqat al-Ṭarīqa min al-Sunna al-'Anīqa*
I. Title

Cover design	Abdallateef Whiteman (www.cwdm.co.uk)
Design and typesetting	ARM (info@whitethreadpress.com)
Printed by	Megaprinters, Istanbul, Turkey (export@mega.com.tr)
Reprinted 2014	

Distributors for UK and Europe
Azhar Academy Ltd.
54–56 Little Ilford Lane +44 (20) 8891 19797
Manor Park sales@azharacademy.com
London E12 5QA www.azharacademy.com

Distributors for America and Canada
White Thread Press
www.whitethreadpress.com
inf@whitethreadpress.com

Distributors for South Africa
Darul-Ihsan Research and Education Centre
www.darulihsan.com +27 (31) 577 7868
motala.m@darulihsan.com +27 (31) 577 6012 (fax)

For My Sheikh
Mawlānā Muḥammad Yūsuf Binnorī,
at whose behest I translated this work.
May Allah illuminate his resting place and
elevate his status in Jannah. Āmīn.

Contents

Translator's Introduction

MAWLĀNĀ ASHRAF ʿALĪ THĀNAWĪ was born in the village of Thānā Bhawan, not far to the south of Delhi, in the Indian district of Muzaffar Nagar, in the year 1863. He had his early schooling in the same village and, at age thirteen or fourteen, began his formal education a few miles away at the institution known as Dār al-ʿUlūm at Deoband with some of the most gifted scholars of Islam ever to appear in the subcontinent.[1]

By the age of twenty-one, Mawlānā Thānawī had satisfied his teachers of his facility with the classical disciplines of Islam and was graduated. In that year he became a teacher at Kānpur[2] and, by written recommendation of his teacher at Deoband, Mawlānā Rashīd Gangohī, was accepted as a spiritual disciple to Hājī 'Imdād Allāh, the sheikh of the Chishti order of Sufis who had sought refuge in Makka after the unsuccessful attempt to dislodge the British imperialists from India in 1857. At the end of his twenty-first year, Mawlānā Thānawī himself went to Makka to perform the Ḥajj, and to benefit from the spiritual care of his sheikh.[3]

On his return to Kānpur, Mawlānā Thānawī busied himself with teaching and writing, alongside his spiritual exercises of *dhikr* and *shughal*, until the latter compelled him to seek once again the companionship of his sheikh at Makka. Thus, he traveled a second time to Makka where he remained for several years in the company of Hājī 'Imdād Allāh. Shortly after Mawlānā Thānawī returned to Kānpūr in 1897, Hājī 'Imdād Allāh wrote to him with the following instructions:

1 Sheikh Muḥammad 'Ikram, *Mawj-e-Kawthar*, Urdu (Lahore, Pakistan: Idārā-e-Thaqāfat-e-Islāmiyya, 1975), p. 204.

2 Ibid., Mawlānā Thānawī taught at both the Fayd-e-ʿĀm Madrasa and at Madrasa Jāmi' al-ʿUlūm in Kānpūr over a period of some fourteen years.

3 Sayyid Sulaymān Nadwī, *Yād-e-Raftagān*, Urdu (Karachi, Pakistan: Maktabā al-Sharq, 1955) p. 284.

> It is better that you go back to Thānā Bhawan. In fact, I hope that a great multitude of people will benefit from you both spiritually and academically. There, you shall bring our mosque and *madrasa* back to life.

On this auspicious note, Mawlānā left Kanpur and returned to his native Thānā Bhawan. True to the hopes of his sheikh, Mawlānā Thānawī revived the mosque and the *madrasa* at Thānā Bhawan and, for the next fifty years benefited the academic and spiritual lives of multitudes of subcontinent Muslims.

The Nature of Islamic Education in the Subcontinent

It is essential at this juncture that the reader understands something of the nature of the training and education received by Mawlānā Thānawī. In fine, the ideal advanced by Islam with regard to the education and upbringing of the individual Muslim is the achievement of moral and spiritual equilibrium. The Qur'ān says: "We have established you as a middlemost nation" (2:143). Thus, the objectives of the founders of Dār al-ᶜUlūm at Deoband included the blending of book learning with character building, of *Sharīᶜa* with *ṭarīqah*, of the *fiqh* of Abū Hanīfa with authentic ḥadīth, of the opinions of the pious predecessors with the revivalist scholars of succeeding ages and so on, in an attempt to tread a middle path between the various Islamic intellectual and spiritual trends and schools of thought.

As the Sharīᶜa and knowledge of the Qur'ān and the Sunna are the basis of all Islamic intellectual activity, the emphasis at Dār al-ᶜUlūm was on the teaching of the classical Islamic disciplines, beginning with Arabic grammar and proceeding with increasing complexity through subjects like rhetoric, logic, philosophy, jurisprudence, theology, and the sciences of the Qur'ān and the Sunna. While the student was engaged in the acquisition of these subjects, he was subjected to a rigorous daily schedule of classroom attendance, group-study sessions, and congregational worship in the mosque. Nearly all students boarded in the madrasa hostels or in the homes of their teachers, and there was very little time for leisurely pursuits.

The Place of Ṭarīqa in the Madrasa System of Education

During the period of study (*taḥṣīl*, or aquisition), however, only the formal and essential modes of worship were encouraged. Nonetheless, it was carefully impressed upon the students that after graduation they were to seek the spiritual guidance of an accomplished sheikh. Nor were the students encouraged to prefer one *ṭarīqa* to another. The important thing in the selection of a sheikh was his adherence to the Sharīᶜa.[4]

4 For Mawlānā Thānawī's own teaching on the subject see his *Qaṣd al-Sabīl*, "The Third Teaching."

Indeed, to the ʿUlamā' of Deoband the value of *taṣawwuf* was in its translating knowledge into action, and learning into deeds. One did not pledge allegiance to a sheikh in order to become a Sufi, but in order to become a practising Muslim. It was not escapist mysticism that the ʿUlamā' of Deoband were seeking for their students, but the way to *iḥsān* or the complementary inner state which gives depth and added meaning to the outer state of Islam. Essentially, the revivalist movement that began in Deoband and which aimed at remedying excesses in Indian Muslim society, was propelled by a group of scholars who added emotional fervor in their practice of Islam to their deep understanding of its sources and principles. It was in this atmosphere of learning and devotion that Mawlānā Ashraf ʿAlī Thānawī grew and prospered.

Mawlānā's Writings

Mawlānā Thānawī's most obvious contribution to the Muslim community of the subcontinent was his incredible output of literature on Islamic subjects.

Jalāl al-Dīn Suyūṭī (d. 911 AH) is generally known as the most prolific author in the history of Islamic scholarship, and his writings are numbered at over five hundred.[5] Mawlānā Thānawī's writings have been variously numbered between six and eight hundred.[6] In addition, he maintained a voluminous daily correspondence with his khalīfahs and murīds, and his published lectures and public addresses number in the hundreds. Moreover, Mawlānā's gifted disciples undertook hundreds of other works at Mawlānā 's insistence, and with his guidance, so that any definite accounting of the number of his works is next to impossible.

The subject matter of Mawlānā's works included all the classical Islamic disciplines. Mawlānā's *Bayān al-Qur'ān*, in three volumes, is undoubtedly the most erudite of all commentaries on the Qur'ān in the Urdu language. At the other end of the spectrum of Qur'ānic scholarship, Mawlānā's *Jamāl al-Qur'ān* became the standard textbook for students of *tajwīd*, or the science of Qur'ānic recitation, throughout the subcontinent; and remains so to this day. Mawlānā's other works on the various Qur'ānic sciences are as numerous as they are instructive.

Likewise, Mawlānā Thānawī wrote with authority on subjects like *ḥadīth*, *fiqh*, *'uṣūl al-fiqh*, *'aqidah*, *logic*, *philosophy*, *rhetoric*, *grammar*, and much else. In the field of *taṣawwuf*, however, the Mawlānā's writings are particularly interesting for their scholarship and variety. Among the works which best represent the breadth

5 Jalāl al-Dīn Suyūṭī, *Fihrist Kutub al-Suyūṭī* (Madras, Maṭbaʿ al-ʿAjā'ib, 1379 AH). See also ʿUmar Riḍā Kuḥālaḥ, *Muʿjam al-Mu'allifīn* (Damascus: Maṭbaʿh al-Taraqqī, 1958), Vol.5, p. 128.

6 Munshī 'Abd al-Raḥmān Khān, *Sīrat-i-Ashraf* (Multan: Idāra-e-Nashr al-Maʿārif, 1956), p. 368. A separate volume of bibliography, entitled *Ta'lifāt-e-Ashrafiyya*, was compiled by Muḥammad ʿAbd al-Haq Fateḥpūrī and published separately in 1353 AH.

of his vision are his *Sīrat-e-Ḥallāj*, a biography of Manṣūr al-Ḥallāj and an exposition of his teachings on *taṣawwuf*, *Sharḥ Fuṣūṣ al-Ḥikam*, *Kalīd-i-Mathnawī*, *ʿIrfān-e-Ḥāfiẓ*, *Masā'il-e-Sulūk*, *al-Takashshuf*, and *al-Tasharruf*. These latter two works will be the subject of detailed discussion later on in this introduction.

Mawlānā's Perception of Taṣawwuf

There is no denying the importance of Mawlānā's written work. Yet, of no less importance to the Muslims of the subcontinent was Mawlānā Thānawī's spiritual guidance. It had become a lamentable fact of life in India that *taṣawwuf* had degenerated to such a degree that there was little to distinguish a yogi from a Sufi. The *ṭarīqas*, or Sufi orders had become social clubs and sources of income for the chosen few. Indeed, in most orders *khilāfah* or spiritual leadership had become a matter of inheritance, like the feudal lordship, which was the bane of Indian society.

Mawlānā Thānawī's contribution was to re-establish in the public mind the connection between *Sharīʿa* and *ṭarīqa*. This he accomplished to a certain extent in his writings. However, the real breakthrough in this potent field for the reform of the individual and society was made by Mawlānā Thānawī, the sheikh and *murshid*, not by Mawlānā Thānawī, the author and scholar.

The difference should be easy to understand. It is one thing to spread the word, and another thing entirely to be an example of the living word. Mawlānā Ashraf ʿAlī Thānawī went a step further. As the result of his attention and guidance, scores of others themselves became living examples of the word of Islam and, in turn, influenced hundreds and thousands of Muslims. The register of Mawlānā Thānawī's spiritual successors (*khalīfahs*) includes some of the most accomplished, learned, pious, and spiritually influential Muslims of the century.[7]

In bringing the Islamic ideal of equilibrium to the field of spiritual guidance, Mawlānā Thānawī established a number of criteria for his disciples. To begin with, all disciples were classified as belonging to one or another of the following four categories:[8] (1) scholar and single, (2) non-scholar and single, (3) scholar and married, (4) non-scholar and married.

The reasons for such a division would have to do with the kind of opportunity a disciple had for attention to spiritual disciplines and exercises and the kind of understanding he/she brought to them. What is significant is the Mawlānā's acceptance of the circumstances and responsibilities of his followers, and his attempt to reasonably accommodate all those interested in pursuing a spiritual relationship. Thereafter, disciples were classified as possessing limited, average,

7 For a complete list of Mawlānā's *Khalīfahs*, see: Munshī ʿAbd al-Raḥmān Khān, op. cit., p. 648–655

8 See *Qaṣd al-Sabīl*, op. cit.

or advanced abilities, and for each group separate sets of disciplines and exercises, as well as reading matter, were prescribed.[9]

One exceptionally lucid work, also entitled *Ḥaqīqat al-ṭarīqa*, or *The Truth About the Way*, was required reading for all of Mawlānā's disciples at the time of their entering the Sufi order.

As this work is quite brief, and yet sheds a good deal of light on Mawlānā Thānawī's teachings, it is translated here into English for the benefit of the reader.

ḤAQĪQAT AL-ṬARĪQA: THE TRUTH ABOUT THE WAY

The Essence of Inner Conduct

1. Neither *kashf* (visions) nor *karāmah* (minor miracles) are required or expected.
2. On the Day of Judgment no one (other than yourself) will be responsible for your salvation.
3. There is no promise that your worldly affairs will improve (as a result of your becoming a disciple of this Sufi order), or through your tying talismans or charms around your necks, or that you will win court cases, or have an increase in income, or be cured of disease, or be granted knowledge of what is in the future.
4. Your behaviour will not be reformed merely through the attentions of your sheikh, nor will you cease to think evil thoughts. You will not automatically engage in worship without even having to resolve to do so. And your knowledge and understanding of the Qur'ān and Islam will not necessarily register any sort of increase.
5. There is no promise that you will attain any inner spiritual states, or even that you will find pleasure in the performance of worship or spiritual exercises, or that you will not be beset by alien thoughts while in worship. There is no guarantee that you will wash your sins away with your tears of remorse.
6. In your performance of spiritual exercises you need never see mystic lights or hear voices from the Unseen.
7. You may never have a sublime or meaningful dream or receive guidance from above.

On the contrary the real objective is to please the Almighty, and the way to achieve this objective is by complete adherence to the Sharīʿa.

---

9 See Thānawī's *al-Takashshuf ʿan muhimmāt al-taṣawwuf* (Lahore: Sajjād Publishers, 1960) p. 30.

Certain of the precepts of the Sharīʿa have to do with the believer's outer state, like prayer, fasting, ḥajj, zakāh, marriage, divorce, discharging marital responsibilities, oaths and their expiation, buying and selling, legal procedures and giving witness, bequests, inheritance, meeting and socializing, greeting and entertaining, and so on. Knowledge of these matters is termed *fiqh*.

Certain others have to do with the inner state, such as one's love for the Almighty, awe of Him, remembrance of Him, acceptance of His decree, or one's decreasing love of the worldly, or lack of greed, or being conscientious in worship, or sincere in religious matters, or one's lack of contempt for others, or lack of conceit, or having control over one's temper, and so on. These matters are termed *sulūk*, or inner conduct.

Then, in the same way that a Muslim is to obey the rules of *fiqh* in his/her outward behaviour, he/she must also obey the rules of inner conduct. Moreover, it is usually as a result of some inner imbalance that irregularities occur in one's behaviour or practice of Islam. For example, a decrease in love for the Almighty might result in a lack of attention to daily prayers, or to one's saying them hurriedly. Likewise, as a result of avarice, one might not give zakāh or go on Ḥajj. Or, owing to one's self-aggrandizement, or to one's inability to check one's anger, one may commit injustice on another or usurp his/her rights. Even if one were to recognise one's fault, and then take care to correct it, the fact remains that unless some sort of inner rectification takes place, one will be sure to lapse in one's efforts to correct the problem.

Thus, for the above reasons, it should be obvious that the rectification of inner conduct is essential. Yet, the problem is that inner ailments are difficult to detect and, even if they are detected, it is no easy matter to prescribe a proper cure for them. In fact, even if the cure were to be known, the taking of the medicine is nearly always distasteful.

For these reasons an accomplished sheikh is required; one who will be able to recognise and diagnose such spiritual maladies and then prescribe for them the appropriate cure. Moreover, the sheikh should have the power to create within his disciple the ability to rectify himself/herself. For this purpose, the sheikh will require the disciple to engage in certain spiritual exercises and disciplines, such as *dhikr*, which in itself is a form of worship.

Basically, then, the disciple will have to do two things. The first is essential, and that is that he/she will have to adhere to the inner and outer precepts of the Sharīʿa. The second is recommended, and that is that he/she engages in much *dhikr*. The result of the first will be the attainment of Allāh's pleasure, and closeness to Him; while the result of the second will be increase in Allāh's pleasure and closeness to Him.

This, then, is the essence of the way to inner conduct, and its essential objectives.[10]

Taṣawwuf and the Study of Ḥadīths

From the foregoing, the reader will have gained a clear understanding of the kind of *taṣawwuf* taught and practised by Mawlānā Thānawī. Further insight into his perceptions in general about *taṣawwuf* may be had from the author's own introduction to this volume, and to his numerous works on the subject. Yet, however one may attempt to characterize Mawlānā Thānawī's brand of *taṣawwuf*, by calling it reformist, fundamentalist, puritanical, or whatever, the fact is that it was, above all, Sharīʿa oriented. As the second source of the Sharīʿa of Islam, the ḥadīths of the Prophet, Allāh bless him and give him peace, play a tremendously important role in defining and clarifying the principles and practices of *taṣawwuf*. It was for this reason that Mawlānā Thānawī turned his attention to writing *taṣawwuf* related commentary on ḥadīth literature.

Taṣawwuf Related Commentary on Ḥadīths

It is interesting to note, furthermore, that the early Sufi writers, if ever they did comment on ḥadīths, did so only in the context of their discussion of other subjects. Thus, while the classical Sufi writers like al-Qushairī, al-Muḥāsibī, Abū Ṭālib al-Makkī and al-Ghazzālī may have quoted profusely from ḥadīth literature, they never wrote separate works of commentary on ḥadīths.

In fact, the reputation of Sufis with regard to ḥadīths is somewhat tarnished. The reason for this, of course, was the admission by several well-known Sufis that they had actually fabricated ḥadīths and then ascribed them to the Prophet, Allāh bless him and give him peace, albeit with the best of intentions. Ibn Nuʿaym's *Ḥilyat al 'Awliyā'* contains several examples of such Sufi-narrators, as do most of the works on *mawḍūʿāt* or spurious ḥadīths, and the works devoted to *ḍuʿafā'*, or the biographies of weak and unreliable narrators.

At the same time, some of the greatest scholars of ḥadīths were themselves Sufis of one order or another. Ḥadīth masters like Sufyān al-Thawrī, Ibn al-Mubārak, Abū Ṭāhir al-Silāfī and others come immediately to mind. Later on, ḥadīth scholars of the calibre of al-Nawāwī, al-Suyūṭī, and al-ʿIrāqī were renowned as Sufis. Indeed, Hindustan had a tradition of producing Sufi scholars of ḥadīths, like al-Ṣāghānī, Sheikh ʿAbd al-Ḥaqq Muḥaddith Dehlawī, Shāh Walī Allāh, Sheikh Ṭāhir al-Pattanī, Shāh ʿAbd al-ʿAzīz, and many others. In fact, of Sheikh Nizām al-'Awliyā', perhaps the most famous of all Indian Sufis, it was written that he had

10 Mawlānā Thānawī, op. cit., p. 33–39.

not only read al-Ṣāghānī's collection of ḥadīth entitled *Mashāriq al-Anwār*, but that he had committed the entire work to memory as well.[11]

Certainly, the ʿUlamā' of Deoband were the inheritors of this tradition. Mawlānā Yaʿqūb, Mawlānā Gangohī, Mawlānā Qāsim Nānautwī, Sheikh al-Hind, Mawlānā Anwar Kashmīrī, Mawlānā Madanī, and Mawlānā Thānawī himself were all examples of Sufi *muḥaddithīn*. Finally, scores if not hundreds of Mawlānā Thānawī's students found fame as scholars of the ḥadīth sciences.

Mawlānā's Works of Commentary on Ḥadīths

It is in the works of Mawlānā Thānawī alone, of all the scholars mentioned in the paragraphs above, that we find works exclusively devoted to *taṣawwuf* related commentary on ḥadīth texts. Among these works are the present volume, *Ḥaqīqat al-ṭarīqa min al-sunna al-ʿanīqa*, or *The Truth About the Way from the Refined Sunna*. In the interest of both brevity and clarity, this title has been revised by the translator to *A Sufi Study of Ḥadīths*. This work is actually a part of a much larger work entitled *al-Takashshuf ʿan muhimmāt al-taṣawwuf* or *Revealing the Important Aspects of Taṣawwuf*. Another work of Mawlānā's commentary is entitled *al-Tasharruf bi maʿrifah aḥādīth al-taṣawwuf*. Before discussing these two books, however, it will be useful to note another important point.

In the monthly magazine of his Sufi order, *al-Hādī*, Mawlānā published a short article entitled "A Notice Regarding the Removal of Ambiguity Concerning *Masā'il al-Taṣawwuf*, *al-Takashshuf*, and *al-Tasharruf*," in which he wrote:

> *Taṣawwuf* is a name for the development of the inner and outer aspects of the individual, and there is not a single Qur'ānic verse or ḥadīth text which is not in some way related to it. So, in every verse, and in every ḥadīth, one or another matter having to do with *taṣawwuf* is sure to be mentioned. However, in these works I have dealt only with those matters which are directly related with what is obviously a question of *taṣawwuf*, and that is how I have made selections of ḥadīths on which to comment.[12]

Both *al-Tasharruf* and *Ḥaqīqat al-ṭarīqa* are collections of selected ḥadīths in which the original Arabic texts are reproduced alongside their Urdu translations, traced to their sources of origin among the major classical collections of ḥadīths, and then commented upon, in Urdu, for their *taṣawwuf* content. Furthermore, in *Ḥaqīqat al-ṭarīqa*, the chapter headings are given in Persian.

---

11 Mīr Khurd, *Siyar al-'Awliyā'*, Urdu trans. by 'Iʿjāz al-Haqq Quddūsī (Lahore: Markazī Urdu Board, 1980) p. 206.

12 *al-Hādī*, Rabiʿ II, 1352 AH.

The classical collection upon which *Ḥaqīqat al-ṭarīqa* is based is *Taysīr al-wuṣūl 'ilā aḥadīth Jāmiʿ al-'Uṣūl*, by al-Shaybānī, which is itself an abridgement of the *Jāmiʿ al-'Uṣūl* by al-Jaza'iri. Moreover, the order of the ḥadīths selected for commentary in *Ḥaqīqat al-ṭarīqa* follows the order of that work. These ḥadīth are taken almost exclusively from the *ṣiḥāḥ al-sittah*, or the six most authentic orthodox collections. Thus, Mawlānā Thānawī never deals with the subject of the authenticity of the ḥadīths he selected for inclusion in *Ḥaqīqat al-ṭarīqa*. The publisher of this translation, however, has deemed it appropriate to provide such information in order to quell doubts or reservations about the provenance of the ḥadīths in this volume.

It may be appropriate to mention that this work seems to have been written especially for inclusion in the larger work, *al-Takashshuf*, as the date given at the end of both works is 1327.[13] It will not be out of place, therefore, to take a brief look at *al-Takashshuf*.

To begin with, *al-Takashshuf* was not designed as a separate work. It is, rather, a collection of shorter works brought together for the purpose of providing Mawlānā's disciples with a basic reader in the most important aspects of *taṣawwuf*. The book is, moreover, divided into three parts for disciples of limited, average and advanced abilities.

Part One of *al-Takashshuf* has thirty pages, Part Two has fourteen, and Part Three has six hundred and seventy pages. Furthermore, in his introduction to the work, Mawlānā recommends that the book be used as a text in formal lessons, rather than merely read in solitude. Thus, it is clear that the book embodies the most essential, as well as many of the most advanced and sensitive, of Mawlānā's teachings about *taṣawwuf*.

As to its contents, the first two parts of *al-Takashshuf* include extracts from several of Mawlānā's works. The contents of the third part, for disciples of advanced ability, include the following works:

1. *al-Anwār wa al-tajallī* (abridged). This is a short philosophical discourse, in Arabic and Persian, on the levels of existence and the comprehensiveness of human beings.
2. *al-Futūḥ fī mā yataʿallaq bi al-rūḥ*: a short treatise on the human soul.
3. *Masā'il al-Mathnawī*: a discussion of the important *taṣawwuf* related couplets in the *Mathnawī* of Mawlānā Rūmī.
4. *ʿIrfān-e-Ḥāfiẓ*: a commentary on the points of *taṣawwuf* raised in the poetry of the *Dīwān* of Ḥāfiẓ Shīrāzī, from the beginning of the collection to the *radīf al-dāl*.[14]

13 Thānawī, op. cit., p. 31 and p. 698.

14 Radif, in Arabic, Persian and Urdu poetry, refers to the consonance of a poem's rhyme. It is the

5. *Ḥaqīqat al-ṭarīqa*: *taṣawwuf* related commentary on ḥadīths of the Prophet, Allāh bless him and give him peace.
6. *al-Nukat al-daqīqa fī mā yataʿallaq bi al-Ḥaqīqa*: a discussion of the legal authority for certain practices of the Sufis which are not expressly mentioned in the Qur'ān or the Sunna.
7. *Ta'yīd al-Ḥaqīqa bi al-ʿāyāt al-ʿatīqa*: commentary on selected verses of the Qur'ān which touch upon *taṣawwuf* related subjects.

Let us now consider the second work, *al-Tasharruf*. To begin with, *al-Tasharruf* was not written as a separate work. Rather, over a period of ten years, from 1343 to 1353 AH (1925–1935 CE), it appeared as a monthly feature in the Urdu language journal, *al-Hādī*. Thereafter, the material was collected and published in a single volume.

Essentially, the work is based on other works of ḥadīth, and is composed of four parts, as outlined below:

1. *Taṣawwuf* based commentary on selected ḥadīths from Zayn al-Dīn al-ʿIrāqī's *Takhrīj aḥadīth al-'Ihyā'*, which is itself a work in which the ḥadīths quoted by al-Ghazzālī in his *'Iḥyā' ʿulūm al-dīn* are traced to their sources and authenticated by al-ʿIrāqī.
2. *Taṣawwuf* based commentary on the ḥadīths mentioned by Mawlānā Rūmī in the *Mathnawī*.
3. *Taṣawwuf* based commentary on ḥadīths mentioned by al-Sakhāwī in his *al-Maqāṣid al-Ḥasana*.
4. *Taṣawwuf* based commentary on ḥadīths in the *Jāmiʿ al-Ṣaghīr* by Jalāl al-Dīn al-Suyūṭī.

Those familiar with these works will know that they include all manner of ḥadīths. It is well known that al-Ghazzālī was not a ḥadīth scholar, and his *'Iḥyā'* includes much that is doubtful and even spurious.[15] Likewise, the poetic license used in the *Mathnawī* may well be said to include the ḥadīths it quotes or refers to, as

---

repetition of the last ryhming word or vowel in any rhyming scheme, most notably used in the Persian and Urdu *ghazal.*

15 ʿAbd al-ʿAzīz al-Khawlī, *Miftāḥ al-Sunna* (Beirut: Dār al-Qalam, 1974) p. 162. However, Imām al-Ghazzālī knew he was not a scholar of ḥadīths. Yet, the way in which āyats and ḥadīths are quoted to establish a point in the *'Iḥyā'* is first an āyat or āyats, then *ṣaḥīḥ*, *ḥasan*, and so on. So the latter though weak do not function as proof but are only included for corroboration. Much the same way that the Mawlānā uses ḥadīths in his work. As he himself said: "In fact, the great majority of Sufi sayings believed popularly to be the words of the Messenger have equivalents, at least in meaning, in the authentic ḥadīths of the Messenger. Therefore, to generalise about the Sufis narrating and popularising spurious material in the name of ḥadīths is decidedly unfair and unwarranted."

well. Finally, both *al-Maqāṣid al-Ḥasana* and *al-Jāmiᶜ al-Ṣaghīr* are collections of popularly quoted ḥadīths and, almost by definition, include what is authentic and what is not.

Nevertheless, Mawlānā's treatment of these ḥadīths was to compare their import with the established principles of the Sharīᶜa. If the meaning was acceptable, and if the ḥadīth scholars had not rejected the ḥadīths outright, then Mawlānā included it among the ḥadīths of *al-Tasharruf* for commentary. In terms of their content, however, the two books are quite similar. Thus, a reading of this volume will provide the reader with a very good idea of what the other book is all about.

What follows is an English translation of *Ḥaqīqat al-ṭarīqa*. Moreover, it is hoped that the information provided in this brief introduction will suffice as a starting point for the reader who is perhaps unfamiliar with the works of Mawlānā Ashraf ᶜAlī Thānawī. I have little doubt that such readers, and all those interested in the subject of *taṣawwuf* will want to look deeper into Mawlānā's works after reading what he has written in the pages that follow.

This, then, has been a brief introduction to one aspect of the works of Mawlānā Ashraf ᶜAlī Thānawī, may Allāh grant him mercy everlasting! Indeed the scope for serious work on the subject of his life, or on any aspect of his works, is vast indeed.

In closing, I should like to record my debt to my teacher, Mawlānā Muḥammad Yūsuf Binnorī, himself a great *muḥaddith* and *faqīh*, as well as a *Mujāz-e-Ṣuḥbat*[16] from Mawlānā Thānawī himself. It was a great personal blessing to have had the opportunity to read the ḥadīths in this volume with Mawlānā Binnorī and it was at his direction, and with his encouragement, that I undertook this translation.[17] May Allāh grant eternal peace to his soul, and to the soul of Mawlānā Thānawī, and to all of the true followers of the Prophet Muḥammad, his family, and his companions!

YUSUF DELORENZO
Virginia USA, 2009

---

16 This term denotes a person who, though he/she may be from another order (in my teacher's case, the Naqshbandi order) has nonetheless been granted permission, *mujāz*, to instruct aspirants from another order. In other words, Mawlānā Thānawī gave his own *murīd*s permission to learn taṣawwuf from Mawlānā Binnorī or, more literally, to benefit from his company, *ṣuḥbat*. YTD.

17 I must also record here my gratitude to Yahya Batha of Turath Publishing who urged me to revive the translation of this work, after it had languished in manuscript form since 1975. I am likewise indebted to Mawlānā Mohammed Mohamedy who translated the final quarter of this book when it was discovered that the original translation had gone missing. Without the help of these two dedicated indivudals, this important work may never have seen the light of day in the English language. May Allāh reward them handsomely in this world and the next. YTD.

Author's Preface

IT IS ESSENTIAL that all Muslims, having seen to the correctness of their beliefs and practice (or outer conduct), also attend to the correctness of their inner conduct. Countless Qur'ānic verses and ḥadīths prove conclusively that this is also essential, though many of those who attend only to externals are heedless of this matter. Certainly, everyone knows that the Qur'ān and the Sunna contain mention of the virtues of things such as abstinence, contentment, humility, sincerity, patience, gratitude, love for the Divine, acceptance of fate, trust, and so forth. Indeed, the Muslim is encouraged by these texts to acquire these qualities and to avoid their opposites, such as greed, pride, hypocrisy, rancour, lust, jealousy, and so forth. Then, can there possibly remain any doubt as to the command or prohibition of these matters by the Sharīʿa? This is what is meant by the reformation of inner conduct. This is the primary goal of the Sufi way. It also happens to be an indisputable obligation.

In addition, experience has proved, and indeed it is the way Allāh has approved, that the single most important factor in the process of inner reformation is that of one's companionship with, and service and obedience to, those who have themselves been reformed. Wherever actual companionship is not feasible, abstract companionship, even in the form of one's reading the biographies of the great Sufis, can conceivably suffice in its place.[18] This is the secret behind the frequent urgings of the Qur'ān and ḥadīths toward the companionship of the good, and their warnings against the companionship of the wicked. For this reason, too, the stories of Allāh's special servants are repeated throughout the texts of the Qur'ān and the Sunna.

18 I should record here that Mawlānā Binnorī once told me that in the absence of anything else, one may take the Kaʿbah in Makka as one's spiritual guide. YTD.

Another fact borne out by experience is that one's companionship of the pious, whether actual or abstract, can only be of benefit when accompanied by conviction and attachment. Otherwise one may spend a lifetime with the best of people and never benefit from their company. Moreover, in the same way that the companionship of refined people is beneficial, the companionship of corrupt people is detrimental.

In our own times, owing to the general lack of knowledge about Islam, and to the predominance of selfish desires, most people never even consider reforming their inner selves. And then, even if they do think of it and seek out the company of a spiritual guide, most of them are barred, owing to imbalances between what they know and what they practise, from making any real progress on the Sufi way. The majority of such people are either too severe or too lax in their approach to Islam. Those who are too severe and narrow-minded often misconstrue the words, deeds, and states of the Sufi masters. Then, having decided for themselves that these things are contrary to the Sunna, the narrow-minded ones shun the Sufi masters and thus remain deprived of their blessings. In fact, it sometimes happens that, owing to their disrespectful and insulting behaviour towards the masters, these narrow-minded people place their well being in serious jeopardy.[19] On the other hand, those who are lax or weak in faith often become the followers of ignorant Sufis who subscribe to false doctrines. Then, without weighing the words, deeds, and states of these Sufi pretenders on the scales of the Sharīʿa, they accept everything they tell them. In this manner, when they decide to serve and accompany ignorant sheikhs, they are actually throwing their religion away.

In view of all this, I have felt it necessary to show the reality of the Sufi way in the light of the Qur'ān and the Sunna, so that hereafter people will no longer deny the perfections of the true Sufi masters, or become the followers of those who pretend to be masters. It is also my wish to remove the doubts harboured by many of our narrow-minded Muslim brothers, many of whom are even scholars, who suppose the Sufi masters to be degenerate, and their ways contrary to the Sharīʿa, and who imagine that there is no basis whatsoever for the Sufi way in orthodox Islam. Finally, I hope to remedy the notions of those whose faith is weak, and who suppose impostors to be masters in spite of their breach of the Sharīʿa. Thus, the difference between truth and falsehood may be rightly measured: in conformance with the standards of the Qur'ān and the Sunna. And in all this it is Allāh from whom I seek assistance.

ASHRAF ʿALĪ THĀNAWĪ

---

19 The Prophet, Allāh bless him and give him peace, said that Allah most High said, "Whoever causes discomfort to a friend (*walī*) of Mine, on such a one I declare war."

Author's Introduction

THE TRUE OBJECTIVE of the "inner way," as I mentioned in the preface, is the reformation of inner conduct. In the language of the Sufis, this inner conduct is termed *akhlāq wa maqāmāt*, or character and stations. Furthermore, as every primary objective is attended by related matters of secondary importance, the aforementioned objective of the Sufis is likewise attended by a great number of related matters of secondary importance. Some of these matters, being of the nature of fruits over which we have no control, are called *aḥwāl* or states. Those matters that are known to produce these fruits, or at least help in producing them, are called *ashghāl* or practices. Those matters, regardless of whether or not we have control over them, which indicate the presence of those fruits are called *ʿalāmāt* or signs. Matters which aim at erasing doubts, remedying inner infirmities, or explaining methods of practice are called *taʿlīmāt* or teachings. Matters in the form of textual evidence from the Qur'ān and ḥadīths which give good tidings to those who possess praiseworthy characters or perform meritorious deeds are called *faḍā'il* or virtues. Matters over which we have control and which are second nature to the Sufis are called *ʿādāt* or habits. Matters in the form of advantageous but unnecessary actions that are permitted by the Sharīʿa and performed by the Sufis are called *rusūm* or customs. Those matters which are purely of an academic nature are called *masā'il* or questions. Matters of a spoken nature are called *aqwāl* or sayings. The explanations of those matters which to all outward appearances seem to transgress the limits of what is permitted by the Sharīʿa, but which in reality do not, are called *tawjīhāt* or interpretations; and if those matters do actually transgress the limits of the Sharīʿa, then the admonition which is then required is called *iṣlāḥ* or reform. Those few remaining matters which do not fit under any of the above-mentioned headings may be termed *mutafarriqāt* or miscellaneous.

Then, to sum up, the list of these primary and secondary matters is as follows: (1) Character, (2) States, (3) Practices, (4) Signs, (5) Teachings, (6) Virtues, (7) Habits, (8) Customs, (9) Questions, (10) Sayings, (11) Interpretations, (12) Corrections, (13) Miscellaneous.

As those of the above-mentioned subjects that have been clearly and specifically mentioned in the Qur'ān and the Sunna are not likely to present any difficulties, there is no need for their repetition here. Satisfactory discussions of those subjects are to be found in all the major works of the Sufis. This book is concerned only with treating those subjects which are not specifically mentioned in the Qur'ān or ḥadīths and which are, indeed, likely to present difficulties to the average Muslim. Therefore, each ḥadīth in this collection will be followed by its translation and, under a separate heading, by brief commentary concerning the authentication of the relevant, problematic, *taṣawwuf* related subject. Though this work does not claim to be comprehensive, it does nonetheless cover many significant subjects. After reading this book, the gifted reader should not have any difficulty in using his/her own powers of reason to come to a proper understanding of the subjects which are not specifically mentioned in these pages.

Undoubtedly, it would have been proper to arrange the ḥadīths in this collection in some kind of logical order. However, for my own ease, and for the purpose of keeping the reader's interest alive, I have chosen not to observe any particular sequence. For the reader's convenience, however, each commentary note has been given two headings: (1) a general heading taken from the list of thirteen primary and secondary matters mentioned above; (2) a particular heading introducing the subject to be discussed in relation to the ḥadīth.

Ashraf ʿAlī Thānawī

A SUFI STUDY *of* ḤADITH

A Translation of At-Tasharruf and Ḥaqīqat aṭ-Ṭarīqa

ḤADĪTH 1

عِنْدَ النَّسَائِيْ فِيْ حَدِيْثِ عُمَرَ بْنِ الْخَطَّابِ رَضِيَ اللهُ عَنْهُ حِيْنَ جَاءَ جِبْرَئِيْلُ عَلَيْهِ السَّلَامُ يَسْأَلُ عَنْ أُمُوْرِ الدِّيْنِ قَوْلُ رَسُوْلِ اللهِ صَلَّى اللهُ عَلَيْهِ وَسَلَّمَ: «وَإِنَّهُ لَجِبْرَئِيْلُ عَلَيْهِ السَّلَامُ نَزَلَ فِيْ صُوْرَةِ دِحْيَةَ الْكَلْبِيِّ».

In the ḥadīth related on the authority of ʿUmar ibn al-Khaṭṭāb ﵁ concerning the arrival of the Angel Jibrīl ﵇ and his questions about the fundamentals of Islam, the Messenger of Allāh ﷺ said, "Of a certainty, he is Jibrīl descended in the form of Diḥyah al-Kalbī." This ḥadīth was related by Nasāʾī.[20]

Questions: Simulation

The appearance of an essence in another (or in another's) form, despite the abiding of its own prior state and attributes, is termed simulation or *tamaththul*, while the form itself is called the simulated form. In dreams and in spiritual visions most things appear in simulated form. Occasionally, however, a miracle occurs and simulation takes place in the ordinary waking world. The ḥadīth above, in which Jibrīl appears in human form, having assumed the appearance of Diḥyah al-Kalbī, is ample proof of this phenomenon. It should be remembered here that Jibrīl was not actually transformed into a man.

The occurrence of simulation is also verified in the following verse of the Qur'ān: "Then we sent unto her our spirit, and it assumed for her the likeness of a perfect man."[21] This, in no way, attests to the validity of the erroneous doctrine of the transmigration of souls. In simulation the state of the essence remains exactly as it was, whereas in transmigration this is not the case.

---

20 *Sunan an-Nasāʾī*: 4994

21 Al-Qur'ān, 19:17

ḤADĪTH 2

عَنْ عَبْدِ اللهِ بْنِ عَمْرِو بْنِ الْعَاص رَضِيَ اللهُ عَنْهُ قَالَ: قَالَ رَسُوْلُ اللهِ صَلَّى اللهُ عَلَيْهِ

وَسَلَّمَ: «الْمُهَاجِرُ مَنْ هَجَرَ مَا نَهَى اللهُ عَنْهُ». (أخرجه الخمسة)

It is related on the authority of ʿAbdullāh ibn ʿAmr ibn al-ʿĀs ☙ that the Messenger of Allāh ☙ said: "The true emigrant (muhājir) is a person who leaves behind everything that Allāh has forbidden." This ḥadīth was related by Bukhārī, Muslim, Tirmidhī, Abū Dāwūd, and Nasāʾī.[22]

Questions: Meaning as the True Object

According to the Sufis, may they enjoy the mercy of Allāh ☙, external form is of no value unless it is accompanied by inner significance. Thus, the true object of our deeds is their inner significance or reality. From the ḥadīth above it is evident that the person who migrates, the muhājir, in the outward sense of leaving home to settle elsewhere, but who pays no heed to the inner significance of abandoning all that is contrary to the pleasure of Allāh ☙, cannot be called a true muhājir. Nonetheless, no one should assume from the ḥadīth above that externals are without value. The proper way to approach the matter is to realise that Allāh has created for every inner meaning a corresponding external form, and that without form the acquisition of inner significance is impossible.

ḤADĪTH 3

عَنِ ابْنِ مَسْعُوْدٍ رَضِيَ اللهُ عَنْهُ قَالُوْا: يَارَسُوْلَ اللهِ! إِنَّ أَحَدَنَا لَيَجِدُ فِي نَفْسِهِ مَا لَأَنْ

يَحْتَرِقَ حتى يَصِيْرَ حُمَمَةً أَو يَخِرَّ مِنَ السَّمَاءِ إلى الأَرْضِ أَحَبُّ إِلَيْهِ مِنْ أَنْ يَتَكَلَّمَ به، قال:

«ذاك مَحْضُ الإِيْمَان». (رواه مسلم)

It is related on the authority of ʿAbdullāh ibn Masʿūd ☙ that when the Companions ☙ said: "O Messenger of Allāh ☙! There are times when we find ourselves thinking of things that, rather than speak of them it would be more desirable to be burned to charcoal, or to plummet to earth from high in the sky", the Messenger ☙ replied, "That is precisely what perfect faith is all about." This ḥadīth was related by Muslim.[23]

---

22 Bukhārī: 10, 6484; Abū Dāwūd: 2481; Nasāʾī: 4999; Ibn Mājah: 3934. Muslim (40, 41, 42) has only the beginning portion of the ḥadīth.

23 Abū Dāwūd: 5112, Muslim: 133. Muslim's report does not have the question put to the noble Mes-

Teachings: Disregarding the Shadows of Doubt

Among the things which most frustrate the traveller on the Sufi way are one's exaggerated attempts to free one's mind of vague and ill-defined suspicions, or *waswasa*, and one's feeling sorry for oneself when these attempts prove unsuccessful. In accordance with the basic wisdoms conveyed in this ḥadīth, Sufi masters treat this problem by first explaining to their disciples that these things are harmless, and then by asking the disciples to ignore such thoughts when they occur. If this is done, then in a very short time the traveller will cease to be troubled by *waswasa*.

ḤADĪTH 4

عن عوف بن مالك الأشجعي رَضِيَ اللهُ عَنْهُ قال: كُنَّا عِنْدَ النَّبِيِّ صَلَّى اللهُ عَلَيْهِ وَسَلَّمَ تِسْعَةً أَوْ ثَمَانِيَةً أَوْ سَبْعَةً فقال: «أَلاَ تُبَايِعُوْنَ رَسُولَ اللهِ؟» فَبَسطْنا أَيْدِينَا وقلنا: على ما نُبَايِعُكَ يارسولَ الله؟ قال: «على أن تَعْبدوا اللهَ، ولا تُشرِكُوا بِإِلٰهِنَا شَيْئاً، وَتُصَلوا الصَلوتِ الخمسَ، وَتَسْمعوا، وَتُطِيعوا» وأَسَرَّ كلمةً خفيةً قال: «وَلاتَسئَلوا الناسَ شَيْئًا» فَلَقَدْ رَأَيْتُ بَعْضَ أولئِكَ النفر يَسْقُطُ سَوْطُ أحدِهم فما يسألُ أحداً يناوِلُه إياه.

(أخرجه مسلم وأبوداؤد والنسائي)

It is related on the authority of ʿAwf ibn Mālik al-Asjaʿī that he said, "We were in the company of the Messenger of Allāh ﷺ, nine, eight, or seven of us, when he ﷺ said, 'Will you not pledge your allegiance to the Messenger of Allāh?' As we had only recently pledged our allegiance to him, we said, 'We have already pledged ourselves to you, O Messenger!' Yet again he asked us, 'Will you not pledge yourselves to the Messenger of Allāh?' So we extended our hands and said, 'To what are we to pledge ourselves, O Messenger of Allāh?' He replied, 'That you worship Allāh ﷻ and not associate anything with Him. That you perform the five daily prayers. And that you hear and obey.' Then he whispered something to us. He said, 'And do not ask anyone for anything.' Since then, I have seen people of that group drop their whips [while mounted] and not ask anyone to hand it up to them." This ḥadīth was related by Muslim, Abū Dāwūd, and al-Nasāʾī.[24]

---

senger ﷺ by the Companions; it is only reported by Abū Dāwūd and Aḥmad. Our author has merged the two narrations into one.

24 Muslim: 1043, Abū Dāwūd: 1642, Nasāʾī: 461, Ibn Mājah: 2867

*Questions: Bay*ʿ*ah*

The type of pledge or *bay*ʿ*ah* taken by Sufis, which amounts to an agreement to obey the injunctions of the Sharīʿa and to faithfully perform certain inward and outward practices, is often made the target of criticism by the narrow-minded. According to these critics, *bay*ʿ*ah* is the same as *bid*ʿ*ah* or blameworthy innovation because there is nothing in the Qur'ān or the Sunna to support it. The only kinds of *bay*ʿ*ah* that they recognise are the *bay*ʿ*ah* of Islam (conversion to Islam from another faith), and the *bay*ʿ*ah* of jihād. However, in the ḥadīth above, the type of *bay*ʿ*ah* mentioned is spiritual *bay*ʿ*ah* because the ones pledging themselves were Companions. Undoubtedly, then, this was not the *bay*ʿ*ah* of Islam. It is also clear from the text that this was not *bay*ʿ*ah* of jihād. Rather, in view of the pledge made by these Companions to obey certain injunctions and to perform certain practices, it is obvious that the *bay*ʿ*ah* of the Sufis does indeed have its precedent in the Sunna.

Practices: Private Instruction

Most Sufi masters are in the habit of taking their disciples aside for private instruction. Sometimes this is done for the purpose of keeping complex matters out of the reach of those who might not appreciate or fathom them, and sometimes because, when special attention is a sign of favour, the disciple will be more likely to take the teachings to heart. Another factor in this kind of private or individualized instruction is that it precludes the possibility of another's overhearing and then taking it upon himself to follow in practice whatever was discussed, even when that practice is unsuited for his condition or circumstances. Anyway, the basis for all of this is found in the ḥadīth above.

Questions: Exaggeration in Carrying Out the Orders of a Master

The natural disposition of most disciples is such that they, when it comes to carrying out the orders of their masters, go to such lengths that they pay as much attention to the letter of the master's words as they do to their meaning. This condition is described in the latter part of the ḥadīth above. Obviously, the intended meaning here was to prohibit those Companions from asking for anything that belonged to others, and not to prohibit them from asking for their own things. Nonetheless, as the words of the prohibition admitted of a literal meaning, even though the context clearly indicated that the literal meaning was not the intended meaning, the Companions chose not to ask even for their own possessions. In another ḥadīth it is related that while the Messenger ﷺ was giving the Friday *khutba*, a man came and stood at the doorway of the mosque.

When the Messenger ﷺ told the man to sit down, he immediately complied by sitting in the doorway. Of course, what the Messenger ﷺ meant was that the man should come inside, find a place, and then sit down and listen, not that he should sit right then and there, blocking the entrance to the mosque. The kind of obedience and respect illustrated here, however, is of utmost importance for anyone who hopes to benefit spiritually from a master.

ḤADĪTH 5

عن عائشة رضي الله تعالى عنها قالت: ما مَسَّ رسولُ اللهِ صَلَّى اللهُ عَلَيْهِ وَسَلَّمَ يَد امْرَأَةٍ قطُّ إلا أن يأْخُذَ عليها فإذا أَخَذ عليها فأَعْطَتْه قال: «اذهَبِي فقد بَايَعْتُكِ». (رواه الشيخان وأبو داود)

ʿĀʾisha ﷺ said, "Never once in his life did the Messenger of Allāh ﷺ touch the hand of a woman who was not related to him. He did, however, take *bayʿah* from them, orally. And when a woman had pledged herself, he would then say to her, 'Go. I have accepted your pledge.'" This ḥadīth was related by Bukhārī, Muslim, and Abū Dāwūd.[25]

Corrections: Taking Bayʿah from Women

It is the practice of certain ignorant and uncircumspect Sufis to hold the hands of women while formally taking *bayʿah* from them. This is completely improper, as it is prohibited to touch an unrelated woman unnecessarily. The ḥadīth above clearly refutes this practice. Who could be a better teacher or more chaste than the Messenger of Allāh ﷺ? Then, when he was so careful about such matters, how can we possibly allow ourselves to be lax about them? When *bayʿah* is actually no more than an agreement, the spoken word will certainly suffice. The masters of latter times have made it their practice, for the purpose of strengthening the master-disciple bond, to hold, when taking formal *bayʿah*, one end of a cloth in their own hands while the female disciple holds the other end. There is really nothing wrong with this practice. Similarly, if it becomes necessary for a man to take *bayʿah* from a master without touching, the same method may be used. However, since it is the Sunna for men to offer their hands when taking *bayʿah*, it is better whenever possible that they do so in that way.

25 Bukhārī: 2713, Muslim: 1866, Abū Dāwūd: 2941, Tirmidhī: 3306, Ibn Mājah: 2875

ḤADĪTH 6

عن أبي هريرةَ رَضِيَ اللهُ عَنْهُ أَنَّهُ دَخلَ السُّوْق فقَالَ: أَرَاكُم ههُنَا ومِيْرَاثُ مُحَمَّدٍ صَلَّى اللهُ عَلَيْهِ وَسَلَّمَ فِي المَسْجدِ، فَذَهَبُوا وانْصَرَفُوا وقالوا: مارَأَينَا شيئاً يَقْسِمُ رَأَيْنَا قومًا يَقْرَؤُنَ القُرآن قال: فذلكم مِيْرَاثُ نَبِيِّكُمْا. (رواه رزين)

It is related on the authority of Abū Hurairā ؓ that he went to the marketplace and asked the people there, "Why do I see you here, when the legacy of Muhammad ﷺ is being distributed in the mosque?" Hearing this, the people in the marketplace went away. In a short while, however, they returned, saying, "We saw nothing being distributed there. All we saw were a few people reciting the Qur'ān." Abū Huraira ؓ replied, "So! There you have the legacy of Muhammad ﷺ." This ḥadīth was related by Imam Razīn.[26]

Practices: The Use of Equivocal Language

In the works of most Sufi masters one can find any number of ambiguous passages which, after one has been made aware of their true meaning, actually begin to make a great deal of sense. At times this kind of veiled language is used involuntarily when the master is under the influence of some spiritual state, though usually it is used either for the purpose of keeping subtleties beyond the reach of those who might not understand them, or for increasing the desire of the true seeker. This is because vagueness is something that is known to increase desire; and that which has been desired greatly will generally have a greater effect on the inner being. Anyway, that there is a basis for the use of this kind of language is clearly attested to in this ḥadīth. Here, for the purpose of increasing the people's desire, Abū Huraira ؓ was ambiguous to the extent that some people came back and told him that he was mistaken. But when he explained to them the true meaning of his words, they realised at once that he had spoken the truth. We should, therefore, never be sceptical about the vague or ambiguous words of the true Sufi masters, and we should certainly never criticise or speak insultingly of them.

ḤADĪTH 7

عن أبي بن كعب رَضِيَ اللهُ عَنْهُ قال: كانَ رَجلٌ مِن الأنصَارِ، بَيتُه أقصى بَيْتٍ فِي المدينة،

26 *Muʿjam al-'Awsaṭ* of aṭ-Ṭabarānī: 7187. Al-Haythamī said in *Majmaʿ az-Zawā'id* (1:129): 'Its chain is good.'

فكَانَ لَا تُخْطِئُهُ الصلوةُ مع رسولِ الله صَلَّى اللهُ عَلَيْهِ وَسَلَّمَ، قال: فَتَوَجَّعْنَا لَهُ، فقلتُ

له: يا فلانُ! لو أنك اشتَرَيتَ حماراً يَقِيْكَ من الرَّمْضَاءِ ويقيكَ مِن هَوَامِّ الأرْضِ قال:

أَمْ واللّٰهِ! ما أُحِبُّ أَنَّ بيتي مُطَنَّبٌ ببيت محمد صَلَّى اللهُ عَلَيْهِ وَسَلَّمَ . قال: فَحَمَلْت به

حِملاً حتى أتيتُ به نبيَّ الله صَلَّى اللهُ عَلَيْهِ وَسَلَّمَ، فَأَخْبَرْتُه، قَالَ: فَدَعَاهُ، فَقَالَ لَهُ مثل

ذلكَ، وَذَكَرَ له أَنَّه يَرْجُوْ فِيْ أثره الأجر. فقال له النبيُّ صَلَّى اللهُ عَلَيْهِ وَسَلَّمَ: «إِنَّ لَكَ

مَا احْتَسَبْتَ». (رواه مسلم)

Ubayy ibn Kaʿb 🍀 related that there was a man from among the Anṣār whose home was the furthest from the center of Madīna, but who never missed a prayer with the Messenger of Allāh 🍀. Ubayy 🍀 said, "As we all felt compassion for the man, one day I said to him, 'Why don't you buy yourself a donkey and spare yourself the trouble of walking among the reptiles and through desert heat?' His reply was, 'By Allāh! Because I do not wish that my house should be any closer to the house of Muhammad 🍀.' I was so annoyed at the man's reply that I went to the Messenger of Allāh 🍀 and told him what the man had said. When the Messenger 🍀 called the man, he repeated what he'd said before. But he added that he hoped to receive a reward in heaven for every step to and from the mosque. So the Messenger 🍀 said to him, 'You will indeed receive the reward you hope for.'" This ḥadīth was related by Muslim.[27]

Practices: Speaking Equivocally

The commentary written for the last ḥadīth (ḥadīth [6]) applies equally to this ḥadīth. Here, the man from the Anṣār expressed himself in such a harsh manner that ʿUbayy 🍀 was genuinely annoyed with him. Still, for reasons known best to himself, the man's words were designed to conceal his true feelings, and state. When questioned by the Messenger 🍀, however, he explained the true meaning behind his words. The poet said: "To our friends we can speak our hearts. Why try and hide pain from a doctor?" Finally, unless there is a good reason for it, no one should intentionally use equivocal language.

HADĪTH 8

عن حنظلةَ بنِ الربيع الأُسَيْدي رَضِيَ اللهُ عَنْهُ - كاتب رسول الله صَلَّى الله عَلَيْهِ

---

27 Muslim: 663, Abū Dāwūd: 557, Ibn Mājah: 783

وَسَلَّمَ – قال: لَقِيَنِيْ أبوبكر فقال: كيف أنتَ؟ قلتُ: نَافَقَ حنظلةُ، قال: سبحان اللهِ! مَاتَقُوْلُ؟ قَالَ: قلتُ: نَكُوْنُ عِنْدَ النَّبِيِّ صَلَّى اللهُ عَلَيْهِ وَسَلَّمَ يُذَكِّرُنا بالنَّارِ وَالْجَنَّةِ كَأَنَّا رَأْيَ عَيْنٍ، فَإِذَا خَرَجْنَا مِنْ عِنْدِهِ، عَافَسْنَا الأَزْوَاجَ وَالأَوْلاَدَ وَالضَّيْعَاتِ، وَنَسِيْنَا كثيراً قالَ: وَاللهِ إِنِّيْ لأجد مثلَ هذا، فَانْطَلَقَا إلى رَسولِ اللهِ صَلَّى اللهُ عَلَيْهِ وَسَلَّمَ، وذَكَرَ لَهُ ذلكَ فقالَ: «وَالَّذِيْ نَفْسِيْ بِيَدِهِ لَوْ تَدُوْمُوْنَ على مَا تَكُوْنُوْنَ عِنْدِيْ أو فِي الذِّكْرِ لَصَافَحَتْكُمُ الْمَلاِئكَةُ عَلَى فُرُشِكُمْ وَفِيْ طُرُقِكُمْ وَلكِنْ، ياحنظلةُ! سَاعَةً وسَاعَةً» ثَلث مَرَّاتٍ. (أخرجه مسلم والترمذي)

It is related that Ḥanẓalah ibn al-Rabīᶜ al-'Usaydī ﵁, scribe to the Messenger ﷺ said, "Abū Bakr met me and asked how I was. In reply, I said, 'Ḥanẓalah has become a hypocrite.' Abū Bakr ﵁ was astonished and said, 'Glory be to Allāh! What are you saying?' I replied, 'When we are with the Messenger of Allāh ﷺ and he reminds us of the Fire and the Gardens of Paradise, at that moment it is as if we are seeing those things with our own eyes. But when we go out from where he is, we again become so involved with our spouses, our children and our property that we forget everything else.' Abū Bakr ﵁ replied, 'By Allāh! I find the same things happening to me.' So the two of us went to the Messenger ﷺ and told him what we had admitted to each other. Then the Messenger of Allāh ﷺ said to us, 'By the One Who holds my life in His hands! If you were to remain in the states you attain while you are in my company, the angels would embrace you in your beds and on the streets! But, O Ḥanẓalah, there is a time for this and a time for that.' He repeated this three times." This ḥadīth was related by Imāms Muslim and Tirmidhī.[28]

Practices: Calling Oneself a Disbeliever

In the writings of the Sufi masters we sometimes find that, in consideration of certain misdeeds or vile states, or with a view to a special or personalised terminology, they refer to themselves as disbelievers. This gives rise to the question of how a person can call himself or herself a disbeliever and still remain a Muslim. But in the ḥadīth above the basis for this practice is evident, because Ḥanẓalah ﵁, in recognition of his changing spiritual states, called himself a hypocrite. Surely, he did not mean to use the term in its strict legal sense of inwardly denying the truth of Allāh's message and the veracity of His Messenger ﷺ. Rather, on

28 Muslim: 2750, Tirmidhī: 2514

the basis of the differences he found between states of presence and absence, he used the term figuratively. An example of the use of the word "disbeliever" as a special term is its use in place of the word "annihilated" or *fāni*, for the reason that one who is *fāni* has been buried in the love of the Almighty; and one of the meanings of the word for disbelief, *kufr*, is to cover over or obliterate something. Since Ḥanẓalah ﷺ found one state obliterating the other from time to time, he termed himself a hypocrite.

Furthermore, the answer given by the Messenger ﷺ was not in refutation of the use of figurative language, but rather of the false premise that the one state was necessarily any better than the other.[29]

States: Spiritual Witnessing

The inner intensification and domination of something in the imagination is called spiritual witnessing or *mushāhadah*. That this actually occurs is attested to in the ḥadīth above in which Ḥanẓalah ﷺ says of the Fire and the Garden, "it is as if we are seeing those things with our own eyes." The meaning here is not that anyone actually saw the Fire and the Garden, but that in their imaginations the thought grew so intense that it possessed them. Many ignorant Sufis suppose spiritual witnessing to be direct vision, but they are clearly mistaken when they attempt to apply a dictionary meaning to a spiritual state.

Miscellaneous: Barakah from Accompanying a Master

In the same way that certain mystical states and conditions follow one's ascetic exertions or spiritual disciplines, they will also be found sometimes to follow one's being in the company of a master. However, unlike the effect of these exercises, the effect of a master's presence or words is not usually long lasting. This was the reason behind Ḥanẓalah's ﷺ complaint that, upon leaving the company of the Messenger ﷺ, he lost much of what he had gained there. Finally, no one should suppose that the reason for Ḥanẓalah's ﷺ lapse was his involvement in worldly affairs because, as we have clarified in the commentary above, the real reason for its occurrence was his parting company with the Messenger of Allāh ﷺ.

Questions: The Transient Nature of Spiritual States

Most travellers on the Sufi way complain at one time or another that a particular state of theirs has lost its former intensity, or has disappeared altogether. Then,

---

29 In other words, there is no reason why one's worldly activities cannot be imbued with the same spiritual significance as an act of prescribed worship, like prayer or fasting. Much of the message of Islam, in fact, is just that. This is what the Messenger ﷺ was referring to when he said that there was to be no monasticism in Islam. YTD.

thinking that they have suffered some sort of spiritual reverse, the travellers become disheartened and confused. This is especially true among neophytes who are far more susceptible to changes in their condition than more experienced travellers. The Sufi masters, however, have established that the ascendancy of spiritual states is at best impermanent. This phenomenon of impermanence is referred to as *talwīn* or variegation, and is something which occurs in varying degrees to even the most experienced Sufis. In this ḥadīth, the Messenger's ﷺ saying, "There is a time for this and a time for that," is in direct reference to *talwīn*. This phenomenon is an inevitable part of the Sufi way and, as such, should never become a cause for concern.

ḤADĪTH 9

عَنْ أَنَسٍ رَضِيَ اللهُ عَنْهُ قَالَ: دَخَلَ رَسُوْلُ اللهِ ﷺ الْمَسْجِدَ، فَإِذَا حَبْلٌ مَمْدُوْدٌ بَيْنَ السَّارِيَتَيْنِ فَقَالَ: «مَا هذَا؟» قَالُوْا: حَبْلٌ لِزَيْنَبَ فَإِذَا فَتَرَتْ تَعَلَّقَتْ فقَالَ : «لاَ، حُلُّوْهُ، لِيُصَلِّ أَحَدُكُمْ نِشَاطَهُ فَإِذَا فَتَرَ فَلْيَقْعُدْ». (أخرجه البخاري وأبوداؤد والنسائي)

It is related on the authority of ʿAnas ؓ that Allāh's Prophet ﷺ once went into the mosque and saw a rope there stretched between two supports. "What is this," he asked. The Companions ﵃ replied, "This is Zaynab's ﵂ rope. When she tires at worship, she props herself up with it." The Messenger of Allāh ﷺ said, "Take it down. You should only worship for as long as you are fresh. When you tire, you should rest." This ḥadīth was related by Bukhārī, Abū Dāwūd, and Nasāʾī.[30]

Teachings: Moderation in Spiritual Disciplines

The Sufi masters are agreed that no one should go to such extremes in their spiritual disciplines as would adversely affect their health or well being. Clearly, this is the lesson of the ḥadīth above. The excesses of certain of the Sufi masters in this matter need not present any difficulties when we realise that, as a result of their sincere desire and love for the Almighty, they were granted the extra strength necessary to perform whatever they did.

ḤADĪTH 10

عن أنس رَضِيَ اللهُ عَنْهُ قال: خَطَّ رَسُوْلُ الله صَلَّى اللهُ عَلَيْهِ وَسَلَّمَ خطًّا، وقال: «هذا

30 Bukhārī: 1150, Muslim: 784, Abū Dāwūd: 1312, Nasāʾī: 1644, Ibn Mājah: 1371

الإنسانُ» وَخَطَّ إلى جَانِبِهِ خَطًّا وَقَالَ: «هذَا أَجلُه» وَخَطَّ آخَرَ بَعِيْداً مِنْهُ وَقَالَ: «هذَا الأَمَلُ» فَبَيْنَمَا هُوَ كَذَالِكَ إِذْ جَاءَهُ الأَقْرَبُ. (أخرجه البخاري والترمذي)

It is related on the authority of ʿAnas ﷺ that the Messenger of Allāh ﷺ drew a line on the ground and said, "This is man." Then he drew a line parallel to the first and said, "This is his appointed time." Then he drew a third line, further than the second, and said, "This is man's wish. So, as man moves toward what he wishes for, he is greeted by the one that is closer to him [his appointed time]. This ḥadīth was related by Bukhārī and Tirmidhī.[31]

Interpretations: The Use of Metaphor to Indicate the Almighty

In the writings, and particularly in the poetry, of many Sufi masters words like sun, moon, ocean, and so forth are used to represent the essence and attributes of the Almighty. On the surface of it, at least, this kind of representation is unbecoming because it equates the Eternal with the ephemeral, and negates the concept of Allāh's unity or *tawḥīd*. The purpose of this, however, is figurative and not literal representation. There is certainly nothing wrong with the figurative representation inherent in the comparison of two essentially unlike things. Witness, for example, the Qur'ānic simile of the lamp: "The similitude of His light is as a niche wherein is a lamp."[32] The most one could say here is that the comparison in the ḥadīth, unlike the one in the Qur'ān, is not made explicit by the use of a word for "like" or "as." This, however, is something which occurs in all good literature.[33] In the ḥadīth above, Allāh's Messenger ﷺ pointed to the lines he had drawn in the dust and said, "This is man, and this is his appointed time," and "This is man's wish." He did not say, "This is like man," or "This is like his appointed time," even though that was what he really meant. Undoubtedly, then, the use of metaphorical language is perfectly acceptable.

There remain here two matters in need of clarification. The first is an explanation of what similarities exist between two essentially unlike things; and the second is an answer to the objection that since the names of the Almighty are self-designated, *tawqīfī*, then where did the Sufi masters get permission to use other, undesignated names?

In brief, the explanation of the first matter is that similarities between the Divine Essence and natural phenomena only seem to be similarities. In actual

31 Bukhārī: 6418, Tirmidhī: 2454

32 Al-Qur'ān: 24:35

33 This is what marks the difference between a simile and a metaphor; both of which are found throughout the Qur'ān. YTD.

fact, they are not. The oneness or unity of Allāh ﷻ, for example, is real, whereas the oneness of the ocean is only a relative sort of oneness. Likewise, the Almighty is a source in the sense that He is the effective and principal cause, whereas the ocean is only a material and secondary cause. And so forth. Certainly, these are significant differences, but they do not prevent comparison or metaphorical representation. For a detailed discussion of this subject, the qualified reader will find nothing better than what Qāḍī Mubārak wrote in his commentary on Muḥib Allāh Bihārī's book, *Sullam al-ʿulūm*.[34] The basis of the simile of the sun, as the source of beneficial light, is obvious.

To clarify the second point, it should be sufficient to point out that designation, *tawqīf*, extends only to the names of the Almighty, and not to every one of His perfect attributes. With the above commentary and clarification in mind, it should be possible to gain a proper understanding of the following verses of mystic poetry, and others like them, without going to the extreme of labelling their authors "disbelievers."

Though the ocean be one, from its fathomless depths
Come the waves with hue and form.
The sun rises, a sign of the sun.
The proof lies in a look at the sun.
Red wine, imbibe, and on the moonfaced, gaze.
Forsake religion and on these beauties gaze.

It should be noted that in these verses "moonfaced beauties" should be understood as representing the manifestations or *tajalliyāt* of the Almighty's perfect attributes.

ḤADĪTH 11

عن ابن عمرَ رَضِيَ اللهُ عَنْهُ قال: أَخَذَ رَسُوْلُ اللهِ صَلَّى اللهُ عَلَيْهِ وَسَلَّمَ بِمَنْكِبِيْ وقَالَ: «كُنْ فِيْ الدُّنْيَا كَأَنَّكَ غَرِيْبٌ أَوْ عَابِرُ سَبِيْلٍ» (أخرجه البخاري والترمذي) وَزَادَ التِّرْمِذِيُّ بعد قوله أوْعَابِرُ سَبِيْلٍ «وَعُدْ نَفْسَكَ مِنْ أَهْلِ الْقُبُوْرِ».

Ibn ʿUmar ﷺ said, "The Messenger of Allāh ﷺ took me by the shoulder and said, 'Live in this world as if you were a stranger, or just a passerby.'" This was related by Bukhārī and Tirmidhī. However, in the version related

34 This is a well-known Ḥanafī text on the subject of legal theory or *ʿuṣūl al-fiqh*. YTD.

by Tirmidhī, after the words, "or just a passerby," the following sentence is added: "And consider yourself to be among the people of the graves."[35]

Sayings: Die Before you Die
This saying is one that Sufis often repeat, and this ḥadīth is the equivalent of its meaning. Therefore, it is not inconceivable that this saying could be a ḥadīth in meaning, even though it is not a ḥadīth in the technical sense of the word. In fact, the great majority of Sufi sayings believed popularly to be the words of the Messenger ﷺ have equivalents, at least in meaning, in the authentic ḥadīths of the Messenger ﷺ. Therefore, to generalise about the Sufis narrating and popularising spurious material in the name of ḥadīths is decidedly unfair and unwarranted.

Character: Contemplation
The heartfelt contemplation of a subject, under all conditions or for a limited period of time, where the intention is to begin acting on the requisites of what is being contemplated, is called *murāqabah*. This is one of the primary objectives of inner conduct. In the ḥadīth above it is *murāqabah* that Ibn ʿUmar ﷺ is being urged to practise, because counting oneself among the dead has to do with inner, not outer, conduct. The results of regular *murāqabah* are a flagging in one's desire for the things of this world, the dwindling away of lust, rancour, and other blameworthy character traits, and an increase in commitment and submission to the will of the Almighty.

ḤADĪTH 12

وعن قيس بن أبي غَرَزَةَ رَضِيَ اللهُ عَنْهُ قَالَ: كُنَّا نُسمَّى فِيْ عَهْدِ رَسُوْلِ اللهِ صَلَّى اللهُ عَلَيْهِ وَسَلَّمَ السَّمَاسِرَةَ فَمَرَّ بِنَا رَسُوْلُ اللهِ صَلَّى اللهُ عَلَيْهِ وَسَلَّمَ فَسَمَّانَا بِاسْمٍ هُوَ أَحْسَنُ مِنْهُ فَقَالَ: «يامَعْشَرَ التُّجَّارِ! إِنَّ الْبَيْعَ يَحْضُرُهُ اللَّغْوُ وَالْحَلْفُ فَشُوْبُوْهُ بِالصَّدَقَةِ». (رواه أبوداؤد، والترمذي والنسائي)

Qays ibn Abī Gharazah ﷺ said, "In the time of Allāh's Messenger ﷺ we were called brokers. Then the Messenger ﷺ stopped by the marketplace one day and gave us a better name, saying, 'O you merchants![36] Surely your buying and selling is sometimes attended by gross exaggeration and

35 Bukhārī: 6416, Tirmidhī: 2333, Ibn Mājah: 4114
36 Note that he called them merchants instead of brokers. YTD.

the swearing of oaths. So, fortify your deals with charity.'" This ḥadīth was related by Abū Dāwūd, Tirmidhī, and Nasā'ī.[37]

Customs: Taking a New Name

In many spiritual families it has become common practice for a disciple to take a new name after taking *bayᶜah* at the hands of a master. The basis for this custom could possibly be derived from the ḥadīth above in which the Messenger of Allāh ﷺ used the word "merchant" instead of "broker" to address the Muslim traders he was visiting.[38]

ḤADĪTH 13

عن أبى هريرة رَضِيَ اللهُ عَنْهُ قال: قَالَ رَسُوْلُ اللهِ صَلَّى اللهُ عَلَيْهِ وَسَلَّمَ: «إِذَا صَلَّى أَحَدُكُمْ فَلْيَجْعَلْ تِلْقَاءَ وَجْهِهِ شَيْئاً فَإِنْ لَمْ يَجِدْ فَلْيَنْصِبْ عَصَاهُ فَإِنْ لَمْ يَكُنْ مَعَهُ عَصًا، فَلْيَخْطُطْ خَطًّا ثُمَّ لَايَضُرُّهُ مَامَرَّ أَمَامَهُ». (رواه أبوداؤد وابن ماجة)

It is related on the authority of Abū Huraira ؓ that the Messenger of Allāh ﷺ said: "When one of you intends to perform the prayer [out in the open], let him first put something in front of himself. If he can find nothing else, then let him put his staff into the ground. If he has no staff, then let him draw a line in front of himself. In that way, nothing that passes in front of him [while he performs prayer] will bother him."[39]

Practices: Collecting One's Thoughts

The state-producing practices prescribed by the Sufi masters all have as their

---

37 Abū Dāwūd: 3326, Tirmidhī: 1208, Nasā'ī: 4468, Ibn Mājah: 2145

38 Prior to Islam traders were free to transact business in any way that they pleased. Thus, in pursuit of greater profits, they committed any number of what, after Islam, would be called unlawful practices. So, in view of the traders having taken to new practices after their conversion to Islam, Allah's Messenger gave them a new name as well. However, since the majority of business transactions, in spite of their technical legality, are rarely free of dubious elements, like the swearing off frivolous oaths, merchants are urged to regularly give a portion of their earnings in charity. This is only one of many examples from the ḥadīth in which Muslims are urged to exercise caution in their worldly affairs, especially where finances are concerned. YTD.

39 Abū Dāwūd: 689. Al-Mundhirī reported from Sufyān ibn ᶜUyayna, who said: 'We have not found anything that would corroborate this report and it has not been narrated but through this chain.' Whenever Ismāᶜīl ibn Umayyah reported this ḥadīth, he would ask: 'Do you have anything that corroborates this?' Imām ash-Shāfiᶜī has also alluded to the weakness of this report. Imām Bayhaqī said: 'This [weakness] does not matter in establishing this ruling.'

object the creation, after dispelling any inner confusion, of a certain presence of mind or oneness of concentration which, once it has become second nature, will greatly facilitate the matter of directing one's attention exclusively to Allāh ﷻ. Obviously, however, as the One to be contemplated is himself Unseen, and as the beginner is rarely able to clear his/her mind of outside thoughts, it takes a great deal of practice before this presence of mind can become second nature. At any rate, the disciplines of the Sufis are basically methods for acquiring this second nature. The ḥadīth above might be the source from which all of this (knowledge) was derived, because the scholars, such as Ibn Humām in his commentary on the *Hidāyah*, have written that among other things, the wisdom behind *sutrah* (putting something in front of oneself when performing prayer in the open) is that it allows one to collect one's thoughts and dispels confusion.

ḤADĪTH 14

عن أبي هريرة رَضِيَ اللهُ عَنْهُ قال: قال رسولُ الله صَلَّى اللهُ عَلَيْهِ وَسَلَّمَ: «إِنَّ الله إِذَا أَحَبَّ عَبْدًا دَعَا جِبْرَئِيْلَ فَقَالَ: إِنِّيْ أُحِبُّ فُلاَنًا فَأَحِبَّهُ قَالَ: فَيُحِبُّهُ جِبْرَئِيْلُ، ثُمَّ يُنَادِيْ فِيْ السَّمَاءِ، فَيَقُوْلُ: إِنَّ الله يُحِبُّ فُلاَنًا فَأَحِبُّوْهُ، فَيُحِبُّهُ أَهْلُ السَّمَاءِ، ثُمَّ يُوْضَعُ لَهُ الْقُبُوْلُ فِيْ الأَرْضِ، وَإِذَا أَبْغَضَ عَبْدًا دَعَا جِبْرَئِيْلَ عَلَيْهِ السَّلاَمُ فَيَقُوْلُ: إِنِّيْ أُبْغِضُ فُلاَنًا فَأَبْغِضْهُ قَالَ: فَيُبْغِضُهُ جِبْرَئِيْلُ عَلَيْهِ السَّلاَمُ ثُمَّ يُنَادِيْ فِيْ أَهْلِ السَّمَاءِ، إِنَّ الله يُبْغِضُ فُلاَنًا فَأَبْغِضُوْهُ قَالَ: فَيُبْغِضُوْنَهُ ثُمَّ يُوْضَعُ لَهُ الْبَغْضَاءُ فِيْ الأَرْضِ». (رواه مسلم)

It is related on the authority of Abū Huraira ﵁ that the Messenger of Allāh ﷺ said: "When Allāh loves someone, He calls Jibrīl ﵇ and says, 'I love so and so. Now, you love him too.' Then Jibrīl, too, loves that person, and calls out to the inhabitants of the heavens, 'Allāh ﷻ loves so and so. Now, you love him too.' So the inhabitants of the heavens come to love that person as well, and the person is accepted all over the earth. When Allāh ﷻ despises someone, He calls Jibrīl and says, 'I despise so and so. Now, you despise him too.' Then Jibrīl, too, despises that person, and calls out to the inhabitants of the heavens, 'Allāh ﷻ despises so and so, now you despise him too.' So the inhabitants of the heavens despise him too, and that person becomes despicable in the eyes of people all over the earth." This ḥadīth was related by Muslim.[40]

40 Muslim: 2637

Signs: Acceptance and Rejection

In the ḥadīth above the *walī* or true spiritual master is distinguished from the non-walī. One should be careful to heed this distinction in one's search for a spiritual guide, and remember always to avoid a guide who is not a true *walī*. When, for no obvious reason, the hearts of many good and decent people are inclined toward a certain person, it is generally a sign that the person has been accepted by the Almighty. Similarly, when for no obvious reason decent people find themselves ill-disposed toward a certain person, it is generally a sign that the person has not been accepted by the Almighty. Of course, if people accept or reject a person on the basis of family ties, wealth, position, or hearsay, then this has nothing to do with that person's standing with the Almighty. Finally, it should be remembered that the inclination or disinclination of people in whom there exist inner infirmities or corruption cannot be considered a valid indicator of anyone's acceptance or rejection by the Almighty.

ḤADĪTH 15

عن مُعاذِ بن جبلٍ رَضِيَ اللهُ عَنْهُ قَالَ: سَمِعْتُ رَسُوْلَ اللهِ صَلَّى اللهُ عَلَيْهِ وَسَلَّمَ يَقُوْلُ: قَالَ اللهُ تَعَالَى: «وَجَبَتْ مَحَبَّتِيْ لِلْمُتَحَابِّيْنَ فِيَّ وَالْمُتَجَالِسِيْنَ وَالْمُتَزَاوِرِيْنَ فِيَّ وَالْمُتَبَاذِلِيْنَ فِيَّ». (رواه مالك)

It is related on the authority of Muʿādh ibn Jabal ﷺ that he heard the Messenger of Allāh ﷺ say: "Allāh ﷻ said, 'Those may be assured of My love who love one another for My sake, who sit with one another for My sake, who visit one another for My sake, and who spend on one another for My sake.'" This ḥadīth was related by Mālik.[41]

Virtues: The Sufis

In the good tidings of this ḥadīth, reference is clearly made to the virtues of the true Sufis, because the attributes mentioned in the ḥadīth are among the chief attributes of the Sufis. For example, the love between a master and his disciple, the affection between fellow disciples, the respect shown by all Sufis for masters other than their own, their generosity in dealing with one another, and their undertaking lengthy journeys for the purpose of visiting one another; all of these things they do for the sake of Allāh, without the slightest trace of worldly motivation.

41 *Muwaṭṭa' Mālik*: 1710

ḤADĪTH 16

عن أَبِي الدَّرْدَاءِ رَضِيَ اللهُ عَنْهُ قَالَ: مَا أَوَدُّ أَنَّ لِيْ مَتْجَراً عَلَى دَرَجَةِ جَامِعِ دِمَشْقَ أُصِيْبُ فِيْهِ كُلَّ يَوْمٍ خَمْسِيْنَ دِيْنَاراً أَتَصَدَّقُ بِهَا فِيْ سَبِيْلِ اللهِ وَلاتَفُوْتُنِيْ الصَّلوةُ فِيْ الْجَمَاعَةِ وَمَا بِيْ تَحْرِيْمُ مَا أَحَلَّ اللهُ تَعَالَى وَلٰكِنِّيْ أَكْرَهُ أَنْ لَا أَكُوْنَ مِنَ الَّذِيْنَ قَالَ اللهُ تَعَالَى فِيْهِمْ: ﴿رِجَالٌ لاَّ تُلْهِيْهِمْ تِجَارَةٌ وَّلاَ بَيْعٌ عَنْ ذِكْرِ اللهِ﴾ (أخرجه رزين)

It is related that Abū Dardā' ﷺ said, "For myself, I have no desire to own a shop on the steps of the Great Mosque in Damascus, even if I could earn fifty dinars a day there to spend in the way of Allāh ﷻ, and never miss performing a single ṣalāh in congregation. It is certainly not my place to prohibit what Allāh ﷻ has legitimised. It is just that I do not like the idea of not being among those described by the Almighty as '. . .people whom neither commerce nor sale divert from the remembrance of Allāh.'" This ḥadīth was related by Razīn.[42]

Practices: Exaggeration in Severing Worldly Ties

The majority of Sufis have never preferred for themselves to have more worldly ties than are absolutely necessary, even though those ties might be perfectly legitimate and acceptable. Instead, it has always been their way to live unencumbered and simple lives, by placing their trust in Allāh. My own master, Hājī Imdād Allāh, may the mercy of Allāh surround his soul, once wrote to a wealthy disciple of his in India who had intimated his intention to move permanently to Makka, that he should arrange for only enough money to be sent to him each month as would cover his basic expenses, and no more; not even for distribution to the needy in charity. Instead, our master told the disciple that if he wanted to help someone financially, he should arrange for the money to be distributed in India directly. In that way, he himself, while living in the holy city of Makka, need never concern himself with anything but worship. Now, many of those who look to nothing but externals will object that the severance of legitimate worldly ties is a form of monasticism (which was clearly prohibited by Allāh's Prophet ﷺ). Who knows what such people would have to say if they read what our master wrote to that wealthy disciple about not taking money for distribution as charity (which is, in itself, a form of worship)? Even so, it is clear from the ḥadīth above that Abū Dardā', who preferred not to own a shop even when he knew that

---

42 Imām Suyūṭī has quoted it in *ad-Durr al-Manthūr* (5/94) from ʿAbd ibn Ḥumayd and Imām Aḥmad's *az-Zuhd*.

it would enable him to give so much in charity every day from his earnings there, was of the same school of thought as our master. Is it possible that a companion of the Prophet ﷺ was guilty of the practice of monasticism or of deliberately preferring not to perform an act of worship? The secret behind all of this is that through an excess of worldly ties an element of confusion is introduced into the state of communion with the Almighty. When Abū Dardā' ؓ said, "And it is certainly not my place to prohibit what Allāh has legalised," he made it clear that he would have no part in monasticism. When he said, "I just do not like the idea of not being among those described by the Almighty as, '. . .people whom neither commerce nor sale divert from the remembrance of Allāh ﷻ,'" he revealed the secret. His interpretation of the Qur'ānic verse is one which took into account the simple fact that most people are unable to transact business while remaining, at the same time, constant in their remembrance of the Almighty.[43]

The following verse of Persian poetry nicely illustrates the point that Abū Dardā' had in mind:

The words that interrupt you when communing with
  Your friend, what matter if of faith, or disbelief!
Or that which screens you from your friend when you would meet,
  What good if it appears a lovely sight or not?

ḤADĪTH 17

عن جابر رَضِيَ اللهُ عَنْهُ فِيْ حَدِيْثٍ طَوِيْلٍ فِيْهِ قِصَّةُ بَيْعِ الْجَمَلِ فَلَمَّا قَدِمْتُ الْمَدِيْنَةَ قَالَ رَسُوْلُ اللهِ صَلَّى اللهُ عَلَيْهِ وَسَلَّمَ لِبِلَالٍ: «أَعْطِهِ أُوْقِيَةَ ذَهَبٍ وَزِدْهُ» فَزَادَنِيْ قِيْرَاطاً فَقُلْتُ: لا تُفَارِقُنِيْ زِيَادَةُ رَسُوْلِ اللهِ صَلَّى اللهُ عَلَيْهِ وَسَلَّمَ فَكَانَ فِيْ كِيْسٍ لِيْ إِلَى أَنْ أَخَذَهُ أَهْلُ الشَّامِ يَوْمَ الْحَرَّةِ . (رواه مسلم)

Jābir ؓ, in a lengthy narration of how he sold his camel, said, "When I arrived at Madīna, the Messenger of Allāh ﷺ said to Bilāl ؓ, 'Give him (Jābir) a measure of gold (in payment for the camel), and add a little extra.' So he gave me a whole carat extra. Then I said to myself, 'Never will I part with this extra carat of gold from the Messenger of Allāh ﷺ!' Thereafter, it remained with me always, in a leather pouch, until it was taken from me

43 Otherwise, the other well know interpretation of this verse, that of Ibn ʿAbbās, takes into account the fact that the first Muslims were both the best of traders and the best of people in their remembrance of Allah. YTD.

(forcibly) by the Syrians at the battle of Ḥarrah." This ḥadīth was related by Muslim.[44]

Practices: Holding Keepsakes

It is the practice of most Sufis to keep something that belongs (or belonged) to their masters as a memento. This is something that is done purely out of love for the master. The precedent for this practice is clearly related in the ḥadīth above.

ḤADĪTH 18

عن عوف بن مالك الأشْجَعِيِّ رَضِيَ اللهُ عَنْهُ قَالَ: قَالَ رَسُوْلُ اللهِ صَلَّى اللهُ عَلَيْهِ وَسَلَّمَ:
«أَنَا وَامْرَأَةٌ سَفْعَاءُ الْخَدَّيْنِ كَهَاتَيْنِ يَوْمَ الْقِيمَةِ، اِمْرَأَةٌ آمَتْ مِنْ زَوْجِهَا ذَاتُ مَنْصَبٍ
وَجَمَالٍ، حَبَسَتْ نَفْسَهَا عَلَى يَتَامَاهَا حَتَّى بَانُوْا أَوْمَاتُوْا» (أخرجه أبو داود)

It is related on the authority of ʿAwf ibn Mālik that the Messenger of Allāh ﷺ said: "I and a woman with parched cheeks [one who has had to toil and suffer] will be like these two [i.e. as close as the index finger is to the middle finger] on the Day of Judgment; a woman whose husband died and left her a widow, a woman who, despite social pressures and her own beauty, refused to remarry for the sake of her children [in order to devote herself to them more completely], until finally they grew up and set out on their own, or died." This ḥadīth was related by Abū Dāwūd.[45]

Practices: Choosing to Remain Unmarried

In order to keep their worldly ties to a minimum, or in order to avoid any kind of real or imagined interference in their relationship with the Almighty, some Sufis never marry. As a result, certain narrow-minded individuals have accused the Sufis of not adhering to the Sunna or way of the Prophet ﷺ. In the above ḥadīth, not only do we find permission for remaining single, we also find that wherever there is a possibility of a child's being neglected, it is better to abstain from marriage. This is, of course, on the condition that one's practice of Islam will not be adversely affected. So, when the possibility that a child will be neglected is a legitimate excuse for not marrying, what then of the possibility that Allāh ﷻ will be neglected?

---

44 Muslim: 715, 1599

45 Abū Dāwūd: 5149. Al-Mundhirī said: 'In its chain, there is Abū 'l-Khaṭṭāb an-Nahhās ibn Qahm al-Baṣrī and his *hadīth*s cannot be argued from.'

ḤADĪTH 19

عن الأحنف بن قَيْسٍ فِيْ حَدِيْثٍ طَوِيْلٍ قَالَ: قُلْتُ: أي لأبي ذَرٍّ رَضِيَ اللهُ عَنْهُ مَا تَقُوْلُ فِيْ هذِهِ الْعَطَاءِ؟ قَالَ: خُذْهُ، فَإِنَّ فِيْهِ الْيَوْمَ مَعُوْنَةً فَإِذَا كَانَ ثَمَنًا لِدِيْنِكَ فَدَعْهُ. (أخرجه الشيخان)

In a lengthy narration, Aḥnaf ibn Qays said, "I said to Abū Dharr ﷺ, 'What do you say about these [monthly or yearly sums granted by rulers as] gifts?' He replied, 'Take them. For nowadays you will find succour in them. But if ever these should become the price of your faith, then drop them.'" This ḥadīth was related by Bukhārī and Muslim.[46]

Practices: Accepting Gifts from the Wealthy

In general, it has been the practice of Sufi masters to accept gifts and stipends. The benefits of their doing so are peace of mind and freedom from having to concern themselves with things that might distract them from their real work. The ḥadīth above is explicit in its giving permission for this practice. However, if the patron has some reason other than sincere love for the master, and actually wants to give money in payment for something he wants from the master, then, under those circumstances, his gifts may not be accepted. Similarly, if the gift is tainted with illegitimate earnings, such as would bring detriment to the name of Islam, then the gift may surely not be accepted. As a general rule, then, a gift may be accepted only when it comes unaccompanied by anything contrary to Islamic teachings.

ḤADĪTH 20

عن عبد الله بن عمرو بْنِ الْعَاصِ رَضِيَ اللهُ عَنْهُ قَالَ: مَرَّ بِيْ رَسُوْلُ اللهِ صَلَّى اللهُ عَلَيْهِ وَسَلَّمَ وَأَنَا أُطَيِّنُ حَائِطاً مِنْ خُصٍّ، فَقَالَ: «مَاهذَا يَا عَبْدَاللهِ؟» فَقُلْتُ: حَائِطٌ أُصْلِحُهُ فَقَالَ: «الأمرُ أَسْرَعُ مِنْ ذلِكَ» وَفِيْ رِوَايَةٍ: «مَاأَرَى الأَمْرَ إِلَّا أَعْجَلَ مِنْ ذلِكَ». (أخرجه أبوداود والترمذي وصححه)

ʿAbdullāh ibn ʿAmr ibn al-ʿĀs said, "The Messenger of Allāh ﷺ passed me by as I was plastering the wall of a hut, and remarked, 'O ʿAbdullāh! What

46 This ḥadīth could not be found in Bukhārī with these words. Muslim: 1657

is this?' I replied, 'Just a wall that needs repairing.' Then he said to me, 'The matter of death is even simpler than that.'" In another version of the same ḥadīth, the Prophet ﷺ says, "I see the matter of death as something even closer than that [wall]." This ḥadīth was related by Abū Dāwūd and Tirmidhī.[47]

Practices: Exaggeration in Severing Worldly Ties

This practice has already been discussed in the commentary of ḥadīth [16]. Obviously, the ḥadīth above refers to the same practice.

ḤADĪTH 21

عن الحارث الأعور، عن علي رَضِيَ اللهُ عَنْهُ قَالَ رَسُوْلُ اللهِ صَلَّى اللهُ عَلَيْهِ وَسَلَّمَ (فِيْ فَضِيْلَةِ الْقُرْآنِ مِنْ حَدِيْثٍ طَوِيْلٍ) «لايَشْبَعُ مِنْهُ الْعُلَمَاءُ، وَلا يَخْلُقُ عَلَيَ كَثْرَةِ الرَّدِّ، وَلاتَنْقَضِيْ عَجَائِبُهُ» الحديث. (أخرجه الترمذي)

It is related on the authority of ʿAlī ؓ that the Messenger of Allāh ﷺ said [among other things in a lengthy ḥadīth], ". . .and the learned will never have their fill of it; and even though it be read and reread, over and over again, it will never seem old, and its wonders will never cease." This ḥadīth was related by Tirmidhī.[48]

States: Spiritual Knowledge

When, through constant remembrance, *dhikr*, and other spiritual practices and disciplines, the darkness of the self and other impurities are dispelled, the heart and soul of the Sufi will enter into a special relationship with the Almighty, so that certain spiritual subtleties and knowledge will be bestowed upon the Sufi from within, as it were, bypassing the usual mediums of learning and study. That this is something which actually occurs is attested to in the ḥadīth above. This is because ordinary, recorded knowledge is limited in scope—once it is digested, that is the end of it, whereas spiritual knowledge is unlimited and, more often than not, impossible to digest.

---

47 Abū Dāwūd: 5235, Tirmidhī: 2335, Ibn Mājah: 4160

48 Tirmidhī: 2906. He said: 'This is a strange ḥadīth; we do not know it but through the report of Ḥamzah az-Zayyāt. And his chain in unknown and there is a doubt in the ḥadīth of Ḥārith.'

ḤADĪTH 22

عن أبي هريرة رَضِيَ اللهُ عَنْهُ أَنَّ رَسُوْلَ اللهِ صَلَّى اللهُ عَلَيْهِ وَسَلَّمَ قَالَ: «مَا اجْتَمَعَ قَوْمٌ فِيْ بَيتٍ مِنْ بُيُوْتِ اللهِ تَعَالى يَتْلُوْنَ كِتبَ اللهِ، وَيَتَدَارَسُوْنَهُ بَيْنَهُمْ إِلاَّ نَزَلَتْ عَلَيْهِمُ السَّكِيْنَةُ وَغَشِيَتْهُمُ الرَّحْمَةُ، وَحَفَّتْهُمُ الْمَلاءِكَةُ، وَذَكَرَهُمُ اللهُ فِيْمَنْ عِنْدَهُ». (أخرجه أبوداؤد)

It is related on the authority of Abū Huraira ؓ that Allāh's Prophet ﷺ said, "Never will a group of people gather in a house from among the houses of Allāh for the recitation of Allāh's Book, or to study it among themselves, except that a state of spiritual tranquility, *sakīna*, will descend upon them, and they are overcome by Divine Mercy, and they are surrounded by angels, and they are mentioned by Allāh as being among those closest to Him." This ḥadīth was related by Abū Dāwūd.[49]

Practices: Group Remembrance

The gathering together of a number of Sufis for the purpose of remembrance, *dhikr*, illuminating their inner beings, enhancing their animation, increasing their determination, and warding off inertia is called group remembrance. The precedent for this practice, along with an indication of its positive spiritual benefits, is to be found in the ḥadīth above.

Customs: Spiritual Retreats

Since the Companions of the Prophet ﷺ and the Followers ؓ had their inner beings enlightened through proximity to the Messenger of Allāh ﷺ, so that they had acquired the ability to maintain states of constant remembrance, they were in no need of seclusion for the purpose of developing this ability. Later on, however, owing to changed conditions, the custom of building retreats became widespread among the Sufi masters, and with good reason. In the ḥadīth above, the words, "houses of Allāh" are usually interpreted to mean mosques. However, since the phrase is figurative, it may be assumed that it refers to the general and not only to the particular. Secondly, when the mosque and retreat are established for more or less the same purposes, they may all be said to share in the description "houses of Allāh." Therefore, in this wise, the ḥadīth may be cited as a precedent for the custom of building retreats.

States: The Inner Condition of Tranquility

Experience has shown that, as a result of one's involvement in constant remem-

---

49 Abū Dāwūd: 1455

brance, a certain strange yet pleasant state comes over the heart and, with continued involvement, will grow stronger and more permanent. In the terminology of the Sufis, this is called *nisba* or affinity. In the ḥadīth above, the word *sakīna* is used to denote the same phenomenon.

ḤADĪTH 23

عن أبي سعيد الْخُدْرِيِّ رَضِيَ اللهُ عَنْهُ قَالَ: قَالَ رَسُوْلُ الله صَلَّى اللهُ عَلَيْهِ وَسَلَّمَ: يَقُوْلُ اللهُ تَعَالَى: «مَنْ شَغَلَهُ الْقُرْانُ عَنْ مَسْئَلَتِيْ أَعْطَيْتُهُ أَفْضَلَ مَا أُعْطِيْ السَّائِلِيْنَ». (أخرجه الترمذي)

It is related on the authority of Abū Saʿīd al-Khudrī 🙵 that Allāh's Prophet 🙵 said, "The Almighty says, 'Whoever is diverted from supplicating Me owing to their preoccupation with recitation of the Qurʾān, will be granted the best of what I grant to those who supplicate.'"[50]

Practices: Non-essential Acts of Worship during Intense Sessions of Remembrance
In most Sufi orders the disciple is given a particular *dhikr*-formula to repeat as a spiritual discipline. While engaged in this discipline, the disciple will forgo many other virtuous acts, like supererogatory prayers, lessons in the Islamic sciences, listening to talks about faith, and so forth. This practice is one which has drawn the criticism of many of those who concern themselves with no more than the externals of Islam. In brief, the reason behind this practice of the Sufis is that at the outset of discipleship, the disciple's internal state is subordinate to the disciple's external state. Over a period of time, however, the opposite will come about, so that the external state will be subordinate to the disciple's internal state. Therefore, if at the outset the disciple is allowed to undertake a number of different activities, it will be next to impossible for the disciple to achieve the mental and spiritual concentration that is at the heart of all Sufi training. The ḥadīth above comes as confirmation of this practice. Therefore, preoccupation with the Qurʾān's recitation, which is itself a kind of *dhikr*,[51] (and to the extent that one neglects as important an act of worship as supplication, *duʿā*) is accorded praise rather than criticism. This is the gist of the practice I have just described.

---

50 Tirmidhī: 2926
51 The Qurʾān describes itself as "…but *dhikr* for all of the worlds" (12:104). YTD.

ḤADĪTH 24

عن عائشةرضي الله تعالى عنها قالت: قَالَ رَسُوْلُ اللهِ صَلَّى اللهُ عَلَيْهِ وَسَلَّمَ: «اَلْمَاهِرُ بِالْقُرْآنِ مَعَ السَّفَرَةِ الْكِرَامِ الْبَرَرَةِ، وَالَّذِيْ يَقْرَأُ الْقُرْآنَ وَيَتَعْتَعُ فِيْهِ وَهُوَ عَلَيْهِ شَاقٌّ لَهُ أَجْرَانِ». (أخرجه الخمسة الا النسائي)

It is related on the authority of ʿĀ'isha ﵂ that the Messenger of Allāh ﷺ said, "One who has mastered the Qur'ān shares the rank of the noble, pious scribes.[52] While one who recites the Qur'ān falteringly, who finds it difficult to recite, for such a one there is a two-fold reward." This ḥadīth was related by Bukhārī, Muslim, Abū Dāwūd, and Tirmidhī.[53]

Teachings: The Irrelevance of Pleasure in Matters of Worship

It sometimes happens, when people find that they are not deriving any pleasure from the act of remembrance, *dhikr*, or the performance of other acts of worship, that they become discouraged and stop doing those things altogether. Sometimes they become so disheartened that they begin thinking that what they were doing was in vain and essentially futile. Such misgivings are anathema to inner, spiritual development because it is confidence that is the key to all such development. The masters have written that the object is *dhikr*, not pleasure. In fact, they say, to maintain one's level of involvement in *dhikr*, even when it is not enjoyable to do so, is of more benefit to the Sufi than if it actually gave him/her great pleasure. Therefore, a lack of pleasure is not necessarily indicative of a corresponding lack of benefit. Rather, the opposite is true. In the ḥadīth above, this truth is clearly set forth in the promise of a double reward for the person who struggles in reciting the Qur'ān; for the reason that there is a proportional relationship between the degree of difficulty and the amount of reward. This is what spiritual disciplines are all about.

ḤADĪTH 25

عَنْ أُسَيْدِ بْنِ حُضَيْرٍ رَضِيَ اللهُ عَنْهُ قَالَ: بَيْنَمَا هُوَ يَقْرَأُ مِن اللَّيْلِ سُوْرَةَ الْبَقَرَةِ وَفَرَسُهُ مَرْبُوْطٌ عِنْدَهُ، إِذْ جَالَتِ الْفَرَسُ فَسَكَتَ فَسَكَنَتْ، فَقَرَأَ فَجَالَتْ، فَسَكَتَ، فَسَكَنَتِ الْفَرَسُ، ثُمَّ قَرَأَ فَجَالَتْ وَكَانَ اِبْنُهُ يَحْيى قَرِيْباً مِنْهَا فَانْصَرَفَ، فَأَخْرَجَهُ ثُمَّ رَفَعَ رَأْسَهُ إِلَى

52 Al-Qur'ān, 80:15.

53 Bukhārī: 3937, Muslim: 798, Abū Dāwūd: 1454, Tirmidhī: 2904, Ibn Mājah: 3779

السَّمَاءِ، فَإِذَا مِثْلُ الظُّلَّةِ فِيْهَا أَمْثَالُ الْمَصَابِيْحِ، فَلَمَّا أَصْبَحَ حَدَّثَ بِهِ النَّبِيَّ صَلَّى اللهُ عَلَيْهِ وَسَلَّمَ فَقَالَ: «أَوَتَدْرِيْ مَاذَاكَ؟» قَالَ: لاَ، فَقَالَ: «تِلْكَ الْمَلائِكَةُ دَنَتْ لِصَوْتِكَ وَلَوْ قَرَأْتَ لأَصْبَحَتْ يَنْظُرُ إِلَيْهَا النَّاسُ لاَ تَتَوَارى مِنْهُمْ». (أخرجه البخاري)

It is related on the authority of Usayd ibn Ḥuḍayr ؓ that as he was reciting one night from the second chapter of the Qur'ān, near where he had tethered his horse for the night, the horse suddenly sprang up [apparently for no reason]. 'Usayd ؓ then stopped his recitation, and the horse grew still. When 'Usayd ؓ began reciting again, the horse sprang up another time. So he stopped, and the horse grew quiet. Usayd ؓ again began to recite, and again the horse sprang up. Then, since his son, Yaḥyā ؓ, was sleeping nearby the horse, 'Usayd ؓ got up and moved him away. It was then that he happened to raise his head up to the sky when, lo and behold, he saw something like a cloud with lamps lit up inside of it. In the morning 'Usayd ؓ related all this to the Messenger of Allāh ﷺ, who said, "Do you know what that was?" "No," Usayd ؓ replied. The Messenger ﷺ said, "Those were angels approaching at the sound of your recitation. If you had continued reciting, the people would have risen this morning and seen them, and they would not have been invisible!" This ḥadīth was related by Bukhārī.[54]

Questions: The Possibility of Angels Revealing Themselves to other than a Prophet

According to the scholars of Islam, not only is it possible for the masters to see the angels, it is also possible for them to converse with the angels. Nor, they add, is this merely a matter of speculation, as such things have actually occurred. The ḥadīth above is an unambiguous account of one such occurrence. In another ḥadīth, related by Muslim, an incident is recorded in which the angels greeted ʿImrān ibn Ḥuṣayn ؓ.

Questions: The Possibility of Being Unable to Interpret One's Own Visions

Another point to be derived from the ḥadīth above is that it often happens that Sufis who have spiritual visions, *kashf*, are incapable of penetrating to the true meaning of those visions. In the ḥadīth above, 'Usayd ؓ actually saw the angels, but was nonetheless unaware that what he had seen were truly angels. Sufi scholars have written that the person who has taken this point to heart will never again rely on his/her own opinion or intellect in the matter of interpreting visions. Indeed, such a person will avoid making many mistakes.[55]

---

54 Bukhārī: 5018

55 In other words, all such visions should be discussed with someone with greater experience. YTD.

ḤADĪTH 26

عَنْ أُبَيِّ بْنِ كَعْبٍ رَضِيَ اللهُ عَنْهُ قَالَ: قَالَ رَسُولُ اللهِ صَلَّى اللهُ عَلَيْهِ وَسَلَّمَ: «يَا أَبَا الْمُنْذِرِ!

أَتَدْرِيْ أَيَّ آيَةٍ مِنْ كِتَابِ اللهِ مَعَكَ أَعْظَمُ؟» قُلْتُ: ﴿اللهُ لاَ إِلَهَ إِلاَّ هُوَ الْحَيُّ الْقَيُّومُ﴾

فَضَرَبَ فِيْ صَدْرِيْ وَقَالَ: «لِيَهْنِئْكَ الْعِلْمُ أَبَا الْمُنْذِرِ». (أخرجه مسلم وأبوداؤد)

It is related on the authority of Ubayy ibn Ka'b ☙, that the Messenger of
Allāh ☙ once said to him, "O Abū Mundhir! Do you know which verse of
Allāh's Book is the greatest you have before you?" 'Ubayy ☙ replied, "Allāh,
there is no god but He, the Living, the Eternal."[56] Then the Prophet ☙ struck
Ubayy on the chest and said, "May this knowledge be a blessing to you, O
Abū Mundhir!" This ḥadīth was related by Muslim and Abū Dāwūd.[57]

States: Spiritual Knowledge
While this subject was discussed in the commentary on Ḥadīth 21, in the ḥadīth
above we find further confirmation of this phenomenon, as the naming of that
particular verse as the greatest in the entire Qur'ān came about through divine
inspiration. Furthermore, in the Prophet's congratulations to 'Ubayy ☙, there is
an obvious reference to the merit of that knowledge.[58]

Note: In this ḥadīth the Āyat al-Kursī[59] is called the greatest verse in the Book of
Allāh on the basis of the blessings to be had from its recitation. Many different
chapters and verses of the Qur'ān have been mentioned in the ḥadīth literature as
possessing blessings of one sort or another. That the blessings of some verses are
greater than those of others is true only in consideration of the different aspects
of each verse or chapter; otherwise every verse of the Qur'ān is equal when you
consider that each is the word of the Almighty, inimitable and miraculous. Thus,
there is no reason to suppose that the various ḥadīths which have come to us concerning the relative merits of one verse or another are in any way contradictory.

ḤADĪTH 27

عَنْ أَبِيْ هُرَيْرَةَ رَضِيَ اللهُ عَنْهُ قَالَ: وَكَّلَنِيْ رَسُولُ اللهِ صَلَّى اللهُ عَلَيْهِ وَسَلَّمَ بِحِفْظِ زَكوةِ

---

56 Qur'ān, 2:255

57 Muslim: 810, Abū Dāwūd: 1460

58 Likewise, in the Prophet's striking Ubay on the chest there is an obvious reference to the source of
that knowledge. YTD.

59 The verse quoted in the Ḥadīth: 2:255, is called the Āyat al-Kursī or the Verse of the Seat (of Power). YTD.

رَمَضَانَ، فَأَتَانِيْ اتٍ فَجَعَلَ يَحْثُوْ مِنَ الطَّعَامِ، فَأَخَذْتُهُ إِلَى أَنْ قَالَ: قَالَ رَسُوْلُ اللهِ صَلَّى اللهُ عَلَيْهِ وَسَلَّمَ: «تَعْلَمُ مَنْ تُخَاطِبُ مُنْذُ ثَلٰثِ لَيَالٍ يَا أَبَا هُرَيْرَةَ؟» قُلْتُ: لَا، قَالَ: «ذَاكَ شَيْطَانٌ». (أخرجه البخاري)

It is related that Abū Huraira ﷺ said, "Allāh's Prophet ﷺ entrusted me with the keeping of the zakāh money given during the month of Ramaḍān. One day, someone came to me and began taking handfuls of the grain [given as zakāh], so I grabbed him. . ." [At this point the ḥadīth continues until Abū Huraira said,] "So the Prophet asked me, 'Do you know whom you have been addressing for the last three days, O Abū Hurairah?' 'No,' I replied. Then he ﷺ said, 'That was Satan.'" This ḥadīth was related by Bukhārī.[60]

Questions: Satan and Simulation
It is clear from the ḥadīth above that Satan assumed a human form and revealed himself as such.

States: Miracles
It is an article of faith with Muslims that miracles may be performed by a *walī*, a true spiritual master. In the ḥadīth above, Abū Huraira's ﷺ capture of Satan was clearly one such miracle.

Questions: The Possibility of Being Unable to Interpret One's Own Miracles
A similar subject was discussed in the commentary on ḥadīth [25]. There, the subject was visions, *kashf*, whereas here the subject is minor miracles, *karāmāt*. In the ḥadīth above, Abū Huraira ﷺ admits his ignorance of the essence of his own *karāma*.

ḤADĪTH 28

عَنْ أَبِيْ أَيُّوْبَ رَضِيَ اللهُ عَنْهُ أَنَّهُ كَانَتْ لَهُ سَهْوَةٌ فِيْهَا تَمْرٌ وَكَانَتْ تَجِيْءُ الْغَوْلُ فَتَأْخُذُ مِنْهُ فَشَكَى ذٰلِكَ إِلَى رَسُوْلِ اللهِ صَلَّى اللهُ عَلَيْهِ وَسَلَّمَ قَالَ: «اِذْهَبْ فَإِذَا رَأَيْتَهَا فَقُلْ بِسْمِ اللهِ أَجِيْبِيْ رَسُوْلَ اللهِ» قَالَ: فَأَخَذَهَا. الحديث (أخرجه الترمذي)

It is related on the authority of Abū Ayyūb al-Anṣārī ﷺ that he had a cellar filled with dates from which the jinn used to take their fill without his permission. When he complained about this to the Prophet ﷺ, he replied,

60 Bukhārī: 2311, 3275, 5010

"Go! And when next you see them, say: 'In the name of Allāh! Answer the call of Allāh's Prophet!'" The narrator of the ḥadīth then said, "And so Abū Ayyūb ﵁ caught the jinn." This ḥadīth was narrated by Tirmidhī.[61]

Customs: Charms and Incantations

Most Sufi masters are called upon to make amulets and charms for people with particular needs, and to perform exorcisms and so forth. In such cases, most masters are too polite to refuse, and so, seeking the help of the Almighty, they do their best to furnish their petitioners with something that will be of use to them in solving their particular problems. In the ḥadīth above, the Messenger of Allāh ﷺ taught Abū Ayyūb ﵁ a formula for exorcising the jinn. Thus, it cannot be said that the custom of the Sufis is in any way contrary to the Sunna. In fact, there are several ḥadīths concerning the use of different charms and incantations.

ḤADĪTH 29

عن جابر رَضِيَ اللهُ عَنْهُ قال: فِينَا نَزَلَتْ ﴿إِذْ هَمَّتْ طَائِفَتَانِ مِنْكُمْ أَنْ تَفْشَلاَ وَاللهُ وَلِيُّهُمَا﴾ قَالَ: نَحْنُ الطَّائِفَتَانِ بَنُوْ حَارِثَةَ وَبَنُوْ سَلِمَةَ وَمَا يَسُرُّنِيْ أَنَّهَا لَمْ تَنْزِلْ لِقَوْلِ اللهِ تَعَالَى ﴿وَاللهُ وَلِيُّهُمَا﴾ (أخرجه الشيخان)

It is related on the authority of Jābir ﵁ that, "Concerning us the verse was revealed, 'When two parties amongst you were about to lose heart, even though Allāh is their Protector.'[62] Yes, we are those two parties, the tribes of Ḥārithah and Salamā. And I am not sorry that this verse was revealed, for has the Almighty not said, 'Allāh is their Protector?'"[63] This ḥadīth was related by Bukhārī and Muslim.[64]

States: Taking Pleasure in Censure by the Beloved

Many Sufis have related how, though it may seem incredible, they have derived pleasure from visions and inspirations in which they were scolded by Allāh or by His Messenger ﷺ. The ḥadīth above, however, should do much toward dispelling our viewing of this phenomenon in the light of incredulity. For, despite the censure of his tribe, it was the one phrase in indication of Allāh's concern with his tribe

61 Tirmidhī: 2880

62 Qur'ān, 3:122

63 Even though the verse mentions a wrong they had committed, and was revealed to censure them its revelation was nonetheless a pleasure to Jabir. YTD.

64 Bukhārī: 4051, Muslim: 2505

which caused Jābir ﵁ to glory in the revelation of the verse. Similarly, when a Sufi is made aware that he/she is being censured, a sign will be given, in one form or another, that the censure is made because the Sufi is cared for. Certainly, if it was Allāh's wrath that the Sufi was being made aware of, he/she would have no cause for rejoicing. Saʿdi tells the story of the Sufi who heard a voice from the Unseen tell him that his years of worship had not found acceptance with the Almighty. The Sufi then continued as before with his worship, saying, 'Accepted or not accepted, there is no other way to go.' At last, from the Unseen came the cry, 'Accepted! Though you remain without perfection. For without Me, you remain without protection!' There is also a story about a disciple of Shāh Abū al-Maʿālī who returned from Madīna and related to him that in a dream he had been visited by the Prophet ﷺ who greeted him and then asked him to convey his greetings to his 'heretical' master. On hearing the dream, Shāh Abū al-Maʿālī began leaping for joy, saying: 'You say I'm no good, and I'm ecstatic! Allāh bless you, you have spoken well. How well sour words beautify sweet, red lips!' Another Sufi was startled when, during a time of intense spiritual contemplation, he heard a voice from the Unseen say, 'You will become a disbeliever and die!' Later the Sufi was told by his master not to worry, and to return to his devotions, for what he had heard was merely a taunt of love, after the fashion of the name-calling practised by lovers everywhere. The following verse of the Mathnawī might also be included under this general heading:

Your displeasure with me is pleasure to my soul,
May my heart be made ransom, my heart in grief!

ḤADĪTH 30

عن جابر رَضِيَ اللهُ عَنْهُ قال: مَرِضْتُ فَأَتَانِيْ رَسُوْلُ اللهِ صَلَّى اللهُ عَلَيْهِ وَسَلَّمَ يَعُوْدُنِيْ وَأَبُوْبَكْرٍ وَهُمَا مَاشِيَانِ فَوَجَدَانِيْ قَدْ أُغْمِيَ عَلَيَّ فَتَوَضَّأَ النَّبِيُّ صَلَّى اللهُ عَلَيْهِ وَسَلَّمَ ثُمَّ صَبَّ وَضُوْءَهُ عَلَيَّ، فَأَفَقْتُ. الحديث (أخرجه الخمسة إلا النسائي)

It is related on the authority of Jābir ﵁ that, "Once, when I had fallen ill, Allāh's Prophet ﷺ walked over with Abū Bakr ﵁ to inquire after my health. I was unconscious when they found me, so the Prophet ﷺ made ablutions and poured the used water over me. At that, I immediately regained consciousness. . . [the ḥadīth continues.] This ḥadīth was related by Bukhārī, Muslim, Abū Dāwūd, and Tirmidhī.[65]

---

65 Bukhārī: 5651, Muslim: 1616, Abū Dāwūd: 2886, Tirmidhī: 2097, Nasā'ī: 138, Ibn Mājah: 2728

Customs: Blessings from Relics

It is the way of most Sufis to secure blessings for themselves from the clothes and other personal effects of their masters and others whose acceptance with the Almighty is obvious. This ḥadīth is explicit in its authentication of this custom; as it was from the blessings of the water used in ablutions by the Prophet ﷺ that Jābir ﵁ regained consciousness.

ḤADĪTH 31

عن عُبَادَةَ بْنِ الصَّامِتِ رَضِيَ اللهُ عَنْهُ قال: كَانَ النَّبِيُّ صَلَّى اللهُ عَلَيْهِ وَسَلَّمَ إِذَا نَزَلَ عَلَيْهِ الْوَحْيُ كُرِبَ لِذَالِكَ وَتَرَبَّدَ وَجْهَهُ. (أخرجه مسلم وأبوداود والترمذي)

> It is related on the authority of ʿUbādah ibn aṣ-Ṣāmit ﵁ that, "When the revelation came to him, the Messenger of Allāh ﷺ was so overwhelmed by the experience that his face turned ashen." This ḥadīth was related by Muslim, Abū Dāwūd, and Tirmidhī.[66]

States: Ecstasy and Effacement

The suspension of senses or faculties which comes about as a result of the descent of spiritual meanings on the heart is called absence or *ghaybah* and effacement or *maḥw* in Sufi terminology. It is this phenomenon, which is so clearly referred to in the ḥadīth above.

ḤADĪTH 32

عن عائشة رضي الله تعالى عنها قالت: كان رسولُ الله صَلَّى اللهُ عَلَيْهِ وَسَلَّمَ يُحْرَسُ (لَيْلاً) حتى نَزَلَ: ﴿وَالله يَعْصِمُكَ مِنَ النَّاس﴾ فَأَخْرَجَ رَسُوْلُ اللهِ صَلَّى اللهُ عَلَيْهِ وَسَلَّمَ رَأْسَهُ مِنَ القُبَّةِ، فَقَالَ: «يَاأَيُّهَا النَّاسُ! انْصَرِفُوْا، فَقَدْ عَصَمَنِيَ الله عز وجل».

(أخرجه الترمذي)

> It is related on the authority of ʿĀ'isha ﵂ that she said, "Allāh's Prophet ﷺ always kept vigil at night until the Almighty revealed the verse: 'Allāh will protect you from mankind.'[67] When that happened, the Prophet ﷺ stuck

66 Muslim: 2334, 1690. It was not found in Abū Dāwūd and Tirmidhī.

67 Al-Qur'ān, 6:68

his head outside the tent and cried, 'Go away, people! The Almighty has granted me his protection.'" This ḥadīth was related by Tirmidhī.[68]

Practices: Rejecting Causative Factors

This type of trust in Allāh ﷻ is not only permissible, but preferable for the strong of heart and faith. Indeed, this has always been the hallmark of the Sufi masters. The ḥadīth above is an extremely lucid account of the reality of such trust, *tawakkul.*

Note: The foregoing of fixed, indispensable causative factors is absolutely prohibited. This has nothing to do with *tawakkul.* The Qur'ānic teaching on the subject is as follows: "And when you are resolved, put your trust in Allāh,"[69] where, undoubtedly, the word "resolved" implies a definite course of action.

ḤADĪTH 33

عن ابن عباس رَضِيَ اللهُ عَنْهُ أَنَّ رَجُلاً أَتيَ النَّبِيَّ صَلَّى اللهُ عَلَيْهِ وَسَلَّمَ، فقال: إِنِّي إِذَا أَصَبْتُ اللَّحْمَ انْتَشَرْتُ لِلنِّسَاءِ وَأَخَذَتْنِي شَهْوَتِي فَحَرَّمْتُ عَلَيَّ اللَّحْمَ، فَأَنْزَلَ الله تَعَالى: ﴿يَا أَيُّهَا الَّذِيْنَ امَنُوْا لاَتُحَرِّمُوْا طَيِّبتِ مَا اَحَلَّ الله لَكُمْ﴾ (أخرجه الترمذي)

It is related on the authority of Ibn ʿAbbās ﷺ that a certain man went to Allāh's Messenger ﷺ and said, "Whenever I eat meat, my appetite for women is stimulated and I am possessed by desire. Therefore, I have forbidden myself from consuming meat." Then the Almighty revealed the verse: "O believers! Forbid not such good things as Allāh has made lawful for you."[70] This ḥadīth was related by Tirmidhī.[71]

Corrections: Prohibition of Excesses in Forsaking Pleasure

Certain harsh and unsparing people have been known to abstain from things which are lawful[72] in the same way that they abstain from things they know to be prohibited, believing that this is something which will bring them closer to Allāh ﷻ. Practically and theoretically, this is religious fanaticism and falls under the category of blameworthy innovation, *bidʿah.* It was in refutation of

68 Tirmidhī: 3046

69 Al-Qur'ān, 3:159

70 Al-Qur'ān, 5:87

71 Tirmidhī: 3054

72 Like meat in general, and beef in particular. YTD.

precisely this type of extremism that the Qur'ānic prohibition of monasticism was revealed.[73] The ḥadīth above explains that it was exactly this sort of monasticism that became the occasion for the revelation of the above mentioned verse of the Qur'ān. The abstinence of the Sufis, especially in the course of their spiritual disciplines, is comparable to nothing so much as the dietary caution exercised by the sick. This is because the sick do not hold it as an article of faith that what they abstain from (while in that state) is prohibited. Nor do they suppose their abstention to be in itself an act of worship. The Sufis' practices in this regard, then, and contrary to the opinion of the shallow formalists, are in no way connected to monasticism.

ḤADĪTH 34

عن ابن عمر رَضِيَ اللهُ عَنْهُ قال: لَمَّا تُوُفِّيَ عَبْدُ اللهِ بْنُ أُبَيٍّ ابْنِ سَلُوْلٍ إِلَى أَنْ قَالَ فَقَامَ عُمَرُ رَضِيَ اللهُ عَنْهُ فَأَخَذَ بِثَوْبِ النَّبِيِّ صَلَّى اللهُ عَلَيْهِ وَسَلَّمَ فَقَالَ: يَا رَسُوْلَ اللهِ! تُصَلِّيْ عَلَيْهِ وَقَدْ نَهَاكَ رَبُّكَ أَنْ تُصَلِّيَ عَلَيْهِ فَقَالَ رَسُوْلُ اللهِ صَلَّى اللهُ عَلَيْهِ وَسَلَّمَ: «إِنَّمَا خَيَّرَنِيَ اللهُ» الحديث. (أخرجه الخمسة إلا أباداود)

It is related on the authority of Ibn ʿUmar ﷺ that, "When ʿAbdullāh ibn Salūl[74] died, [such and such took place. The ḥadīth continues until finally Ibn ʿUmar ﷺ continues...] Then ʿUmar ﷺ stood up and grasped the cloak of the Prophet ﷺ saying, 'O Messenger of Allāh ﷺ! Are you praying for him even when your Lord has forbidden you to pray for him?'[75] The Prophet ﷺ replied, 'On the contrary, Allāh ﷻ has given me a choice.'" This ḥadīth was related by Bukhārī, Muslim, Tirmidhī, and Nasā'ī.[76]

States: Intoxication Resulting from Spiritual Meanings

Intoxication, *sukr*, is the name given to that loss of discretion which sometimes takes place at the time of the descent of spiritual meanings on the heart. The return of discretion is called sobriety, *ṣaḥw*. In the ḥadīth above, a situation is described in which ʿUmar's ﷺ heart was so overwhelmed by antipathy for the

73 Al-Qur'ān, 57:27

74 Ibn Salūl was a well known hypocrite in Madīna who, despite his profession of Islam, was despised by many of the believers. YTD.

75 The reference made by ʿUmar ﷺ is to the Qur'ānic verse at 9:80: ". . .ask forgiveness for them, or ask not forgiveness. . ." YTD.

76 Bukhārī: 1269, 4670, 4672, Muslim: 2774, Tirmidhī: 3098, Nasā'ī: 1901, Ibn Mājah: 1523

enemies of Allāh that he paid no attention to the way, both in word and deed, that he approached Allāh's Prophet ﷺ. Indeed, to all outward appearances, ʿUmar's ؓ behaviour was extremely disrespectful. The Prophet ﷺ, however, knowing the reason for ʿUmar 's ؓ behaviour, excused him. Later, when the state of *sukr* was replaced by *ṣaḥw*, ʿUmar ؓ marvelled at how reckless he had been, and was most repentant.

ḤADĪTH 35

عن عبدالله بن كعب عن كعب رَضِيَ اللهُ عَنْهُ فِيْ حَدِيْثِ تَخَلُّفِهِ عَنْ تَبُوْكَ أَنَّهُ نَهى رَسُوْلُ اللهِ صَلَّى اللهُ عَلَيْهِ وَسَلَّمَ الْمُسْلِمِيْنَ عَنْ كَلاَمِنَا أَيُّها الثَّلثةُ وَفِيْهِ قَالَ: لَمَّا جَائَنِيْ الَّذِيْ سَمِعْتُ صَوْتَهُ يُبَشِّرُنِيْ نَزَعْتُ لَهُ ثَوْبَيَّ فَكَسَوْتُهُمَا اِيَّاهُ بِبَشَارَتِهِ ﴿حَتّى إِذَا ضَاقَتْ عَلَيْهِمُ الْأَرْضُ بِمَا رَحُبَتْ﴾ (أخرجه الخمسة)

On the authority of ʿAbdullāh ibn Kaʿb ؓ it is related that his father, Kaʿb ؓ [in the course of telling the story of how he had remained behind during the military campaign to Tabūk,] said, "So Allāh's Prophet ﷺ forbade the Muslims to engage any of the three of us in conversation." Later, in the same ḥadīth, Kaʿb ؓ said, "When the one whose voice I had heard came to give me the good tidings [of forgiveness for having missed the campaign], I stripped off my robe and dressed him in it, out of joy for his having been the one to inform me." In the same ḥadīth, Kaʿb ؓ cites the following verse of the Qur'ān to describe how he and the other two felt: ". . .until, for all of its breadth, the earth became strait for them."[77] This ḥadīth was related by Bukhārī, Muslim, Tirmidhī, Abū Dāwūd, and Nasā'ī.[78]

Practices: Discipline by Disassociation

It is related concerning most Sufi masters that at one time or another they were forced to discipline someone from among their disciples by banishment, or by enforced silence, or by some other apposite disciplinary action. The object of this sort of discipline is no more than admonishment, and it is certainly never based on any kind of personal or animosity or malice. That this practice is a good one is attested to by the ḥadīth above, as Allāh's Prophet ﷺ disciplined three of his Companions in much the same way.

---

77 Al-Qur'ān, 9:118

78 Bukhārī: 4418, Muslim: 2769, Abū Dāwūd: 2773, Tirmidhī: 3102, Nasā'ī: 3855

Customs: Presentation of Gifts to Bearers of Good Tidings

It is customary among many Sufis to offer garments or small sums of money to those, such as the reciters of inspired poetry, who bring them pleasure with their glad tidings. This is no different than Kaʿb's giving his robe to the one who brought him the news of his forgiveness.

States: Contraction

The contraction of the heart at the coming of the signs of Divine majesty, *jalāl*, is called *qabḍ* by the Sufis. The straitened conditions of the three men described by Kaʿb in his narrative correspond exactly to the *qabḍ* of the Sufis, as the reason for those conditions was the delay in the acceptance of the three men's repentance; for this delay was a sign, among many others, of Divine majesty. Indeed, the phrase used in the narrative to describe this state is a metaphor for restriction and depression. The opposite of *qabḍ* is *basṭ* or expansion, which denotes joy and pleasure in the heart at the coming of the signs of Divine bounty. This was the state experienced by Kaʿb after he learned that his repentance had been accepted. All of this is clear from the ḥadīth above in which it is related that, as a sign of how he felt, he gave away his robe.

ḤADĪTH 36

عن ابن عباس رَضِيَ اللهُ عَنْهُ أن النبي صَلَّى اللهُ عَلَيْهِ وَسَلَّمَ قال: «لَمَّا أَغْرَقَ الله فِرْعَوْنَ قَالَ: آمَنَتْ أَنَّهُ لاَ اِلهَ اِلاَّ الَّذِيْ آمَنَتْ بِهِ بَنُوْ اِسْرَائِيْلَ، قَالَ جِبْرَئِيْلُ: يَا مُحَمَّدُ لَوْ رَأَيتَنِيْ وَأَنَا آخُذُ مِنْ حَالِ الْبَحْرِ وَأَدُسُّهُ فِيْ فِيْهِ مَخَافَةَ أَنْ تُدْرِكَهُ الرَّحْمَةُ». (أخرجه الترمذي)

It is related on the authority of Ibn ʿAbbās that Allāh's Messenger said, "When Pharaoh saw that he was going to drown, he cried out, 'I believe that there is no god but the One in whom the Israelites believe!' Then the angel Jibrīl said to me, 'O Muḥammad! If only you could have seen me as I took mud from the ocean floor and stuffed it into his mouth for fear of his being overtaken at the last moment of his life by the mercy of Allāh!'" This ḥadīth was related by Tirmidhī.[79]

States: Intoxication

In spite of the heart's position as the point on which revolves the acceptance of one's confession of faith, if it is not the time for the acceptance of repentance, it

79 Tirmidhī: 3107

will avail nothing to confess one's faith aloud. If the time is right, however, for the acceptance of one's repentance, even a silent confession of faith will suffice.[80] Jibrīl's 🕊 attempt to silence Pharaoh, in spite of his knowledge that his doing so would have no bearing on Pharaoh's ultimate destiny, came as a result of his being in the state of *sukr*, concerning the reality of which I have spoken already in my commentary on a previous ḥadīth [34]. In this case, too, it was Jibrīl's 🕊 extreme antipathy for the enemies of Allāh that led him to do what he did.

ḤADĪTH 37

عن ابن عباس رَضِيَ اللهُ عَنْهُ قال: قال أبوبكر: يَارَسُوْلَ الله! قَدْ شِبْتَ قَالَ: «شَيَّبَتْنِيْ هُوْدُ وَالْوَاقِعَةُ» الحديث. (أخرجه الترمذي)

It is related on the authority of Ibn ʿAbbās 🕊 that Abū Bakr 🕊 said, "O Messenger of Allāh! You have aged!" Then he 🕊 replied, "The chapters of Hūd and the Event have aged me!"[81] This ḥadīth was related by Tirmidhī.[82]

States: Awe
On a higher spiritual plane than, but corresponding to, *qabḍ* and *basṭ* (contraction and expansion) are the feeling of awe brought on by the manifestation of Divine majesty or *hayba* and intimacy or *uns*. As the spiritual states of the Prophet 🕊 were of the highest levels of spiritual development, it is better to refer to his awe for the Almighty, which is one of the early signs of *qabḍ*, as *hayba*.

Character: Spiritual Vigilance
Complete reflection on, and attention to, any particular subject, along with a continued effort to take its meaning to heart is called vigilance or *murāqabah*. Obviously, the ageing mentioned here as a result of awe depends chiefly on constant and concentrated attention to the subject. In this wise, the ḥadīth points clearly to the practice of *murāqabah*.

---

80 Therefore, as Pharaoh's confession of faith came too late, it mattered nothing that he confessed it aloud. See Qurʾān, 10:91–2. YTD.

81 The chapter entitled Hūd (11), the first of these two chapters, contains mention of how former nations were punished and made the objects of Divine wrath, while the chapter entitled The Event (56), details the Hereafter and conditions in the Fire and Garden. YTD.

82 Tirmidhī: 3297

ḤADĪTH 38

عن أبي سعيد رَضِيَ اللهُ عَنْهُ أن رسولَ الله صَلَّى اللهُ عَلَيْهِ وَسَلَّمَ قال: «اتَّقُوْا فِرَاسَةَ الْمُؤْمِنِ فَإِنَّهُ يَنْظُرُ بِنُوْرِ اللهِ تَعَالي». (أخرجه الترمذي)

It is related on the authority of Abū Saʿīd al-Khudrī ؓ that the Messenger of Allāh ﷺ said, "Beware the intuition of a believer, for the believer sees with the light of Allāh." This ḥadīth was related by Tirmidhī.[83]

States: Intuition

Through the purity of heart, which is, in fact, the fruit of constant remembrance and heeding, it quite often happens that a Sufi is able to perceive obscure spiritual truths. A branch of *kashf*, or spiritual vision, this is known in Sufi parlance as intuition or *firāsa*. The ḥadīth above mentions this faculty explicitly. Furthermore, the "light of Allāh" mentioned in the ḥadīth refers directly to the purity of heart which is brought about through remembrance, *dhikr*, and heedfulness, *taqwā*.

ḤADĪTH 39

عن عائشة رضي الله تعالى عنها أنها قالت: قلتُ يا رسولَ اللهِ ﴿اَلَّذِيْنَ يُؤْتُوْنَ مَا اتَوْ وَقُلُوْبُهُمْ وَجِلَةٌ﴾ أَهُمُ الَّذِيْنَ يَشْرَبُوْنَ الْخَمْرَ وَيَسْرِقُوْنَ؟ قَالَ: «لَا، يَابِنْتَ الصِّدِّيقِ! وَلكِنَّهُمُ الَّذِيْنَ يَصُوْمُوْنَ وَيَتَصَدَّقُوْنَ وَيَخَافُوْنَ ألاَّ يُقْبَلَ مِنْهُمْ: أولِئكَ الَّذِيْنَ يُسَارِعُوْنَ فِي الْخَيْرَاتِ». (أخرجه الترمذي)

It is related on the authority of ʿĀ'isha ؓ that, "I asked the Messenger of Allāh if the people referred to in the verse: 'Those who give of what they are given, with their hearts quaking,' were those who drink wine and practise thievery. He ﷺ answered me, saying, 'No, O daughter of al-Siddīq! Rather, they are the ones who keep fasts and give alms, and then fear that perhaps their deeds will not be accepted of them. Those are the ones who truly vie in good deeds.'" This ḥadīth was related by Tirmidhī.[84]

Character: Fear and Humility

This ḥadīth is clear in its bespeaking these two characteristics of the Sufis, as it contains mention of those who, when they look on the lowliness and insignificance

83 Tirmidhī: 3127

84 Tirmidhī: 3175

of their own condition, and then on the majesty of the Almighty, are overcome by fear of the possibility that their works will not avail them in the Hereafter.

Signs: Those Nearest to Allāh

In the Qurʾānic verse quoted above, Allāh described certain characteristics as the attributes of His closest servants. These characteristics, then, are among the signs that indicate the true Sufi masters.

ḤADĪTH 40

عن ابن عباس رَضِيَ اللهُ عَنْهُ فِي قِصَّةِ هِلالِ بْنِ أُمَيَّةَ قَالَ: وَالَّذِيْ بَعَثَكَ بِالْحَقِّ إِنِّي لَصَادِقٌ وَلَيُنْزِلَنَّ اللهُ تَعَالى مَا يُبَرِّئُ ظَهْرِيْ مِنَ الْحَدِّ فَنَزَلَ جِبْرَيْلُ عَلَيْهِ السَّلَامُ وَفِيْهِ قَالَ النَّبِيُّ صَلَّى اللهُ عَلَيْهِ وَسَلَّمَ: «لَوْلَا مَامَضى مِنْ كِتَابِ اللهِ لَكَانَ لِيْ وَلَهَا شَأْنٌ».

(أخرجه البخاري والترمذي وأبوداؤد)

It is related on the authority of Ibn ʿAbbās 🙏 that when Hilāl ibn Umayyah 🙏 was unable to produce witnesses, after accusing his wife of adultery, the Messenger of Allāh 🙏 told him that if he was unable to produce witnesses, he would have to face the penalty for false accusation.[85] So, Hilāl 🙏 said, "By the One Who sent you with the true faith! I am telling the truth. Surely, the Almighty will reveal something to exonerate me and spare me from that penalty!" Just then, Jibrīl 🙏 descended.[86] In the same ḥadīth it is related that[87] the Prophet 🙏 said, "Had it not been for what was revealed in the Book of Allāh, this woman and I would have had business together."[88] This ḥadīth was related by Bukhārī, Abū Dāwūd, and Tirmidhī.[89]

---

85 The specific *ḥadd* penalty for false accusation, *qadhf*, in cases of adultery is eighty lashes. See Qurʾān, 24:6. YTD.

86 Jibrīl 🙏 brought revelation exonerating Hilal from the penalty in exchange for his oath and that of his wife. See Qurʾān, 24:6. YTD.

87 This is what the Prophet 🙏 said when Hilāl's 🙏 wife gave birth to a child who displayed the exact signs that the Prophet 🙏 had said would confirm its descent from one other than Hilāl. YTD.

88 In other words, she might have been punished. However, as she had taken the oath, as required by the law of *liʿān* in the verse that was revealed when Hilāl 🙏 first complained to him, the matter was closed until the Day of Judgment. It should be recognised here that the Prophet was speaking to Hilāl 🙏 and telling him that he knew him to be truthful. Otherwise, from a purely legal perspective, there was no case. For unless there are witnesses to testify to adultery, the appearance of signs on a child are not sufficient to convict in a case involving *ḥudūd*, especially when the general rule in such cases is that the least modicum of doubt will suffice to put aside the penalty. YTD.

89 Bukhārī: 4747, Abū Dāwūd: 2254, Tirmidhī: 3179, Ibn Mājah: 2597

States: Miracles

If Hilāl's ؓ statement, "Surely the Almighty will reveal something to exonerate me and spare me from that penalty!" is taken as a declarative statement, and it is most likely that it was, then his foretelling the descent of the angel of revelation was a miracle, *karāma*. If the sentence is understood as exclamatory in nature, however, then the acceptance of his plea may be understood as a miracle.

Corrections: Legal Before Spiritual Considerations

By means of revelation it was revealed to the Prophet ﷺ that if a child with certain distinguishing traits were born to Hilāl's ؓ wife, it would be illegitimate. Obviously, in a matter of such gravity, the Prophet ﷺ would never have relied on his own opinions or assumptions. When a child with exactly those traits was born to the woman, then, in spite of the certainty of his knowledge, the Prophet ﷺ deferred to the ruling of the Sharīʿa. This is a very important point, that the Prophet ﷺ put the Sharīʿa before the *Ḥaqīqa* or, in this case, the certainty that the woman was guilty, and it is one on which many of our deeds and beliefs depend. Furthermore, this is actually a great mercy for us. Were it not so, there would be no order in the world. For example, the reality or *Ḥaqīqa* of the matter is that everything in existence is the possession of Allāh ﷻ, and that when we ascribe things to ourselves or to others, we are only speaking figuratively. Then, if we were to do away with this counterfeit coin of figurative language and thought, and begin to transact all of our affairs in the currency of the *Ḥaqīqa*, all distinction between what is rightfully our own and what belongs to others—rights, responsibilities, and even families—would all fall away. The resulting chaos, scandal and corruption is all too predictable. So Allāh, in His wisdom and mercy, has given us the Sharīʿa to protect us from these evils. Those who are incapable of understanding this essential wisdom behind the Sharīʿa often end up in heresy and worse.

ḤADĪTH 41

عن عائشة رضي الله تعالى عنها في حَدِيْثِ الإِفْكِ حِيْنَ نَزَلَ بَرَائَتُهَا قَالَتْ: فَقَالَتْ لِيْ أُمِّيْ: قُوْمِيْ إِلى رَسُوْلِ اللهِ، فَقُلْتُ: وَاللهِ لاَ أَقُوْمُ إِلَيْهِ، لاَ أَحْمَدُ إِلاَّ اللهَ هُوَ الَّذِيْ أَنْزَلَ بَرَائَتِيْ . (أخرجه الخمسة إلا أبا داود)

It is related on the authority of ʿĀ'isha ؓ concerning the events surrounding the incident in which she was slandered: "So, my mother said to me, 'Go now to Allāh's Prophet!' I replied, 'I will not go to him! Nor will I praise any other than Allāh! He was the One who revealed my innocence.'" This ḥadīth was related by Bukhārī, Nasā'ī, and Tirmidhī.[90]

States: Ecstatic Pronouncements
The ecstatic pronouncements made by Sufi masters while under the influence of one spiritual state or another, whether made in prose or poetry, which when construed literally seem presumptuous or rash, are termed *shaṭaḥāt*. Here, the statement made by ʿĀ'isha ﵂ was of this kind. The reason she said what she did was that she was extremely unhappy that the Prophet ﷺ being only human and not possessing knowledge of all things, had himself been troubled and puzzled by the whole incident. In other words, ʿĀ'isha's ﵂ distress was at what she believed to be the Prophet's ﷺ uncertainty about her. When the Qur'ānic verses concerning her innocence were revealed, she was so elated that she said what she said (as narrated in the ḥadīth above). Finally, that the Messenger of Allāh ﷺ did not refute or rebuke her for what she had said is ample proof that those who let such pronouncements, *shaṭaḥāt*, escape from their lips may certainly be excused.

ḤADĪTH 42

عن أبي هريرة رَضِيَ اللهُ عَنْهُ في قوله تعالى ﴿إِنَّكَ لَا تَهْدِي مَنْ أَحْبَبْتَ﴾ قَالَ: نَزَلَتْ فِيْ رَسُوْلِ اللهِ صَلَّى اللهُ عَلَيْهِ وَسَلَّمَ حَيْثُ يُرَاوِدُ عَمَّهُ أَبَاطَالِبٍ عَلَى الإِسْلَامِ. (أخرجه مسلم والترمذي)

It is related on the authority of Abū Huraira ﵁ concerning the verse: "No, you surely cannot guide whomsoever you wish. . ."[91] that the Messenger of Allāh ﷺ had been attempting to guide his uncle, Abū Ṭālib, to accept Islam. This ḥadīth was related by Muslim and Tirmidhī.[92]

Corrections: Spiritual Administration
Many ignorant people make the mistake of believing that Sufi masters have the ability to direct communication of Divine effusion, *fayḍ*, whenever, and to whomever, they please. That this belief is false is made evident in the ḥadīth above for, when the Prophet was not so empowered, how is it possible that others should be? Therefore, when the matter of ensuring spiritual welfare, which is the primary

90 Bukhārī: 4141, Muslim: 2770, Tirmidhī: 3180, Nasā'ī: 8931
91 Qur'ān, 28:56
92 Muslim: 25, Tirmidhī: 3188

function of a Sufi master, is outside the sphere of his direct influence, then with all the more reason the matter of promoting temporal welfare must undoubtedly be understood to be beyond the power of the Sufi master. Nowadays, so many ignorant Sufis are caught up in the presumption, and I seek refuge in Allāh from the enormity of their beliefs, that the Sufi masters are in possession of all the powers of divinity. The ḥadīth above should suffice to repudiate all such notions.

ḤADĪTH 43

عن ابن عباس رَضِيَ اللهُ عَنْهُ في قوله تعالى: ﴿مَا جَعَلَ اللهُ لِرَجُلٍ مِّنْ قَلْبَيْنِ فِيْ جَوْفِهِ﴾ قَالَ: قَامَ نَبِيُّ اللهِ صَلَّى اللهُ عَلَيْهِ وَسَلَّمَ يَوْمًا يُصَلِّيْ، فَخَطَرَ خَطْرَةً، الحديث (أخرجه الترمذي)

> It is related on the authority of Ibn ʿAbbās ﷺ that he said, concerning the following verse: "Allāh has not assigned to any person two hearts within his breast."[93] "One day, Allāh's Messenger ﷺ was standing in prayer when certain thoughts crossed his mind. . ." This ḥadīth was related by Tirmidhī.[94]

Questions: Stray Thoughts

Some people think that it is conditional to the proper performance of prayer that no stray thoughts enter the mind of the one performing it. That this is not so should be perfectly clear from the ḥadīth above. An intentional lapse in concentration, however, will certainly impair the value of the prayer. Still, the coming to mind of stray thoughts is something that is beyond our control. What is, however, within our control is our pursuing or ignoring these thoughts as they occur; for, if we pursue them, we may impair our prayer. That over which we exercise no control will neither enhance nor detract from our worship. There are sometimes periods in which no such stray thoughts occur, and this is the result of a certain absorption which is a praiseworthy spiritual state, but which is not something to be sought in itself. In fact, sometimes a thought-filled prayer is better than a thought-free one, for it is quite a taxing matter to ignore stray thoughts and remain concentrated on prayer. I have already explained that the rewards to be had from an act of worship are proportionate to the degree of difficulty or effort expended on performing it.

93 Qur'ān, 33:4

94 Tirmidhī: 3199

ḤADĪTH 44

عن أبي هريرة رَضِيَ اللهُ عَنْهُ قال: إِنَّ نَبِيَّ اللهِ صَلَّى اللهُ عَلَيْهِ وَسَلَّمَ قَالَ: «إِذَا قَضَى الله تَعَالى الْأَمْرَ فِيْ السَّمَاءِ ضَرَبَتِ الْمَلَئِكَةُ عَلَيْهِمُ السَّلاَمُ بِأَجْنِحَتِهَا خُضْعَاناً لِقَوْلِهِ كَأَنَّهُ سِلْسِلَةٌ عَلَى صَفْوَانٍ». (أخرجه البخاري)

It is related on the authority of Abū Huraira ﷺ that Allāh's Prophet ﷺ said, "When the Almighty gives a command in heaven, the angels fold their wings in humble deference to the word of Allāh, which sounds like the noise of a chain dragged over rock." This ḥadīth was related by Bukhārī.[95]

Questions: The Eternal Manifested in the Form of the Temporal

It is obvious that while the "word" of Allāh ﷻ is eternal, the sound (form) of a chain being dragged over rock is temporal. Then, in this ḥadīth, through the comparison of the eternal "word" to the temporal "sound," confirmation is found for the matter, so often referred to by the Sufi masters, of the manifestations of the Eternal Being in the temporal universe; a phenomenon referred to in Sufi terminology as representative manifestation or *tajallī-e-mithalī*. Now, the reality of this manifestation has nothing to do with transformation, incarnation, or the assertion that Allāh ﷻ is all, because every one of those notions is false, according to reason and revelation alike. Rather, what we have here is something which, with respect to certain of its attributes, bears a resemblance to the Eternal; a resemblance through which something created acts in such a way as to shed light on the attributes of the Eternal. In the light of this commentary, it should not be difficult to interpret the meaning of the following ḥadīth, or of others like it: Said the Prophet ﷺ, "I saw my Lord in the best possible form." Finally, that there is nothing improper in the use of similes to describe Allāh ﷻ will be evident to anyone who has read the Qur'ān.

ḤADĪTH 45

عن ابن مسعود رَضِيَ اللهُ عَنْهُ قال: قال رسول الله صَلَّى اللهُ عَلَيْهِ وَسَلَّمَ: «إِذَا تَكَلَّمَ الله تَعَالى بِالْوَحْيِ سَمِعَ أَهْلُ السَّمَاءِ صَلْصَلَةً كَجَرِّ السِّلْسِلَةِ عَلى الصَّفَا فَيُصْعَقُوْنَ». الحديث (أخرجه أبوداود)

95 Bukhārī: 4701, Tirmidhī: 3223, Ibn Mājah: 194

It is related on the authority of Ibn Masʿūd ﵁ that the Messenger of Allāh ﷺ said, "When Allāh reveals His Word the heavenly hosts first hear a clanking like the sound of a chain being dragged over rock, and then they lose their senses. . . ." This ḥadīth was related by Abū Dāwūd.[96]

States: Ecstasy and Effacement
It sometimes happens, when there has been a particularly forceful descent of spiritual meanings on the heart, that the Sufi will lose consciousness. This is a part of the states known as *ghaybah* and *maḥw* discussed in the commentary on ḥadīth [31] above. That this is not merely an excess invented by Sufis in the name of Islam is lucidly attested to (". . .and then they lose their senses. . .") in this ḥadīth.

ḤADĪTH 46

عن أنس رَضِيَ اللهُ عَنْهُ قال: نَزَلَ عَلَى النَّبِيِّ صَلَّى اللهُ عَلَيْهِ وَسَلَّمَ ﴿إِنَّا فَتَحْنَا لَكَ فَتْحاً مُبِيْناً﴾ وَفِيْهِ: فَالْفَتْحُ الْمُبِيْنُ هُوَ فَتْحُ الْحُدَيْبِيَّةِ. (أخرجه الشيخان والترمذي)

It is related on the authority of 'Anas ﵁ that the verse: "Surely, We have given you a manifest victory,"[97] was revealed to Allāh's Prophet ﷺ and that surely the "manifest victory" referred to in the verse was the victory of Ḥudaybiya. This ḥadīth was related by Bukhārī, Muslim and Tirmidhī.[98]

Teachings: Uneasiness Over Contraction
The events which took place at Ḥudaybiya are well known.[99] To all outward appearances, the Muslims were forced into signing a non-aggression pact with the disbelievers there. However, in view of Anas' ﵁ commentary, it is clear that the Almighty referred to the truce of Ḥudaybiya for the reason that it included several subtle considerations. In fact, events later proved that Ḥudaybiya was the first step in the liberation of Makka, a manifest victory if there ever was one. In all this we have a glimpse at the foundation of the teaching by Sufi masters that

96 Abū Dāwūd: 4378. Al-Mundhirī said: 'Bukhārī, Tirmidhī and Ibn Mājah have also reported a similar ḥadīth from ʿIkrimah, the freedman of Ibn ʿAbbās ﵁, from Abū Hurairah ﵁.

97 Qur'ān, 48:1

98 Bukhārī: 4172, 4834, Muslim: 1786, Tirmidhī: 3262

99 In brief, Ḥudaybiya was the site of a treaty between the Muslims and the idolators of Makka. For details, see the commentaries on verse 48:1. YTD.

although the state of contraction, or *qabḍ*, seems outwardly to be an indication of decline, it is in reality a praiseworthy state, like expansion, *basṭ*, and one from which the experienced Sufi may derive great benefit. Indeed, the first step on the way to *basṭ* is *qabḍ*.

Mawlānā Rūmī wrote:

When *qabḍ* comes it'll be, O wayfarer,
For your benefit, so be not dismayed.
When *qabḍ* comes, see in it the best,
Stay diligent, and keep your composure.

ḤADĪTH 47

عن ابن عباس رَضِيَ اللهُ عَنْهُ في قوله تعالى: ﴿اِعْلَمُوْا أَنَّ اللهَ يُحْيِي الْأَرْضَ بَعْدَ مَوْتِهَا﴾ قَالَ: لِيْنُ الْقُلُوْبِ بَعْدَ قَسْوَتِهَافَيَجْعَلُهَا مُخْبِتَةً مُنِيْبَةً، يُحْيِي الْقُلُوْبَ الْمَيْتَةَ بِالْعِلْمِ وَالْحِكْمَةِ، وَإِلاَّ فَقَدْ عُلِمَ إِحْيَاءُ الأَرْضِ بِالْمَطَرِ مُشَاهَدَةً (أخرجه رزين)

It is related on the authority of Ibn ʿAbbās that he said, concerning the verse: "Know that Allāh revives the earth after it was dead,"[100] that: "Allāh softens the hearts after they have grown hard, and makes them humble and repentant. He it is Who brings inert hearts to life with knowledge and with wisdom. Nonetheless, that the earth is revived by the rain is a phenomenon easily perceived through observation." This ḥadīth was related by Razīn.[101]

Summary

In the verse preceding the verse mentioned in this ḥadīth, the believers are urged to create within their hearts a sense of submission to the will of the Almighty. This is followed by the verse concerning the revival of the earth. There are two possible explanations for this sequence. The first is that the revival of the earth, as a universally recognised phenomenon, is mentioned here as an example of how the heart may also come back to life. The second is that the heart is represented there figuratively by the earth, as Ibn ʿAbbās opined in the ḥadīth, so that the verse is essentially a metaphor.

100 Qur'ān, 57:17

101 *Ad-Durr al-Manthūr*, 6:254

Sayings: The Heart is Allāh's Wide Earth

Certain Sufi masters have referred to the heart as "Allāh's wide earth."[102] This ḥadīth may simply have been the source of this saying.

Miscellaneous: Esoteric Commentary on the Qur'ān

In the works and discourses of the Sufi masters one may find any number of Qur'ānic verses and ḥadīths interpreted in rather unconventional ways. This has always been a cause of much consternation among rigid formalists. This ḥadīth, however, clearly indicates that there is nothing wrong with this kind of Sufi commentary. In the first volume of my commentary, *The Key to the Mathnawī*, I have discussed this subject at length.[103]

---

102 E.g., Qur'ān, 29:56 and 39:10. –Trans. "O My servants who believe, surely My earth is vast. So, Me alone you must worship." and "Say (on My behalf) "O My servants who believe, fear your Lord. Those who do good deeds in this world will have a good return, and the earth of Allah is wide. Certainly those who observe patience will be given their reward in full without measure."

103 In the story of the Khalīfa's Seeing Laylā, Mawlānā Rūmī wrote the following verses: "The Qur'ānic text: 'Cleanse My House,' you two, is/ the explanation of such purity: it (the purified heart)/ is a treasure of (divine) light, though its form is of this earth." Now, the Qur'ānic text quoted in the couplet is from the second chapter of the Qur'ān, (2:125), and is in the form of a command directed to the Prophet Ibrāhīm ﷺ and his son, Ismaʿīl ﷺ, concerning the purification of the Kaʿbah. Mawlānā Thānawī, in his Urdu commentary on the Mathnawī wrote that the verse also contains reference to the purification of the heart, but that that reference is indirect, and indicated rather than designated. Mawlānā Thānawī then writes: "You should know that this kind of esoteric commentary is something which is found throughout the works of the Sufi masters. Regarding this, however, there are two major misconceptions. The first is the belief that the only true interpretation of the Qur'ān is the Sufi interpretation, and that whatever the other scholars have written is wrong. Undoubtedly, this belief is entirely erroneous, and a sure sign of deviation. The second misconception results in people reviling the Sufis and accusing them of having tampered with the Qur'ān. It is essential, therefore, to study the matter more closely. To begin with, the proper commentary of the Qur'ān is the commentary written for it by conventional, orthodox Qur'ānic scholars or *mufassirīn*. However, it sometimes happens that the intended meaning of the Qur'ān will bring to mind another, similar meaning. If, for example, Zayd and ʿAmr each bear a likeness to one another, then one might automatically think of ʿAmr when speaking of Zayd. So, as a result of this sort of mental association, the intended meaning of the Qur'ān may call to mind a similar meaning, subject in the same way to the same things as the intended meaning. Therefore, it is decidedly not the intention of the Sufi masters to impose their own interpretations on the texts of the Qur'ān or the Ḥadīths, but rather merely to draw parallels and illustrative instances wherever possible. For example, from the above quoted Qur'ānic text, ". . .cleanse My House," the mind easily passes on to that part of the human body, the heart, which resembles the Kaʿbah through its being the place of descent for spiritual meanings and light. Then, the inference may be drawn that just as the command has been given to cleanse the Kaʿbah, so that it becomes a finer receptacle for heavenly manifestations, so also the command is given to cleanse the heart. Now, this sort of lore is known as contemplative knowledge or ʿilm al-iʿtibār; and it is this which is mentioned in the Qur'ān itself: "Therefore, contemplate, O you who are possessed of vision!" (59:2). Indeed, the very same process is used by the formalist scholars of law in their interpretations of the Sharīʿa. See, Ashraf ʿAlī Thānawī, *Kalīd-i-Mathnawī* (Deoband, India: Matbaʿ-e-Ashrafī, n.d.) vol. 1, pp.90–91.

ḤADĪTH 48

عن أبي هريرة رَضِيَ اللهُ عَنْهُ في قوله تعالى ﴿وَيُؤْثِرُوْنَ عَلى أَنْفُسِهِمْ وَلَوْ كَانَ بِهِمْ خَصَاصَةٌ﴾ الاية، إِنَّ رَجُلاً مِنَ الْأَنْصَارِ بَاتَ بِهِ ضَيْفٌ وَلَمْ يَكُنْ عِنْدَهُ إِلاَّ قُوْتُهُ وَقُوْتُ صِبْيَانِهِ ، فَقَالَ لامْرَأَتِهِ : نَوِّمِيْ الصِّبْيَةَ ، وَاطْفِئِ السِّرَاجَ ، وَقَرِّبِيْ لِلضَّيْفِ مَاعِنْدَكَ ، فَنَزَلَتْ الآيَةُ . (أخرجه الترمذي وصححه)

It is related on the authority of Abū Huraira ﵁ concerning the verse: "...and who prefer others over themselves, even though poverty be their lot,"[104] that "A man from the Anṣār had a guest for the night but no food to offer him, except for a few morsels he had put aside for his children. The man said to his wife, 'Put the children to sleep, put out the light, then serve our guest whatever we have.' Then the verse was revealed." This ḥadīth was related by Tirmidhī.[105]

Practices: Non-disclosure of Good Deeds

It has always been the practice of Sufi masters to do their utmost to conceal the good that they do. This ḥadīth is clear in its confirmation of such a practice.

Character: Altruism

This ḥadīth also substantiates the selflessness, or preference for the welfare of others which is characteristic of the Sufis in general.

ḤADĪTH 49

عن ابن عباس رَضِيَ اللهُ عَنْهُ في قوله تعالى: ﴿وَلاَسُوَاعاً وَلاَيَغُوْثَ وَيَعُوْقَ وَنَسْراً﴾ قال: وَكُلُّهَا أَسْمَاءُ رِجَالٍ صَالِحِيْنَ مِنْ قَوْمِ نُوْحٍ عَلَيْهِ السَّلاَمُ، فَلَمَّا هَلَكُوْا أَوْحَى الشَّيْطَانُ إِلى قَوْمِهِمْ أَنْ انْصِبُوْا إِلى مجَالِسِهِمْ الَّتِيْ كَانُوْا يَجْلِسُوْنَ فِيْهَا أَنْصَابًا وَسَمُّوْهَا بِأَسْمَاءِهِمْ، فَفَعَلُوْا، فَلَمْ تُعْبَدْ، حَتَّى إِذَا هَلَكَ أولئِكَ وَتَنَسَّخَ الْعِلْمُ عُبِدَتْ. (أخرجه البخاري)

It is related on the authority of Ibn ʿAbbās ﵁ concerning the verse: "...and do not leave Wadd, nor Suwaʿ, Yaghūth, Yaʿūq, nor Nasr," that: "All of these are the names of pious men from the nation of the Prophet Nūḥ

104 Qur'ān, 59:9
105 Tirmidhī: 3304

🕮. When they died, Satan prompted their followers to erect statues of them in the places where they used to rest, and to name them with their names. So, the people did as Satan bid them, but they never worshipped the statues. Still, when those people passed away and knowledge of true religion had been forgotten, people began worshipping the statues." This ḥadīth was related by Bukhārī.[106]

Corrections: The Prohibition Concerning Pictures

It is the practice of some Sufis nowadays to keep pictures of their masters. This ḥadīth shows clearly how this practice can be, and has actually been, corrupted into great evil. According to the Sharīʿa, pictures are not to be shown respect.[107] However, as those Sufis who keep pictures of their masters also treat those pictures with great respect, they are clearly acting in defiance of the Sharīʿa.

ḤADĪTH 50

عن أبي هريرة رَضِيَ اللهُ عَنْهُ أن رسولَ اللهِ صَلَّى اللهُ عَلَيْهِ وَسَلَّمَ قالَ: «إنَّ الْعَبْدَ إذَا أَخْطَأَ خَطِيْئَةً نُكِتَتْ فِي قَلْبِهِ نُكْتَةٌ، فَإِذَا هُوَ نَزَعَ وَاسْتَغْفَرَ وَتَابَ صُقِلَ قَلْبُهُ، وَإِنْ عَادَ زِيْدَ فِيْهَا حَتّى تَعْلُوَ قَلْبَهُ وَهُوَ الرَّانُ الَّذِيْ ذَكَرَ اللهُ تَعَالى». (أخرجه الترمذي وصححه)

It is related on the authority of Abū Huraira 🕮 that the Messenger of Allāh 🕮 said, "Whenever a servant commits an act of wrongdoing, a black spot appears on his/her heart; and when he/she desists, and asks forgiveness, and repents, his/her heart will become clear. But, if instead [of remaining committed to repentance] he/she again commits the same wrongs, more and more black marks will accumulate until they overshadow his/her heart. This is the rust which the Almighty speaks of in the Qurʾān."[108] This ḥadīth was related by Tirmidhī.[109]

Miscellaneous: The Heart in Light and Darkness

In the writings of many Sufi masters, the heart is spoken of as being either "illu-

---

106 Bukhārī: 4940

107 Mawlānā Thānawī's own *fatwā* or legal verdict on the subject of photographs was that they are allowed only when they are a necessity, as in a passport, or identity card, etc. The traditional fiqh ruling on pictures of living beings in general is that they are permitted, but must not be displayed in places that command respect. Thus, they had no objection to pictures on rugs, for example, since these are used on the floor and under people's feet.–Trans.

108 Qurʾān, 83:4

109 Tirmidhī: 3334, Ibn Mājah: 4244

mined" through worship and devotion, or "darkened" through wrongdoing and neglect. In this ḥadīth, the same things are mentioned. This light or darkness, then, does register on the heart—as a result of one's own deeds. But not in any perceptible way.

ḤADĪTH 51

عن ابن عباس رَضِيَ اللهُ عَنْهُ في قولِهِ تعالى: ﴿لَتَرْكَبُنَّ طَبَقاً عَنْ طَبَق﴾ قال: حَالٌ بَعْدَ حَالٍ قَالَ: هذَا نَبِيُّكُمْ صَلَّى اللهُ عَلَيْهِ وَسَلَّمَ. (أخرجه البخاري)

It is related on the authority of Ibn ʿAbbās ؓ concerning the verse: "Surely, you shall traverse, stage after stage,"[110] that, "This means, state after state. And the person to whom this was addressed was your Prophet ﷺ." This ḥadīth was related by Bukhārī.[111]

Questions: A Sufi Can Always Make More Progress

In the writings and discourses of the Sufi masters it is often noted that there is no end to the progress that might be made by a Sufi. The words of this ḥadīth, when applied generally, are certainly consistent with this observation. The phrase, "stage after stage" refers neither to only two stages, nor to any other definite number of stages, but is rather intended to denote an unending succession of stages. This is what is referred to in the works of the Sufi masters.

ḤADĪTH 52

عن أبي ذرٍّ رَضِيَ اللهُ عَنْهُ قلتُ يارسولَ الله! ومَا كَانَتْ صُحُفُ إِبْرهِيْمَ وَمُوْسى؟ قَالَ: «كَانَتْ عِبَراً كُلَّهَا، عَجِبْتُ لِمَنْ أَيْقَنَ بِالْمَوْتِ ثُمَّ يَفْرَحُ، عَجِبْتُ لِمَنْ أَيْقَنَ بِالنَّارِ كَيْفَ يَضْحَكُ؟ عَجِبْتُ لِمَنْ رَأَى الدُّنْيَا وَتَقَلُّبَهَا بِأَهْلِهَا ثُمَّ يَطْمَئِنُّ إِلَيْهَا، عَجِبْتُ لِمَنْ أَيْقَنَ بِالْقَدْرِ ثُمَّ يَنْصِبُ، عَجِبْتُ لِمَنْ أَيْقَنَ بِالْحِسَابِ ثُمَّ لايَعْمَلُ». (أخرجه رزين)

It is related on the authority of Abū Dharr ؓ that he said to Allāh's Prophet ﷺ, "O Messenger of Allāh! What were the scrolls of Ibrahim and Mūsā?" The Prophet ﷺ replied, "They were admonition entirely. I am amazed at people who, although certain of death, persist nonetheless

110 Qur'ān, 84:19
111 Bukhārī: 4940

in making merry. And I am amazed at those who, although convinced of the existence of the Fire, persist nonetheless in laughter. I am amazed at those who, although acquainted with the way fortunes may change at a moment's notice in this world, persist nonetheless in their complacency. I am amazed at those who, although convinced that their daily bread is predestined, persist nonetheless in striving to earn more and more. And I am amazed at those who, although they believe in a final reckoning, persist nonetheless in making no effort to do good deeds." This ḥadīth was related by Razīn.[112]

Teachings: Contemplation

The sort of contemplation known as *murāqabah* that is taught and practised by Sufis is essentially thoughtful consideration. Experience has shown that before one can become adept at *murāqabah* one must practise it diligently for a certain period of time each day. The principles on which this practice is based are to be found in this ḥadīth, for the matter of associating peoples' ways with their beliefs is one that requires a certain amount of reflection which is, in fact, at the heart of the practice of *murāqabah*.

ḤADĪTH 53

عن ابن عمر رَضِيَ اللهُ عَنْهُ أنَّ رَجُلاً مِنْ أَصْحَابِ رَسُوْلِ اللهِ صَلَّى اللهُ عَلَيْهِ وَسَلَّمَ أُرُوْا لَيْلَةَ الْقَدْرِ فِيْ الْمَنَامِ فِيْ السَّبْعِ الْأَوَاخِرِ فَقَالَ صَلَّى اللهُ عَلَيْهِ وَسَلَّمَ: «أَرى رُؤْيَاكُمْ قَدْ تَوَاطَئَتْ فِيْ السَّبْعِ الْأَوَاخِرِ، فَمَنْ كَانَ مُتَحَرِّيَهَا فَلْيَتَحَرَّهَا فِيْ السَّبْعِ الْأَوَاخِرِ». (أخرجه الثلاثة والترمذي)

It is related on the authority of Ibn ʿUmar ﵁ that a number of the Companions ﵃ were shown in their dreams that the "Night of Power"[113] was one of the last seven nights in the month of Ramaḍān. When they told the Messenger of Allāh ﷺ of what they had dreamt, he replied, "I see that your dreams are in agreement on the last seven nights. Then, whoever seeks it, let them seek it on the last seven nights." This ḥadīth was related by Bukhārī, Muslim, Mālik, and Tirmidhī.[114]

---

112 *Ad-Durr al-Manthūr*, 6:571

113 al-Qur'ān, 97:3

114 Bukhārī: 2015, Muslim: 1165, Muwaṭṭa': 616. Tirmidhī has not recorded this ḥadīth of Ibn ʿUmar ﵁, but a similar report from ʿĀ'isha ﵂, but has alluded to this report in his comment: 'On this issue, there is also a ḥadīth by Ibn ʿUmar ﵁.

Questions: The Reliability of Concurrent Visions

While it is the firm belief of the Sufi masters that spiritual vision, *kashf*, is unacceptable as legal evidence, they are agreed on the reliability of concurrent visions in regard to extralegal matters. This ḥadīth is clearly indicative of this point of view.

ḤADĪTH 54

عن ابن عباس رَضِيَ اللهُ عَنْهُ قال: قال رسولُ اللهِ صَلَّى اللهُ عَلَيْهِ وَسَلَّمَ: «اَلشَّيْطَانُ جَاثِمٌ عَلى قَلْبِ ابْنِ ادَمَ فَإِذَا ذَكَرَ اللهَ تَعَالى خَنَسَ، وَإِذَا غَفَلَ وَسْوَسَ». (أخرجه البخاري تعليقاً)

It is related on the authority of Ibn ʿAbbās ﷺ that Allāh's Messenger ﷺ said, "Satan will perch himself on a person's heart. Then, if the person mentions the name of Allāh ﷻ, Satan will slink away. But if the person is negligent [in remembering Allāh], Satan will begin whispering to that person." This ḥadīth was related by Bukhārī.[115]

Teachings: Silencing the Whisperings of Satan through Remembrance

It should be abundantly clear from this ḥadīth that *dhikr* is an effective remedy for the whisperings or *waswasa* that often cause concern and worry and that could, therefore, lead to frustration and even to one's abandoning one's spiritual disciplines. Therefore, it is clearly important that one fortify oneself with *dhikr* rather than suffer as a result of *waswasa* regardless of its variety, including evil but resistible whisperings, neutral but resistible whisperings, and irresistible whisperings. Now, while there is no danger of wrongdoing resulting from the "neutral" variety of whisperings, it is still to be feared for its debilitating effect on the heart, which might eventually lead to wrongdoing. While it is true that the irresistible varieties of *waswasa* are not immediately harmful, they are, nonetheless, quite often the cause of much concern and worry and could, therefore, lead to frustration and even to one's abandoning one's spiritual disciplines. Therefore, it is clearly important that one fortify oneself with *dhikr* rather than suffer as a result of *waswasa*.

ḤADĪTH 55

عن أبي سعيد رَضِيَ اللهُ عَنْهُ قال: اِعْتَكَفَ رَسُوْلُ اللهِ صَلَّى اللهُ عَلَيْهِ وَسَلَّمَ فِيْ الْمَسْجِدِ،

115 Bukhārī: As a chapter-heading on Sūra an-Nās in the Book of Qur'ānic Interpretation.

فَسَمِعَهُمْ يَجْهَرُوْنَ بِالْقُرْآنِ فَكَشَفَ السِّتْرَ فَقَالَ : «أَلا إِنَّ كُلَّكُمْ يُنَاجِي رَبَّهُ فَلاَ يُؤْذِيَنَّ بَعْضُكُمْ بَعْضاً وَلايَرْفَعُ بَعْضُكُمْ عَلى بَعْضٍ فِيْ الْقِرَاءَةِ أَوْ فِيْ الصَّلوةِ. (أخرجه أبو داؤد)

It is related on the authority of Abū Saʿīd ﷺ that while the Prophet ﷺ was sequestered in the mosque, he heard others noisily reciting the Qur'ān. Opening the curtain from his makeshift compartment, he said, "Listen! Each one of you is conversing with his Lord. So, do not disturb each other, and do not raise your voices one above the other while reciting the Qur'ān or in prayer." This was related by Abū Dāwūd.[116]

Teachings: Contingencies in Permission for Audible Dhikr

In this ḥadīth, the reason given for the prohibition on reciting aloud was the matter of causing inconvenience to others. From this we may derive the following two conclusions. First, that the Sharīʿa permits the practice of making remembrance aloud, *dhikr-e-jalī*. Secondly, permission for such *dhikr* may be given only when others will not be disturbed by it. This is the middle way between the two positions on either extreme. One group insists that audible *dhikr* is contrary to the Sunna, and that those who practise it become so enchanted by it that they begin to give it more importance than prayer. The point to remember here is that what is of importance is *dhikr* itself, and not any particular kind of *dhikr*. Audible *dhikr* is not in itself an act of worship, though it does have its advantages. Its effect on the heart, for example, is greater; it is effective in nullifying unwanted thoughts, and so forth. However, should it become a nuisance to other people, then the spiritual drawback of causing discomfort to another will far outweigh the advantages of making *dhikr* aloud. Therefore, at such times, the *dhikr* should be inaudible. Finally, as to the question of whether audible or inaudible *dhikr* is better, the answer that comes to us from other ḥadīths is that inaudible *dhikr* is superior.

ḤADĪTH 56

عن عائشة رضي الله تعالى عنها قالت: قَامَ رَجُلٌ مِنَ اللَّيْلِ فَقَرَأَ الْقُرْآنَ وَرَفَعَ صَوْتَهُ فَلَمَّا أَصْبَحَ قَالَ رَسُوْلُ اللهِ صَلَّى اللهُ عَلَيْهِ وَسَلَّمَ: «يَرْحَمُ الله فُلاناً كَأَيٍّ مِنْ آيَةٍ أَذْكَرَنِيْهَا اللَّيْلَةَ كُنْتُ أُسْقِطْتُهَا. (رواهُ الشيخان وأبو داؤد وهذا لفظه)

116 Abū Dāwūd: 1332

It is related on the authority of ʿĀʾisha 🙲 that a man once woke during the night and began to recite the Qurʾān aloud. So, in the morning, Allāh's Prophet 🙲 said, "May Allāh bless so and so. Last night he reminded me of a number of verses that had slipped my mind." This ḥadīth was related by Bukhārī, Muslim, and Abū Dāwūd.[117]

Questions: A Novice as the Means for a Master's Development
We may learn from this ḥadīth that a spiritual master will sometimes become the recipient of divine effusion, *fayḍ*, through a less developed intermediary. There should be no difficulty in our understanding this matter when it takes place without the intermediary's having intended it, as was the case in the ḥadīth quoted here. Obviously, the source of all *fayḍ* is the Almighty Himself, and the novice is only an intermediary. In this case, the one receiving *fayḍ* is actually (under normal conditions) the means by which *fayḍ* passes on to the novice; and it is clear that whenever a follower is benefited by a guide, the reward for the benefit will go to the guide by means of the follower. Similarly, even when this takes place as a result of the novice's own intentions, there should still be no reason to suspect that the novice is more accomplished than the master. There are many ḥadīths in which there is record of the Prophet 🙲 benefiting from the advice of his Companions 🙲. In spite of that, the question of who among them was the most excellent, the closest to Allāh, etc. has never arisen. Someone's becoming an intermediary in some particular matter is certainly in no way prejudicial to established virtue and excellence. Of course, when we are speaking of other than the Prophet there is nothing to prevent us from allowing that a disciple might, in certain areas, actually be more accomplished than his/her master. Finally, since it is possible to receive *fayḍ* through an intermediary, it is clear that even a master may benefit from the company of the righteous. Indeed, it often happens that a master will benefit from a disciple.

ḤADĪTH 57

عن ابن مسعود رَضِيَ اللهُ عَنْهُ قال: قال رسولُ اللهِ صَلَّى اللهُ عَلَيْهِ وَسَلَّمَ: «اقْرَءْ عَلَيَّ الْقُرْآنَ» فَقُلْتُ: أَقْرَأُ عَلَيْكَ وَعَلَيْكَ أُنْزِلَ؟ فَقَالَ: «إِنِّي أُحِبُّ أَنْ أَسْمَعَهُ مِنْ غَيْرِيْ» فَقَرَأْتُ عَلَيْهِ وَفِيهِ : فَإِذَا عَيْنَاهُ تَذْرِفَانِ. (أخرجه الخمسة إلا النسائي)

It is related on the authority of ʿAbdullāh ibn Masʿūd 🙲 that the Prophet

---

117 Bukhārī: 5037, Muslim: 788, Abū Dāwūd: 131

ﷺ said to him, "Recite the Qur'ān for me." When ʿAbdullāh ؓ replied, "What? You want me to read what was revealed to you?" the Messenger of Allāh ﷺ said, "It's just that I love to hear it from someone else. . ." Further on, in the same narration, Ibn Masʿūd ؓ reports that as he was reciting for the Prophet ﷺ, ". . .his eyes suddenly filled with tears." This ḥadīth was related by Bukhārī, Muslim, Abū Dāwūd, and Tirmidhī.[118]

Questions: The Special Properties of Audition

It is human nature that people often derive more pleasure from listening to something recited to them than from reading or reciting the same thing themselves. For this reason, audition or *samāʿ* is sometimes prescribed for a disciple who needs to have a particular state intensified, or to have his/her desire or *shawq* renewed, or to attain a certain spiritual composure. The fact that certain types of *samāʿ* are prohibited is another matter.

States: Ardour

One's being overcome by a peculiar but praiseworthy spiritual state is called ardour or *wajd*. The last sentence in this ḥadīth is clearly indicative of *wajd*, and may be cited as a precedent from the Sunna for this state.[119]

ḤADĪTH 58

عن أسماءَ رضي الله تعالى عنها قالت: مَا كَانَ أَحَدٌ مِنَ السَّلَفِ يُغْشى عَلَيْهِ، وَلا يَصْعَقُ عِنْدَ تِلاوَةِ الْقُرْآنِ، وَإِنَّمَا كَانُوْا يَبْكُوْنَ وَيَقْشَعِرُّوْنَ ثُمَّ تَلِيْنُ جُلُوْدُهُمْ وَقُلُوْبُهُمْ إِلى ذِكْرِ اللهِ. (أخرجه رزين)

It is related on the authority of Asmā' ؓ that, "Among the first Muslims no one ever fainted or cried out in ecstasy when the Qur'ān was being recited. The most that would happen was that people would cry or shiver until their skin and their hearts would soften to the remembrance of Allāh." This ḥadīth was related by Razīn.[120]

Questions: The Ardour of the Masters

The meaning of *wajd* was given in the commentary on the previous ḥadīth. Here,

---

118 Bukhārī: 4582, Muslim: 800, Abū Dāwūd: 3668, Tirmidhī: 3024, Ibn Mājah: 4194

119 See ḥadīth [93]. YTD.

120 Ibn Saʿd, *aṭ-Ṭabaqāt al-Kubrā*: 8:188

in this ḥadīth, the kind of *wajd* being described is the *wajd* of the spiritually adept. It is this kind of *wajd* which is described in the Qur'ān.[121] The fainting and shouting that most people associate with *wajd* is *wajd* of a middling degree, and is known to have occurred very infrequently among the first Muslims. In a ḥadīth related by Imam Tirmidhī, for example, there is mention of an incident in which Abū Huraira ﷺ fainted as a result of *wajd*.

ḤADĪTH 59

عن أبي هريرة رَضِيَ اللهُ عَنْهُ قال: قال رسولُ اللهِ صَلَّى اللهُ عَلَيْهِ وَسَلَّمَ: «إِذَا قَامَ أَحَدُكُمْ مِنَ اللَّيْلِ فَاسْتَعْجَمَ الْقُرْآنُ عَلَى لِسَانِهِ فَلَمْ يَدْرِ مَايَقُوْلُ فَلْيَضْطَجِعْ».(أخرجه مسلم وأبوداؤد)

It is related on the authority of Abū Huraira ﷺ that Allāh's Messenger ﷺ said, "If any one of you rises at night to pray, and then finds himself slurring the words of the Qur'ān, and incapable of comprehending what he is reading, then let him lie down and go back to sleep." This ḥadīth was related by Abū Dāwūd and Muslim.[122]

Teachings: The Prohibition of Excess in Spiritual Disciplines

Some people go to such extremes in their disciplines, like denying themselves food and drink, and sleep, and so on, that they never give a thought to the possibility that what they are doing may be harmful in some way. Surely, there is a lesson for these people in this ḥadīth. Two points should be kept in mind here. The first is that more often than not the result of such excesses will be to impair one's health and no more, so that one becomes incapable of performing even the prescribed acts of worship. The second is that when one is so tired as to be incapable of reciting the words properly, there is no way that the full benefits of recitation will be forthcoming; and when that is the case, one's staying awake will have been in vain.

ḤADĪTH 60

عن عبد الرحمن بن عَبْدٍ الْقَارِيِّ قَالَ: سَمِعْتُ عُمَرَ بْنَ الْخَطَّابِ رَضِيَ اللهُ عَنْهُ يَقُوْلُ:

121 al-Qur'ān, 39:23

122 Muslim: 787, Abū Dāwūd: 1311, Ibn Mājah: 1372

قَالَ رَسُوْلُ اللهِ صَلَّى اللهُ عَلَيْهِ وَسَلَّمَ: «مَنْ نَامَ عَنْ حِزْبِهِ مِنَ اللَّيْلِ وَعَنْ شَيْءٍ مِنْهُ فَقَرَأَهُ مَابَيْنَ صَلوةِ الْفَجْرِ وَصَلوةِ الظُّهْرِ كُتِبَ لَهُ كَأَنَّمَا قَرَأَهُ مِنَ اللَّيْلِ».(أخرجه الستة إلا البخاري)

It is related on the authority of ʿAbd al-Raḥmān ibn ʿAbd al-Qārī that he heard ʿUmar ﵁ say: "I heard the Messenger of Allāh say, 'Whenever one of you sleeps through his/her nightly devotions, or through a part of them, then, if you perform them anytime between dawn and afternoon prayer, you will receive the same reward as you would for performing them at night.'" This ḥadīth was related by Mālik, Muslim, Abū Dāwūd, Tirmidhī, and Nasā'ī.[123]

Teachings: Making Up Missed Devotions

The real message in this ḥadīth is that one should never miss one's daily (or nightly) devotions, even though they are categorised as superogeratory. If, however, they cannot be performed at the regular time, then they may be performed later. But to miss them entirely is to miss great blessings. As it is said: "Those who have no devotions, will have no experiences."

ḤADĪTH 61

عن الحارثِ بْنِ سُوَيْدٍ قال: حَدَّثَنَا عَبْدُ اللهِ بْنُ مَسْعُوْدٍ رَضِيَ اللهُ عَنْهُ قَالَ: سَمِعْتُ رَسُوْلَ اللهِ صَلَّى اللهُ عَلَيْهِ وَسَلَّمَ يَقُوْلُ: «للهُ أَفْرَحُ بِتَوْبَةِ عَبْدِهِ الْمُؤْمِنِ مِنْ رَجُلٍ نَزَلَ فِيْ أَرْضٍ دَوِّيَّةٍ» إلي قَوْلِهِ «فَإِذَا رَاحِلَتُهُ عِنْدَهُ عَلَيْهَا زَادُهُ وَشَرَابُهُ» ثُمَّ قَالَ: «اَللّٰهُمَّ أَنْتَ عَبْدِيْ وَأَنَا رَبُّكَ أَخْطَأَ مِنْ شِدَّةِ الْفَرْحِ». (رواه الترمذي)

It is related on the authority of Ḥārith ibn Suwayd ﵁ that he heard ʿAbdullāh ibn Masʿūd ﵁ say that he heard Allāh's Prophet ﷺ say, "Allāh's elation at the repentance of His believing servant is greater even than the happiness of that person who spends the night in the desert and awakes in the morning to discover that his camel has wandered off with all of his provisions, and who finally, after much trepidation and anxiety, gives up hope and lies down to die. . . only to awaken to the sight of the camel and

123 Muslim: 142, Abū Dāwūd: 1313, Tirmidhī: 530, Nasā'ī: 1791, Ibn Mājah: 1343, *Muwaṭṭa'*: 686

provisions, exclaiming: 'O Allāh! You are my slave, and I am your Master!' thus erring in his excitement."' This ḥadīth was related by Tirmidhī.[124]

States: Ecstatic Pronouncements
It sometimes happens, when a Sufi is overcome by the intensity of one spiritual state or another, that he or she will utter, in ecstasy, words whose meaning will be difficult, if not impossible, to reconcile with the Sharīʿa and its teachings. From this ḥadīth, both the validity and the irreproachability of this type of ecstasy may be ascertained for, after quoting what the man said, the Prophet ﷺ excused the man's words rather than condemn them.

ḤADĪTH 62

عن ابن عمر رَضِيَ اللهُ عَنْهُ قال: قال رسول الله صَلَّى اللهُ عَلَيْهِ وَسَلَّمَ: «رَأَيْتُ اِمْرَأَةً سَوْدَاءَ ثَائِرَةَ الرَّأْسِ خَرَجَتْ مِنَ الْمَدِيْنَةِ حَتّى نَزَلَتْ بِمَهْيَعَةَ وَهِيَ الجُحْفَةُ ، فَأَوَّلْتُ أَنَّ وَبَاءَ الْمَدِيْنَةِ نُقِلَ إِلَيْهَا» . (أخرجه البخاري والترمذي)

It is related on the authority of Ibn ʿUmar ﷺ that Allāh's Prophet ﷺ said, "In a dream I saw a black woman with dishevelled hair depart Madīna and travel to Juḥfah. My interpretation of this dream is that Madīna's notoriously unhealthy climate has relocated to Hujfah."[125] (Commentary for this and the next ḥadīth follows the translation of ḥadīth [63]).

ḤADĪTH 63

عَنْ أُمِّ الْعَلاَءِ الأَنْصَارِيَّةِ رضي الله تعالى عنها قَالَتْ: لَمَّا قَدِمَ الْمُهَاجِرُوْنَ طَارَ لَنَا عُثْمَانُ بْنُ مَظْعُوْنٍ فِيْ السُّكْنِي، فَاشْتكى فَمَرَّضْنَاهُ حَتّى تُوُفِّيَ قَالَتْ: فَرَأَيْتُ لِعُثْمَانَ فِيْ الْمَنَامِ عَيْناً تَجْرِيْ فَأَخْبَرْتُ رَسُوْلَ اللهِ صَلَّى اللهُ عَلَيْهِ وَسَلَّمَ فَقَالَ : «ذَاكِ عَمَلُهُ يَجْرِيْ لَهُ». (أخرجه البخاري)

It is related on the authority of Umm al-ʿAlā' ﷺ that she said, "When the Muslims migrated to Madīna it fell to our lot to share our home with

124 Bukhārī: 6308, Muslim: 2744, Tirmidhī: 2497. The last portion of this ḥadīth, 'O Allāh! You are my slave. . .' is not reported in Ibn Masʿūd's ﷺ ḥadīth, but by Anas ﷺ as recorded by Muslim (2747).

125 Bukhārī: 7038, 7039, 7040, Tirmidhī: 229, Ibn Mājah: 3924

ʿUthmān ibn Mazʿūn 🌸. When he became ill, we cared for him until, after a time, he died. Then we prepared him for burial." Her narration continues, until she relates, "Then I went to sleep and saw in a dream that ʿUthmān 🌸 was in possession of a gushing fountain. The next day I went to Allāh's Messenger 🌸 and told him what I had dreamed. So he told me that 'Those were ʿUthmān's good deeds, gushing for him in Paradise.'" This ḥadīth was related by Bukhārī.[126]

Questions: The World of Manifest Meaning

In the ḥadīth above, and in the one which preceded it, the truth of the world of manifest meaning, ʿālam al-mithāl, where spiritual and other meanings are made manifest in a variety of forms, is further confirmed.

ḤADĪTH 64

عَنْ أَنَسٍ رَضِيَ اللهُ عَنْهُ قَالَ: قَالَ رسولُ اللهِ صَلَّى اللهُ عَلَيْهِ وَسَلَّمَ : «لاَ يَتَمَنَّيَنَّ أَحَدُكُمُ

الْمَوْتَ مِنْ ضُرٍّ أَصَابَهُ». الحَدِيثَ . (أخرجه الخمسة)

It is related on the authority of Anas 🌸 that Allāh's Prophet 🌸 said, "No one should ever wish to die just because hardship has befallen him." This ḥadīth was related by Muslim, Bukhārī, Abū Dāwūd, Tirmidhī and Nasāʾī.[127]

Questions: Wishing to Die

In the writings and discourses of many Sufi masters the wish to die is often expressed. This, apparently, is done in contradiction to the explicit directive of the Sharīʿa. The qualifying condition, ". . .just because hardship has befallen him," in this ḥadīth should suffice to clarify any doubts on the matter. In other words, the prohibition against wishing to die is qualified by the aforementioned condition. Then, whenever the condition is satisfied, the prohibition will be applicable. If the condition is not satisfied, however, the prohibition will be void, unless there is another legitimate reason for it not to be so. The wish expressed by the Sufi masters is nothing more than the result of their true desire to meet Allāh 🌸, and is therefore in no way contrary to the Sharīʿa. Rather this (wish of the masters) is more precisely a spiritual state that is itself the result of basṭ or spiritual expansion.

---

126 Bukhārī: 7018
127 Bukhārī: 5671, Muslim: 2680, Abū Dāwūd: 3018, Tirmidhī: 971, Nasāʾī: 1821, Ibn Mājah: 4265

ḤADĪTH 65

عن أُسَامَةَ بن زَيْدٍ رَضِيَ اللهُ عَنْهُ قَالَ: قَالَ رَسُوْلُ الله صَلَّى اللهُ عَلَيْهِ وَسَلَّمَ: «مَنْ صُنِعَ إِلَيْهِ مَعْرُوْفٌ فَقَالَ لِفَاعِلِهِ جَزَاكَ الله خَيْرًا فَقَدْ أَبْلَغَ فِي الثَّنَاءِ» (أخرجه الترمذي)

It is related on the authority of Usāmah ibn Zayd ﷺ that Allāh's Messenger ﷺ said, "Whoever is done a favour, and then says to the one who did the favour, 'May Allāh gift you with a good reward,' will certainly have done his/her utmost to praise that person." This ḥadīth was related by Tirmidhī.[128]

Teachings and Practices: Supplications for the Bearer of Gifts

It is the custom of the Sufi masters to show their appreciation to those who serve them, or present them with gifts, by evincing their pleasure and, at the same time, by making *duʿā* for the person who favoured them. In this, aside from the obvious blessings, moral virtue, and adherence to the Sunna, there is also the matter of gratitude to the one performing the favour, itself an act of worship. The lack of appreciation and the haughtiness evinced by some so-called masters is therefore most uncharacteristic, unworthy and, in some respects, a sure sign of ingratitude to the Almighty.

ḤADĪTH 66

عن أبي سعيد رَضِيَ اللهُ عَنْهُ قَالَ: قِيْلَ يَا رَسُوْلَ الله! أَيُّ النَّاسِ أَفْضَلُ؟ قَالَ: «مُؤْمِنٌ مُجَاهِدٌ بِنَفْسِهِ وَمَالِهِ فِيْ سَبِيْلِ الله» قِيْلَ: ثُمَّ مَنْ؟ قَالَ: «رَجُلٌ فِيْ شِعْبٍ مِنَ الشِّعَابِ يَتَّقِي الله وَيَدَعُ النَّاسَ مِنْ شَرِّهِ». (أخرجه الخمسة)

It is related on the authority of Abū Saʿīd ﷺ that when Allāh's Prophet ﷺ was asked who was the best of people, he replied, "A believer, a doer of jihad with his/her life and wealth in the way of Allāh." Abū Saʿīd ﷺ also related that when the Messenger ﷺ was asked who was the next best, he replied, "A person who dwells in a canyon among canyons, who fears Allāh, and who spares other people his/her own evil." This ḥadīth was related by Muslim, Bukhārī, Abū Dāwūd, Tirmidhī and Nasāʾī.[129]

---

128 Tirmidhī: 2035

129 Bukhārī: 2786, Muslim: 1888, Abū Dāwūd: 2485, Tirmidhī: 160, Nasāʾī: 3107, Ibn Mājah: 3978

Practices: Retreat

It has been the practice of most Sufis to avoid as much as possible the company of others, and to live their lives in relative seclusion. That this is permitted by the Sharīʿa and, within certain limits, even considered praiseworthy may be ascertained from the ḥadīth related here. By analogy it may be assumed that permission to live in seclusion may also be given to one who is not spared from the evil of people in general. Furthermore, the ḥadīth suggests that a life of intercourse and association is better for the person from whom people can be expected to benefit. Indeed, it was for this reason that the doer of jihad was said to be better than the person in retreat. In summary, then, it may be said that the person who can be of benefit to Muslims in general should remain in their society, while one who will not be of any special benefit to them, but who is likely to suffer because of them, or cause them to suffer, may live in isolation.

ḤADĪTH 67

عَنْ شَدَّادِ بْنِ الْهَادِ: أَنَّ رَجُلاً مِنَ الأعْرَابِ جَاءَ فَامنَ بِالنَّبِيِّ صَلَّى اللهُ عَلَيْهِ وَسَلَّمَ إِلى قَوْلِهِ وَلكِنِّيْ اتَّبَعْتُكَ على أَن أُرْمى إِلى ههُنَا - وَأَشَارَ بِيَدِهِ إِلى حَلَقِهِ- بِسَهْمٍ فَأَمُوْتَ فَأَدْخُلَ الْجَنَّةَ، فقَالَ: «إِنْ تَصْدُقِ الله يَصْدُقْكَ» فَلَبِثُوْا قَلِيْلاً ثُمَّ نَهَضُوْا فِيْ قِتَالِ الْعَدُوِّ فَأُتِيَ بِهِ النَّبِيُّ صَلَّى اللهُ عَلَيْهِ وَسَلَّمَ مَحْمُوْلاً قَدْ أَصَابَهُ سَهْمٌ حَيْثُ أَشَارَ، فَقَالَ النَّبِيُّ صَلَّى اللهُ عَلَيْهِ وَسَلَّمَ: «أَهُوَ هُوَ؟» قَالُوْا: نَعَمْ. قَالَ: «صَدَقَ الله فَصَدَقَهُ» ثُمَّ كُفِّنَ فِيْ جُبَّةِ النَّبِيِّ صَلَّى اللهُ عَلَيْهِ وَسَلَّمَ . الحديث (أخرجه النسائي)

It is related on the authority of Shaddād ibn al-Hād that one of the bedouins went to Allāh's Prophet ﷺ and proclaimed his faith in him. The narrator of this ḥadīth then went on to detail how when the bedouin was apportioned a share of the spoils of war, he went to the Prophet ﷺ and said, "It was not for this that I have followed you! Rather, I have followed you to be pierced here [pointing to his neck] by an arrow so that I die and then go straight to the Eternal Garden!" In reply, the Messenger of Allāh ﷺ said, "If you have spoken the truth, Allāh will verify it." After a short passage of time, the Muslims again took up arms against their enemies. Then the man was brought before the Prophet ﷺ, borne by his comrades at arms, and pierced through by an arrow in exactly the place he had pointed to earlier. When he saw him, the Prophet ﷺ asked, "Is this the same man?" The people gathered there said, "Yes." Then Allāh's Prophet

ﷺ declared, "He spoke the truth, and Allāh has verified it." Then he ﷺ directed that the man be buried in his own (the Prophet's) cloak. This ḥadīth was related by Nasāʾī.[130]

States: Miracles
As the circumstances of this Companion's martyrdom were to a great extent miraculous, the ḥadīth may be cited as a genuine instance of a miracle.

Customs: Keepsakes
The burial of the Companion in the Prophet's ﷺ cloak may be considered as the precedent for all such customs retained by the Sufis; their possessing keepsakes and mementos of their masters for the sake of blessings, both during his lifetime and after.

ḤADĪTH 68

عَنْ ابْنِ عُمَرَ رَضِيَ اللهُ عَنْهُ أَنَّ رَسُوْلَ اللهِ صَلَّى اللهُ عَلَيْهِ وَسَلَّمَ قَامَ يَعْنِيْ يَوْمَ بَدْرٍ فَقَالَ:
«إِنَّ عُثْمَانَ انْطَلَقَ فِيْ حَاجَةِ اللهِ وَحَاجَةِ رَسُوْلِ اللهِ صَلَّى اللهُ عَلَيْهِ وَسَلَّمَ وَإِنِّيْ أُبَايِعُ لَهُ».
(أخرجه أبو داؤد)

It is related on the authority of ʿAbdullāh ibn ʿUmar ؓ that Allāh's Prophet ﷺ stood up on the day of the battle of Badr and said, "Today ʿUthmān is away on Allāh's business, and on His Prophet's business. So, I will pledge for him myself!" This ḥadīth was related by Abū Dāwūd.[131]

Customs: Spiritual Pledges for those not Present
The custom of accepting requests for *bayʿah* from those who, for one reason or another, are unable to present themselves before a master is one that is quite widespread among Sufis. Concerning the legality of *bayʿah* in absentia, the ḥadīth above is unambiguous for ʿUthmān ؓ was clearly not present. Since, however, he wished to be present, the Prophet took his pledge anyway. Obviously, the *bayʿah* described in the ḥadīth was the *bayʿah* of jihad. There is, nonetheless, no reason to suppose that there are any procedural differences between the different kinds of *bayʿah*. Finally, the reason for ʿUthmān's ؓ absence was the illness of his wife, the daughter of the Prophet ؓ.

130 Nasāʾī: 1955
131 Abū Dāwūd: 2726

ḤADĪTH 69

عن عَبْدِ اللهِ بْنِ عَمْرِو بْنِ الْعَاصِ رَضِيَ اللهُ عَنْهُ قَالَ: كَانَ عَلَى ثَقَلِ النَّبِيِّ صَلَّى اللهُ عَلَيْهِ وَسَلَّمَ رَجُلٌ يُقَالُ لَهُ كِرْكِرَةُ، فَمَاتَ فَقَالَ رَسُوْلُ اللهِ صَلَّى اللهُ عَلَيْهِ وَسَلَّمَ: «هُوَ فِيْ النَّارِ» فَذَهَبُوْا يَنْظُرُوْنَ إِلَيْهِ فَوَجَدُوْا عَبَاءَةً قَدْ غَلَّهَا. (أخرجه البخاري)

It is related on the authority of ʿAbdullāh ibn ʿAmr that, "There was a man in charge of the Prophet's baggage whose name was Kirkirah. When he died, the Prophet said, 'He has gone to the Fire.' Then the Companions went and looked in the man's possessions, where they found a cloak he had misappropriated from the spoils of war." This ḥadīth was related by Bukhārī.[132]

Corrections: The Futility of Bayʿah without Proper Practice

Many ignorant Sufis proudly proclaim that they are the disciples of such and such a master, and then, as if their association with such a master were in itself such a great virtue, suppose that there is no need for them to do anything else. The magnitude of the mistake these people make should be apparent from this ḥadīth. What more blessed association could one hope for than to serve Allāh's Prophet? Yet, even to the servant of the Prophet the retribution meted out was in proportion to the crime. What then of one's association with master so and so, when the deeds of the disciple amount to nothing?

ḤADĪTH 70

عن أبي أمامةَ رَضِيَ اللهُ عَنْهُ قَالَ: قَالَ رَسُوْلُ اللهِ صَلَّى اللهُ عَلَيْهِ وَسَلَّمَ: «مَنْ تَرَكَ الْمِرَاءَ وَهُوَ مُبْطِلٌ بُنِيَ لَهُ بَيْتٌ فِيْ رَبَضِ الْجَنَّةِ، وَمَنْ تَرَكَهُ وَهُوَ مُحِقٌّ بُنِيَ لَهُ فِيْ وَسَطِهَا، وَمَنْ حَسَّنَ خُلُقَهُ بُنِيَ لَهُ فِيْ أَعْلاهَا». (أخرجه الترمذي)

It is related on the authority of Abū Umāmah al-Bāhilī that Allāh's Messenger said, "A person who chooses not to argue when they know that they are wrong will have a house built for them on the outskirts of the Eternal Garden. And a person who chooses not to argue even when they know they are right will have a house built for them in the middle of the Garden. And a person who works consciously to improve their character

132 Bukhārī: 3074

will have a house built for them in the highest (and best) part of the Eternal Garden." This ḥadīth was related by Tirmidhī.[133]

Practices: Avoiding Debate
It has always been the way of the Sufi masters, even when right, to remain silent in the face of those who wish only to debate or quarrel with them. That this practice is one that is encouraged by the Sharīʿa should be more than obvious from the ḥadīth cited here.

ḤADĪTH 71

عَنْ سَهْلِ بْنِ سَعْدٍ رَضِيَ اللهُ عَنْهُ قَالَ: قَالَ رَسُوْلُ اللهِ صَلَّى اللهُ عَلَيْهِ وَسَلَّمَ: «مَا مِنْ مُسْلِمٍ يُلَبِّيْ إِلاَّ لَبّى مَا عَنْ يَمِيْنِهِ وَشِمَالِهِ مِنْ حَجَرٍ أَوْ شَجَرٍ أَوْ مَدَرٍ حَتّى تَنْقَطِعَ الأَرْضُ مِنْ هٰهُنَا وَهٰهُنَا. (أخرجه الترمذي)

It is related on the authority of Sahl ibn Saʿd ؓ that Allāh's Prophet ﷺ said, "Whenever a Muslim says '*labbayk*' whatever is on their right says '*labbayk*', and then whatever is on their left, whether rock, or tree, or sand. . . until the word travels out over all the world." This ḥadīth was related by Tirmidhī.[134]

Questions: The Speech of the Inanimate
This ḥadīth should be more than sufficient to confirm the veracity of the visions had by many Sufi masters in which rocks and other inanimate objects appear to speak.

ḤADĪTH 72

عَنْ نَافِعٍ أَنَّهُ سَمِعَ أَسْلَمَ مَوْلى عُمَرَ رَضِيَ اللهُ عَنْهُ يَقُوْلُ ابْنُ عُمَرَ رَضِيَ اللهُ عَنْهُ: رَأى عُمَرُ رَضِيَ اللهُ عَنْهُ عَلى طَلْحَةَ رَضِيَ اللهُ عَنْهُ ثَوْباً مَصْبُوْغاً وَهُوَ مُحْرِمٌ فَقَالَ: مَاهٰذَا؟ فَقَالَ: هُوَ مَعْرَةٌ أَوْ مِدْرَةٌ فَقَالَ: إِنَّكُمْ أَيُّهَا الرَّهْطُ أَئِمَّةٌ يَقْتَدِيْ بِكُمُ النَّاسُ، فَلَوْلاَ أَنَّ رَجُلاً جَاهِلاً رَأى هٰذَا لَقَالَ إِنَّ طَلْحَةَ بْنَ عُبَيْدِ اللهِ كَانَ يَلْبَسُ الثِّيَابَ الْمُصْبَغَةَ فِيْ الإِحْرَامِ فَلاَ تَلْبَسُوْا أَيُّهَا الرَّهْطُ مِنْ هٰذِهِ الثِّيَابِ. (أخرجه مالك)

---

133 Abū Dāwūd: 4800, Tirmidhī: 1993, Ibn Mājah: 51

134 Tirmidhī: 828, Ibn Mājah: 2921

It is related on the authority of Nāfiᶜ that he heard Aslam say to Ibn ᶜUmar ؓ that ᶜUmar ؓ once saw Ṭalḥah ؓ wearing a dyed garment as *iḥrām*, so ᶜUmar ؓ asked him about it. Ṭalḥah ؓ replied, "It's brick-dust dye." ᶜUmar ؓ then replied, "You are looked upon as a leader, and people follow your example. Now, if an ignorant person were to see you in these clothes, he might go around telling people that Ṭalḥah ibn ᶜUbaydullāh ؓ wears a dyed garment for *iḥrām*. Therefore, Ṭalḥah, do not wear any sort of dyed garments [as *iḥrām*].[135] This ḥadīth was related by Mālik.[136]

Corrections: The Need for Circumspection

From this ḥadīth it is evident that the people who are looked up to as leaders in Islam have more need for prudence and piety than do the majority of Muslims. Since the Sufis are looked up to by most Muslims, it is clear that they need to be extra careful in their practice of Islam. Unfortunately, however, in our own times the reverse has become the norm. Indeed, it is negligence and unconcern which characterise most of our present day Sufis. Some have even gone so far as to deny the necessity of the Sharīᶜa and its emphasis on externals. May Allāh deliver us from their ignorance!

ḤADĪTH 73

عَن الصَّعْبِ بْنِ جَثَّامَةَ رَضِيَ اللهُ عَنْهُ أَنَّهُ أَهْدى إِلى رَسُوْلِ اللهِ صَلَّى اللهُ عَلَيْهِ وَسَلَّمَ حِماراً وَحْشِياًّ وَهُوَ بِالْأَبْوَاءِ أَوْ بِوَدَّانَ فَرَدَّهُ عَلَيْهِ فَلَمَّا رَأى مَا فِيْ وَجْهِهِ قَالَ: «إِنَّا لَمْ نَرُدَّهُ عَلَيْكَ إِلاَّ أَنَّا حُرُمٌ». (أخرجه الستة إلا أباداؤد)

It is related on the authority of Ṣaᶜb ibn Jaththāmah ؓ who gifted a wild ass to Allāh's Prophet ﷺ while he was at Abwā' or Waddān, that when the Prophet ﷺ returned the gift, and saw what was on the man's face, he explained, "We return this to you only because we are in *iḥrām*." This ḥadīth was related by Mālik, Muslim, Bukhārī, Nasā'ī and Tirmidhī.[137]

---

135 The use of incense during Ḥajj is prohibited, and in the early days of Islam most dyed garments were dyed with incense of one form or another. Thus, though Ṭalḥah wore a garment dyed with brick dust, it was not inconceivable that some people would have supposed it to have been dyed in incense and then deduce for themselves that, if someone of the stature of Ṭalḥah could wear it, then there must not be anything wrong with their wearing such garments. YTD.

136 *Muwaṭṭa'*: 626

137 Bukhārī: 1825, Muslim: 1193, Tirmidhī: 849, Nasā'ī: 2821, Ibn Mājah: 3090

Teachings: Returning Gifts

From this ḥadīth we learn that the reason for returning a gift, if it is valid, should be made known to the giver, so that he/she does not become insulted or discouraged. The excuse presented by the Messenger ﷺ lends itself to two explanations. The first is that if the ass was alive, its acceptance was prohibited and contrary to the conditions of *iḥrām*. The second is that if the ass was dead when presented, the possibility that it had been hunted down especially for presentation to the Prophet ﷺ could not have been discounted. Under those conditions, the jurists of the Shafiʿī school have opined that its acceptance is prohibited, while the jurists of the Ḥanafī school hold that to accept it is permitted, while noting that the more prudent course would be to refuse or return it.

ḤADĪTH 74

عَنْ ابْنِ عُمَرَ رَضِيَ اللهُ عَنْهُ قَالَ: سَمِعْتُ رَسُوْلَ اللهِ صَلَّى اللهُ عَلَيْهِ وَسَلَّمَ يُهِلُّ مُلَبِّداً إلى قَوْلِهِ وَلاَيَزِيْدُ على هذِهِ الْكَلِمَاتِ. زَادَ فِيْ رِوَايَةٍ عَنْ عَبْدِ اللهِ بْنِ عُمَرَ رَضِيَ اللهُ عَنْهُ يَقُوْلُ بَعْدَ هذِهِ الْكَلِمَاتِ: لَبَّيْكَ، اَللّٰهُمَّ لَبَّيْكَ، لَبَّيْكَ، وَسَعْدَيْكَ، وَالْخَيْرُ فِيْ يَدَيْكَ، وَالرَّغْبَاءُ إِلَيْكَ وَالْعَمَلُ. وَفِيْ رِوَايَةِ أَبِيْ دَاوُدَ قال: وَالنَّاسُ يَزِيْدُوْنَ ذَالْمَعَارِجِ وَنَحْوَهُ مِنَ الْكَلامِ وَالنَّبِيُّ صَلَّى اللهُ عَلَيْهِ وَسَلَّمَ يَسْمَعُ وَلايَقُوْلُ شَيْئاً. (أخرجه البخاري)

It is related on the authority of ʿAbdullāh ibn ʿUmar ؓ that he heard the Messenger of Allāh ﷺ make the ritual chant of the Ḥajj in a certain manner. The ḥadīth continues until Ibn ʿUmar ؓ says, ". . . and he added nothing to these words." In another ḥadīth on the subject, Ibn ʿUmar ؓ related that he had it on the authority of his father, ʿUmar ؓ, that he added some other words to the ritual chant. Another narration, related by Abū Dāwūd on the authority of Jābir ؓ, contains the following statement, ". . .and the people [all of whom were Companions] added words of their own which the Prophet heard and did not object to." The ḥadīths related by Ibn ʿUmar ؓ were related by Bukhārī and Muslim.[138]

Miscellaneous: Original Composition

Certain critics of the Sufis have charged them with *bidʿah* or blameworthy innovation because they compose their own supplications, *dhikr*, and daily recita-

138 Bukhārī: 5915, Muslim: 1184, Abū Dāwūd: 1812, Tirmidhī: 826, Nasā'ī: 2751, Ibn Mājah: 2918. Jābir's ؓ ḥadīth is reported by Abū Dāwūd: 1813.

tions. From the ḥadīths quoted here, however, it should be clear that there is in fact permission for this kind of innovation. The blameworthy sort of innovation comes about when people attempt to make innovations in the body of the religion itself. Clearly, even when the innovations are in themselves unobjectionable, this is prohibited; and even more so when the innovations are dubious or clearly objectionable.

ḤADĪTH 75

عن جابرٍ رَضِيَ اللهُ عَنْهُ في حديث طويل فقال صَلَّى اللهُ عَلَيْهِ وَسَلَّمَ: «لَوْ اسْتَقْبَلْتُ مِنْ أَمْرِيْ مَااسْتَدْبَرْتُ مَا اهْتَدَيْتُ». (أخرجه الخمسة إلا الترمذي وهذا لفظ الشيخين)

It is related on the authority of Jābir ﷺ, as a part of a lengthy narration concerning the Farewell Ḥajj, that Allāh's Prophet ﷺ said, "If I had known then what I know now, I would not have brought these animals with me for sacrifice."[139] This ḥadīth was related by Muslim, Bukhārī, Abū Dāwūd, and Nasā'ī.[140]

Corrections: The Impermanence of Spiritual Visions

It is the belief of many over-zealous Sufis that the *kashf* or spiritual visions of the Sufi masters is something which the masters can turn on or off at will. Some even believe that their masters know everything that happens, as it happens. The absurdity of these beliefs should be apparent to anyone who has read the ḥadīth related here by Jābir ﷺ, as the Messenger of Allāh ﷺ clearly admitted to his not having known what was in store for him. Those who hold to such erroneous beliefs should see to their rectification.

ḤADĪTH 76

عن ابن عباسٍ رَضِيَ اللهُ عَنْهُ قال: لَمَّا قَدِمَ رَسُوْلُ اللهِ صَلَّى اللهُ عَلَيْهِ وَسَلَّمَ أَبى أَنْ يَّدْخُلَ الْبَيْتَ وَفِيْهِ الْالِهَةُ، فَأَمَرَ بِهَا فَأُخْرِجَتْ وَأَخْرَجُوْا صُوْرَةَ إِبْرَاهِيْمَ وَإِسْمعِيْلَ عَلَيْهِمَا السَّلَامُ فِيْ أَيْدِيْهِمَا الْأَزْلَامُ، فَقَالَ رَسُوْلُ اللهِ صَلَّى اللهُ عَلَيْهِ وَسَلَّمَ: «قَاتَلَهُمُ اللهُ،

139 When a Ḥajj pilgrim takes animals along for sacrifice at the Ḥajj, he/she may not remove his/her ihram until after the animals have been sacrificed. Evidently, on the Farewell Pilgrimage, this presented problems to the Prophet. YTD.

140 Bukhārī: 1651, Muslim: 1216, Abū Dāwūd: 1789, Nasā'ī: 2713, Ibn Mājah: 3074

أَمَ وَ اللهِ لَقَدْ عَلِمُوْا أَنَّهُمَا لَمْ يَسْتَقْسِمَا بِهَا قَطُّ» فَدَخَلَ الْبَيْتَ فَكَبَّرَ فِيْ نَوَاحِيْهِ. (أخرجه البخاري)

It is related on the authority of Ibn ʿAbbās ﷺ that when Allāh's Messenger ﷺ entered Makka [following its liberation] he refused to go inside the Kaʿbah as long as idols remained inside of it. When he gave the order that the idols be removed, he noticed that one of the things his Companions ﷺ took out was a painting that depicted the prophets, Ibrāhīm ﷺ and Ismāʿīl ﷺ, divining with arrows. As soon as he saw the picture, Allāh's Prophet ﷺ exclaimed, "May Allāh damn them [the idolaters]! By Allāh! They knew that those two never once practised divination by arrows!" Then he ﷺ entered the Kaʿbah and recited the words "Allāh is Great" in every direction.[141]

Corrections: The Veneration of Images

Nowadays, many ignorant Sufis have taken to keeping pictures of their masters and to accord to those pictures so much respect that it borders on sanctification. The ḥadīth here makes it quite clear that the Messenger of Allāh ﷺ would have no part of such veneration. The fact that he refused to enter the Kaʿbah as long as that picture was inside is sufficient to indicate his position on the matter.

ḤADĪTH 77

عَنِ الْأَسْلَمِيَّةِ رضي الله عنها قَالَتْ: قُلْتُ لِعُثْمَانَ بْنِ طَلْحَةَ رَضِيَ اللهُ عَنْهُ: مَا قَالَ لَكَ رَسُوْلُ اللهِ صَلَّى اللهُ عَلَيْهِ وَسَلَّمَ حِيْنَ دَعَاكَ؟ قَالَ: قَالَ: «إِنِّيْ نَسِيْتُ أَنْ آمُرَكَ أَنْ تُخَمِّرَ الْقَرْنَيْنِ فَإِنَّهُ لَيْسَ يَنْبَغِيْ أَنْ يَكُوْنَ فِيْ الْبَيْتِ شَيْءٌ يَشْغُلُ الْمُصَلِّيْ». (أخرجه أبوداود)

It is related on the authority of Al-Aslamiyyah ﷺ that she once asked ʿUthmān ibn Ṭalḥah ﷺ what the Prophet ﷺ had said to him when he called him. ʿUthmān ﷺ replied, "He told me he had forgotten to ask me to cover over those two horns.[142] 'For indeed,' he said, 'there should be nothing inside here which might distract people from performing their prayers.'" This ḥadīth was related by Abū Dāwūd.[143]

---

141 Bukhārī: 1601

142 These were two horns found inside the Kaʿbah and said to be from the goat sacrificed by the Prophet Ibrāhīm ﷺ instead of his son, Ismāʿīl ﷺ.

143 Abū Dāwūd: 2030

Teachings: Empty Rooms for Worship

It is the teaching of the Sufi masters that the rooms or cubicles set aside for worship and spiritual disciplines should be bare except for a single mat on which to sit, so that the disciple's mind will be less likely to wander while he/she is engaged with disciplines. The basis for this practice is clearly presented in the ḥadīth.

ḤADĪTH 78

عن عائشة رضي الله تعالى عنها قالت: كَانَتْ قُرَيْشٌ وَمَنْ دَانَ دِيْنَهَا وَهُمُ الْحُمْسُ يَقِفُوْنَ بِالْمُزْدَلِفَةِ وَيَقُوْلُوْنَ: نَحْنُ قَطِيْنُ اللهِ فَلا نَخْرُجُ مِنْ حَرَمِهِ . (أخرجه رزين)

It is related on the authority of ʿĀ'isha ﷺ that, "The Quraysh and those who followed them, collectively called the *ḥums*, used to halt at Muzdalifah and say, 'We are the ones who dwell in Allāh's sacred precincts, therefore we shall not step outside of them."[144] This ḥadīth was related by Razīn.[145]

Corrections: Baseless Practices by Those Living Near the Graves of Sufi Masters

The people mentioned in this ḥadīth based their claim that they, unlike the rest of the Ḥajj pilgrims, need not go to ʿArafah on the fact that they were the servants and inhabitants of the sacred precincts. Their claim, however, was refuted by the Qur'ān.[146]

From all of this we may deduce that the practices, many of which are contrary to the Sharīʿa, invented and perpetuated by those who live nearby the graves of people revered as saints, *awliyā'*, are completely unfounded.

ḤADĪTH 79

عن أنس رَضِيَ اللهُ عَنْهُ أَنَّ النَّبِيَّ صَلَّى اللهُ عَلَيْهِ وَسَلَّمَ أَتَى الْجَمْرَةَ فَرَمَاهَا إِلى قَوْلِهِ قَالَ لِأَبِيْ طَلْحَةَ: «اَقْسِمْهُ بَيْنَ النَّاسِ». (أخرجه الخمسة إلا النسائي)

It is related on the authority of Anas ﷺ that Allāh's Messenger ﷺ said [after having his hair cut off at the completion of the Ḥajj] to Abū Ṭalḥah

144 The Ḥajj pilgrims proceed from Muzdalifah to ʿArafah during the Ḥajj. But Muzdalifah lies within the haram, or the sacred precints, while ʿArafah does not. In refusing to continue on to ʿArafah during the Ḥajj, the pagan Quraysh attempted to assert their tribal superiority over the rest of the pilgrims. YTD.

145 Tirmidhī: 884

146 al-Qur'ān, 2:198

ﷺ, "Distribute the hairs among the people." This was related by Bukhārī, Muslim, Abū Dāwūd and Tirmidhī.[147]

Practices: The Presentation of Blessed Gifts
It is the practice of most Sufi masters to present gifts for the sake of blessings to those of their disciples in whom they find sincere desire. This ḥadīth may be cited as the basis for this practice. This does not necessarily mean that the masters think of themselves as "blessed". Rather, their purpose in presenting such gifts is to keep their disciples in good spirits. Of course, where the Prophet is concerned, there is no doubt that he was indeed blessed and a source of true *barakah*. This is an article of faith with all Muslims, and it is corroborated by impeccable textual evidence.

ḤADĪTH 80

عن ابن عباسٍ رَضِيَ اللهُ عَنْهُ قَالَ: أُتِيَ عُمَرُ رَضِيَ اللهُ عَنْهُ بِمَجْنُوْنَةٍ قَدْ زَنَتْ وَفِيْهِ قَالَ عَلِي رَضِيَ اللهُ عَنْهُ: يَا أَمِيْرَ الْمُؤْمِنِيْنَ لَقَدْ عَلِمْتَ أَنَّ رَسُوْلَ اللهِ صَلَّى اللهُ عَلَيْهِ وَسَلَّمَ قَالَ: «رُفِعَ الْقَلَمُ عَنْ ثَلٰثَةٍ: عَنِ الصَّبِيِّ حَتّٰى يَبْلُغَ، وَعَنِ النَّائِمِ حَتّٰى يَسْتَيْقِظَ، وَعَنِ الْمَعْتُوْهِ حَتّٰى يَبْرَأَ» وَإِنَّ هٰذِهِ مَعْتُوْهَةُ بَنِيْ فُلانٍ، لَعَلَّ الَّذِيْ أَتَاهَا أَتَاهَا وَهِيَ فِيْ بَلاءِهَا فَخَلّٰى سَبِيْلَهَا. (أخرجه أبو داود)

It is related on the authority of Ibn ʿAbbās ؓ that a mad woman who had committed adultery was brought before ʿUmar ؓ, and that ʿAlī ؓ said to him, "You know that Allāh's Prophet ﷺ said that, 'The pen is lifted[148] for three; for a child until he/she reaches maturity, for a sleeper until he/she wakes, and for an insane person until he/she comes to their senses.' This woman is known by her tribe as a madwoman. So it is certainly possible that when she committed this act, she was out of her senses." This ḥadīth was related by Abū Dāwūd.[149]

Questions: Toleration for the Spiritually Intoxicated
Just as the mind is subject to becoming clouded by different physical and psy-

147 Bukhārī: 171, Muslim: 1305, Abū Dāwūd: 1981, Tirmidhī: 912

148 The intended meaning is that there are three kinds of people who are not to be held responsible for their deeds. The lifting of the pen refers to the record of their deeds, and how certain deeds will not be recorded. YTD.

149 Abū Dāwūd: 4402

chological stimuli, it can also become clouded at the arrival of certain spiritual states. Among these states is the state of spiritual intoxication, *sukr*. Then, in the same way that the Sharīʿa excuses the insane, it also excuses the rash utterances, *shaṭaḥāt*, made by those in states of ecstasy, and the errors of omission and commission made by Sufis who have come under the influence of extremely overwhelming states of ecstasy like *sukr*. Furthermore, such a state, like insanity, will oftentimes be impossible to detect. It was for this reason that ʿUmar ﵁ was in doubt in regard to the state of the woman brought before him, until ʿAlī ﵁ spoke up and clarified the matter. The teaching of the ḥadīth is simply that if there are indications of the possibility that someone may be excused by the Sharīʿa, it is far better to give that person the benefit of the doubt. That was what ʿAlī ﵁ did in the case of the mad woman, as it was well known that she was often subject to fits of insanity. Therefore, the deeds and sayings of the spiritually intoxicated may be excused or interpreted favourably when there is evidence of true *sukr* (something the person's spiritual master would know immediately), and of the person's virtues, good character and adherence to the Sunna. When, on the other hand, a person is known to be a wrongdoer and is scornful of the Sunna, no excuse or favourable interpretation should be allowed, as there is nothing to indicate the person's deserving it. Were it not this way, the door of legal censure and punishment would be closed; and that is clearly absurd.

ḤADĪTH 81

عَنْ أَنَسٍ رَضِيَ اللهُ عَنْهُ أَنَّ رَجُلاً كَانَ يُتَّهَمُ بِأُمِّ وَلَدِ رَسُوْلِ اللهِ صَلَّى اللهُ عَلَيْهِ وَسَلَّمَ فَقَالَ لِعَلِيٍّ رَضِيَ اللهُ عَنْهُ: «اذْهَبْ فَاضْرِبْ عُنُقَهُ» فَأَتَاهُ عَلِيٌّ فَإِذَا هُوَ فِيْ رَكِيٍّ يَتَبَرَّدُ فَقَالَ لَهُ عَلِيٌّ رَضِيَ اللهُ عَنْهُ: اخْرُجْ، فَنَاوَلَهُ يَدَهُ فَأَخْرَجَهُ، فَإِذَا هُوَ مَجْبُوْبٌ لَيْسَ لَهُ ذَكَرٌ، فَكَفَّ عَنْهُ وَأَخْبَرَ بِهِ النَّبِيَّ صَلَّى اللهُ عَلَيْهِ وَسَلَّمَ فَحَسَّنَ فِعْلَهُ. زَادَ في روايةٍ: وقَالَ: «الشَّاهِدُ يَرى مَالا يَرى الْغَائِبُ». (أخرجه مسلم)

It is related on the authority of Anas ﵁ that a man was accused of committing adultery with one of the maid servants from the household of the Prophet ﷺ. So the Prophet ﷺ said to ʿAlī ﵁, "Go and cut off his head." When ʿAlī ﵁ went after the man, he found him bathing in a well. Offering the man his hand, ʿAlī ﵁ said, "Come out." Then, while helping the man out of the water, ʿAlī ﵁ noticed that the man's penis had been cut off. So he let the man go. Later, when the Prophet ﷺ was informed of what had transpired, he congratulated ʿAlī ﷺ for the job he had done, and then said, "An eyewitness will see what others cannot." This was related by Muslim.[150]

Corrections: Attention to the Spirit Rather than the Letter of a Command

In this ḥadīth, the command of the Prophet ﷺ was absolute and unqualified by legal conditions or other restraints. ʿAlī ﷺ was to find the man and punish him. At face value, the orders provided for no more and no less than that. To the superficial observer, anything more or less would appear to be disobedience. Thus, many of the Sufis whose greatest concern is with the externals of obedience to their masters will ignore entirely the factors underlying those orders, even to the point of failing to discriminate between what is allowed and what is not allowed by the Sharīʿa. Such careless disciples are considered by true Sufi masters to be less than obedient. On the other side of the coin, there are some obedient disciples who will be considered by people to be disobedient because they followed the spirit and not the letter of their masters' commands. It is clear, however, from the congratulations received by ʿAlī ﷺ that such absolute commands are actually qualified, at least to the extent that they are consistent with the principles and precepts of the Sharīʿa. Then, when the orders of the Prophet ﷺ were so qualified, is it conceivable that the orders of an ordinary master would not also be qualified in the same way? Especially when it is the teaching of all true masters that adherence to the Sharīʿa is essential in all matters. Then, in such matters, though something other than absolute obedience may appear to be disobedience, it is in reality the very essence of obedience.

ḤADĪTH 82

عَنْ عَلِيٍّ رَضِيَ اللهُ عَنْهُ قَالَ: قَالَ رَسُوْلُ اللهِ صَلَّى اللهُ عَلَيْهِ وَسَلَّمَ: «رُفِعَ الْقَلَمُ عَنْ ثَلٰثةٍ: عَنِ النَّائِمِ حَتّٰى يَسْتَيْقِظَ، وَعَنِ الصَّبِيِّ حَتّٰى يَحْتَلِمَ، وَعَنِ الْمَجْنُوْنِ حَتّٰى يَعْقِلَ».

(أخرجه أبوداود والترمذي وزاد أبوداود في الأخرى: عن الخَرِف)

It is related on the authority of ʿAlī ﷺ that Allāh's Prophet ﷺ said, "For three, the pen is lifted: for a sleeper until he/she wakes, for a child until he/she matures, and for an insane person until he/she returns to their senses. This ḥadīth was related by Abū Dāwūd and Tirmidhī, with the difference that in Abū Dāwūd's version the words, "and a person who has become senile," are also related.[151]

---

150 Muslim: 2771

151 Abū Dāwūd: 4403, Tirmidhī: 1423

Questions: Pardon for the Spiritually Overcome

This question was discussed in detail in the commentary on the eightieth ḥadīth. From the addition in the narration related by Abū Dāwūd, however, it becomes even more evident that the loss of reason excused by the Sharīᶜa is not limited to insanity only, but to senility as well. Then, when it is clear that there is no such limitation, the spiritual state which overcomes the mind should also be considered as belonging to the same category, and deserving of the same treatment.

ḤADĪTH 83

عن النَّوَّاسِ بْنِ سَمْعَانَ رَضِيَ اللهُ عَنْهُ قال: سَأَلتُ رَسولَ اللهِ صَلَّى اللهُ عَلَيْهِ وَسَلَّمَ عَنِ الْبِرِّ وَالإِثْمِ، فَقَالَ: «اَلْبِرُّ حُسْنُ الْخُلُقِ وَالإِثْمُ مَاحَاكَ فِيْ صَدْرِكَ، وَكَرِهْتَ أَنْ يَطَّلِعَ عَلَيْهِ النَّاسُ». (أخرجه مسلم والترمذي)

It is related on the authority of Nawwās ibn Samᶜān ﷺ that he asked Allāh's Messenger ﷺ about piety and impiety. In reply, the Prophet ﷺ said, "Piety is good character. Impiety is whatever pricks your conscience, and what you would not like others to know about." This ḥadīth was related by Muslim and Tirmidhī.[152]

Questions: Accrediting the Judgment of the Spiritually Pure

The type of impiety referred to in this ḥadīth has to do with those acts of wrongdoing for which no specific textual prohibition exists but which one suspects to be contrary to the fundamental principles of Islam. The answer given to the question was designed to enable all Muslims to recognise this kind of wrongdoing for themselves. But the key to proper recognition, as alluded to by the fact that it was the Companions for whom the answer was given, is inner purity. From this ḥadīth it should be apparent that the judgment of a spiritually developed Muslim may be accredited and acted upon in those matters for which there are no explicit Sharīᶜa directives. It is on the basis of this principle that most masters, when petitioned for discipleship, look into their own hearts for an answer and, accordingly, either accept or reject petitions for initiation into the Sufi order.

ḤADĪTH 84

عن أبي ذرٍّ رَضِيَ اللهُ عَنْهُ قال: قال رسولُ اللهِ صَلَّى اللهُ عَلَيْهِ وَسَلَّمَ: «يَا أَبَاذَرٍّ! إِنِّي

152 Muslim: 2553, Tirmidhī: 2389

أَرَاكَ ضَعِيْفاً وَإِنِّيْ أُحِبُّ لَكَ مَا أُحِبُّ لِنَفْسِيْ لا تَأْمُرَنَّ عَلى اثْنَيْنِ وَلاتَوَلَّيَنَّ مَالَ يَتِيْمٍ».

(أخرجه أبوداود)

It is related on the authority of Abū Dharr ﷺ that Allāh's Prophet ﷺ said, "O Abū Dharr! I can see that you are weak.[153] And truly, I want for you only that which I want for myself. So, never judge between two parties, and never become responsible for the welfare of an orphan." This ḥadīth was related by Abū Dāwūd.[154]

Practices: Abstinence from Worldly Affairs

It is the practice of most Sufis to disassociate themselves from all non-essential affairs of the world. This is something which their formalist critics never fail to mention in their attacks on the Sufi way, charging that as a result of this retirement from worldly affairs the Sufis are of no benefit whatsoever to the Muslim community in general. This ḥadīth, however, clearly shows the approval of the Prophet for the practice of non-involvement. At the heart of the matter lies the fact that while, undoubtedly, it is a good thing to be of benefit to others, it quite often happens that this same 'being of benefit' becomes the cause of evil (love of fame, power, influence, position, etc.). It is also quite obvious that the repulsion of evil must be put before the acquisition of good. This ruling, however, is not binding in the case of persons whose spiritual state is such that they are no longer susceptible to this kind of evil. Indeed, the first Caliphs of Islam were excellent examples of such insusceptibility. In this ḥadīth, the words, "I can see that you are weak," clearly indicate a measure of susceptibility. Finally, as it is a mistake to rely on one' s own opinion before one has attained a high degree of spiritual competence, one should leave all important decisions to one's spiritual master.

ḤADĪTH 85

عَنْ جُبَيْرِ بْنِ مُطْعِمٍ رَضِيَ اللهُ عَنْهُ قَالَ: أَتَتْ امْرَأَةٌ النَّبِيَّ ﷺ، فَكَلَّمَتْهُ فِيْ شَيْءٍ فَأَمَرَهَا أن تَرْجِعَ، قَالَتْ: فَإِنْ لَمْ أَجِدْكَ كَأَنَّهَا تَعْنِيْ الْمَوْتَ قَالَ: «فَإِنْ لَمْ تَجِدِيْنِيْ فَأْتِيْ أَبَابَكْرٍ».

(أخرجه الشيخان والترمذي)

It is related on the authority of Jubayr ibn Mutʿim ﷺ that a woman went to Allāh's Prophet ﷺ and spoke with him about something. When they

153 i.e., that you are unable to bear too many worldly relationships.

154 Muslim: 1826, Abū Dāwūd: 2868, Nasā'ī: 3697

had finished talking, the Prophet ﷺ asked the woman to come and talk to him again. The woman then asked, "And if I do not find you?" as if to refer to his death. So the Prophet ﷺ replied, "If you do not find me, then go to Abū Bakr." This ḥadīth was related by Bukhārī, Muslim and Tirmidhī.[155]

Practices: Spiritual Successors

It is the practice of most Sufi masters to name a successor or several successors from among their disciples who will be responsible for carrying on their work in the Sufi order. The basis for this practice may be seen in the ḥadīth related here by Jubayr ؓ. It is, of course, essential that those so designated be qualified in every way for the responsibility. Nowadays, it happens all too often that after a master passes away, his disciples and relatives gather together to choose his successor from those among them who were closest to the master, regardless of whether or not that person is truly qualified. This is clearly injurious to all concerned, and a blot on the name of Sufis everywhere.

ḤADĪTH 86

عن عائشة رضي الله تعالى عنها فِيْ حَدِيْثٍ طَوِيْلٍ قَالَتْ: وَكَانَ لِعَلِيٍّ رَضِيَ اللهُ عَنْهُ مِنَ النَّاسِ وَجْهٌ حَيوةَ فَاطِمَةَ فَلَمَّا مَاتَتْ انْصَرَفَتْ وُجُوْهُ النَّاسِ عَنْهُ. (أخرجه الشيخان واللفظ لمسلم)

It is related on the authority of ʿĀ'isha ؓ, as part of a lengthy narration, that, "While Fatimah was alive, ʿAlī ؓ enjoyed a great deal of prestige among the Muslims. But after she died, that prestige diminished somewhat." This was related by Bukhārī and Muslim.[156]

Practices: Respect for the Relatives of a Master

To the Sufis, the giving of respect to all those related to their masters is a matter of second nature. It is evident from the ḥadīth here that this is something that was found among the Companions as well.

ḤADĪTH 87

عن عائشة رضي الله تعالى عنها مِنْ خُطْبَةِ عُمَرَ رَضِيَ اللهُ عَنْهُ قَالَ فِيْهَا: أَنَا عُمَرُ وَلَمْ

155 Bukhārī: 2659, Muslim: 2386, Tirmidhī: 3676

156 Bukhārī: 4240, 4241, Muslim: 1759

أَحْرِصْ عَلى أَمْرِكُمْ، وَلكِنَّ الْمُتَوَفّى أَوْصى إِلَيَّ بِذلِكَ، وَاللهُ أَلْهَمَهُ ذلِكَ، وَلَيْسَ أَجْعَلُ أَمَانَتِيْ إِلَى أَحَدٍ لَيْسَ لَهَا بِأَهْلٍ وَلكِن أَجْعَلُهَا إِلى مَنْ تَكُوْنُ رَغْبَتُهُ إِلى التَّوْقِيْرِ لِلْمُسْلِمِيْنَ، أُولئِكَ أَحَقُّ بِهِمْ مِمَّنْ سِوَاهُ. (أخرجه مالك)

It is related on the authority of ʿĀ'isha ﷺ that ʿUmar ﷺ said in one of his last addresses, "I am ʿUmar. I never coveted being appointed your leader. But then the dying man [Abū Bakr] willed it to me; and it was Allāh ﷻ who inspired him [to do so]. Therefore, I will not bestow this trust on anyone who is not truly worthy of it. Rather, I will bestow it on someone whose sole interest is the honour and welfare of the Muslims." This ḥadīth was related by Mālik.[157]

Questions: Inspiration

Certain of the Sufi masters are known to have received inspiration, *ilhām*. This ḥadīth clearly mentions one such instance of a spiritually advanced Muslim receiving *ilhām*.

Corrections: Appointing Successors

Many so-called Sufis appoint successors solely for the purpose of perpetuating their orders, regardless of whether or not the one so appointed is actually worthy of the position. This ḥadīth clearly indicates the error of this practice. Those who are guilty of such excesses should see to their rectification.

ḤADĪTH 88

عن ابن عُمَرَ رَضِيَ اللهُ عَنْهُ فِيْ حَدِيْثٍ طَوِيْلٍ عَنْ عُمَرَ رَضِيَ اللهُ عَنْهُ قَالَ: إِنَّ اللهَ تَعَالى يَحْفَظُ دِيْنَهُ، وَإِنِّيْ لَئِنْ لا أَسْتَخْلِفُ فَإِنَّ رَسُوْلَ اللهِ صَلَّى اللهُ عَلَيْهِ وَسَلَّمَ لَمْ يَسْتَخْلِفْ، وَإِنْ أَسْتَخْلِفْ فَإِنَّ أَبَابَكْرٍ رَضِيَ اللهُ عَنْهُ قَدْ اسْتَخْلَفَ. الحديث (أخرجه الخمسة إلا النسائي)

It is related on the authority of Ibn ʿUmar ﷺ, in a lengthy narration, that his father, ʿUmar ﷺ said, "Undoubtedly, Allāh, Most High, is going to see to the preservation of His religion. So, if I fail to name a successor, well, the Prophet ﷺ did not name a successor either. And if I do name a suc-

---

157 Ibn Ḥibbān, *ath-Thiqāt*, Chapter on the inauguration of ʿUmar ﷺ.

cessor, Abū Bakr 🕮 also named a successor." This ḥadīth was related by Bukhārī, Muslim, Abū Dāwūd and Tirmidhī.[158]

Practices: Not Naming a Successor

It is the practice of many Sufi masters not to name a specific successor, trusting that Allāh 🕮 will put those of their disciples who are worthy of it in positions to carry on the work of their orders. This ḥadīth may be cited as the precedent for this practice. Furthermore, it is the teaching of the Sufis that to become a spiritual successor, *khalīfah*, it is not essential to have been appointed by the master himself (though this, of course, is the exception rather than the rule), on the condition that one has given the master one's spiritual allegiance, *bayʿah*, and then proved oneself worthy of becoming a *khalīfah*.

ḤADĪTH 89

عَنْ عُمَرَ بْنِ مَيْمُوْنَ الْأَوْدِيِّ فِي حَدِيثٍ طَوِيلٍ قَالَ عُمَرُ رَضِيَ اللهُ عَنْهُ لِعَبْدِ اللهِ بْنِ
عُمَرَ رَضِيَ اللهُ عَنْهُ: انْطَلِقْ إِلَى أُمِّ الْمُؤْمِنِيْنَ عَائِشَةَ رضي الله عنها وَقُلْ: يَسْتَأْذِنُ عُمَرُ
بْنُ الْخَطَّابِ أَنْ يُدْفَنَ مَعَ صَاحِبَيْهِ إِلَى قَوْلِهِ فَقَالَتْ: كُنْتُ أُرِيدُهُ لِنَفْسِيْ وَلَأُوْثِرَنَّهُ الْيَوْمَ
الخ.(رواه البخاري)

It is related on the authority of ʿUmar ibn Maymun that ʿUmar 🕮 said to his son, "Go to the Mother of the Muslims, and say to her that ʿUmar ibn al-Khaṭṭāb 🕮 asks permission to be buried at the side of his two companions." In the same narration it is related that ʿĀʾisha 🕮 replied, "I had wanted that place for myself, but today I prefer that he should have it." This was related by Bukhārī.[159]

Customs: Burial in a Blessed Place

A great many of the Sufi masters have directed in their wills that arrangements be made for their burial in certain blessed places, or at the side of certain pious predecessors. The ḥadīth above indicates that this custom is not without precedence in the Sunna.

Customs: Self Sacrifice

Another widespread Sufi custom is their courtesy in allowing themselves to be

---

158 Bukhārī: 7218, Muslim: 1823, Abū Dāwūd: 2939, Tirmidhī: 2526
159 Bukhārī: 3700

preceded by those who are their betters in the performance of good deeds. For example, when a master comes and stands in the second row for congregational prayers, quite often a Sufi in the front row will offer his place to the master, and then perform the prayer in the second row. That there is nothing wrong with this should be evident from the ḥadīth above. Some scholars, however, have written that it is better not to practise this kind of self-sacrifice in matters of worship, as it indicates a lack of desire. In matters of blessings, *barakah*, however, there is nothing wrong with it. It is clear, moreover, that what ʿĀ'isha 🙵 did pertained to a matter of *barakah*. The opinion of our greatest scholars, however, is that respect for a superior is itself an act of worship. Then, if a greater act of worship is preferred to a lesser act of worship, this surely cannot be called a lack of desire. Of course, a lesser act of worship should never be preferred over a greater act.

HADĪTH 90

عَنِ ابْنِ عَبَّاسٍ رَضِيَ اللهُ عَنْهُ قَالَ: قَالَ رَسُوْلُ اللهِ صَلَّى اللهُ عَلَيْهِ وَسَلَّمَ: «لَاتَسْتُرُوْا الْجُدُرَ». (رواه أبو داؤد)

It is related on the authority of Ibn ʿAbbās 🙵 that, "Allāh's Prophet 🙵 said, "Do not cover your walls with cloth." This ḥadīth was related by Abū Dāwūd.[160]

Corrections: Covering Memorials and Tombs
It is evident from this ḥadīth that the practice of covering tombs and memorials with decorative trappings is not a good one.

HADĪTH 91

عَنْ أَبِيْ مُوْسَى رَضِيَ اللهُ عَنْهُ قَالَ: كُنَّا فِيْ سَفَرٍ فَجَعَلَ النَّاسُ يَجْهَرُوْنَ بِالتَّكْبِيْرِ، فَقَالَ النَّبِيُّ صَلَّى اللهُ عَلَيْهِ وَسَلَّمَ: «أَرْبَعُوْا عَلَى أَنْفُسِكُمْ إِنَّكُمْ لَاتَدْعُوْنَ أَصَمَّ وَلَاغَائِبَ إِنَّكُمْ تَدْعُوْنَ سَمِيْعاً بَصِيْراً وَهُوَ مَعْكُمْ وَالَّذِيْ تَدْعُوْنَهُ أَقْرَبُ إِلَى أَحَدِكُمْ مِنْ عُنُقِ رَاحِلَتِهِ». (أخرجه الخمسة إلا النسائي)

It is related on the authority of Abū Mūsā 🙵 that while the Companions 🙵 were on a journey, some people began shouting "Allāh is Great" aloud,

---

160 Abū Dāwūd: 1485

so Allāh's Prophet ﷺ said, "Be kind to yourselves! You are not calling a deaf or absent one, you are calling the All-hearing, the All-seeing, and He is with you! In fact, the One you are calling is closer to you than the necks of the camels you are riding." This ḥadīth was related by Bukhārī, Muslim, Abū Dāwūd and Tirmidhī.[161]

Corrections: Audible Dhikr

The practice of doing *dhikr* aloud is one which is well supported by evidence from the Qur'ān and the Sunna, so there is really no need to discuss its status in the Sharīʿa. However, what needs to be discussed is the matter of exaggerated or overly loud *dhikr*. Certain overly enthusiastic Sufis believe that volume in *dhikr* is itself an act of worship. Accordingly, it is their belief that the louder the *dhikr* the greater the benefit. In this, they are completely indifferent to the right of others to peace and quiet. On the other hand, there are any number of dry formalists who are of the opinion that audible *dhikr* is a form of blameworthy innovation or *bidʿah*.The truth of the matter is that this kind of exaggerated audible *dhikr* is neither worship nor *bidʿah*, as long as one does not hold the belief that it is actually an act of worship.[162] Rather, the practice of doing overly loud *dhikr* is a spiritual remedy that is known to produce special effects on the heart, like sensitivity and increased concentration.

Then, on this basis, the practice may be said to be permitted. However, wherever there is permission for something, it will always be conditional on the absence of nullifying factors. Thus, in this matter as well, permission is given only on the condition that no one is inconvenienced by it. The implied prohibition in the ḥadīth here should be interpreted as applying to the belief that volume in *dhikr* is an integral part of the act of worship. Nor does the prohibition in the ḥadīth negate in any way the benefit of this practice as a remedy for spiritual ailments, as this aspect of loud *dhikr* is not specifically mentioned.

There remains here the question of why, when this remedial aspect of loud *dhikr* is so desirable and useful, no mention of it is made in other ḥadīths? In fine, the answer is that the Companions were not in need this particular remedy, as they had advanced beyond the particular spiritual sphere in which this remedy is effective.[163] Only later on did the need for this sort of remedy arise.

---

161 Bukhārī: 2992, Muslim: 2704, Abū Dāwūd: 1526, Tirmidhī: 3461

162 The *dhikr* itself it worship, but the exaggerated audible part is not. So, what the author is warning about is the mistaken belief that the audible part is actually an act of worship. YTD.

163 Another explanation is that there might well have been cases where the Prophet, Allah bless him and give him peace, prescribed this sort of *dhikr*, but that no one recorded it as a ḥadīth; or, if they did, the ḥadīth may have been rejected early on by the *muḥaddithīn* for technical or other reasons. YTD.

Questions: Proximity

Essentially, the proximity and closeness of the Almighty is beyond human comprehension. It can certainly not be called subjective or spatial proximity, though some theologians have labelled it 'attributive' proximity. The way of the early Sufi masters, however, was to refrain from attempting to classify the attributes of the Almighty, and to leave unexplained whatever the Almighty left unexplained. In the few instances where the masters spoke of this proximity in terms suggesting limitation, their intention was not to ascribe human characteristics to the Almighty but to allow their readers to come to a more complete understanding of the matter. Toward that end they used figurative language. The ḥadīth here clearly indicates[164] that there is nothing wrong with the use of this sort of figurative expression with regard to the Almighty.

ḤADĪTH 92

عن أبي هريرة رَضِيَ اللهُ عَنْهُ فِيْ دُعَاءِ رَسُوْلِ اللهِ صَلَّى اللهُ عَلَيْهِ وَسَلَّمَ: «اَللّٰهُمَّ اغْسِلْنِيْ مِنْ خَطَايَايَ بِالْمَاءِ وَالثَّلْجِ وَالْبَرْدِ». (أخرجه الخمسة إلا الترمذي وهذا لفظ الشيخين)

It is related on the authority of Abū Huraira that Allāh's Messenger ﷺ recited the following supplication, "O Allāh! Cleanse me of my mistakes with water, snow and sleet." This ḥadīth was related by Muslim, Bukhārī, Nasā'ī and Abū Dāwūd.[165]

Interpretations: Figurative Representation of the Divine Attributes

In the poetry of many Sufi masters the Divine essence and attributes are represented figuratively by water and the ocean, as in the following verses:

> Though the ocean be one, from its great depths
> waves rise in a multitude of hues and forms.

The purpose of this figurative representation is not to suggest a complete unanimity of similarities; indeed, the Almighty is far beyond compare. Rather, it is to illustrate His attributes, by means of similarities, in ways that are clear and instructive. For example, the ocean is a 'single, non-composite entity which is the source of many varied phenomena, and the same is true of the Almighty; though it is obvious that, in nature, the sources are as different from one another as they could possibly be. Permission for the use of this kind of figurative rep-

164 "...closer to you than the necks of the camels you are riding."

165 Bukhārī: 6375, Muslim: 598, Abū Dāwūd: 781, Tirmidhī: 3494, Nasā'ī: 60, Ibn Mājah: 805

resentation may clearly be ascertained from the ḥadīth cited here. Water, snow and sleet are figurative representations of the Divine attribute of mercy, and the quality common to all is purification. Then, when it has been established that figurative representation of the Divine attributes is permitted, it follows that figurative representation of the Divine essence is also permissible, as there is no difference between the attributes and essence of the Divine.

ḤADĪTH 93

عَنْ زَيْدِ بْنِ ثَابِتٍ رَضِيَ اللهُ عَنْهُ أَمَرَهُ صَلَّى اللهُ عَلَيْهِ وَسَلَّمَ بِالتَّسْبِيْحِ وَغَيْرِهِ دُبُرَ الصَّلَوتِ قَالَ: فَلَمَّا أُمِرُوْا بِذلِكَ، رَأى رَجُلٌ مِنَ الأَنْصَارِ فِيْ مَنَامِهِ أَنَّ رَجُلاً يَقُوْلُ: اجْعَلُوْهَا خَمْساً وَعِشْرِيْنَ وَاجْعَلُوْا فِيْهَا التَّهْلِيْلَ، فَلَمَّا أَصْبَحَ ذَكَرَ ذلِكَ لِرَسُوْلِ اللهِ صَلَّى اللهُ عَلَيْهِ وَسَلَّمَ فَقَالَ: «اجْعَلُوْهَا كَذلِكَ». (أخرجه النسائي)

It is related on the authority of Zayd ibn Thābit ﵁ concerning the Prophet's ﷺ teaching that one should say 'Glory be to Allāh,' after every prayer, a man from among the Muslims of Madīna saw in a dream that someone told him to say 'Glory be to Allāh' twenty five times after every prayer, and to add the words, 'There is no god but Allāh,' as well. The next morning, when the man related his dream to Allāh's Messenger ﷺ, he said, "Then do it that way." This ḥadīth was related by Nasā'ī.[166]

Miscellaneous: Informing One's Master of One's Dreams

The Sufi masters have written in their works on the etiquette of the Sufi way that when a disciple receives instructions in a dream, the disciple should consult with the master before acting upon those instructions. This ḥadīth clearly corroborates this practice. It is essential in such instances that the disciple not be deluded into thinking that (as the instructions were vouchsafed to him/her alone) more was revealed to them than was revealed to the master. For even though that is possible, it does not mean that the disciple is in any way more accomplished than the master. For the disciple such thinking is indeed injurious, and they should refrain from it, thinking instead that the vision or dream was the result of spiritual blessings or progress brought about in them by the master. Furthermore, it should be evident to the disciple that the master is far more qualified to grasp the true significance of their dreams and visions. For that reason, the

166 Nasā'ī: 1351

disciple should always inform the master of dreams and visions, and abide by whatever the master says concerning them.

ḤADĪTH 94

عَنْ عَائِشَةَ رَضِيَ الله تَعَالى عَنْهَا قَالَتْ: كَانَ رَسُوْلُ اللهِ صَلَّى اللهُ عَلَيْهِ وَسَلَّمَ إِذَا أَخَذَ مَضْجِعَهُ، نَفَثَ فِيْ يَدَيْهِ وَقَرَأَ الحديث (أخرجه الستة إلا النسائي)

It is related on the authority of ʿĀ'isha ﷺ that when Allāh's Prophet ﷺ went to bed, he would blow into his hands and recite a supplication. This was related by Mālik, Bukhārī, Muslim, Abū Dāwūd and Tirmidhī.[167]

Customs: Incantation and Sufflation

While the ritual recitation of Qur'ānic verses to produce a favourable effect is not in itself among the objectives of the Sufi way, it is a form of service to humanity and, as such, is something which the Sufis almost never refuse to do. From the evidence of this ḥadīth, it is certain that this practice is condoned by the Sharīʿa, and that there is nothing wrong in its being performed for one's own benefit. The secret behind all such charms and recitations is that, essentially, they represent a form of dependence upon, humility before, and subservience to the Almighty.

ḤADĪTH 94

عَنْ مَالِكٍ فِيْ دُعَاءِهِ صَلَّى اللهُ عَلَيْهِ وَسَلَّمَ «اَللّٰهُمَّ ازْوِ لَنَا الأَرْضَ» الحديث.

It is related on the authority of one of the Companions that the Messenger of Allāh ﷺ used the following words in a prayer of supplication, "O Allāh! Fold up the earth for us." This ḥadīth was related by Imam Mālik.[168]

Sayings: Traversing the Earth

Many stories are told about masters who miraculously travel great distances in short amounts of time. As a matter of course, the starched formalists deny all such narrations. The Sufis, however, and many other scholars claim not only that such journeys are possible but that they have actually occurred as well. The ḥadīth quoted here would seem to bear out the claim of the Sufis, as the 'folding of the earth' is something which has no fixed quantitative value. Thus, as a variable, it is not confined to any one specific distance; and in the absence of any

167 Bukhārī: 6319, Muslim: 2192, Abū Dāwūd: 5056, Tirmidhī: 3402, Ibn Mājah: 3875

168 *Muwaṭṭa'*: 3583, Tirmidhī: 3438

evidence to suggest limitation, it will remain a variable. It is a principle of Islamic legal theory that the general, unless proven to be specific, will remain general. Thus, in general, such traversing of the earth is possible.

ḤADĪTH 95

عَنْ جَابِرٍ رَضِيَ اللهُ عَنْهُ قَالَ: صَنَعَ أَبُوْالْهَيْثَمِ طَعَاماً، فَدَعَا رَسُوْلَ اللهِ صَلَّى اللهُ عَلَيْهِ وَسَلَّمَ وَأَصْحَابَهُ، فَلَمَّا فَرَغُوْا قَالَ: «أَثِيْبُوْا أَخَاكُمْ» قَالُوْا: وَمَا إِثَابَتُهُ؟ قَالَ: «إِنَّ الرَّجُلَ إِذَا دَخَلَ بَيْتَهُ وَأَكَلَ طَعَامَهُ وَشَرَابَهُ، فَدَعَا لَهُ فَتِلْكَ إِثَابَتُهُ». (رواه أبوداود)

It is related on the authority of Jābir ؓ that Abū Laytham ؓ once prepared a meal and invited the Messenger of Allāh ﷺ and his Companions ؓ to partake of it. When they had finished eating, the Messenger ﷺ said, "Repay your brother." The Companions ؓ asked, "And how do we repay him?" Allāh's Prophet ﷺ replied, "When you enter someone's house, eat their food, drink their drink, and then pray for them. That is how you repay them." This ḥadīth was related by Abū Dāwūd.[169]

ḤADĪTH 96

عن أنسٍ رَضِيَ اللهُ عَنْهُ قَالَ: أَكَلَ النَّبِيُّ صَلَّى اللهُ عَلَيْهِ وَسَلَّمَ عِنْدَ سَعْدِ بْنِ عُبَادَةَ خُبْزاً وَزَيْتاً ثُمَّ قَالَ: «أَفْطَرَ عِنْدَكُمُ الصَّائِمُوْنَ، وَأَكَلَ طَعَامَكُمُ الأَبْرَارُ، وَصَلَّتْ عَلَيْكُمُ الْمَلائِكَةُ». (أخرجه أبوداود)

It is related on the authority of Anas ؓ that the Messenger ﷺ ate a meal of bread and olive oil with Saʿd ibn ʿUbādah ؓ, and then recited the following supplication, "May the fasting break their fasts with you, may the pious partake of your food, and may the angels pray for you." This ḥadīth was related by Abū Dāwūd.[170]

Practices: Supplicating for One's Host

It is the practice of the Sufis to offer supplication, *duʿā'*, after eating, for the one who has fed them. The ḥadīth above corroborates this practice. Another ḥadīth concerning the same practice follows.

---

169 Abū Dāwūd: 3853

170 Abū Dāwūd: 3853

ḤADĪTH 97

عَنْ قَتَادَةَ رَضِيَ اللهُ عَنْهُ قَالَ: كَانَ رَسُوْلُ اللهِ صَلَّى اللهُ عَلَيْهِ وَسَلَّمَ إِذَا رَأَى الْهِلَالَ صَرَفَ وَجْهَهُ عَنْهُ. (رواه أبو داؤد)

It is related on the authority of Qatādah that when the Messenger of Allāh ﷺ saw the moon, he would turn his head away. This ḥadīth was related by Abū Dāwūd.[171]

Teachings: Ignoring Illuminations

The Sufi masters teach that one should never pay attention to mystic illuminations which may come while one is in a state of contemplation. Concerning these illuminations they teach that the veil of light is worse than the veil of darkness. This teaching is substantiated by the ḥadīth related by Qatādah. The reason that the Messenger ﷺ turned away from the moon was that many Arabs in those times used to gaze on the heavens so intently, and with such veneration, that they were diverted from ever directing their attention toward the Creator. Here, with regard to mystic illuminations, a similar situation exists wherein attention is diverted from the true objective.

ḤADĪTH 98

عَنْ عِمْرَانَ بْنِ حُذَيْفَةَ رَضِيَ اللهُ عَنْهُ قَالَ: كَانَتْ مَيْمُوْنَةُ تَدَّانُ وَتُكْثِرُ فَقَالَ لَهَا أَهْلُهَا فِيْ ذٰلِكَ وَلَامُوْهَا، فَقَالَتْ: لَا أَتْرُكَ الدِّيْنَ وَقَدْ سَمِعْتُ خَلِيْلِيْ وَصَفِيِّيْ صَلَّى اللهُ عَلَيْهِ وَسَلَّمَ يَقُوْلُ: «مَا مِنْ أَحَدٍ يَدَّانُ دَيْناً فَعَلِمَ اللهُ أَنَّهُ يُرِيْدُ قَضَاءَهُ إِلاَّ أَدَّاهُ اللهُ تَعَالَى عَنْهُ فِيْ الدُّنْيَا». (أخرجه النسائي)

It is related on the authority of ʿImrān ibn Hudhayfah ؓ that Maymūnah ؓ was borrowing a lot of money, until finally her family reproved her. Then she said, "No, I will not refrain from borrowing. For I have heard my dear friend and sincere companion (i.e. her husband, the Messenger ﷺ) say, "Whenever someone borrows money, and Allāh knows that they truly intend to repay the debt, Allāh will see to it that it is paid in this world." This ḥadīth was related by Nasā'ī.[172]

---

171 Abū Dāwūd: 5093

172 Nasā'ī: 4690

Practices: Borrowing Money for Guests and the Needy
Many Sufi masters borrow freely in order to entertain guests and provide for the needy. This ḥadīth alone should suffice to vouch for this practice. It is well known that Maymūnah ﷺ was not given to frivolous spending."[173]

ḤADĪTH 99

عَنْ أَبِيْ هُرَيْرَةَ رَضِيَ اللهُ عَنْهُ فِيْ حَدِيْثِ فَضِيْلَةِ الذِّكْرِ قَالَ رَسُوْلُ اللهِ صَلَّى اللهُ عَلَيْهِ وَسَلَّمَ: «فَيَقُوْلُ مَلَكٌ: مِنْهُمْ فُلانٌ، عَبْدٌ خَطَّاءٌ لَيْسَ مِنْهُمْ، إِنَّمَا مَرَّلِحَاجَةٍ فَجَلَسَ، فَيَقُوْلُ: وَلَهُ قَدْ غَفَرْتُ، هُمُ الْقَوْمُ لا يَشْقى جَلِيْسُهُمْ». (أخرجه الشيخان)

It is related on the authority of Abū Hurairah ﷺ in a lengthy ḥadīth from the Prophet ﷺ concerning the virtues of *dhikr* that an angel said, after being told by the Almighty that He had forgiven the sins of all of those present in a certain group of people engaged in His remembrance, *dhikr*, "But there is a certain one among them, a wrongdoer, who is not really one of them, but who was passing by on his own business and simply decided to sit there and rest." The reply of the Almighty to the angel was, "And I forgive him too! Even those who come only to sit with these people will not be deprived." This ḥadīth was related by Bukhārī, Muslim and Tirmidhī.[174]

Customs: Initiation into Sufi Orders
It has been the way of the Sufi masters to also initiate into their spiritual orders people from whom little can be expected in the way of spiritual advancement. While this may appear to be little more than an exercise in futility, there is at least the advantage of the blessings which come to them through their association with a Sufi order. This kind of *bayʿah*, then, is given only for the sake of *barakah*. This practice is clearly supported by the ḥadīth quoted here, as even those who sit in the company of Allāh's special servants will not be deprived. Certainly, when a person takes *bayʿah* from a Sufi master it is more than likely that the person will attach themselves to the master at least to the extent of sitting and conversing with the master from time to time.

---

173 Among the wives of the Messenger ﷺ, Maymūnah bint al-Ḥārith ﷺ was perhaps best known for kindness and generosity. Of her, ʿĀ'isha ﷺ said, "She was the most God-fearing among us, and the most attached to her relatives." YTD.

174 Bukhārī: 6408, Muslim: 2689, Tirmidhī: 3600

ḤADĪTH 100

عَنْ أَبِيْ هُرَيْرَةَ رَضِيَ اللهُ عَنْهُ قَالَ: قَالَ رَسُوْلُ اللهِ صَلَّى اللهُ عَلَيْهِ وَسَلَّمَ: «أَوَّلُ مَنْ يُّدْعى يَوْمَ الْقِيَامَةِ» الحديث. وَفِيْهِ قَالَ «شُفَيٌّ»: فَأَخْبَرْتُ مُعَاوِيَةَ رَضِيَ اللهُ عَنْهُ بِهذَا الْحَدِيْثِ عَنْ أَبِيْ هُرَيْرَةَ رَضِيَ اللهُ عَنْهُ فَقَالَ: قَدْ فُعِلَ بِهولاءِ هذَا فَكَيْفَ بِمَنْ بَقِيَ مِنَ النَّاسِ؟ ثُمَّ بَكى مُعَاوِيَةُ رَضِيَ اللهُ عَنْهُ بُكَاءً شَدِيْداً حَتّى ظَنَنَّا أَنَّهُ هَالِكٌ، ثُمَّ أَفَاقَ وَمَسَحَ عَنْ وَجْهِهِ. (أخرجه مسلم والترمذي واللفظ له والنسائي)

It is related on the authority of Shufayy al-Asbuḥī that he related a ḥadīth to Muʿāwiyah ﵁ concerning the first people to be questioned on the Day of Judgment in exactly the way he had heard it from Abū Huraira ﵁, and that Muʿāwiyah ﵁ had said, "If that is what is going to happen to them, then what about the rest of us?" Then Muʿāwiyah ﵁ broke down and cried so much that people thought he was going to die. But he eventually regained his composure, wiped his face, and said, "Allāh and His Messenger are right." Then he quoted from the Qur'ān: "Whoso desires the life of this world and its temptations, We will pay them in full for their works therein, and they shall not be defrauded there: they are those for whom in the world to come there is only the Fire. Their deeds will have failed them, and void will be their works."[175] This ḥadīth was related by Muslim, Nasā'ī and Tirmidhī.[176]

States: Spiritual Ardour

Spiritual ardour, or *wajd* has been defined as one's being overwhelmed by a peculiar but praiseworthy spiritual state. While there are many different forms and degrees of *wajd*, only that which is free of dissemblance may be considered praiseworthy. Muʿāwiyah's ﵁ state, as described in this ḥadīth, is an example of true *wajd*.

ḤADĪTH 101

عَنْ أَبِيْ هُرَيْرَةَ رَضِيَ اللهُ عَنْهُ فِيْ قِصَّةِ مُنَاظَرَةِ أَبِيْ بَكْرٍ رَضِيَ اللهُ عَنْهُ وَعُمَرَ رَضِيَ اللهُ عَنْهُ فِيْ قِتَالِ مَانِعِيْ الزَّكوةِ قَالَ عُمَرُ: فَوَ اللهِ مَاهُوَ إِلاَّ أَنْ رَأَيْتُ أَنَّ اللهَ شَرَحَ صَدْرَ أَبِيْ بَكْرٍ رَضِيَ اللهُ عَنْهُ لِلْقِتَالِ فَعَرَفْتُ أَنَّهُ الْحَقُّ. (رواه البخاري وغيره)

175 al-Qur'ān, 11:15

176 Muslim: 1905, Tirmidhī: 2382, Nasā'ī: 3139

It is related on the authority of Abū Hurairah ﵁, concerning the difference of opinion between Abū Bakr ﵁ and ʿUmar ﵁ on the question of whether or not to make war on those who withheld payment of Zakāh, that ʿUmar ﵁ said, "By Allāh! When I saw that Allāh had opened the heart of Abū Bakr ﵁ to the waging of war, I knew that he was right." This ḥadīth was related in its entirety by Mālik, Muslim, Bukhārī, Nasāʾī, Abū Dāwūd and Tirmidhī.[177]

States: Divine Guidance

The biographies of the Sufi masters contain innumerable references to incidents of divine guidance, or *ilhām*. What is termed in the ḥadīth above as Allāh's opening the heart of Abū Bakr ﵁ clearly attests to the validity of the *ilhām* of the masters. Essentially, *ilhām* is divine guidance exerted directly upon the heart. In the argument referred to in the ḥadīth, it would appear that both Abū Bakr ﵁ and ʿUmar ﵁ were made recipients of divine guidance. First, Abū Bakr ﵁ received it and then, through the spiritual effusion of Abū Bakr's ﵁ words, the *ilhām* was passed to ʿUmar ﵁. Moreover, since the outcome of their *ilhām* was in no way contrary to the Sharīʿa, they acted upon it.

ḤADĪTH 102

عَنْ أَبِيْ ذَرٍّ رَضِيَ اللهُ عَنْهُ قَالَ: قَالَ رَسُوْلُ اللهِ صَلَّى اللهُ عَلَيْهِ وَسَلَّمَ: «لَيْسَتِ الزَّهَادَةُ فِيْ الدُّنْيَا بِتَحْرِيْمِ الْحَلالِ وَلاَ إِضَاعَةِ الْمَالِ وَلكِنِ الزَّهَادَةُ أَنْ تَكُوْنَ بِمَا فِيْ يَدِ اللهِ تَعَالى أَوْثَقُ مِنْكَ بِمَا فِيْ يَدِكَ، وَأَنْ تَكُوْنَ فِيْ ثَوَابِ الْمُصِيْبَةِ إِذَا أُصِبْتَ بِهَا أَرْغَبُ مِنْكَ فِيْهَا لَوْ أَنَّهَا أُبْقِيَتْ لَكَ» (أخرجه الترمذي) وزاد رزين: لأَنَّ الله تَعَالى يَقُوْلُ: ﴿لِكَيْلاَ تَأْسَوْا عَلى مَافَاتَكُمْ وَلاَتَفْرَحُوْا بِمَا اتكُم﴾

It is related on the authority of Abū Dharr ﵁ that Allāh's Messenger ﷺ said, "Asceticism is not simply a matter of your denying yourself what is lawful, or of spurning wealth. Asceticism is your having more faith in what is in the hand of Allāh than in what you hold in your own hand. And asceticism is your desiring more a reward for your enduring affliction than an end to it." This ḥadīth was related by Tirmidhī.[178]

177 Bukhārī: 4986

178 Tirmidhī: 2340, Ibn Mājah: 4100

Character: Signs of Mastery: Trust in Allāh
The realities of asceticism, *zuhd*, and trust in Allāh, *tawakkul*, two qualities of the Sufi masters which are so inseparable from true mastery as to be unmistakable as distinguishing traits of the true master, are concisely explained in this ḥadīth. In fact, this ḥadīth should go a long way toward eliminating the misconceptions people have concerning ascetics as people who shun all lawful pleasures as completely as they do unlawful ones, who immediately give away whatever they receive, and who never lift a finger to extract themselves from difficulty. From the ḥadīth quoted here, it is clear that these matters are in no way essential to true *zuhd*, which is one's having more faith in what is in the hands of Allāh ﷻ than in what is in one's own hands, and one's being happier with misfortune than without it for the sake of the reward to be had for being patient under the strain of it.

ḤADĪTH 103

عَنْ عَطِيَّةَ السَّعْدِيِّ رَضِيَ اللهُ عَنْهُ قَالَ: قَالَ رَسُوْلُ اللهِ صَلَّى اللهُ عَلَيْهِ وَسَلَّمَ: «لايَبْلُغُ الْعَبْدُ حَقِيْقَةَ التَّقْوى حَتّى يَدَعَ مَا لابَأْسَ بِهِ حَذْراً لِمَا بِهِ بَأْسٌ». (أخرجه الترمذي)

It is related on the authority of ʿAṭiyyah al-Saʿdī that the Messenger of Allāh ﷺ said, "A believer will never truly be heedful unless he/she forsakes what is unobjectionable as a precaution against what is objectionable." This ḥadīth was related by Tirmidhī.[179]

Miscellaneous: Rebutting the Objection to the Denouncement of Lawful Pleasures
Most strait-laced formalists take exception to the Sufi practice of renouncing worldly pleasures, saying that this is contrary to the Sunna. However, the truth of the matter as disclosed by the ḥadīth above is that this practice is indeed a part of the Sunna, and the way to true *taqwā*, or heedfulness.

ḤADĪTH 104

عَنْ عَبَّادِ بْنِ تَمِيْمٍ أَنَّ أَبَا بَشِيْرٍ الأَنْصَارِيِّ رَضِيَ اللهُ عَنْهُ أَخْبَرَهُ أَنَّهُ كَانَ مَعَ رَسُوْلِ اللهِ صَلَّى اللهُ عَلَيْهِ وَسَلَّمَ فِيْ سَفَرٍ فَأَمَرَ مُعَاوِيَةَ: «لاتَبْقَيَنَّ فِيْ رَقَبَةِ بَعِيْرٍ قِلادَةٌ مِنْ وَتَرٍ أَوْ قِلادَةٌ إِلاَّ قُطِعَتْ» . (أخرجه الثلثة وأبوداود)

179 Tirmidhī: 2451, Ibn Mājah: 4215

It is related on the authority of 'Abbād ibn Tamīm that Abū Bashīr ؓ was once on a journey with Allāh's Prophet ﷺ, when it was announced that there was not to remain on the neck of any camel any kind of collar except that it be cut off. This was related by Mālik, Bukhārī and Abū Dāwūd.[180]

Reform: Unlawful Charms

Most commentators on this ḥadīth have explained that the announcement was made because the Arabs from before the advent of Islam were accustomed to tying protective charms around the necks of their animals; charms which, for the most part, could not be tolerated by the Sharīʿa of Islam. This ḥadīth, then, proclaims the prohibition of all amulets, charms and talismans that are in any way antithetical to the Sharīʿa.[181] Many of today's so-called Sufis would do well to take note of this.

ḤADĪTH 105

عَنْ كَبْشَةَ الْأَنْصَارِيَّةِ رَضِيَ الله تَعَالَى عَنْهَا قَالَتْ: دَخَلَ عَلَيَّ النَّبِيُّ صَلَّى اللهُ عَلَيْهِ وَسَلَّمَ فَشَرِبَ مِنْ فِيْ قِرْبَةٍ مُعَلَّقَةٍ قَائِماً فَقُمْتُ إِلَى فِيْهَا فَقَطَعْتُهُ. (أخرجه الترمذي)

It is related on the authority of Kabashah ؓ that Allāh's Messenger ﷺ once entered her house and, while standing, drank from the mouth of a water bag that was hanging from a peg on the wall. Later, she cut the leather away from the mouth of the water bag. This much of the ḥadīth was related by Tirmidhī. In the version of the ḥadīth related by Razīn, Kabashah ؓ added, "Then I made from the leather a small flask from which I used to drink."[182]

Customs: Blessings from what is Used by a Master

The belief of many disciples that there are blessings to be had from whatever their master touches, or drinks from, or wears, is verified by this ḥadīth.

Reform: Permission to Use What Was Used by a Master

Many of those who use such articles do so only occasionally. There is nothing

---

180 Bukhārī: 3005, Muslim: 2115, Abū Dāwūd: 2552, *Muwaṭṭa'*: 3456

181 The author is speaking here of unlawful charms, i.e. charms in the name of other than Allāh ﷻ, or in the shape of humans, etc. Otherwise, in his commentary on ḥadīths [28] and [94], he has discussed how, in fact, the practice of making charms is a part of the Sunna. YTD.

182 Tirmidhī: 1892, Ibn Mājah: 3423

wrong with this if it is done as a measure to conserve the effects of the blessings. However, if it is done out of a belief that frequent use is in some way disrespectful, then the words, "from which I used to drink" from the ḥadīth should suffice to dispel that groundless belief.

ḤADĪTH 106

عَنْ جَابِرٍ رَضِيَ اللهُ عَنْهُ قَالَ: دَخَلَ النَّبِيُّ صَلَّى اللهُ عَلَيْهِ وَسَلَّمَ حَائِطَ رَجُلٍ مِنَ الْأَنْصَارِيِّ وَهُوَ يُحَوِّلُ الْمَاءَ فِيْ حَائِطِهِ فَقَالَ رَسُوْلُ اللهِ صَلَّى اللهُ عَلَيْهِ وَسَلَّمَ: «إِنْ كَانَ عِنْدَكَ مَاءٌ بَاتَ هٰذِهِ اللَّيْلَةَ فِيْ شَنٍّ وَإِلاَّ كَرَعْنَا»؟ الحديث. (رواه البخاري وأبوداود)

It is related on the authority of Jābir ﷺ that Allāh's Messenger ﷺ once entered a vegetable garden owned by a man from the Anṣār of Madīna who was, at that moment, drawing water from his well. The Emissary ﷺ said, "If you have some water which has stood overnight in a water bag, I'd prefer to drink that. But, if you don't, I'll just ask you for a drink from that well."[183] This ḥadīth was related by Bukhārī and Abū Dāwūd.[184]

Miscellaneous: Latitude in Partaking of Worldly Pleasures

A number of Sufi masters are known to have been quite liberal in matters of food and drink, giving nearly ceremonious attention to the ways in which food was prepared and served. Certain purists have objected that this sort of behaviour has nothing to do with self denial or any of the other concerns of a true master. The Prophet's ﷺ showing of a preference for one kind of water over another is certainly indicative of a certain degree of latitude in such matters, especially with regard to the spiritually developed. The wisdom behind all of this is that through one's partaking of these delights, one's love for the True Provider is increased, while at the same time one's dependence on Him is demonstrated in a practical manner. Both of these qualities may be numbered among the objectives of the Sufi way. Actually, in the same way that there is a great deal which is beneficial in forsaking worldly pleasures, there is also a great deal which is beneficial in partaking of them. Finally, only a master should decide how much of each will be suitable for him/herself or for his/her disciples.

---

183 Well water left overnight will be clearer, as the dust particles have a chance to settle to the bottom, whereas freshly drawn water from a desert well will often be murky. YTD.

184 Bukhārī: 5613, Abū Dāwūd: 3724, Ibn Mājah: 3432

ḤADĪTH 107

عن أبي هريرة رَضِيَ اللهُ عَنْهُ قَالَ: قالَ النَّبِيُّ صَلَّى اللهُ عَلَيْهِ وَسَلَّمَ: «أُتِيْتُ لَيْلَةَ أُسْرِيْ بِيْ بِقَدَحَيْنِ مِنْ خَمْرٍ وَلَبَنٍ، فَأَخَذْتُ اللَّبَنَ فَقَالَ الْمَلَكُ: اَلْحَمْدُ للهِ الَّذِيْ هَدَاكَ لِلْفِطْرَةِ لَوْ أَخَذْتَ الْخَمْرَ لَغَوَتْ أُمَّتُكَ». (أخرجه النسائي)

It is related on the authority of Abū Huraira that the Messenger of Allāh said, "On the night I was taken up into the heavens, I was given two cups; one of wine and one of milk. When I drank the cup of milk, an angel said, "Praise be to Allāh Who guided you to Islam. Had you taken the wine, the community of your followers would have gone astray." This ḥadīth was related by Nasā'ī.[185]

Questions: The World of Manifest Meaning

The particular meaning-form of Islam is milk, while the meaning-form of worldly pleasures is wine. Thus, the world of manifest meaning, so often referred to by Sufi masters, finds confirmation in the ḥadīth related here.

ḤADĪTH 108

عَنْ جَابِرٍ رَضِيَ اللهُ عَنْهُ أَنَّهُ سَمِعَ رَسُوْلَ اللهِ صَلَّى اللهُ عَلَيْهِ وَسَلَّمَ يَقُوْلُ: «بَيْنَ الرَّجُلِ وَبَيْنَ الشِّرْكِ تَرْكُ الصَّلوةِ». (أخرجه مسلم)

It is related on the authority of Jābir that Allāh's Messenger said, "Between a person and disbelief there is one's abandonment of regular prayer." This ḥadīth was related by Muslim and Tirmidhī.[186]

Sayings: Calling a Misdeed Disbelief

In the works of many Sufi masters misdeeds are referred to as disbelief. For example,

> On the Way, it's disbelief to bear enmity,
> With us the heart's a mirror, that's our policy.

As the same thing has been done in this ḥadīth (one does not become a disbeliever by missing one's prayers), it may be said to corroborate this figurative usage

185 Bukhārī: 3394, Muslim: 168, Tirmidhī: 3130, Nasā'ī: 5660

186 Muslim: 82, Abū Dāwūd: 4678, Tirmidhī: 2691

of words. In the same way that the ḥadīth can be explained,[187] so also the sayings and writings of the Sufis can be explained or interpreted in one way or another.

ḤADĪTH 109

عَنْ أَبِي ذَرٍّ رَضِيَ اللهُ عَنْهُ أَنَّ رَسُوْلَ اللهِ صَلَّى اللهُ عَلَيْهِ وَسَلَّمَ قَامَ حَتَّى أَصْبَحَ بِآيَةٍ ﴿إِنْ تُعَذِّبْهُمْ فَإِنَّهُمْ عِبَادُكَ وَإِنْ تَغْفِرْ لَهُمْ فَإِنَّكَ أَنْتَ الْعَزِيْزُ الْحَكِيْمُ﴾ (أخرجه النسائي)

It is related on the authority of Abū Dharr ﷺ that Allāh's Prophet ﷺ stood all night in prayer, reciting one verse over and over again until morning. The verse was: "If you punish them, they are your servants; and if you forgive them, you are the Almighty, All Wise." This ḥadīth was related by Nasāʾī.[188]

Miscellaneous: Spiritual Disciplines

It is a frequent charge of the formalists that the rigorous variety of spiritual disciplines, or *mujāhadah* practised by the Sufis is a blameworthy form of innovation, *bidʿah*. From the ḥadīth above it should be more than evident that such discipline was practised by the Prophet ﷺ himself, which makes it a part of the Sunna. The few ḥadīth which mention the prohibition of such practices also clarify that the prohibition is only for those who are physically unable to perform those practices or are otherwise not in a position to perform them regularly.

ḤADĪTH 110

عَنْ عَلِيِّ بْنِ عَبْدِ الرَّحْمٰنِ قَالَ ابْنُ عُمَرَ رَضِيَ اللهُ عَنْهُ يَحْكِيْ صَلوةَ رَسُوْلِ اللهِ صَلَّى اللهُ عَلَيْهِ وَسَلَّمَ أَشَارَ بِإِصْبَعِهِ الَّتِيْ تَلِيْ الإِبْهَامَ فِيْ الْقِبْلَةِ وَرَمى بِبَصَرِهِ إِلَيْهَا. (أخرجه النسائي)

It is related on the authority of ʿAlī ibn ʿAbd al-Raḥmān that ʿAbdullāh ibn ʿUmar ﷺ said in his description of how the Prophet ﷺ used to perform the prayer, *ṣalāh*, that he ﷺ used to point toward the *qiblah* with the forefinger, and then keep his gaze fixed on that finger. This ḥadīth was related by Nasāʾī.[189]

---

187 The explanation given by most commentators is that non-performance of *ṣalāh* may be taken to mean complete abandonment of *ṣalāh* as a practice and a part of faith, in which case, the non-performer becomes a disbeliever. YTD.

188 Nasāʾī: 1011

189 Nasāʾī: 1161

ḤADĪTH 111

عَنْ ابْنِ الزُّبَيْرِ رَضِيَ اللهُ عَنْهُ فِيْ صَلوةِ رَسُوْلِ اللهِ صَلَّى اللهُ عَلَيْهِ وَسَلَّمَ لايُجَاوِزُ بَصَرُهُ إِشَارَةً. (أخرجه أبو داؤد)

It is related on the authority of Ibn Zubayr ﵁ concerning the prayer of Allāh's Prophet ﷺ that his gaze never went beyond the tip of the finger he was pointing with. This ḥadīth was related by Abū Dāwūd and Nasā'ī.[190]

Practices: Increasing Concentration

Among the many spiritual disciplines practised by the Sufis is their looking fixedly at a single object. The purpose of this particular exercise, and many others like it, is to increase the powers of concentration and absorption. The two ḥadīth quoted here would seem to confirm this practice.

ḤADĪTH 112

عَنِ الْفَضْلِ بْنِ عَبَّاسٍ رَضِيَ اللهُ عَنْهُ قَالَ: قَالَ رَسُوْلُ اللهِ صَلَّى اللهُ عَلَيْهِ وَسَلَّمَ: «اَلصَّلاةُ مَثْنى مَثْنى، تَشَهُّدٌ فِيْ كُلِّ رَكْعَتَيْنِ، وَتَخَشُّعٌ وَتَمَسْكُنٌ» وَفِيْهِ: «وَمَنْ لَمْ يَفْعَلْ فَهِيَ خِدَاجٌ». (أخرجه الترمذي)

It is related on the authority of al-Faḍl ibn ʿAbbās ﵁ that Allāh's Messenger ﷺ said, "*Ṣalāh* is performed in twos, with one's witnessing after every two cycles, and with humility and devotion. The prayer of those who do not do these things will be stillborn. This ḥadīth was related by Tirmidhī.[191]

Questions: The Need for Humility

While most Sufis hold that complete concentration is essential to the proper performance of prayer and other acts of worship, the formalists insist that it is not. The ḥadīth above makes it perfectly clear that this is indeed essential, as without it prayer is stillborn and imperfect.

ḤADĪTH 113

عَنْ عَائِشَةَ رَضِيَ الله تَعَالى عَنْهَا قَالَتْ: صَلَّى رَسُوْلُ اللهِ صَلَّى اللهُ عَلَيْهِ وَسَلَّمَ فِيْ خَمِيْصَةٍ

190 Abū Dāwūd: 990

191 Tirmidhī: 385

لَهَا أَعْلاَمٌ، فَنَظَرَ إِلَى أَعْلاَمِهَا نَظْرَةً فَقَالَ: «اذْهَبُوْا بِخَمِيْصَتِيْ هٰذِهِ إِلَى أَبِيْ جَهْم وَائْتُوْنِيْ بِأَنْبِجَانِيَّتِهِ فَإِنَّهَا أَلْهَتْنِيْ اٰنِفاً عَنْ صَلوتِيْ». وفي رواية مالك وأبي داؤد «كُنْتُ أَنْظُرُ إِلَيْهَا وَأَنَا فِي الصَّلوةِ فَأَخَافُ أَنْ تَفْتِنَنِيْ». (أخرجه الستة إلا الترمذي)

It is related on the authority of ʿĀʾisha 🙽 that Allāh's Messenger 🙽 performed prayer while dressed in an embroidered robe. When he caught himself gazing at the embroidery, he said, "Take this robe of mine away to Abū Jahm ibn Hudhayfah and exchange it for a simple woollen robe. This thing has just distracted me from my prayer!" This ḥadīth was related by Mālik, Muslim, Bukhārī, Nasāʾī and Abū Dāwūd. In the version related by Mālik and Abū Dāwūd, the last sentence reads, "I was looking at it as I performed prayer and became afraid that it might distract me."[192]

Practices: Foregoing Whatever Interferes with Concentration
This ḥadīth clearly endorses the reduction in factors that distract from the remembrance of Allāh 🙽 which is practised by so many of the Sufi masters.

Questions: Whispering and Vague Suspicions
Another matter that becomes evident from this ḥadīth is that occasionally mild forms of *waswasa*, whisperings and vague suspicions, are visited upon the spiritually developed. This is certainly not in any way to be construed as detracting from their virtues and perfection.

Character: Publicising One's Condition
It is a part of sincerity and humility to make one's own seemingly imperfect condition known to one's followers and disciples. There is a provision to this, however, and that is that there be no danger of someone's misunderstanding and then having doubts about the Sufi way or Islam. If the imperfect condition is one of wrongdoing, then it is essential that it not be made known to others, as there are many ḥadīth which expressly prohibit the broadcasting of one's own or another's wrongdoing.

ḤADĪTH 114

عَنْ أَبِيْ هُرَيْرَةَ رَضِيَ اللّٰهُ عَنْهُ قَالَ: قَالَ رَسُوْلُ اللّٰهِ صَلَّى اللّٰهُ عَلَيْهِ وَسَلَّمَ: «لَعَنَ اللّٰهُ الْيَهُوْدَ وَالنَّصَارى اتَّخَذُوْا قُبُوْرَ أَنْبِيَاءِهِمْ مَسَاجِدَ». (أخرجه الخمسة إلا الترمذي)

---

192 Bukhārī: 373, Muslim: 556, Abū Dāwūd: 914, Nasāʾī: 772, Muwaṭṭaʾ: 324, 325. The addition in Mālik and Abū Dāwūd alluded to above are actually in Mālik and Bukhārī.

It is related on the authority of Abū Hurairah ﷺ that the Messenger of Allāh ﷺ said, "May the curse of Allāh be on those Christians and Jews who worship the graves of their prophets!" This ḥadīth was related by Bukhārī, Muslim, Abū Dāwūd and Nasā'ī.[193]

Reform: Grave Worship

This ḥadīth should suffice as admonishment to the ignorant Sufis of our times who prostrate themselves at the graves of past Sufi masters, regardless of whether they do so with the intention of worship, which is clearly disbelief, or with the intention of greeting, which is a major act of wrongdoing and no more than a step removed from disbelief.

ḤADĪTH 115

عَنْ أَبِيْ الدَّرْدَاءِ رَضِيَ اللهُ عَنْهُ قَالَ: قَامَ رَسُوْلُ اللهِ صَلَّى اللهُ عَلَيْهِ وَسَلَّمَ يُصَلِّيْ وَفِيْهِ قَالَ: «إِنَّ عَدُوَّ اللهِ إِبْلِيْسَ جَاءَ بِشِهَابٍ مِنْ نَارٍ لِيَجْعَلَهُ فِيْ وَجْهِيْ». الحديث (رواه مسلم)

It is related on the authority of Abū Dardā' ﷺ that Allāh's Messenger ﷺ once stood and began to perform his prayer. When he had finished, he ﷺ reported to his Companions, "Iblīs, the enemy of Allāh, brought a flame from the Fire of hell and tried to put it in my face." This ḥadīth was related by Muslim and Nasā'ī.[194]

Miscellaneous: No One is Safe from the Promptings of Satan

From this ḥadīth it should be clear that regardless of how perfectly developed a person may be spiritually, one should never underestimate the disruptive power of Satan, *Iblīs*. On the contrary, one should constantly be on guard against Satan's causing one to do wrong. Look at the insolence of the wretch who dared even to come into the presence of Allāh's Messenger ﷺ, threatening him with burning fire while he was at prayer! As the prophets are protected from wrongdoing, Satan had to resort to the threat of physical violence in order to cause distress to the Prophet ﷺ.

ḤADĪTH 116

عَنْ ابْنِ عَبَّاسٍ رَضِيَ اللهُ عَنْهُ قَالَ: قَالَ رَسُوْلُ اللهِ صَلَّى اللهُ عَلَيْهِ وَسَلَّمَ: «مَنْ سَمِعَ

193 Bukhārī: 1390, Muslim: 530, Abū Dāwūd: 3227, Nasā'ī: 704, 2049

194 Muslim: 542

الْمُنَادِيْ فَلَمْ يَمْنَعْهُ مِنِ اتِّبَاعِهِ عُذْرٌ لَمْ تُقْبَلْ مِنْهُ الصَّلٰوةُ الَّتِيْ صَلَّاهَا» قِيْلَ، وَمَا الْعُذْرُ؟

قَالَ «خَوْفٌ أَوْ مَرَضٌ». (أخرجه أبو داود)

It is related on the authority of Ibn ʿAbbās 🙾 that Allāh's Messenger 🙼 said, "The prayer performed by someone who hears the call to prayer and, without an excuse, fails to answer that call will not be accepted." One of the Companions asked what a valid excuse was, so the Prophet replied, "Fear, or sickness." This ḥadīth was related by Abū Dāwūd.[195]

Reform: Performing the Prayer in a Mosque
Many of our modern-day Sufis rarely if ever go to a mosque to perform their prayer. It is quite clear from this ḥadīth that these dervishes need correcting; for when their prayer *is* imperfect to the point of being unacceptable, of what avail will their *dhikr* and other disciplines be to them?

ḤADĪTH 117

عَنْ ابْنِ عَبَّاسٍ رَضِيَ اللهُ عَنْهُ وَسُئِلَ عَنْ رَجُلٍ يَصُوْمُ النَّهَارَ وَيَقُوْمُ اللَّيْلَ وَلَايَشْهَدُ الْجَمَاعَةَ وَلَا الْجُمُعَةَ فَقَالَ: هٰذَا مِنْ أَهْلِ النَّارِ. (أخرجه الترمذي)

It is related on the authority of Ibn ʿAbbās 🙾 that when he was asked about someone who spent his days fasting and his nights in prayer, but who never went to a mosque for congregational prayers, he answered, "He is one of the people of the Fire." This ḥadīth was related by Tirmidhī.[196]

Reform: Prayer in the Mosque
The same subject that was mentioned in the ḥadīth above is again mentioned here, but with even greater emphasis.

ḤADĪTH 118

عَنْ عِتْبَانَ بْنِ مَالِكٍ رَضِيَ اللهُ عَنْهُ قَالَ: قُلْتُ يَا رَسُوْلَ اللهِ! إِنَّ السُّيُوْلَ تَحُوْلُ بَيْنِيْ وَبَيْنَ مَسْجِدِ قَوْمِيْ، فَأُحِبُّ أَنْ تَأْتِيَنِيْ فَتُصَلِّيْ فِيْ مَكَانٍ مِنْ بَيْتِيْ أَتَّخِذُهُ مَسْجِدًا، فَقَالَ صَلَّى اللهُ عَلَيْهِ وَسَلَّمَ: «سَنَفْعَلُ». الحديث (أخرجه الثلاثة والنسائي)

---

195 Abū Dāwūd: 547

196 Even though this narration quotes Ibn ʿAbbas, it is considered a ḥadīth for the reason that Ibn ʿAbbās 🙾 would never have said what he did unless he had heard it from Allāh's Prophet. YTD.

It is related on the authority of ʿUtbān ibn Mālik that when he told Allāh's Messenger that the rains prevented him from making his way to the mosque for prayers and that he would like the Emissary to come to his home and perform prayer with him in the place where he usually performed it, Allāh's Messenger replied, "Yes, we will do it." This ḥadīth was related by Mālik, Muslim, Bukhārī and Nasāʾī.

Practices: Designating a Place Especially for Devotions

In spite of the fact that ʿUtbān might have chosen to perform prayer with the Prophet in any place in his home, he preferred that it be performed in the place in which he was accustomed to performing it when alone. The reason for this is that a designated place is a sure aid to increased concentration. Thus, when making *dhikr* or performing other spiritual disciplines it is better that one sit in a specially designated place. First, it should never be supposed that this designation is in itself an act of worship. Secondly, such a place should be chosen as will not interfere with the rights or comforts of others.

Customs: Taking a Place of Blessings

Another reason for ʿUtbān's asking the Prophet to perform the prayer with him in that particular place was so that it would become a place of blessings (having once been occupied by the blessed person of Muḥammad al-Muṣṭafā) The reason for this is that it is better that one be in a place of blessings when performing spiritual exercises such as *dhikr* and so on. Here also, however, the condition is that one does not exceed proper bounds in either what one believes about the subject or in one's practices related to it. If this condition is not met, one may very easily fall into the mistake of *bidʿah*.

ḤADĪTH 119

عَنْ أَنَسٍ رَضِيَ اللهُ عَنْهُ قَالَ: قَالَ رَسُوْلُ اللهِ صَلَّى اللهُ عَلَيْهِ وَسَلَّمَ: «إِنِّيْ لَأَدْخُلُ فِيْ الصَّلوةِ وَأَنَا أُرِيْدُ أَنْ أُطِيْلَهَا فَأَسْمَعُ بُكَاءَ الصَّبِيِّ فَأَتَجَوَّزُ فِيْ صَلوتِيْ لِمَا أَعْلَمُ مِنْ وَجْدِ أُمِّهِ مِنْ بُكَاءِهِ». (أخرجه الخمسة إلا أبا داؤد)

It is related on the authority of Anas that Allāh's Prophet once said, "When I begin performing prayer I feel like prolonging it. But sometimes I hear the crying of a child, and so I shorten the prayer because I realise how upset the child's mother [who may possibly be performing the prayer in the congregation] must be." This ḥadīth was related by Muslim, Bukhārī, Nasāʾī and Tirmidhī.[197]

Questions: The Prayers of the Masters

Many people suppose complete mental involvement to be the true objective of prayer, and thus believe it to be one of the qualities essential to spiritual mastery. From this ḥadīth, however, it is plain to see that this is neither an objective nor an essential quality. Had this sort of absorption been essential for mastery, then how was it that the greatest of all, Allāh bless him and give him peace, was not completely absorbed in his prayer? Why did he pay attention to the crying of a child? Why did he imagine in his mind's eye the anxiety of a child's mother? Nonetheless, absorption is certainly worthy of praise. But because something is praiseworthy does not mean that it is an end in itself.

ḤADĪTH 120

عَنْ ابْنِ عُمَرَ رَضِيَ اللهُ عَنْهُ قَالَ: قَالَ رَسُوْلُ اللهِ صَلَّى اللهُ عَلَيْهِ وَسَلَّمَ: «أَقِيْمُوْا الصُّفُوْفَ وَحَاذُوْا بَيْنَ الْمَنَاكِبِ وَسُدُّوْا الْخَلَلَ وَلِيْنُوْا بِأَيْدِيْ إِخْوَانِكُمْ وَلَاتَذَرُوْا فُرُجَاتِ الشَّيْطَانِ». الحديث (أخرجه أبوداؤد)

It is related on the authority of Ibn ʿUmar 🙴 that the Messenger of Allāh 🙵 said, "Straighten the rows, line up the shoulders, fill in the empty spaces, don't push against your neighbour, and don't leave any space in between for Satan." This ḥadīth was related by Abū Dāwūd.[198]

Miscellaneous: Audible Group Dhikr

It is the teaching of the Sufi masters that when doing audible group *dhikr* the participants should sit as closely together as possible. That teaching is borne out by the words of the Prophet in the ḥadīth quoted here, "Fill in the empty spaces." Certain masters have taught that empty spaces in the group are invitations to *waswasa* or vague misgivings. This is also supported by the ḥadīth: "Don't leave any space in between for Satan."

---

197 Bukhārī: 709, 710, Muslim: 470, Tirmidhī: 237, Ibn Mājah: 989, Nasāʾī:826
198 Abū Dāwūd: 666

ḤADĪTH 121

عَنْ عَبْدِ اللهِ بْنِ مُغَفَّلٍ الْمُزَنِيِّ رَضِيَ اللهُ عَنْهُ قَالَ: قَالَ رَسُوْلُ اللهِ صَلَّى اللهُ عَلَيْهِ وَسَلَّمَ: «صَلُّوْا قَبْلَ الْمَغْرِبِ رَكْعَتَيْنِ» ثُمَّ قَالَ: «صَلُّوْا قَبْلَ الْمَغْرِبِ رَكْعَتَيْنِ لِمَنْ شَاءَ» خَشْيَةَ أَنْ يَتَّخِذَهَا النَّاسُ سُنَّةً. (أخرجه أبوداؤد بهذا اللفظ) وَفِيْ أُخْرى لِلشَّيْخَيْنِ. قَالَ: «صَلُّوْا قَبْلَ صَلوةِ الْمَغْرِبِ» ثُمَّ قَالَ فِيْ الثَّالِثَةِ: «لِمَنْ شَاءَ كَرَاهِيَةَ أَنْ يَتَّخِذَهَا النَّاسُ سُنَّةً».

It is related on the authority of ʿAbdullāh ibn Mughaffal ؓ that Allāh's Prophet ﷺ said, "Perform two cycles of prayer before sunset." The narrator added, "Then he said, 'Perform two cycles of prayer before sunset, if you wish,' so that no one would think that they had been ordered to do so." This ḥadīth was related by Abū Dāwūd. In another version related by Muslim and Bukhārī, the Prophet ﷺ said, "Perform prayer before sunset," three times, and then said, "If you wish," so that people would not think that to do so was Sunna.[199]

Reform: Discounting Supposedly Requisite Practices

Although the practice of performing two cycles of prayer before sunset was mentioned expressly, the Companions ؓ were made to understand that they were not to assume it was a duty. Then, concerning those practices for which there is no mention, express or otherwise, in the Qur'ān or the Sunna, how is it possible that the Prophet could have intended that people obligate themselves to perform them? Furthermore, experience has shown that until people completely abandon these practices, they are not fully able to free themselves from the belief that they are somehow obligated to perform them. For this reason it is essential that they discontinue these practices, whatever they may be.

ḤADĪTH 122

عَنِ الْمُغِيْرَةِ بْنِ شُعْبَةَ رَضِيَ اللهُ عَنْهُ قَالَ: قَامَ رَسُوْلُ اللهِ صَلَّى اللهُ عَلَيْهِ وَسَلَّمَ حَتّى تَوَرَّمَتْ قَدَمَاهُ فَقِيْلَ لَهُ: «قَدْ غُفِرَلَكَ مَاتَقَدَّمَ مِنْ ذَنْبِكَ وَمَا تَأَخَّرَ» قَالَ: «أَفَلا أَكُوْنُ عَبْداً شَكُوْراً»؟ (أخرجه الخمسة إلا أباداؤد)

It is related on the authority of Mughīrah ibn Shuʿbah ؓ that Allāh's Messenger ﷺ stood so long in night prayer that his feet swelled up. So one of

199 Abū Dāwūd: 1281, Bukhārī: 1183, Muslim: 838

the Companions asked him why, if his former and his latter wrongs had been forgiven, did he have need of such rigorous devotions? Allāh's Messenger ﷺ replied, "Am I not to be an appreciative servant?" This ḥadīth was related by Bukhārī, Muslim, Nasā'ī and Tirmidhī.[200]

Miscellaneous: Rigorous Spiritual Disciplines
The commentary on *mujāhadah* at Ḥadīth 109 applies equally to this ḥadīth.

ḤADĪTH 123

عَنْ عَائِشَةَ رضي الله تعالى عنها قَالَتْ: كَانَ رَسُوْلُ اللهِ صَلَّى اللهُ عَلَيْهِ وَسَلَّمَ لاَيَدَعُ قِيَامَ اللَّيْلِ وَكَانَ إِذَا مَرِضَ أَوْ كَسِلَ صَلَّى قَاعِداً. (أخرجه أبوداؤد)

It is related on the authority of ʿĀ'isha ؓ that Allāh's Prophet ﷺ never missed a night prayer, *tahajjud*. If he was ill or fatigued, he performed the night prayer from a sitting position. This ḥadīth was related by Abū Dāwūd.[201]

Teachings: Taking Rest
When it becomes apparent to a master that a disciple's ardour is flagging, then, in accordance with the teachings of the Sufi masters, he should decrease the disciple's disciplines and allow him/her to take more rest. The ḥadīth quoted here may be cited as containing the foundation of this teaching, as the Prophet himself ﷺ used sometimes (when fatigued) to take the liberty of performing the night prayer in a sitting position.

ḤADĪTH 124

عَنْ عُثْمَانَ بْنِ أَبِيْ الْعَاصِ رَضِيَ اللهُ عَنْهُ قَالَ: قُلْتُ يَا رَسُوْلَ اللهِ! إِنَّ الشَّيْطَانَ قَدْ حَالَ بَيْنِيْ وَبَيْنَ صَلاَ تِيْ وَبَيْنَ قِرَائَتِيْ يُلَبِّسُهَا عَلَيَّ، فَقَالَ رَسُوْلُ اللهِ صَلَّى اللهُ عَلَيْهِ وَسَلَّمَ: «ذلِكَ شَيْطَانٌ يُقَالُ لَهُ خِنْزِبٌ فَإِذَا أَحْسَسْتَهُ فَتَعَوَّذْ بِاللهِ مِنْهُ وَاتْفُلْ عَلى يَسَارِكَ ثَلثاً» قَالَ: فَفَعَلْتُ ذلِكَ، فَأَذْهَبَهُ اللهُ تَعَالى عَنِّيْ. (أخرجه مسلم)

It is related on the authority of ʿUthmān ibn ʿAbū al-ʿĀṣ ؓ that he said

200 Bukhārī: 4836, Muslim: 2819, Tirmidhī: 412, Nasā'ī: 1645, Ibn Mājah: 1419
201 Abū Dāwūd: 1307

to Allāh's Messenger, Allāh bless him and give him peace, "Satan comes between me and my prayer, interfering with my recitation of the Qur'ān, so that I become confused." So Allāh's Messenger ﷺ replied to him, "That is the satan called Khanzab. When you sense his presence, seek refuge in Allāh from him and spit three times to your left." ʿUthmān ؓ said, "So, I did that. And when I did, Allāh made him (the satan) go away." This ḥadīth was related by Muslim.[202]

Miscellaneous: A Cure for Whisperings

There are a number of methods for curing *waswasa*, including the method recommended in the ḥadīth here. The basic element in all of these cures, however, is one's directing one's attention to Allāh ﷻ and ignoring the *waswasa*. Whatever specific methods are mentioned in the numerous ḥadīth which have come to us on the subject are all essentially related to this one simple principle. In the particular method mentioned in the ḥadīth related by ʿUthmān ؓ, the directive to seek refuge in Allāh ﷻ is a way of turning one's attention toward Allāh ﷻ, while the directive to spit on the left is a way of ignoring the whisperings. It would also seem apparent that this method is best applied prior to one's beginning the prayer.

ḤADĪTH 125

عَنْ أَبِيْ هُرَيْرَةَ رَضِيَ اللهُ عَنْهُ قَالَ: سَأَلَ رَجُلٌ رَسُوْلَ اللهِ صَلَّى اللهُ عَلَيْهِ وَسَلَّمَ عَنِ الْمُبَاشَرَةِ لِلصَّائِمِ، فَرَخَّصَ لَهُ فَأَتَاهُ آخَرُ فَسَأَلَهُ، فَنَهَاهُ وَكَانَ الَّذِيْ رَخَّصَ لَهُ شَيْخاً كَبِيْراً وَالَّذِيْ نَهَاهُ شَاباً. (أخرجه أبوداؤد)

It is related on the authority of Abū Hurairah ؓ that a man went to Allāh's Prophet ﷺ and asked if there was permission for one fasting to embrace one's wife. So the Prophet ﷺ gave the man permission to do so. But when another man came and asked the same thing, the Prophet ﷺ refused to give him permission. The man he gave permission to was an old man, while the man he refused was a young one. This ḥadīth was related by Abū Dāwūd.[203]

202 Muslim: 2203

203 Abū Dāwūd: 2387

Practices: Each According to His Own

It has been the practice of the Sufi masters to instruct their disciples each according to his/her own particular spiritual development, state, and abilities. The event described in this ḥadīth is quite obviously based on the same underlying principle. Furthermore, the ḥadīth lends support to the practice of most Sufi masters of giving instruction to their disciples in private. It is not difficult to imagine the confusion which would result if novices of limited abilities and spiritual stature were to begin with practices and disciplines meant for advanced Sufis. Furthermore, private instruction is often more effective for the reason that the rapport between teacher and student can be more firmly established in private.

ḤADĪTH 126

عَنْ أَبِي هُرَيْرَةَ رَضِيَ اللهُ عَنْهُ قَالَ: قَالَ رَسُوْلُ اللهِ صَلَّى اللهُ عَلَيْهِ وَسَلَّمَ: «لاتَخُصُّوْا اللَّيْلَةَ الْجُمُعَةَ مِنْ بَيْنِ اللَّيَالِيْ وَلاَ تَخُصُّوْا يَوْمَ الْجُمُعَةَ بِصِيَامٍ مِنْ بَيْنِ الْأَيَّامِ إِلاَّ أَنْ يَكُوْنَ فِيْ صَوْمٍ يَصُوْمُ أَحَدُكُمْ. (أخرجه مسلم)

It is related on the authority of Abū Hurairah ﷺ that the Messenger of Allāh ﷺ said, "Do not single out the night of Jumuʿah from among all other nights for standing in prayer. And do not single out the day of Jumuʿah from among all other days for fasting. Fast on Jumuʿah only when a fast that you regularly keep[204] falls on that day." This ḥadīth was related by Muslim.[205]

Reform: Turning Practice into Belief

When, concerning a matter of practice, there is nothing in the Sharīʿa to limit its performance to a certain time or place, then to make it a belief that the practice should be performed at only a certain time or place, or to intend to perform it only at a certain time or place even if one is not regular in doing so, or to be regular in performing it at a certain time even if one does not intend to be doing so, or to give those who do not know the impression that the practice is in some way limited to a certain time or place, is clearly prohibited by the Sharīʿa. In our own times not only the Muslims in general, but many Sufis as well have become entangled in this affliction.

---

204 For example, if one regularly fasts in the middle of the month, or after every three days, as recommended in the Sunna. YTD.

205 Muslim: 1144

ḤADĪTH 127

عَنْ أَبِيْ هُرَيْرَةَ رَضِيَ اللهُ عَنْهُ قَالَ: قَالَ رَسُوْلُ اللهِ صَلَّى اللهُ عَلَيْهِ وَسَلَّمَ فِيْ حَدِيْثٍ طَوِيْلٍ: «إِنَّ اللهَ لاَ يَنْظُرُ إِلى صُوَرِكُمْ وَأَجْسَادِكُمْ وَلكِنْ يَنْظُرُ إِلى قُلُوْبِكُمْ وَأَعْمَالِكُمْ، اَلتَّقْوى ههُنَا وَيُشِيْرُ إِلى صَدْرِهِ». الحديث (رواه الستة إلا النسائي وهذا لفظ مسلم)

It is related on the authority of Abū Hurairah ﵁, as a part of a lengthy narration, that Allāh's Prophet ﷺ said, "Assuredly it is not your bodies or forms which concern Allāh, but your hearts and your deeds. Piety (*taqwa*) is here! Piety is here! Piety is here!" And he pointed to his chest. This ḥadīth was related by Bukhārī, Muslim, Abū Dāwūd and Tirmidhī.[206]

Questions: Inner Meaning

In this ḥadīth as well there is clear support for the Sufi way. Indeed, what the ḥadīth alludes to is the very same purification of the heart and cultivation of good character and deeds which are promoted by *taṣawwuf*. Another point to be gleaned from this ḥadīth is that the writings of many Sufi masters may be viewed in much the same way, i.e. for their content rather than their form. Indeed, there are many examples of the use of this sort of language by the Prophet ﷺ himself.

ḤADĪTH 128

عَنْ أَنَسٍ رَضِيَ اللهُ عَنْهُ قَالَ: بَعَثَنِيْ رَسُوْلُ اللهِ صَلَّى اللهُ عَلَيْهِ وَسَلَّمَ فِيْ حَاجَةٍ فَأَبْطَأْتُ عَلى أُمِّيْ، فَلَمَّا جِئْتُ قَالَتْ: مَاحَبَسَكَ؟ قُلْتُ: بَعَثَنِيْ رَسُوْلُ اللهِ صَلَّى اللهُ عَلَيْهِ وَسَلَّمَ فِيْ حَاجَةٍ وَقَالَتْ: وَمَاهِيَ؟ قُلْتُ: إِنَّهَا سِرٌّ، قَالَتْ: لاتُحَدِّثَنَّ بِسِرِّ رَسُوْلِ اللهِ صَلَّى اللهُ عَلَيْهِ وَسَلَّمَ أَحَداً. (أخرجه الشيخان)

It is related on the authority of Anas ﵁ that Allāh's Prophet ﷺ sent him on a mission for something he needed done. When Anas ﵁ was late in returning, his mother asked him what had delayed him, so Anas explained that he had been sent by the Prophet ﷺ to do something for him, and that it was a secret. Then Anas' ﵁ mother said, "Don't ever reveal a secret of the Prophet ﷺ to anyone." This was related by Bukhārī and Muslim.[207]

---

206 Muslim: 2564, Abū Dāwūd: 4882, Tirmidhī: 1927, Ibn Mājah: 4143

207 This account was not found in these words in Bukhārī. Muslim: 2482

Teachings: Keeping Secrets

The keeping of secrets is something which is greatly emphasised by Sufi masters, regardless of whether the secrets have to do with the instructions one receives from one's master, or with one's visions, or dreams, or with experiences one has while under the instruction of a master.

ḤADĪTH 129

عَنْ عُمَرَ رَضِيَ اللهُ عَنْهُ قَالَ: قَالَ رَسُوْلُ اللهِ صَلَّى اللهُ عَلَيْهِ وَسَلَّمَ: «إِنَّ مِنْ عِبَادِ اللهِ لأُنَاساً مَاهُمْ بِأَنْبِيَاءَ وَلاَ شُهَدَاءَ يَغْبِطُهُمُ الْأَنْبِيَاءُ وَالشُّهَدَاءُ يَوْمَ الْقِيمَةِ لِمَكَانِهِمْ مِنَ اللهِ تَعَالي» قَالُوْا: يَارَسُوْلَ اللهِ! تُخْبِرُنَا مَنْ هُمْ؟ قَالَ: «هُمْ قَوْمٌ تَحَابُّوْا بِرُوْحِ اللهِ عَلى غَيْرِ أَرْحَامٍ بَيْنَهُمْ، وَلاأَمْوَالٍ يَتَعَا طَوْنَهَا فَوَ اللهِ إِنَّ وُجُوْهَهُمْ لَنُوْرٌ، وَإِنَّهُمْ لَعَلى نُوْرٍ، لاَ يَخَافُوْنَ إِذَا خَافَ النَّاسُ، وَلاَ يَحْزَنُوْنَ إِذَا حَزِنَ النَّاسُ» وَقَرَأَ هذِهِ الايَةَ: ﴿أَلاَ إِن أَوْلِيَاءَ اللهِ لاَخَوْفٌ عَلَيْهِمْ وَلاَ هُمْ يَحْزَنُوْنَ﴾ (أخرجه أبوداؤد)

It is related on the authority of ʿUmar that Allāh's Messenger said, "Verily, there are people among the servants of Allāh who are neither prophets nor martyrs, but whose good fortune will be coveted on the Day of Judgment by the prophets and martyrs because of the positions they will hold nearby the Almighty." The Companions said, "Tell us, O Allāh's Messenger, who these people are!" So the Emissary replied, "They are a people who love one another for no other reason than for the sake of Allāh, who have no blood or financial ties between them. By Allāh! Their faces and everything else about them will be light! When most people fear, they will have no fear; and when most people sorrow, they will have no sorrow!" Then the Emissary recited the following verse: "Surely, the friends of Allāh; no fear shall beset them, neither shall they sorrow."[208] This was related by Abū Dāwūd.[209]

Virtues: The Friends of Allāh

It is hardly necessary to point out here that the people referred to in this ḥadīth are the great Sufi masters. No one should suspect that the words, ". . .whose good fortune will be coveted of the Day of Judgment by the prophets," point somehow to the inferiority of the prophets, as that is clearly nonsense.

---

208 al-Qur'ān, 10:62

209 Abū Dāwūd: 3527

ḤADĪTH 130

عَنْ أَبِي ذَرٍّ رَضِيَ اللهُ عَنْهُ قَالَ: قُلْتُ يَا رَسُولَ اللهِ! الرَّجُلُ يُحِبُّ الْقَوْمَ وَلَايَسْتَطِيعُ
أَنْ يَعْمَلَ عَمَلَهُمْ، قَالَتْ: «أَنْتَ يَا أَبَاذَرٍّ مَعَ مَنْ أَحْبَبْتَ» (أخرجه أبوداود) وَفِيْ لَفْظِ
التِّرْمِذِيِّ عَنْ صَفْوَانَ بْنِ عَسَّالٍ رَضِيَ اللهُ عَنْهُ: «اَلْمَرْءُ مَعَ مَنْ أَحَبَّ».

It is related on the authority of Abū Dharr 🙏 that he once said, "O Allāh's
Prophet! What about someone who really loves a certain group of peo-
ple, but is unable to do what they do?" The Prophet 🙏 replied, "You, O
'Abū Dharr, will always be with those you love." This was related by Abū
Dāwūd. The words of Tirmidhī's report from Ṣafwān ibn 'Assāl 🙏 are:
"Man will be with whom he loves."[210]

Virtues: Those Who Love the Masters

This ḥadīth points clearly to the virtue of those who love and follow the great Sufi
masters. We have seen by experience how most disciples begin to love their masters from the time of their initiation into the order, *bay'ah*. Quite often, a master
will initiate a person from whom little can be expected in the way of spiritual
disciplines and development, solely for the reason that they possess the requisite
desire. Finally, our deeds are judged by our intentions.

ḤADĪTH 131

عَنْ أَبِي هُرَيْرَةَ رَضِيَ اللهُ عَنْهُ قَالَ: قَالَ رَسُولُ اللهِ صَلَّى اللهُ عَلَيْهِ وَسَلَّمَ: «اَلْأَرْوَاحُ
جُنُودٌ مُجَنَّدَةٌ فَمَا تَعَارَفَ مِنْهَا ائْتَلَفَ وَمَا تَنَاكَرَ مِنْهَا اخْتَلَفَ». (أخرجه مسلم وأبوداؤد
وأخرجه البخاري عن عائشة)

It is related on the authority of Abū Huraira 🙏 that the Messenger of Allāh
🙏 said, "The souls of humankind were [in the spirit world] as an army gathered. Then those who were acquainted with one another [in that world] will
harmonise [in this world], and those who were unknown to one another
there will fall into discord here." This ḥadīth was related by Muslim and
Abū Dāwūd. Bukhārī related a similar ḥadīth from 'Ā'isha 🙏.[211]

---

210 Abū Dāwūd: 5126, Tirmidhī: 2387
211 Bukhārī: 3336, Muslim: 2638, Abū Dāwūd: 4834

Questions: Spiritual Harmony

Experience has shown that the success of any master-disciple relationship depends on there being some sort of natural harmony between the two. This harmony will be seen to have been attributed in this ḥadīth to prior acquaintance in the spirit world.[212] Furthermore, in cases where this natural harmony is found to be lacking, it often happens that a master will decline to grant initiation, *bayʿah*, preferring instead to recommend that the prospective disciple seek out another master.

ḤADĪTH 132

عَنْ أَبِي هُرَيْرَةَ رَضِيَ اللهُ عَنْهُ قَالَ: قَالَ رَسُوْلُ اللهِ صَلَّى اللهُ عَلَيْهِ وَسَلَّمَ: «لَمَّا خَلَقَ اللهُ

ادَمَ عَلَى صُوْرَتِهِ». الحديث . (أخرجه البخاري)

It is related on the authority of Abū Huraira 🙏 that the Messenger of Allāh 🙏 said, "When Allāh created Adam as a manifestation of His attributes. . ." (the ḥadīth continues). This ḥadīth was related by Bukhārī.[213]

Sayings: Man is the Manifestation of the Divine

The meaning most widely agreed upon by the commentators on this ḥadīth is one which clearly lends support to the saying of the Sufis that the reality of humans is that they are manifestations of the Divine. Briefly speaking, the human being is a singular and even astonishing creation of the Almighty. The presence of this creation, in turn, indicates the presence and perfect attributes of a Creator. Then, in view of these facts, the created may be said to be a manifestation of the Creator, i.e., the means of His manifestation. In this same wise, all of creation may be said to be the manifestation of the Almighty. There are a number of other interpretations that may be given to the words of this ḥadīth, according to one of which only the most accomplished of Sufi masters may be said to be a manifestation of the Divine. I have discussed this subject at length in my Urdu commentary on Mawlānā Rūmī's, *Mathnawī*, entitled *Kalīd-i-Mathnawī*, or *The Key to the Mathnawī*. In any case, the ḥadīth should be viewed as the basis for all commentary on this saying, as the word *ṣūrah* (often mistakenly interpreted to mean "image") actually means manifestation.

---

212 al-Qurʾān, 7:172
213 Bukhārī: 6227

ḤADĪTH 133

عَنِ ابْنِ عُمَرَ رَضِيَ اللهُ عَنْهُ أَنَّهُ نَظَرَ يَوْماً إِلَى الْكَعْبَةِ فَقَالَ: مَا أَعْظَمَكِ وَمَا أَعْظَمَ حُرْمَتَكِ

وَالْمُؤْمِنُ أَعْظَمُ حُرْمَةً عِنْدَ اللهِ تَعَالَى مِنْكِ. (أخرجه الترمذي)

It is related on the authority of Ibn ʿUmar 🙵 that Allāh's Messenger 🙵 once remarked, while gazing at the Kaʿbah in the Sacred Mosque, "How magnificent you are! And, to think that the sanctity of a believer is even more sublime!" This ḥadīth was related by Tirmidhī.[214]

Sayings: One Heart is Better than a Thousand Kaʿbahs
This well-known Sufi saying is clearly exonerated by the ḥadīth quoted here, as the reason for the believer's being more sacred than the Kaʿbah is the believer's faith. Then, as the heart is said to be the place where faith resides, there should be no difficulty in understanding why the believer's heart is more sacred than the Kaʿbah. Furthermore, since the ḥadīth said that the believer's heart is more sublime, without specifying exactly how much more, then it is certainly within the realm of possibility that it be a thousand times more sacred. It should, however, be understood that this is a partial excellence only, and not one which necessarily implies that humans may also be prostrated to, in the same way that humans bow down before the Kaʿbah.

ḤADĪTH 134

عَنْ أَبِي هُرَيْرَةَ رَضِيَ اللهُ عَنْهُ قَالَ: قَالَ رَسُولُ اللهِ صَلَّى اللهُ عَلَيْهِ وَسَلَّمَ: «الْمَرْءُ عَلَى دِينِ

خَلِيلِهِ فَلْيَنْظُرْ أَحَدُكُمْ مَنْ يُخَالِلُ». (أخرجه أبو داود والترمذي)

It is related on the authority of Abū Hurairah 🙵 that Allāh's Prophet 🙵 said, "A person will adopt the ways of his friend. Be, therefore, wary of those you choose to befriend." This ḥadīth was related by Abū Dāwūd and Tirmidhī.[215]

Reform: Caution in the Choice of a Master
Obviously, when mere friendship can be such a powerful influence on one's lifestyle, then the infinitely closer relationship of the disciple and master will surely be a very influential one. Experience has shown that the beliefs, deeds, and char-

214 Tirmidhī: 2032, Ibn Mājah: 3931
215 Abū Dāwūd: 4833, Tirmidhī: 2378

acter of a master all have a certain effect on the disciple which, if nothing else, will at least amount to the disciple's viewing those beliefs, deeds and characteristics in a favourable light. Obviously, then, if the beliefs, for example, of a master are erroneous, the beliefs of his disciples are certainly not likely to be entirely correct. This is why one must be very careful in choosing a master.

ḤADĪTH 135

عَنْ عُمَرَ رَضِيَ اللهُ عَنْهُ قَالَ: قَالَ رَسُوْلُ اللهِ صَلَّى اللهُ عَلَيْهِ وَسَلَّمَ: «أَلا لايَخْلُوَنَّ رَجُلٌ بِامْرَأَةٍ إلاَّ كَانَ ثَالِثَهُمَا الشَّيْطَانُ». (أخرجه الشيخان وأبوداؤد)

It is related on the authority of Ibn ʿUmar ﵄ that ʿUmar ﵁ once addressed the Muslims at a place called Jābiyah and said, "Listen, O believers! As I am standing here among you now, Allāh's Messenger ﷺ once stood among us and said, "Beware! Whenever a man contrives to be alone with a woman, they will inevitably be joined by a third; Satan."[216]

Reform: Female Disciples to Veil Themselves Before Male Masters
Under certain circumstances it is not entirely unlikely that a master could be left alone with a female disciple, or at least be figuratively left alone if the only others present are also women. For this reason it is essential that women disciples always wear veils before their masters. Obviously, very little in the way of spiritual progress can be expected in the presence of Satan! The lax attitudes of many of our present day Sufis are certainly in need of correction.

ḤADĪTH 136

عَنْ أَبِيْ مُوْسي رَضِيَ اللهُ عَنْهُ قَالَ: قَامَ فِيْنَا رَسُوْلُ اللهِ صَلَّى اللهُ عَلَيْهِ وَسَلَّمَ بِخَمْسِ كَلِمَاتٍ وَفِيْهَا: «حِجَابُهُ النُّوْرُ لَوْ كَشَفَهُ لَأَحْرَقَتْ سُبُحَاتُ وَجْهِهِ مَا انْتَهى إِلَيْهِ بَصَرُهُ مِنْ خَلْقِهِ». (أخرجه مسلم)

It is related on the authority of Abū Mūsā ﵁ that Allāh's Prophet ﷺ stood among the Companions ﵃ and spoke of five things, [the last of which was that] Allāh's veil is of light. If ever He lifted it, the splendour of His

216 Tirmidhī: 2165, Ibn Mājah: 2363, Nasāʾī: 10418

countenance would incinerate whatever of His creation He gazed upon. This ḥadīth was related by Muslim.[217]

Questions: Visions of the Almighty
A great many ignorant Sufis hold to the belief that a Sufi traveller is capable of seeing Allāh in this world in the same way that all believers will see Him in the next. This ḥadīth clearly disproves their claim.

ḤADĪTH 137

عَنْ عُمَرَ بْنِ ثَابِتٍ الأَنْصَارِيِّ أَنَّهُ أَخْبَرَهُ بَعْضُ أَصْحَابِ رَسُوْلِ اللهِ صَلَّى اللهُ عَلَيْهِ وَسَلَّمَ أَنَّ رَسُوْلَ اللهِ صَلَّى اللهُ عَلَيْهِ وَسَلَّمَ قَالَ يَوْمَ حَذَّرَ النَّاسَ الدَّجَّالَ: «إِنَّهُ مَكْتُوْبٌ بَيْنَ عَيْنَيْهِ كَافِرٌ يَقْرَأُهُ مَنْ كَرِهَ عَمَلَهُ، أَوْ يَقْرَأُهُ كُلُّ مُؤْمِنٍ» . . . وَقَالَ: «تَعَلَّمُوْا أَنَّهُ لَنْ يَرى أَحَدٌ مِنْكُمْ رَبَّهُ حَتّى يَمُوْتَ». (رواه مسلم)

It is related on the authority of ʿUmar ibn Thābit ﷺ that he was told by one of the Companions that Allāh's Messenger ﷺ said, while warning the Muslims of the Dajjāl, "Written between his two eyes is the word "Disbeliever" readable to anyone who dislikes his [Dajjāl's] works, or to anyone who believes. Know, then, that none of you will be able to see your Lord until you die, whereas anyone will be able to see the Dajjāl. Therefore, do not be tricked into believing that the Dajjāl is your Lord." This ḥadīth was related by Muslim.[218]

Questions: Visions of the Almighty
The impossibility of one's seeing the Almighty in this world is further substantiated in this ḥadīth.

ḤADĪTH 138

عَنْ أَبِيْ هُرَيْرَةَ رَضِيَ اللهُ عَنْهُ أَنَّ أَعْرَابِيًّا دَخَلَ الْمَسْجِدَ، وَرَسُوْلُ اللهِ صَلَّى اللهُ عَلَيْهِ وَسَلَّمَ جَالِسٌ، فَصَلَّى رَكْعَتَيْنِ ثُمَّ قَالَ: اللّهُمَّ ارْحَمْنِيْ وَمُحَمَّداً وَلاتَرْحَمْ مَعَنَا أَحَداً، فَقَالَ النَّبِيُّ صَلَّى اللهُ عَلَيْهِ وَسَلَّمَ «لَقَدْ تَحَجَّرْتَ وَاسِعاً» ثُمَّ لَمْ يَلْبَثْ أَنْ بَالَ فِيْ الْمَسْجِدِ

217 Muslim: 179, Ibn Mājah: 196
218 Muslim: 7365

فَأَسْرَعَ إِلَيْهِ النَّاسُ، فَنَهَاهُمْ رَسُوْلُ اللهِ ا، وَقَالَ: «إِنَّمَا بُعِثْتُمْ مُيَسِّرِيْنَ وَلَمْ تُبْعَثُوْا مُعَسِّرِيْنَ، صُبُّوْا عَلَيْهِ سِجْلاً مِنْ مَاءٍ» أَوْقَالَ: «ذَنُوْباً مِنْ مَاءٍ». (أخرجه الخمسة إلا مسلماً وهذا لفظ أبي داوُد والترمذي)

It is related on the authority of Abū Huraira ﷺ that a bedouin entered the mosque while Allāh's Prophet ﷺ was sitting there. The bedouin performed two cycles of prayer, and then prayed aloud, "O Allāh! Have mercy on me and Muhammad! And show mercy to no one else." Afterwards, the Prophet ﷺ remarked to the bedouin, "Do you think you can confine what is boundless?" Just then, the bedouin urinated on the floor of the mosque, and all those present hastened toward him. But the Prophet ﷺ stopped them from doing harm to the man, saying, "Remember! You are charged with being facilitators, not with being aggravators! Just pour a bucket of water over it." This ḥadīth was related by Mālik, Bukhārī, Abū Dāwūd, Nasā'ī and Tirmidhī.[219]

Character: Tolerance for the Deeds and Words of the Ignorant

It is not the way of the Sufi masters to be harsh with the ignorant people with whom they occasionally come into contact. On the contrary, their reactions to such people are always tempered with forbearance. Indeed, certain critics have even accused some masters of indulging the ignorant. The ḥadīth quoted here should dispel all such misgivings.

ḤADĪTH 139

عَنْ أَبِيْ هُرَيْرَةَ رَضِيَ اللهُ عَنْهُ أَنَّ رَسُوْلَ اللهِ صَلَّى اللهُ عَلَيْهِ وَسَلَّمَ قَالَ بَعْدَ ذِكْرِ فَضْلِ بَعْضِ الأَعْمَالِ: «فَذٰلِكُمُ الرِّبَاطُ، فَذٰلِكُمُ الرِّبَاطُ، فَذٰلِكُمُ الرِّبَاطُ». (أخرجه مسلم ومالك والترمذي والنسائي)

It is related on the authority of Abū Huraira ﷺ that the Messenger of Allāh ﷺ said [after mentioning the virtues of certain practices], "This is your post! This is your post! This is your post!" This ḥadīth was related by Mālik, Muslim, Tirmidhī and Nasā'ī.[220]

---

219 Bukhārī: 220, Muslim: 285, Abū Dāwūd: 380, Tirmidhī: 147, Nasā'ī: 56, Ibn Mājah: 529

220 Muslim: 251, Tirmidhī: 51, Nasā'ī: 14, *Muwaṭṭa'*: 557

Sayings: Jihād Against Satan

My own master, Hājī ʿImdād Allāh, wrote a treatise on *The Greater Jihād*, in which he established that the *jihād* of the Sufi traveller is with the armies of Satan. The ḥadīth quoted here, since it speaks of a post, indicates clearly that a Muslim is always at war with Satan.

ḤADĪTH 140

عَنْ جَابِرٍ رَضِيَ اللهُ عَنْهُ فِيْ حَدِيْثٍ طَوِيْلٍ، فَلَمَّا خَرَجَ الرَّجُلانِ إِلى فَمِ الشِّعْبِ اضْطَجَعَ الْمُهَاجِرِيُّ، وَقَامَ الأَنْصَارِيُّ يُصَلِّيْ، فَأَتى الرَّجُلُ، فَلَمَّا رَأى شَخْصَهُ عَرَفَ أَنَّهُ رَبِيْئَةٌ فَرَمَاهُ بِسَهْمٍ، فَوَضَعَهُ فِيْهِ، فَنَزَعَهُ حَتّى رَمَاهُ بِثَلَثَةِ أَسْهُمٍ ثُمَّ رَكَعَ وَسَجَدَ، ثُمَّ نَبَّهَ صَاحِبَهُ، فَلَمَّا عَرَفَ أَنَّهُمْ قَدْ نَذِرُوْا بِهِ هَرَبَ، فَلَمَّا رَأى الْمُهَاجِرِيُّ مَا بِالأَنْصَارِيِّ مِنَ الدِّمَاءِ قَالَ: سُبْحَانَ اللهِ! أَلاَ أَنْبَهْتَنِيْ أَوَّلَ مَارَمى لَكَ! قَالَ: كُنْتُ فِيْ سُوْرَةٍ أَقْرَؤُها فَلَمْ أُحِبَّ أَنْ أَقْطَعَهَا. (أخرجهُ أبو داود)

It is related on the authority of Jābir who said, in his narration of the Dhāt al-Ruqāʿ campaign, "When the two men reached the mouth of the canyon, the Muhājir lay down while the Anṣārī stood up to pray. Just then, one of the enemy approached and, seeing that the man standing was a sentinel, fired an arrow at him which lodged itself in his side. When the sentinel pulled it out, the archer fired three more arrows into him. Then the sentinel moved into the bowing (*rukūʿ*) and then the prostration (*sajdah*) position until finally, after completing the prayer, the sentinel woke his sleeping partner. By this time, the enemy had gone away, knowing that the alarm would be given. When the Muhājir saw the blood on his partner, he said, "Allāh be praised! Why did you not tell me the first time you were shot?" The Anṣārī replied, "I was reciting a chapter from the Qur'ān that I especially like, and did not want to interrupt the recitation." This ḥadīth was related by Abū Dāwūd.[221]

States: Savouring Recitation

To take pleasure in reciting the Qur'ān in prayer, or in any other act of worship is often indicative of a very advanced spiritual state, as should be obvious from the ḥadīth quoted here.

---

221 Abū Dāwūd: 198

ḤADĪTH 141

عَنْ عَلِيٍّ رَضِيَ اللهُ عَنْهُ أَنَّ رَسُوْلَ اللهِ صَلَّى اللهُ عَلَيْهِ وَسَلَّمَ قَالَ: «مَنْ تَرَكَ مَوْضِعَ شَعْرَةٍ مِنْ جَنَابَةٍ لَمْ يَغْسِلْهَا فُعِلَ بِهِ كَذَا وَكَذَا مِنَ النَّارِ» قَالَ عَلِيٌّ: فَمِنْ ثَمَّ عَادَيْتُ رَأْسِيْ ثَلَثاً وَكَانَ يَجُزُّ شَعْرَهُ. (أخرجه أبوداؤد)

It is related on the authority of ʿAlī ؓ that Allāh's Prophet ﷺ said, "Whoever fails to wash even an area the size of a hair when performing the ritual bath will suffer such and such a penalty in the Fire." ʿAlī ؓ commented, "After hearing that, I became my hair's worst enemy." Another narrator in the chain said, "It became the practice of ʿAlī ؓ, after that, to keep his head shaved." This ḥadīth was related by Abū Dāwūd.[222]

Practices: Shaving the Head

It is the practice of most Sufi masters to keep their heads shaved. The precedent for this practice comes from the example of ʿAlī ؓ who, as is evident from the ḥadīth, did so with the tacit approval of the Prophet ﷺ. Furthermore, aside from the benefit mentioned in the ḥadīth (of facilitating the perfect performance of the ritual bath), the other benefits of shaving the head are freedom from having to care for it, from becoming attached to it, and not having to worry about its causing perspiration during the performance of certain rigorous disciplines.

ḤADĪTH 142

عَنْ عُثَيْمِ بْنِ كَثِيْرِ بْنِ كُلَيْبٍ عَنْ أَبِيْهِ، عَنْ جَدِّهِ أَنَّهُ جَاءَ رَسُوْلَ اللهِ صَلَّى اللهُ عَلَيْهِ وَسَلَّمَ فَقَالَ: قَدْ أَسْلَمْتُ فَقَالَ لَهُ رَسُوْلُ اللهِ صَلَّى اللهُ عَلَيْهِ وَسَلَّمَ «أَلْقِ عَنْكَ شَعْرَ الْكُفْرِ» يَقُوْلُ: احْلِقْ. الحديث. (أخرجه أبوداؤد)

It is related on the authority of ʿUthaym ibn Kathīr ibn Kulayb, on the authority of his father, Kathīr, that his [ʿUthaym's] grandfather, Kulayb ؓ went to Allāh's Messenger ﷺ and said, "I commit myself to the way of Islam." At that, Allāh's Messenger ﷺ said, "Then get rid of that disbelieving hair," by which he meant to say, "Shave it off." This ḥadīth was related by Abū Dāwūd.[223]

---

222 Abū Dāwūd: 249, Ibn Mājah: 599

223 Abū Dāwūd: 356

Customs: Shaving for Initiation
Certain masters require that their disciples shave their heads as a part of the
initiation and pledging *bayʿah* formalities. That this is not without a sound basis
in the Sunna is attested to by this ḥadīth. It may be that the logic behind this
custom is that it emphasises the individual's desire to rid himself of all traces of
what went before, be it disbelief, or wrongdoing, or imperfect devotion.

ḤADĪTH 143

عَنْ أَسْلَمَ قَالَ فِيْ حَدِيْثٍ طَوِيْلٍ، وَكَانَ عِنْدَ عُمَرَ رَضِيَ اللهُ عَنْهُ صِحَافٌ تِسْعٌ فَلاتَكُوْنُ

فَاكِهَةٌ وَلاطَرِيْفَةٌ إِلاَّ جَعَلَ مِنْهَا فِيْ تِلْكَ الصِّحَافِ، فَيَبْعَثُ بِهَا إِلى أَزْوَاجِ النَّبِيِّ صَلَّى اللهُ

عَلَيْهِ وَسَلَّمَ الحديث. (أخرجه مالك)

It is related on the authority of Aslam, as part of a lengthy narration, that
ʿUmar ☘ had nine large trays which he used to fill with fruit and other
delicacies and then send to the wives of Allāh's Prophet ﷺ. This ḥadīth
was related by Mālik.[224]

Practices: Serving the Family of One's Deceased Master
It has always been the practice of the Sufis to offer their services to the family of
their deceased or absent masters. The ḥadīth quoted here clearly indicates the
praiseworthiness of this practice.

ḤADĪTH 144

عَنْ عُمَرَ رَضِيَ اللهُ عَنْهُ قَالَ: إِيَّاكُمْ وَاللَّحْمَ فَإِنَّ لَهُ ضَرَاوَةً كَضَرَاوَةِ الْخَمْرِ وَإِنَّ الله

يُبْغِضُ أَهْلَ الْبَيْتِ اللَّحْمِيَّيْنِ. (أخرجه مالك)

It is related on the authority of ʿUmar ☘ that he said, "Be wary of eating
meat! For the habit of eating meat is as hard to break as the habit of drink-
ing wine. Allāh likes not those who are in the habit of eating meat." This
ḥadīth was related by Mālik.[225]

Practices: Avoiding Meat
There are many Sufis who do not eat meat. Concerning this matter it will be nec-

---

224 Mālik: 970
225 Mālik: 3450

essary to understand the following points. If the reason for a Sufi's abstention is the same as given in the ḥadīth, i.e., to avoid falling into a base habit which might itself become a factor in leading to other base habits, then the Sufi's abstention is perfectly all right. Nonetheless, such a Sufi should partake of meat from time to time so as not to seem as if he/she were prohibiting that which Allāh ﷻ has permitted. If, however, the Sufi should abstain out of a belief that abstinence from meat is in itself an act of devotion, then this is blameworthy innovation, *bidʿah*. And if the Sufi does so as a part of the working of a spell or charm, then that is mere nonsense added to nonsense. And if the Sufi does so out of a belief that the slaughter of animals is cruel and unnatural, then that is clearly heresy.

ḤADĪTH 145

عَنْ جَابِرٍ رَضِيَ اللهُ عَنْهُ قَالَ: أَدْرَكَنِيْ عُمَرُ رَضِيَ اللهُ عَنْهُ وَفِيْهِ قَالَ: أَوَ كُلَّمَا اشْتَهَيْتَ شَيْأً اشْتَرَيْتَهُ؟ حَسَبَ أَحَدِكُمْ مِنَ السَّرِفِ أَنْ يَّأْكُلَ كُلَّمَا اشْتَهى . (أخرجه مالك)

It is related on the authority of Jābir ؓ that one day, as he was returning from the marketplace with a package of meat, ʿUmar ؓ met him and asked what he was carrying. Jābir ؓ replied, "We had a craving for meat, so, for a dirham, I bought some." Then ʿUmar ؓ replied, "And is it that whenever you have a craving for something, you go out and buy it? For the likes of us, it is extravagance enough that we eat everything we desire." This ḥadīth was related by Mālik.[226]

Practices: Foregoing Pleasures

It is the practice of nearly all Sufis to devote a good deal of time and energy to the matter of combatting their desires. This is what this particular ḥadīth is all about.

ḤADĪTH 146

عَنْ أَبِيْ سَعِيْدٍ رَضِيَ اللهُ عَنْهُ قَالَ: كُنَّا فِيْ سَفَرٍ وَفِيْ الْحَدِيْثِ قِصَّةُ اللَّدِيْغِ وَفِيْهِ فَقَالَ: مَارَقِيْتُ إِلاَّ بِأُمِّ الْكِتَابِ، قُلْنَا: لاتُحَدِّثُوْا شَيْئًا حَتّى نَأْتِيَ رَسُوْلَ اللهِ صَلَّى اللهُ عَلَيْهِ وَسَلَّمَ فَنَسْأَلُهُ، فَلَمَّا قَدِمْنَا ذَكَرْنَاهُ لَهُ فَقَالَ: وَمَايُدْرِيْكَ أَنَّهَا رُقْيَةٌ؟ اقْسِمُوْا وَاضْرِبُوْا لِيْ بِسَهْمٍ.

(أخرجه الخمسة الا النسائي)

226 *Muṣannaf Ibn Abī Shaibah*: 25012

It is related on the authority of Abū Saʿīd who, in his narration of the events of a journey he had taken, told the story of a man who was bitten by a poisonous snake and then cured by a member of Abū Saʿīd's party. Abū Saʿīd relates that when the man was asked what charm he had used to cure the victim, he replied, "The only charm I used was the Opening Chapter of the Qur'ān." Later, when the victim had recovered, he gifted the Muslim party a hundred goats. 'Abū Saʿīd said, "So we said to one another, 'Let us not do anything about these goats until we have asked Allāh's Messenger ﷺ about the matter.'" When we returned from our mission, and told Allāh's Messenger ﷺ what happened with the snakebite victim, he said to us, "How did you know it was a charm? Distribute the goats among your party, and give me a share too!" This ḥadīth was related by Bukhārī, Muslim, Tirmidhī and Abū Dāwūd.[227]

Customs: Taking Money for Charms

Some Sufis take money from people who come to them asking for charms. That this is permitted, and in no way degrading, is obvious from the ḥadīth quoted here. There are, however, two conditions that must be met: 1) that the charm and what it is employed to help bring about are in no way contrary to the Sharīʿa and; 2) that there be no deception involved. It should be remembered here that for anyone but an accomplished master, the business of making charms and attending to the problems of the public are quite often very distressing at a spiritual level.

ḤADĪTH 147

عَنْ أَنَسٍ رَضِيَ اللهُ عَنْهُ قَالَ: قَالَ رَسُوْلُ اللهِ صَلَّى اللهُ عَلَيْهِ وَسَلَّمَ: «لاعَدْوى وَلاطِيَرَةَ وَيُعْجِبُنِيْ الفَأْلُ» قَالُوْا: وَمَا الْفَأْلُ؟ قَالَ: «كَلِمَةٌ طَيِّبَةٌ». (أخرجه الخمسة إلا النسائي)

It is related on the authority of Anas ؓ that Allāh's Prophet ﷺ said, "There is nothing to [the spread of disease by] contagion, and nothing to omens. Signs, however, are of interest to me." The Companions ؓ asked, "What do you mean by 'signs'?" The Prophet ﷺ replied, "Any sort of encouraging word."[228] This ḥadīth was related by Bukhārī, Muslim, Abū Dāwūd and Tirmidhī.[229]

---

227 Bukhārī: 5736, Muslim: 2201, Abū Dāwūd: 3418, Tirmidhī: 2063, Ibn Mājah: 2156

228 For example, if someone looking for something they had lost, hears someone cry out "finders keepers," that would be an "encouraging word"; and it may be taken as a good sign and nothing more. YTD.

229 Bukhārī: 5756, Muslim: 2224, Abū Dāwūd: 2915, Tirmidhī: 1615, Ibn Mājah: 3537

Customs: Seeking Signs in the Qur'ān or the Works of the Sufi Masters

Many Sufis have been known to seek signs about their worldly or spiritual needs in the pages of the Qur'ān, the *Divān* of Ḥāfiẓ, or the *Mathnawī* of Mawlānā Rūmī. The validity of this practice should be evident from the ḥadīth. If there is nothing more to one's seeking than that, there is nothing wrong with the custom. The important thing is never to lose sight of the fact that only Allāh ﷻ can bring these things to pass, both the sign and what it portends. However, if one should overstep this point and suppose that, for example, Mawlānā Rūmī is ever-present and all-seeing, or that the signs one receives from a book are really omens of something sure to take place, then this is the worst sort of *bidʿah*, and very near to disbelief.

ḤADĪTH 148

عَنْ عَلِيٍّ رَضِيَ اللهُ عَنْهُ قَالَ: قَالَ رَسُوْلُ اللهِ صَلَّى اللهُ عَلَيْهِ وَسَلَّمَ: «نِعْمَ الرَّجُلُ الْفَقِيْهُ فِي الدِّيْنِ إِنْ احْتِيْجَ إِلَيْهِ نَفَعَ، وَإِنِ اسْتَغْنى عَنْهُ أَغْنى نَفْسَهُ (أخرجه رزين)

It is related on the authority of ʿAlī ؓ that Allāh's Messenger ﷺ said, "What an excellent person is one learned in the ways of Islam! When needed, they are useful; and when others have no need of them, they can be of use to themselves." This ḥadīth was related by Razīn.[230]

Practices: Correcting Without Rancour

In the matter of giving advice or friendly admonition, it has never been the way of the Sufis to harass or antagonise anyone. For the Sufis, it is enough to say what they feel they must, once or twice, and to leave the matter at that. If their advice is heeded, fine; and if it is not, then they have better things to do. The words in the ḥadīth, ". . .when others have no need of them, they can be of use to themselves," clearly indicate the correctness of this practice. The following Qur'ānic verse may also be cited in this connection: "As for he who thinks himself to be self-sufficient, you give your attention to him, even though you are not accountable for his failure to attain purity.[231]

230 *Musnad al-Firdaws*: 6742

231 al-Qur'ān, 80:4

ḤADĪTH 149

عَنْ أَبِي الدَّرْدَاءِ رَضِيَ اللهُ عَنْهُ قَالَ: سَمِعْتُ رَسُوْلَ اللهِ صَلَّى اللهُ عَلَيْهِ وَسَلَّمَ يَقُوْلُ: «إِنَّ الْعُلَمَاءَ وَرَثَةُ الأَنْبِيَاءِ». (أخرجه أبوداؤد)

It is related on the authority of Abū Dardā' ﷺ that he heard the Messenger of Allāh ﷺ say, "Verily, the learned are the heirs of the prophets." This was related by Abū Dāwūd and Tirmidhī.[232]

Questions: Transmission of Affinity

It is an accepted truth among the Sufis that the spiritual affinity which is passed on from master to master began as the legacy of the Messenger of Allāh. In this ḥadīth, the word "learned" refers particularly to those who have attained spiritual knowledge. When they are termed the "heirs" to the prophets, it is quite obvious that it is the transmission of spiritual knowledge which is alluded to. In this way, the Sufi maxim concerning the transmission of spiritual affinity from breast to breast is confirmed by the Sunna of the Prophet Muhammad, Allāh bless him and give him peace and blessings everlasting.

ḤADĪTH 150

عَنْ عَلِيٍّ رَضِيَ اللهُ عَنْهُ قَالَ: حَدِّثُوْا النَّاسَ بِمَا يَعْرِفُوْنَ أَتُحِبُّوْنَ أَنْ يُكْذَبَ اللهُ وَرَسُوْلُهُ. (أخرجه البخاري)

It is related on the authority of ʿAlī ﷺ that he said, "Speak to people of things they can understand. Would you like it if people started doubting Allāh and His Prophet?"[233] This ḥadīth was related by Bukhārī.[234]

Corrections: Avoiding Mention of the Obscure

Certain indiscreet Sufis have been known to sit in public and speak about recondite problems of *taṣawwuf* before people who either, thinking what they hear to be contrary to the Sharīʿah, become hostile to *taṣawwuf* or, in spite of their inability to comprehend what is being said, become antagonistic toward the Sharīʿah. In either case, and the latter of the two is surely the worse, these peo-

232 Abū Dāwūd: 3641, Ibn Mājah: 223

233 In other words, do not speak to them about abstruse theological issues, for example, which are more likely to create, rather than put to rest, doubts in the minds of any but the most accomplished scholars.

234 Bukhārī: 127

ple are actually showing antagonism to Allāh and His Prophet ﷺ. Therefore, as is evident from the ḥadīth above, abstruse points of *taṣawwuf* should never be mentioned in front of those who are incapable of comprehending them.

ḤADĪTH 151

عَنْ ابْنِ مَسْعُوْدٍ رَضِيَ اللهُ عَنْهُ أَنَّهُ قَالَ: مَا أَنْتَ بِمُحَدِّثٍ قَوْماً حَدِيْثاً لاتَبْلُغُهُ عُقُوْلُهُمْ، إِلاَّ كَانَ لِبَعْضِهِمْ فِتْنَةً. (أخرجه مسلم)

On the authority of Ibn Masʿūd ﵁ who said, "When you speak to people about things they do not understand, you may be certain that some of them will be led astray." Imam Muslim related it.[235]

Commentary

This and the preceding ḥadīth [150] point to what has already been mentioned in the commentary on ḥadīth [150].

ḤADĪTH 152

عَنْ ابْنِ عَمْرِو بْنِ الْعَاصِ رَضِيَ اللهُ عَنْهُ قَالَ: كُنْتُ أَكْتُبُ كُلَّ شَيْءٍ سَمِعْتُهُ مِنْ رَسُوْلِ اللهِ صَلَّى اللهُ عَلَيْهِ وَسَلَّمَ فَنَهَتْنِيْ قُرَيْشٌ وَقَالُوْا: أَتَكْتُبُ كُلَّ شَيْءٍ تَسْمَعُهُ وَرَسُوْلُ اللهِ صَلَّى اللهُ عَلَيْهِ وَسَلَّمَ بَشَرٌ يَتَكَلَّمُ فِيْ الرِّضَا وَالْغَضَبِ، فَأَمْسَكْتُ عَنِ الْكِتَابَةِ حَتّى ذَكَرْتُ ذٰلِكَ لِرَسُوْلِ اللهِ صَلَّى اللهُ عَلَيْهِ وَسَلَّمَ فَأَوْمَأَ بِإِصْبَعِهِ إِلى فَمِهِ وَقَالَ: «اُكْتُبْ فَوَالَّذِيْ نَفْسِيْ بِيَدِهِ مَايَخْرُجُ مِنْهُ إِلاَّ حَقٌّ». (أخرجهُ أبوداوٗد)

On the authority of ʿAmr ibn al-ʿĀṣ ﵁ who said, "I used to write everything I heard from the Prophet ﷺ. But the Quraysh stopped me, saying, 'You write everything, even though the Prophet ﷺ is only human and may sometimes say things in anger?' So I stopped writing until I had a chance to ask the Prophet ﷺ about it myself. Then he ﷺ pointed his finger to his mouth and said, 'Go ahead and write! By the One who holds my life in His hands, nothing comes out of here but the truth." Abū Dāwūd related it.[236]

---

235 Muslim: 14 [Muqaddimah]

236 Abū Dāwūd: 3646

Customs: Recording Discourses

Many disciples are in the habit of recording (on paper or otherwise) the discourses of their masters. It should be clear from this ḥadīth that while this is permitted, there is every need for caution as masters, like other humans, are subject to mistakes and are certainly not *maʿṣūm* (protected from wrongdoing).

ḤADĪTH 153

عَنْ أَبِي هُرَيْرَةَ رَضِيَ اللهُ عَنْهُ قَالَ: خَطَبَ رَسُوْلُ اللهِ ، فَذَكَرَ قِصَّةً الحديث، فَقَالَ أَبُوْ شَاه: أُكْتُبُوْا لِيْ يَارَسُوْلَ اللهِ! فَقَالَ: «أُكْتُبُوْا لِأَبِيْ شَاه». (أخرجه الترمذي وصححه)

It is related on the authority of Abū Huraira ﵁ who said, "Allāh's Messenger ﷺ addressed us. . ." [the narrator then related the address in its entirety, after which one of those present, a man named Abū Shāh said,] "O Allāh's Messenger! Write [this sermon] for me." Then he ﷺ said [to one of his scribes] "Write it down for Abū Shāh." Imam Tirmidhī related this ḥadīth and considered it sound.[237]

Customs: Documenting Matters of Importance

The Prophet's command to put his words into writing validates a number of Sufi practices like recording the sermons of the masters, writing out supplications and forms of remembrance, *dhikr*, for aspirants, transcribing the family trees of Sufi orders, and writing out records of spiritual succession, *khilāfah*. Thus, all of these may be said to be a part of the Sunna.

ḤADĪTH 154

عَنْ أَبِي أَيُّوْبَ رَضِيَ اللهُ عَنْهُ قَالَ: قَالَ رَسُوْلُ اللهِ صَلَّى اللهُ عَلَيْهِ وَسَلَّمَ: «لَوْلاَ أَنَّكُمْ تُذْنِبُوْنَ لَذَهَبَ اللهُ تَعَالَى بِكُمْ وَخَلَقَ خَلْقاً يُذْنِبُوْنَ فَيَغْفِرُ لَهُمْ». (أخرجه مسلم والترمذي) ولمسلم عن أبي هريرة رَضِيَ اللهُ عَنْهُ نحوه وزَادَ فَيَسْتَغْفِرُوْنَ. زاد رزين قَالَ رَسُوْلُ اللهِ صَلَّى اللهُ عَلَيْهِ وَسَلَّمَ: «وَالَّذِيْ نَفْسِيْ بِيَدِهِ لَوْ لَمْ تُذْنِبُوْا لَخَشِيْتُ عَلَيْكُمْ مَاهُوَ أَشَدُّ مِنْهُ وَهُوَ الْعُجُبُ».

It is related on the authority of Abū Ayyūb ﵁ that he said, "Allāh's Mes-

237 Tirmidhī: 2666

senger 🕮 said, 'Were it not for your wrongdoing, Allāh most High would have done away with you and created creatures to whom He could grant forgiveness.'" Imams Tirmidhī and Muslim related it. In another version related by Imām Muslim on the authority of Abū Huraira 🕮, the last sentence is as follows; "...He would have created creatures who seek forgiveness, so that He could forgive them." Imam Razīn related a version in which Allāh's Messenger 🕮 said, "By the One Who holds my life in His hand! If you did not do wrong, I would fear something even worse from you: pride."[238]

Questions: The Creation of Evil and Manifestation of the Divine Attributes
In our discussion of the two questions [in the heading] above we will refer to the version of the ḥadīth related by Imams Muslim and Tirmidhī. With regard to the first, scholars have asserted that from the perspective of the Sharīʿa, faith and righteousness are of significance in this world. However, from the perspective of creation (or nature), things like disbelief and wrongdoing are also of significance and must be allowed to come into being. With regard to the second question, which may be viewed as the wisdom behind the first, the scholars write that all the names of Allāh are becoming, *jamīl*, and, as such, require manifestation. The manifestation of each name (attribute) will then become the cause for the occurrence of different kinds of events. The connection between the ḥadīth and the first question should be fairly evident, as the ḥadīth emphasises the need for the occurrence of wrongdoing. Furthermore, upon closer examination, the words, "to whom He could grant forgiveness," will be seen to relate to the second question, as the wisdom or secret behind His creation of evil has to do with forgiveness. Among the names of Allāh is *al-Ghaffār* or The Forgiving, which can only be manifested in connection with the occurrence of wrongdoing. The poet of Shīraz, *Ḥāfiẓ*, alluded nicely to both of these issues in the following verses:

In the workshop of rapture, for *kufr* there must be room.
Were there no Abū Lahab, who would the flames consume?

The "workshop of rapture" here refers to the physical world. This is because of the following statement that is commonly ascribed to the Almighty, "I was as a buried treasure until I had a desire to be known. That was when I created creation." So the reason for the creation of the world was the Almighty's desire to be known; and rapture and desire are synonymous. To summarise, therefore, since

---

238 Muslim: 2748, Tirmidhī: 3539. Razīn's addition has been recorded by adh-Dhahabī in *Mīzān al-iʿtidāl* under the biography of Sallām ibn Abī aṣ-Ṣahbāʾ.

among the names of Allāh is *Al-Muntaqim* or The Avenger, the manifestation of the same requires the occurrence of *kufr*, disbelief, and rebellion. It should be remembered that when we speak of "requiring" in connection with the Almighty we are not speaking literally because Allāh most High is far above being required to do anything. Nor do we mean to encourage anyone to do wrong because we refer to this as something "required" or "necessary". The texts of the Qur'ān and ḥadīth are nothing if not clearly in opposition to such a notion. (Similarly, it should be remembered that Allāh's desiring something is entirely different from the desire we know as humans.) Rather, what is intended here is an explanation of the wisdom behind this phenomenon, in addition to encouragement for those who commit wrongdoing and are then sincerely repentant.

Teachings: The Reason for Certain Kinds of Spiritual Contraction

The topic to be discussed here has as its starting point the wording of the ḥadīth above as related by Imām Razīn. The Sufi masters teach that one kind of contraction, *qabḍ*, is that which attends the commission of an act of wrongdoing. It often happens that after performing such an act the disciple will become so depressed and disgusted with himself that if he is not checked there is every possibility that he will either cause harm to himself or lose hope and abandon everything he acquired on the Sufi way. At such a time it is essential that he be made to understand that he needs only to repent of his wrongs and sincerely seek forgiveness from Allāh; and that afterwards there will be no reason for him to be upset. This is because there is actually a good reason for wrongdoing. Indeed, were it not for one's occasional wrongdoings one would almost certainly become the victim of pride. Therefore, the Sufi who does wrong can be said to have received treatment for something worse. Once this is understood, the Sufi should have no difficulty in shaking off his depression and attending to the more important business of seeking forgiveness.

ḤADĪTH 155

عَنِ ابْنِ عَبَّاسٍ رَضِيَ اللهُ عَنْهُ قَالَ: حَدَّثَنِي عُمَرُ بْنُ الْخَطَّابِ رَضِيَ اللهُ عَنْهُ قَالَ: لَمَّا كَانَ يَوْمُ بَدْرٍ نَظَرَ رَسُوْلُ اللهِ صَلَّى اللهُ عَلَيْهِ وَسَلَّمَ إِلى الْمُشْرِكِيْنَ وَهُمْ أَلْفٌ، وَأَصْحَابُهُ ثَلثُ مِائَةٍ وَتِسْعَةَ عَشَرَ رَجُلاً، فَاسْتَقْبَلَ الْقِبْلَةَ، ثُمَّ مَدَّ يَدَيْهِ، فَجَعَلَ يَهْتِفُ بِرَبِّهِ يَقُوْلُ: «اللّٰهُمَّ أَنْجِزْلِيْ مَا وَعَدْتَّنِيْ، أَللّٰهُمَّ إِنْ تَهْلِك هذِهِ الْعِصَابَةُ مِنَ الْمُسْلِمِيْنَ لاتُعْبَدْ فِيْ الْأَرْضِ» فَمَا زَالَ يَهْتِفُ بِرَبِّهِ مَادًّا يَدَيْهِ حَتّى سَقَطَ رِدَاؤُهُ عَنْ مَنْكَبَيْهِ. الحديث (أخرجه مسلم والترمذي)

It is related on the authority of Ibn ʿAbbās 🙵 that he related on the authority of ʿUmar ibn al-Khaṭṭāb 🙵 said, "On the day of the battle of Badr, Allāh's Messenger 🙵 looked in the direction of the pagan enemy who numbered a thousand, when his own forces numbered only three hundred and nineteen. Then he turned toward the direction of the Qibla, extended his arms, and began beseeching his Lord, saying, 'O Allāh! Fulfil Your promise to me. O Allāh! Bring to pass what You promised me. O Allāh! If You destroy this band of believers, no one will be left on earth to worship You.' In this wise, he 🙵 continued to beseech his Lord until his cloak fell off of his shoulders." Imams Muslim and Tirmidhī related it.[239]

States: Taking Liberties with the Almighty
Idlāl, which literally means coquetry or taking liberties with a loved one, is the name of a spiritual state which sometimes comes over those Sufis who are so immersed in the love of Allāh 🙵 that they, in effect, forget who they are and behave toward the Almighty with the familiarity of a lover for the beloved. The ḥadīth above may be interpreted in the context of this state, *idlāl*, (as the Prophet 🙵 seemed to all outward appearances to have been threatening the Almighty; which was clearly not the case!). The Sufi poet, *Ḥāfiẓ* of Shīrāz, speaks of this spiritual state in the following couplet:

> If the shadow (succour and favour) of the Beloved (the Almighty) should
> fall on the lover
> What of it? After all, while we need Him, He is not without desire for us.

In other words, what is desired is our obedience and devotion. And the word "desire" is used in this verse of poetry to refer to the divine will.

ḤADĪTH 156

عَنْ أَنَسٍ رَضِيَ اللهُ عَنْهُ فِي قِصَّةِ غَزْوَةِ أُحُدٍ قَوْلُ أَنَسِ بْنِ النَّضْرِ قَالَ: يَاسَعْدَ بْنَ مُعَاذٍ! الْجَنَّةَ وَرَبِّ النَّضْرِ، إِنِّي لَأَجِدُ رِيْحَهَا مِنْ دُوْنِ أُحُدٍ. الحديث . (أخرجه الشيخان والترمذي)

It is related on the authority of Anas ibn Mālik 🙵 who, in his narration concerning the battle of ʿUḥud, related the words of his uncle, ʿAnas ibn an-Naḍar 🙵, who said [to his companion in battle], "O Saʿd ibn Muʿādh!

---

239 Muslim: 1763, Tirmidhī: 3081

Paradise, by the Lord of Naḍar, I detect its fragrance by the foot of Mount ʻUḥud." Imams Muslim, Bukhārī and Tirmidhī related it.[240]

States: The World of the Unseen
The unveiling of things from the world of the Unseen, *ʿālam al-ghayb*, indicates that the recipient of these communications, on condition that he/she is a Muslim who devotedly adheres to the Sharīʿa, has attained an elevated spiritual station.

ḤADĪTH 157

عَنْ سَعْدِ بْنِ أَبِيْ وَقَّاصٍ رَضِيَ اللهُ عَنْهُ قَالَ: رَأَيْتُ عَلى يَمِيْنِ رَسُوْلِ اللهِ صَلَّى اللهُ عَلَيْهِ وَسَلَّمَ وَعَلى شِمَالِهِ يَوْمَ أُحُدٍ رَجُلَيْنِ، عَلَيْهِمَا ثِيَابٌ بِيْضٌ، يُقَاتِلاَنِ كَأَشَدِّ الْقِتَالِ مَا رَأَيْتُهُمَا قَبْلُ وَلاَبَعْدُ، يَعْنِيْ جِبْرَئِيْلَ وَمِيْكَائِيْلَ. (أخرجه الشيخان)

It is related that Saʿd ibn Abī Waqqāṣ said, "On the day of [the Battle of] ʻUḥud I saw two men in white fighting on the left and the right of Allāh's Messenger ﷺ. I had never seen them before, and I never saw them again; Jibrīl and Mikā'īl." Imams Muslim and Bukhārī related it.[241]

States: Unveiling Angels and Questions: Assimilation
From the ḥadīth above it is clear that Jibrīl and Mikā'īl were actually seen by Saʿd. The question of assimilation has already been discussed in the commentary of ḥadīth [1]. In the case of the sighting reported in the ḥadīth above, we may assume that if others also saw the two angels, then the ḥadīth in which assimilation is mentioned explains what happened. If others did not see the two angels, then this is explained by the preceding ḥadīth [156].

ḤADĪTH 158

عَنْ أَبِيْ هُرَيْرَةَ رَضِيَ اللهُ عَنْهُ فِيْ قِصَّةِ غَزْوَةِ الرَّجِيْعِ مِنَ الْحَدِيْثِ الطَّوِيْلِ عَنْ بَعْضِ بَنَاتِ الْحَارِثِ كَانَتْ تَقُوْلُ: مَارَأَيْتُ أَسِيْراً قَطُّ خَيْراً مِنْ خُبَيْبٍ، لَقَدْ رَأَيْتُهُ يَأْكُلُ مِنْ قِطْفِ عِنَبٍ، وَمَا بِمَكَّةَ يَوْمَئِذٍ ثَمَرَةٌ وَإِنَّهُ لَمُوْثَقٌ بِالْحَدِيْدِ، وَمَاكَانَ إِلاَّ رِزْقاً رَزَقَهُ اللهُ خُبَيْباً، وَفِيْهِ: وَبَعَثَتْ قُرَيْشٌ إِلى عَاصِمٍ لِيُؤْتَوْا بِشَيْءٍ مِنْ جَسَدِهِ بَعْدَ مَوْتِهِ وَكَانَ قَتَلَ

240 Bukhārī: 2805, Muslim: 1903, Tirmidhī: 3200
241 Bukhārī: 4054, Muslim: 2306

عَظِيْماً مِنْ عُظَمَاءِهِمْ يَوْمَ بَدْرٍ فَبَعَثَ اللهُ عَلَيْهِمْ مِثْلَ الظُّلَّةِ مِنَ الدَّبْرِ فَحَمَتْهُ مِنْ رُسُلِهِمْ، فَلَمْ يَقْدِرُوْا مِنْهُ على شَيْءٍ . (أخرجه البخاري وأبوداؤد)

Abū Huraira related in his account of the Battle of al-Rajīʿ that one of the daughters of al-Ḥārith used to say, "Never have I seen a better prisoner than Khubaib. I have seen him bound in chains, eating from a cluster of grapes at a time when fruit was not to be found in all of Makka. Verily, that could have been nothing other than provision provided to him by Allāh most High." Later in the same narration, [but concerning ʿĀṣim], Abū Huraira said, "Then the Quraysh commanded that a piece of ʿĀṣim's [dead] body be brought to them, for ʿĀṣim had killed one of their chiefs in the battle of Badr. But Allāh sent a cloud of hornets to cover his corpse so that it was protected from the Quraysh. In this wise, they were unable to do anything to him." Imams Bukhārī and Abū Dāwūd related it.[242]

States: Karāmah

The compelling miracles mentioned in the ḥadīth above in regard to Khubaib and ʿĀṣim are indicative, as both men were steadfast in their adherence to the Sharīʿa, of the elevated spiritual states which they had attained.

ḤADĪTH 159

عَنْ أَنَسٍ رَضِيَ اللهُ عَنْهُ فِيْ قِصَّةِ غَزْوَةِ بِئْرِ مَعُوْنَةَ قَالَ: بَعَثَ رَسُوْلُ اللهِ صَلَّى اللهُ عَلَيْهِ وَسَلَّمَ قَوْماً مِنْ بَنِي سُلَيْمٍ إِلى بَنِيْ عَامِرٍ. وَفِيْ رِوَايَةٍ: بَعَثَ خَالِيْ حَرَاماً أَخاً لِأُمِّ سُلَيْمٍ فِيْ سَبْعِيْنَ رَاكِباً، فَلَمَّا قَدِمُوْا، قَالَ لَهُمْ خَالِيْ: أَتَقَدَّمُكُمْ فَإِنْ أَمَّنُوْنِيْ حَتّى أُبَلِّغَهُمْ عَنْ رَسُوْلِ اللهِ صَلَّى اللهُ عَلَيْهِ وَسَلَّمَ وَإِلاَّ كُنْتُمْ مِنِّيْ قَرِيْباً، فَتَقَدَّمَ فَأَمَّنُوْهُ فَبَيْنَمَا هُوَ يُحَدِّثُهُمْ عَنْ رَسُوْلِ اللهِ صَلَّى اللهُ عَلَيْهِ وَسَلَّمَ إِذَا أَوْمَئُوْا إِلَيَ رَجُلٍ مِنْهُمْ فَطَعَنَهُ فَأَنْفَذَهُ فَقَالَ: اللهُ أَكبَرُ، فُزْتُ وَرَبِّ الْكَعْبَةِ. الحديث (أخرجه الشيخان) وفي رواية البخاري عن أنس رَضِيَ اللهُ عَنْهُ يَقُوْلُ: لَمَّا طُعِنَ حَرَامُ بْنُ مِلْحَانَ يَوْمَ بِئْرِ مَعُوْنَةَ قَالَ (أي أخذ) بِالدَّمِ هكَذَا فَنَضَحَهُ عَلى وَجْهِهِ وَرَأْسِهِ، ثُمَّ قَالَ: فُزْتُ وَرَبِّ الْكَعْبَةِ.

It is related on the authority of Anas concerning the battle at the Well

242 Bukhārī: 3045, Abū Dāwūd: 2660

of Maʿūna, that Allāh's Messenger ﷺ sent a group of Muslims from Banī Sulaim to [the unbelieving] Banī ʿĀmir [for the purpose of calling them to Islam]. Another version of Anas' ؓ account begins like this: "My uncle, Ḥarām ibn Malḥān ؓ, the brother of my mother, Umm Sulaym ؓ, was sent on a mission with seventy horsemen. When they arrived, my uncle said to the others, 'I will go ahead on my own. If they promise to keep me safe, and allow me to address the tribe about the teachings of Allāh's Messenger ﷺ then fine. But, if they do not, then you will not be far from me [and may soon come to my aid].' In this manner, he approached them, and they promised to keep him safe. As he, Ḥarām, was speaking to them about Allāh's Messenger ﷺ a signal was given by his hosts, and one of the tribe ran him through with a sword. At that, Ḥarām exclaimed, 'Allāhu Akbar! I have succeeded. By the Lord of the Kaʿbah!'" Imams Bukhārī and Muslim related it.

In another version of the ḥadīth related by Imām Bukhārī, Anas ؓ says, "When Ḥarām ibn Malḥān was stabbed at the Well of Maʿūna, he took his own blood in his hands and wiped it on his face and head and then said, 'I have succeeded. By the Lord of the Kaʿbah!'"[243]

States: Yearning for Death

From the words and deeds of Anas' ؓ uncle it is quite evident that he had an exceptionally fervent desire to end his life in the favour of Allāh ﷻ and that when death did come to him in this way he was overjoyed. It is this very same desire which becomes the basis for the death wishes expressed by the Sufi masters in their poetry and other works.

Sayings: Ablutions in Blood

Certain Sufis have written about performing their ablutions with blood rather than water. If there is any need to corroborate the metaphorical with the literal, the example of Ḥarām ؓ wiping his face and head in his own blood is certainly about as literal as one can be.

ḤADĪTH 160

عَنْ أَنَسٍ رَضِيَ اللهُ عَنْهُ قَالَ: خَرَجَ النَّبِيُّ صَلَّى اللهُ عَلَيْهِ وَسَلَّمَ إِلَي الْخَنْدَقِ، فَإِذَا الْمُهَاجِرُوْنَ وَالأَنْصَارُ يَحْفِرُوْنَ فِيْ غَدَاةٍ بَارِدَةٍ، وَلَمْ يَكُنْ لَهُمْ عَبِيْدٌ يَعْمَلُوْنَ ذٰلِكَ لَهُمْ،

243 Bukhārī: 2801, 4092, Muslim: 677

فَلَمَّا رَأَى مَا بِهِمْ مِنَ النَّصَبِ وَالْجُوْعِ قَالَ: «اللّٰهُمَّ إِنَّ الْعَيْشَ عَيْشُ الاخِرَةِ فَاغْفِرْ لِلأَنْصَارِ وَالْمُهَاجِرَةِ» فَقَالُوْا مُجِيْبِيْنَ لَهُ: «نَحْنُ الَّذِيْنَ بَايَعُوْا مُحَمَّداً عَلَى الْجِهَادِ مَا بَقِيْنَا أَبَداً» (أخرجه الشيخان والترمذي)

Anas ﷺ said, "When the Prophet ﷺ went out to the trench, the Muhājirs and Anṣār were digging there in the morning cold, as they had no prisoners or slaves to do the work. When the Prophet ﷺ found that they were tired and hungry, he said [in verse], 'O Allāh! Surely the life is the life to come. Forgive, then, the Anṣār and the Muhājirs!' At that, the diggers answered him, saying, [also in verse], 'We are the ones who are pledged to Muhammad, to fight for him as long as we live!'" Imams Bukhārī, Muslim and Tirmidhī related it.[244]

Practices: Samāʿ to Stimulate the Soul

Certain Sufis are of the conviction that when, owing to circumstances of a temporary nature, the disciple or aspirant becomes spiritually irresolute, lax, or contracted, then in order to remedy the situation the aspirant may, while strictly adhering to the conditions[245] under which *samāʿ* is permissible, indulge in *samāʿ*. In this way, the aspirant's irresolution may be dispelled, and a desire to worship will be facilitated. Thus, *samāʿ* should be understood to be the means to an end, when the end, or objective, is worship. The ḥadīth above will be seen to record a precedent for this practice. The digging of the Trench was the objective; while fatigue and hunger might have led to irresolution. And the recitation of the rhymed and metered verses performed the function of lifting spirits and preventing indolence. In view of these factors, then, this would seem to be the wisdom behind this practice. It must be remembered, however, that to suppose *samāʿ* itself to be the objective, or to practise it without concern for propriety, is tantamount to tampering with religion.

ḤADĪTH 161

عَنْ عَائِشَةَ رَضِيَ اللهُ تَعَالَى عَنْهَا قَالَتْ: لَمَّا رَجَعَ النَّبِيُّ صَلَّى اللهُ عَلَيْهِ وَسَلَّمَ مِنَ الْخَنْدَقِ،

---

244 Bukhārī: 2834, Muslim: 1805, Tirmidhī: 3857

245 *Samāʿ* may be defined as audition, or one's listening to rhymed and metered verse that is recited by a professional. Such verse, when recited professionally, will obviously have rhythmic and musical qualities. During the author's time, and throughout Muslim history, the institution of *samāʿ* has suffered many abuses, both from those who support it and those who oppose it. What the author is pointing to here, however, is the straightforward recitation of poetry without frivolity. YTD.

الحديث. وَفِيهِ: كَانَ سَعْدٌ أُصِيبَ يَوْمَ الْخَنْدَقِ فِي أَكْحَلِهِ فَضَرَبَ عَلَيْهِ صَلَّى اللهُ عَلَيْهِ

وَسَلَّمَ خَيْمَةً فِي الْمَسْجِدِ لِيَعُودَهُ مِنْ قَرِيبٍ، فَقَالَ سَعْدٌ: اللّٰهُمَّ إِنَّكَ تَعْلَمُ أَنَّهُ لَيْسَ قَوْمٌ

أَحَبَّ إِلَيَّ أَنْ أُجَاهِدَهُمْ فِيكَ مِنْ قَوْمٍ كَذَّبُوا رَسُولَكَ وَأَخْرَجُوهُ، اللّٰهُمَّ فَإِنِّي أَظُنُّ أَنَّكَ

قَدْ وَضَعْتَ الْحَرْبَ بَيْنَنَا وَبَيْنَهُمْ فَإِنْ كَانَ بَقِيَ مِنْ حَرْبِ قُرَيْشٍ شَيْءٌ فَأَبْقِنِي لَهُ حَتَّى

أُجَاهِدَهُمْ فِيكَ، وَإِنْ كُنْتَ وَضَعْتَ الْحَرْبَ فَافْجُرْهَا وَاجْعَلْ مَوْتِي فِيهَا فَانْفَجَرَتْ

مِنْ لَيْلَتِهِ فَلَمْ يَرُعْهُمْ وَفِي الْمَسْجِدِ إِلاَّ الدَّمُ يَسِيلُ إِلَيْهِمْ فَإِذَا سَعْدٌ يَغِذُّ جُرْحُهُ دَمًا فَمَاتَ

فِيهَا. (أخرجه الشيخان)

ʿĀʾisha 🙵 in her narration concerning the Battle of the Trench, said, "When Allāh's Messenger 🙵 returned from the Trench [he found out that] the medial vein in Saʿd ibn Muʿādh's 🙵 arm had been severed [in the fighting]. Therefore, the Prophet 🙵 ordered that a tent be erected in the masjid for Saʿd 🙵 so that he 🙵 could attend to Saʿd 🙵 from close by. Then Saʿd 🙵 prayed, 'O Allāh! Surely you know that there is no one I like to fight more than the people who discredited your Prophet and turned him out. O Allāh! It now appears to me that You have put an end to the fighting between us [the Muslims and Quraysh]. But if I am wrong about this, and there is to be more fighting, then let me live so that I may fight for You against them. And if the fighting is truly at an end, then let my wound continue to flow so that I may die of it.' That night his wound opened so that the people in the masjid were startled at the sight of his blood flowing toward them. That was the night Saʿd 🙵 succumbed to his wound and died." Imams Bukhārī and Muslim related it.[246]

ḤADĪTH 162

عَنْ جَابِرٍ رَضِيَ اللهُ عَنْهُ قَالَ: إِنَّ سَعْدَ بْنَ مَعَاذٍ رُمِيَ يَوْمَ الْأَحْزَابِ قَطَعُوا أَكْحَلَهُ أَوْ

أَبْجَلَهُ، فَحَسَمَهُ رَسُولُ اللهِ صَلَّى اللهُ عَلَيْهِ وَسَلَّمَ بِالنَّارِ، فَانْتَفَخَتْ يَدُهُ فَتَرَكَهُ، فَنَزَفَهُ

الدَّمُ فَحَسَمَهُ أُخْرَى فَانْتَفَخَتْ يَدُهُ فَلَمَّا رَأَى ذَلِكَ قَالَ: اللّٰهُمَّ لَاتُخْرِجْ نَفْسِي حَتَّى تُقِرَّ

عَيْنِي مِنْ بَنِي قُرَيْظَةَ، فَاسْتَمْسَكَ عِرْقُهُ فَمَا قَطَرَ قَطْرَةً حَتَّى نَزَلُوا عَلَى حُكْمِهِ، فَحَكَمَ

فِيهِمْ أَنْ يُقْتَلَ رِجَالُهُمْ وَتُسْتَحْي نِسَاؤُهُمْ فَقَالَ صَلَّى اللهُ عَلَيْهِ وَسَلَّمَ: «أَصَبْتَ حُكْمَ

---

246 Bukhārī: 4122, Muslim: 1769, Nasāʾī: 711

اللهِ فِيْهِمْ» وَكَانُوْا أَرْبَعَ مِائَةٍ فَلَمَّا فَرَغَ مِنْ قَتْلِهِمْ انْفَتَقَ عِرْقُهُ فَمَاتَ. (أخرجه الترمذي وصححه)

Jābir ﵁ said, Saʿd ibn Muʿādh ﵁ was wounded by an arrow on the Day of the Hosts (during the Battle of the Trench) so that the medial vein in his arm was severed. Therefore, Allāh's Messenger ﷺ attempted to cauterize it. However, when he did, the arm began to swell, and after a short while the blood was flowing again. Again an attempt was made to cauterize the wound, and again the arm grew swollen. When Saʿd ﵁ saw what had happened, he said, "O Lord! Don't take my life until my eyes have been soothed by the sight of Banī Qurayza.[247] Then the blood ceased to flow from his wound, and not a single drop of blood seeped from it until [finally, after having been brought to their knees by the Muslim blockade of their quarter] Banī Qurayza agreed to submit to whatever Saʿd ﵁ decided concerning them.[248] Then Saʿd ﵁ decided that their men must be put to death, and that their women [and children] be allowed to live. Allāh's Messenger ﷺ said, 'You have decided their fate in conformance with the decision of Allāh.' The number of their men was four hundred. When [the sentence had been carried out and] the men of Qurayza had been executed, Saʿd's ﵁ wound began to flow as before. A short while later, he died of it. Imam Tirmidhī related it and attested to its authenticity.[249]

States: Kashf and Karāmah

An example of *kashf* may be found in Saʿd's ﵁ saying, "It now appears to me that You have put an end to the fighting between us." Indeed, with the Battle of the Trench all fighting between the Muslims and the idolators of Quraysh had come to an end. There was a brief skirmish at Makka (about two years later), but most historians hesitate even to call it that. There are two examples of *karāmah* in the story of Saʿd ﵁. One was the stoppage of the flow of blood mentioned in the second ḥadīth [162], and the second was the re-opening of the closed

247 The Qurayza were a Hebrew tribe living in Madīna with the Muslims under a truce, who had traitorously sided with the idolators against the Muslim defenders of the city in the Battle of the Trench. Therefore, when the siege had been lifted, Allah's Messenger ﷺ directed that the quarter of Madīna in which the Qurayza resided be surrounded. Thus, the meaning of Saʿd's ﵁ prayer was that he wished to live to see Banī Qurayza punished for their treachery.

248 The Qurayza sent word to Allah's Messenger ﷺ that they would surrender only if the terms were dictated by Saʿd ibn Muʿādh ﵁. Since the Qurayza had always maintained cordial relations with Saʿd ﵁ in the days before the advent of Islam, they evidently hoped that he would be lenient with them on the basis of their prior relationship.

249 Tirmidhī: 1582

wound mentioned in the first ḥadīth [161]. Furthermore, there is no reason to suppose that there is any contradiction in the prayers of Saʿd ﷺ as recorded in the two ḥadīths above. What happened first was that the blood flowing from his wound stopped as a result of his prayer, as recorded in the second ḥadīth. Then, as a result of his prayer, as mentioned in the first ḥadīth, the blood again started to flow. Thus, in the second ḥadīth, the narrator's saying, "When the men of Qurayza. . ." should be viewed as his own condensation of events. Actually, the full story would read more like this: When the men of Qurayza had been executed, and Saʿd ﷺ had supplicated his Lord with the prayer mentioned in the first ḥadīth, Saʿd's ﷺ wound began to flow as before.

States: The Love of Life and the Love of Death

While certain of the writings of the Sufi masters clearly indicate a love of life on their part, certain other of their works would seem to indicate the opposite. From the prayer of Saʿd ﷺ, however, the rationale behind both points of view is expressed quite clearly. Thus, their love of life springs from their love of involvement in the practices of worship and devotion. Saʿd ﷺ said, "Then let me live so that I may fight for You against them," when *jihād* is a form of worship. Their desire for death is based on no more than their wish to preserve their religion and be united with the Almighty.

ḤADĪTH 163

عَنْ عُرْوَةَ بْنِ الزُّبَيْرِ عَنِ الْمِسْوَرِ بْنِ مَخْرَمَةَ وَمَرْوَانَ، (الحديث الطويل) وَفِيْهِ قِصَّةُ الْحُدَيْبِيَّةِ ثُمَّ إِنَّ عُرْوَةَ بْنَ مَسْعُوْدٍ جَعَلَ يَرْمُقُ أَصْحَابَ النَّبِيِّ صَلَّى اللهُ عَلَيْهِ وَسَلَّمَ بِعَيْنَيْهِ قَالَ: فَوَ اللهِ مَايَنْتَخِمُ رَسُوْلُ اللهِ بِنُخَامَةٍ إِلاَّ وَقَعَتْ فِيْ كَفِّ رَجُلٍ مِنْهُمْ فَدَلَكَ بِهَا وَجْهَهُ وَجِلْدَهُ، وَإِذَا أَمَرَهُمْ ابْتَدَرُوْا أَمْرَهُ، وَإِذَا تَوَضَّأَ كَادُوْا يَقْتَتِلُوْنَ عَلى وَضُوْءِهِ، وَإِذَا تَكَلَّمَ خَفِضُوْا أَصْوَاتَهُمْ عِنْدَهُ، وَمَايُحِدُّوْنَ النَّظَرَ إِلَيْهِ تَعْظِيْماً لَهُ، وَفِيْ هذَا الحَدِيْثِ: قَالَ عُمَرُ بْنُ الْخَطَّابِ. فَأَتَيْتُ نَبِيَّ اللهِ صَلَّى اللهُ عَلَيْهِ وَسَلَّمَ فَقُلْتُ: يَا نَبِيَّ اللهِ! أَلَسْتَ نَبِيَّ اللهِ حَقاًّ؟ قَالَ: «بَلي» قُلْتُ: أَلَسْنَا عَلَيَ الْحَقِّ وَعَدُوُّنَا عَلَيَ الْبَاطِلِ؟ قَالَ: «بَلي» قُلْتُ: فَلِمَ نُعْطِيْ الدَّنِيَّةَ فِيْ دِيْنِنَا إِذَنْ؟ قَالَ: «إِنِّيْ رَسُوْلُ اللهِ وَلَسْتُ أَعْصِيْهِ وَهُوَ نَاصِرِيْ» قُلْتُ: أَوَ لَيْسَ كُنْتَ تحَدَّثْتَنَا أَنَّا سَنَأْتِيْ الْبَيْتَ وَنَطُوْفُ بِهِ؟ قَالَ: «بَلي» أَفَأَخْبَرْتُكَ أَنَّكَ تَأْتِيْهِ الْعَامَ؟» قُلْتُ: لا، قَالَ: «فَإِنَّكَ اتِيْهِ وَمُطَوِّفٌ بِهِ» فَأَتَيْتُ أَبَابَكْرٍ، فَقُلْتُ: يَا أَبَا بَكْرٍ، أَلَيْسَ هذَا

نَبِيَّ اللهِ حَقًّا، قَالَ: بَلي، قُلْتُ: أَلَسْنَا عَليَ الْحَقِّ وَعَدُوُّنَا عَليَ الْبَاطِلِ؟ قَالَ: بَلي، قُلْتُ: فَلِمَ نُعْطِيْ الدَّنِيَّةَ فِيْ دِيْنِنَا إِذَنْ؟ فَقَالَ: أَيُّهَا الرَّجُلُ إِنَّهُ رَسُوْلُ اللهِ وَلَيْسَ يَعْصِيْ رَبَّهُ وَهُوَ نَاصِرُهُ فَاسْتَمْسِكْ بِغَرْزِهِ فَوَ اللهِ إِنَّهُ عَليَ الْحَقِّ، قُلْتُ: أَلَيْسَ كَانَ يُحَدِّثُنَا أَنَّا سَنَأْتِيْ الْبَيْتَ وَنَطُوْفُ بِهِ؟ قَالَ: بَلي، أَفَأَخْبَرَكَ أَنَّكَ تَأْتِيْهِ الْعَامَ؟ قُلْتُ: لاَ، قَالَ: فَإِنَّكَ اتِيْهِ وَمُطَوِّفٌ بِهِ، قَالَ عُمَرُ: فَعَمِلْتُ لِذلِكَ أَعْمَالاً. الحديث. (أخرجه البخاري وأبو داؤد)

ʿUrwah ibn al-Zubayr ﷺ related from al-Miswar ibn Makhramah and Marwān a lengthy narration concerning the Treaty of al-Ḥudaybiyyah in which it is recorded that: " [a leader of the Makkan idolators who had been sent to determine the strength and numbers of the believers gathered at Ḥudaybiyyah] began staring at the Companions of the Prophet ﷺ and reported, 'By Allāh! The Prophet ﷺ could not even sneeze without having his mucus fall into the hands of one of his Companions who would then rub it over his face and skin. If he ordered them to do anything, they would all attempt to be the first to comply. If he performed ablutions, they would nearly kill each other for the water he had used. If he spoke, they immediately lowered their voices in his presence. And never, out of their respect for him, did they stare at him." In the same narration [of the Treaty of Hudaibiyyah in which the terms dictated by the pagan Quraysh were accepted, some of which appeared unfavourable to the believers], it is also recorded that ʿUmar ibn al-Khattab ﷺ said, "So I went to Allāh's Prophet ﷺ and [in a state of agitation over the terms of the treaty] said, 'O Messenger of Allāh! Are you not truly the Messenger of Allāh?' He replied, 'I certainly am.' Then I said, 'Are we not followers of the truth while our enemies are followers of falsehood?' He replied, 'Certainly.' Then I said, 'So why do we agree to humiliation with respect to our religion?' He replied, 'Verily, I am Allāh's Prophet, and verily I will never disobey Him! [In other words, whatever I have done or agreed to do has been in accordance with the will of Allāh.] He will always be my Helper.' So, I said, 'But didn't you tell us that we will go to the House [i.e., the Kaʿbah in Makka and perform *tawāf* there?' He replied, 'Certainly, I did. But did I say that you'd go to it this year?' So I said, 'No.' Then he replied, 'You will go to it. And you will circumambulate it.' At that, I went to Abū Bakr ﷺ and said, 'O Abū Bakr! Is he not truly the Messenger of Allāh?' Abū Bakr ﷺ replied, 'Verily, he is.' Then I said, 'Are we not followers of the truth while our enemies are followers of falsehood?' Abū Bakr ﷺ replied, 'Certainly.' Then I said, 'So why do we agree to humiliation with respect to our religion?' He replied, 'Listen, man! Verily, he is Allāh's Prophet ﷺ, and verily he will never disobey His Lord. As long as he obeys, Allāh will be his Helper. So be steadfast in your obedience to him because, by Allāh, he is doing the right thing.' So I said, 'But didn't he say to us that we would visit the House and circumambulate it?' He replied, 'Verily. But did he say that you would visit it this year?' I replied, 'No.' Abū Bakr ؓ said, 'Then you will visit it. And you will circumambulate it.'" ʿUmar ؓ said, "For that [i.e., in order to make up for my having questioned the Prophet in that manner] I did many, many good deeds." Bukhārī and Abū Dāwūd related this ḥadīth.[250]

Customs: Excess in Love for and Devotion to the Master

From the behaviour of the Companions ؓ described in the beginning of this ḥadīth it is clearly established that the Sufis' love for their masters, even to the point of giving their lives for him, so that their loyalty to him is greater than that for any worldly authority. Obviously, however, such devotion must never go beyond the bounds established by the Sharīʿa.

States: Losing Oneself in Love for the Sheikh

While the ḥadīth does not address this matter specifically, it is clear when one ponders the matter, that this may certainly be understood from the text of the ḥadīth. In other words, from the words spoken by Abū Bakr ؓ at the end of the ḥadīth in reply to ʿUmar's ؓ questions, it is obvious that his heart and mind were at one with the heart and mind of the Prophet ﷺ. A connection of this sort, in view of the habits of the especially gifted Sufi masters, is what is known as "Losing oneself in love for one's master." The existence of an attribute, moreover, is a certain indicator, *dalīl qatʿī*, that there are those who actually possess that attribute. When such a connection is established by the text of a ḥadīth, then this state (of losing oneself in love for one's spiritual master) is also established. The reality of this state may be witnessed in the affinity of an aspirant for his or her spiritual guide, as expressed (and developed) by means of love and devotion.

ḤADĪTH 164

عَنْ سَلَمَةَ بْنِ الْأَكْوَعِ رَضِيَ اللهُ عَنْهُ قَالَ: قَدِمْنَا الْحُدَيْبِيَّةَ مَعَ رَسُوْلِ اللهِ الحديث. وَفِيْهِ:
ثُمَّ إِنَّ رَسُوْلَ اللهِ صَلَّى اللهُ عَلَيْهِ وَسَلَّمَ دَعَا لِلْبَيْعَةِ فِيْ أَصْلِ الشَّجَرَةِ فَبَايَعْتُهُ فِيْ أَوَّلِ

250 Bukhārī: 2731, 2732, Abū Dāwūd: 2765

النَّاسُ، ثُمَّ بَايَعَ وَبَايَعَ، حَتَّى إِذَا كَانَ فِي وَسَطٍ مِنَ النَّاسِ قَالَ: «بَايِعْ يَا سَلَمَةُ!» قُلْتُ:

قَدْ بَايَعْتُكَ، يَا رَسُوْلَ الله! فِيْ أَوَّلِ النَّاسِ، قَالَ: «وَأَيْضاً» وَرَآنِيْ رَسُوْلُ الله صَلَّى اللهُ

عَلَيْهِ وَسَلَّمَ عُزْلاً، فَأَعْطَانِي حَجَفَةً، ثُمَّ بَايَعَ، حَتَّى إِذَا كَانَ فِيْ آخِرِ النَّاسِ قَالَ: «أَلاَ

تُبَايِعُنِيْ يَا سَلَمَةُ؟» قَالَ: قُلْتُ: قَدْ بَايَعْتُكَ، يَارَسُوْلَ الله! فِيْ أَوَّلِ النَّاسِ، وَفِيْ أَوْسَطِ

النَّاسِ قَالَ:« وَأَيْضاً» فَبَايَعْتُهُ الثَّالِثَةَ. الحديث . (أخرجه مسلم)

Salamah ibn al-Akwaʿ ⚬ said, "We approached Ḥudaibiyyah with Allāh's Prophet ⚬ . . . and so on." In the same narration, Salamah ⚬ said, "Allāh's Prophet ⚬ called upon us to swear allegiance to him beneath a tree, and so I swore allegiance among the first of those who swore it. Then the Prophet ⚬ continued taking oaths of allegiance from more and more people until, when he was through half of them, he called out to me, 'O Salamah! Swear allegiance.' I replied, 'I have already sworn allegiance, among the first people to do so.' He replied, 'Do it again.' So I again swore allegiance to him and, when he noticed I was without a weapon, he gave me a shield. Then he returned to taking the oath of allegiance from more and more people until he reached the last of them. Then he said to me, 'O Salamah! Why don't you swear allegiance to me?' So I said, 'O Allāh's Prophet! I swore allegiance to you among the first of those who swore it! And then again among those in the middle! Do you now want me to swear with those at the end?' He replied, 'Again.' So he took my oath, and in that manner I swore allegiance three times!'" This was related by Muslim.[251]

Customs: Renewing Bayʿah for Emphasis
At times it may be beneficial to have even a seasoned aspirant renew the oath of allegiance, *bayʿah*. This ḥadīth openly establishes the precedent for such a practice.

ḤADĪTH 165

عَنْ عَلِيٍّ رَضِيَ اللهُ عَنْهُ فِيْ قِصَّةِ كِتَابِ حَاطِبٍ وَقَالَ عُمَرُ رَضِيَ اللهُ عَنْهُ دَعْنِيْ يَا رَسُوْلَ

الله! أَضْرِبْ عُنُقَ هذَا الْمُنَافِقِ، فَقَالَ رَسُوْلُ الله صَلَّى اللهُ عَلَيْهِ وَسَلَّمَ: «إِنَّهُ قَدْ شَهِدَ

بَدْراً وَمَا يُدْرِيْكَ لَعَلَّ الله تَعَالَى اطَّلَعَ عَلَى أَهْلِ بَدْرٍ فَقَالَ: اعْمَلُوْا مَاشِئْتُمْ فَقَدْ غَفَرْتُ

لَكُمْ». (أخرجه الخمسة إلا النسائي)

---

251 Muslim: 1807

ʿAlī ﷺ related, in his narrative concerning Ḥāṭib's ﷺ letter,[252] "'Umar said, 'Let me, O Allāh's Prophet ﷺ, strike that hypocrite's neck!' So Allāh's Prophet ﷺ said, 'Verily, he fought at the Battle of Badr. So, how are you to know if Allāh saw what they did and then said to them, "Go and do whatever you wish. For I have forgiven you."'" This was included in five of the six most authentic collections, excluding al-Nasā'ī.[253]

Reform: The Invalidity of the Belief in Infallibility

According to certain ignorant Sufis and heretics, when a person attains 'perfection' he is free to do as he wishes and, for such a one, nothing is unlawful. This school of thought is known as *al-Ibāḥiyyah*, and the amazing thing is that its adherents present this ḥadīth as proof of their claim. It is as if they are saying, 'See what the ruling was for those who fought at Badr.' The truth of the matter, however, is that this ḥadīth openly refutes their claim because the words 'I have forgiven. . .' mean that the deeds they commit will have to be unlawful for them to receive forgiveness. Owing to the extreme generosity of the Almighty, He (may have) made this particular promise to only this particular group of people. Otherwise, there is no need to forgive what is lawful. If, on the other hand, the Almighty had said, 'I have made this lawful for you,' it might have been possible to draw such a conclusion. Moreover, it is not possible to compare those who fought at Badr with anyone else because there is textual evidence to confirm the promise of forgiveness that was made to them, whereas no such evidence exists for anyone else. So how can anyone possibly compare themselves with the veterans of Badr? In fact, this article of faith by the *Ibāḥiyyah* is *kufr*, disbelief; and anyone who holds it will require correction.

ḤADĪTH 166

عَنْ وَهَبٍ قَالَ: سَأَلْتُ جَابِراً رَضِيَ اللهُ عَنْهُ عَنْ شَأْنِ ثَقِيْفٍ إِذَا بَايَعَتْ قَالَ: اشْتَرَطَتْ أَنْ لاصَدَقَةَ عَلَيْهَا وَلاَ جِهَادَ وَأَنَّهُ سَمِعَ رَسُوْلَ اللهِ صَلَّى اللهُ عَلَيْهِ وَسَلَّمَ يَقُوْلُ: «سَيَتَصَدَّقُوْنَ وَيُجَاهِدُوْنَ إِذَا أَسْلَمُوْا» . (أخرجه أبوداؤد)

Wahb said, "I questioned Jābir ﷺ concerning the oath of allegiance sworn

252 Ḥāṭib ﷺ had written to the pagans in Makka describing some of the military plans of the Prophet ﷺ. When the letter was intercepted, Ḥāṭib ﷺ was taken by the Companions to the Prophet ﷺ for questioning. At that time, Ḥāṭib's ﷺ explanation was accepted. Even so, ʿUmar ﷺ still wanted to kill the man as a traitor.

253 Bukhārī: 3007, Muslim: 2494, Abū Dāwūd: 2650, Tirmidhī: 3305

by the Thaqīf [tribe]. He said, 'They stipulated that they would do so only if they did not have to pay zakah or participate in Jihad.' And he heard Allāh's Prophet ﷺ say, 'They will pay [zakāh] and fight [in jihād], if they truly convert to Islam.'[254] This was related by Abū Dāwūd.[255]

Habits: Occasional Leniency in Regard to Essentials

At times, Masters have been known to exhibit restraint, even to the point of ignoring the shortcomings of those they deal with on both an occasional and a regular basis. For people in this state, the Masters have even prescribed special recitations and *dhikr* without waiting for them to actually discontinue their incorrect practices. This has prompted some people to suspect that the Masters are guilty of hypocrisy. The truth of this matter, however, is that the Masters use their God-given insight to decide when the good practices they prescribe for people will, step by step, erase the incorrect behaviour that those people exhibit. The Masters are also sensitive to the fact that severity on their parts may have the effect of preventing people from doing what is right, and may even discourage them from repenting of their errant ways. Thus, whatever good can be found in such people should be encouraged. Indeed, some people simply do not have the strength to resolve suddenly to refrain from sinful acts. Such resolve, then, needs to be developed by stages. This ḥadīth may help to explain how the Masters deal with such cases.

ḤADĪTH 167

عَنْ أَبِي مُوْسي رَضِيَ اللهُ عَنْهُ قَالَ لِمُعَاذٍ: كَيْفَ تَقْرَأُ أَنْتَ؟ قَالَ: سَأُنَبِّئُكَ بِذلِكَ، أَمَّا أَنَا فَأَنَامُ ثُمَّ أَقُوْمُ فَأَقْرَأُ، وَأَحْتَسِبُ فِيْ نَوْمَتِيْ مَا أَحْتَسِبُ فِيْ قَوْمَتِيْ. (أخرجه الخمسة إلا الترمذي)

Abū Mūsā ؓ related that he once asked Muʿādh ؓ [when both were deputed to govern in Yemen], "How do you recite [your night prayers]?" He replied, "I will tell you about that. For myself, first I sleep [in other words, I do not stay awake all night long] and then I stand [in prayer] and recite. In this manner, I earn as many blessings from my sleep as I do

254 In other words, it is not necessary to let details get in the way of someone's conversion or practice of Islam. Rather, once they have converted, have gained a better understanding of the religion and its ways, and have been in the company of the believers, it may be hoped that they will begin to appreciate the religion in all of its various aspects.

255 Abū Dāwūd: 3025

from my prayers." This was related by Bukhārī, Muslim, Abū Dāwūd and al-Nasā'ī.[256]

Questions: The Habits of the Masters as Worship

From the ḥadīth above, it should be clear that when one's knowledge matures to the point of propriety, such that even mundane activities are undertaken with a higher purpose in mind, then those activities will acquire the characteristics of worship; and they will occasion blessings and bring one closer to the Almighty. Thus, one's sleep, if it is undertaken for the purpose of rest and renewal of strength for worship, may actually be accounted an act of worship. Likewise, at times the purpose may be to exhibit one's frailty and need. At other times, the purpose may be to conserve strength for service to others, or to humanity in general. In all such cases, one's sleep may surely be accounted an act of worship. In the same way, other deeds may take on the aspect of worship. The sayings of the Masters attest to this, and the ḥadīth above indicates the same.

ḤADĪTH 168

عَنْ جَرِيْرِ بْنِ عَبْدِ اللهِ رَضِيَ اللهُ عَنْهُمَا قَالَ: قَالَ رَسُوْلُ اللهِ صَلَّى اللهُ عَلَيْهِ وَسَلَّمَ: «أَلا تُرِيحُنِيْ مِنْ ذِيْ الْخَلَصَةِ؟» وَكَانَ بَيْتاً فِيْهِ خَثْعَمُ يُسَمَّى الْكَعْبَةَ الْيَمَانِيَّةَ، فَانْطَلَقْتُ فِيْ خَمْسِيْنَ وَمِائَةِ رَاكِبٍ مِنْ أَحْمَسَ، - وَكَانُوْا أَصْحَابَ خَيْلٍ - وَكُنْتُ لا أَثْبُتُ عَلَى الْخَيْلِ، فَضَرَبَ فِيْ صَدْرِيْ حَتّى رَأَيْتُ أَثَرَ أَصَابِعِهِ فِيْ صَدْرِيْ وَقَالَ: «اللّهُمَّ ثَبِّتْهُ وَاجْعَلْهُ هَادِياً مَهْدِياً» فَانْطَلَقَ إِلَيْهَا فَكَسَرَهَا وَحَرَّقَهَا. (أخرجه الشيخان وأبو داوٗد)

Jarīr ibn ʿAbdullāh ﷺ related that Allāh's Prophet ﷺ said, "Will you not rid us of Dhi 'l-Khalṣah?" which was a temple in the territory of Khathʿam that was also known as the Kaʿbah of Yemen. Jarīr ﷺ said, "So I went with a party of one hundred and fifty riders from [the tribe of] Aḥmas who were true horsemen while I was barely able to keep myself in the saddle. So he ﷺ struck my breast so hard that I could see the impression of his fingers on [the skin of] my chest, and recited, 'O Allāh, stabilise him[257] and make him one who is a guide and rightly-guided!' Thereafter, the unit

256 Bukhārī: 4341, Muslim: 1732, Abū Dāwūd: 4354, Nasā'ī: 5598

257 It is evident from the context that the purpose of the prayer was to ask for stability for Jarīr ﷺ in both the saddle and religion.

went to the temple and destroyed it, setting it on fire." This was related by Bukhārī, Muslim and Abū Dāwūd.

Questions: Natural Characteristics are not Erased from those who Attain Perfection
Scholars have stated that just because one attains a state of spiritual perfection[258] this does not mean that such a person will no longer be subject to human nature. Nonetheless, that person will undoubtedly be less susceptible to the sort of human frailties that will lead him or her to act contrary to the Sharīʿah. From the ḥadīth above, it is clear that the Prophet ﷺ felt the effects of outside influences on his heart and soul. At the same time, however, he would never have acted without a clear reason from the Sharīʿah to do so. Still, he needed from time to time to bring his impulses under control. Thus, it should be clear that the efforts of certain Sufis to attain absolute perfection are akin to their attempting to catch the wind and hold it in their fists! Stories concerning the perfection of certain Sufis actually describe their coming under the influence of a temporary state rather than anything of a permanent nature.

ḤADĪTH 170

عَنْ عَامِرِ بْنِ سَعِيْدٍ قَالَ: دَخَلْتُ عَلى قُرْظَةَ بْنِ كَعْبٍ رَضِيَ اللهُ عَنْهُ وَأَبِيْ مَسْعُوْدٍ الأَنْصَارِيِّ رَضِيَ اللهُ عَنْهُ فِيْ عُرْسٍ، فَإِذَا جَوَارٍ يُغَنِّيْنَ، فَقُلْتُ: أَنْتُما صَاحِبَا رَسُوْلِ اللهِ صَلَّى اللهُ عَلَيْهِ وَسَلَّمَ وَمِنْ أَهْلِ بَدْرٍ يُفْعَلُ هذَا عِنْدَكُمْ؟ فَقَالاَ: اجْلِسْ إِنْ شِئْتَ فَاسْمَعْ مَعْنَا، وَإِنْ شِئْتَ اذْهَبْ فَقَدْ رُخِّصَ لَنَا فِيْ اللَّهْوِ عِنْدَ الْعُرْسِ. (أخرجه النسائي)

ʿĀmir ibn Saʿīd ﷺ narrated, "I visited Qurazah ibn Kaʿb and Abū Saʿūd al-Anṣāri ﷺ during a wedding where girls were singing, so I said, 'The two of you are Companions of the Prophet ﷺ and veterans of the Battle of Badr. So how could such a thing happen in your presence?' The two of them answered me. 'Sit with us, if you like. Or go. For we have been given license to do such things on these occasions.'" This ḥadīth was related by al-Nasāʾī.[259]

---

258 Obviously, spiritual perfection may be defined in a variety of ways. Suffice it to say, however, that all the Sufi masters acknowledge the fact that no human is capable of perfection in every respect. Thus, the meaning of perfection here may be understood as a high degree of accomplishment in spirituality. YTD.

259 Nasāʾī: 3385

ḤADĪTH 171

عَنْ مُحَمَّدِ بْنِ الْمُنْكَدِرِ قَالَ: بَلَغَنِي أَنَّ اللهَ تَعَالَى يَقُوْلُ يَوْمَ القِيمَةِ: أَيْنَ الَّذِيْنَ كَانُوْا يُنَزِّهُوْنَ أَسْمَاعَهُمْ عَنِ اللَّهْوِ وَمَزَامِيْرِ الشَّيْطَانِ أَدْخِلُوْهُمْ فِيْ رِيَاضِ المِسْكِ ، ثُمَّ يَقُوْلُ لِلْمَلائِكَةِ : أَسْمِعُوْهُمْ حَمْدِيْ ، وَخَبِّرُوْهُمْ : أَنْ لاَّ خَوْفٌ عَلَيْهِمْ وَلاَ هُمْ يَحْزَنُوْنَ.

(أخرجه رزين)

Muḥammad ibn al-Munkadīr said, "I have heard it said that the Almighty will say on Judgment Day, 'Where are those who protected their ears from indulging in pleasure[260] and from the instruments of Satan? Allow them to enter into gardens of musk. Then he will say to the angels, 'Let them hear My praises! And tell them they have nothing to fear. . . nor shall they grieve!'" This ḥadīth was related by Razīn.[261]

Habits: The Samāᶜ of the Chishtī Order and the Opposition of the Naqshbandī

The opinions of the rightly-guided followers of both of these orders, those who approve of audition and those who disapprove, are derived from authentic sources of evidence. In one instance, however, the aspect of spiritual exuberance, *shawq* is dominant; while in the other instance, it is prudence that is dominant. The first of the two ḥadīths above, ḥadīth [170], would seem to indicate the first order's preference, while the second, ḥadīth [171], would seem to indicate the preference of the other Sufi order. Logically, when a degree of physical diversion is allowed (by the Sharīᶜa), it would seem to follow that a degree of spiritual diversion must also be allowed. The actual degrees to which such activity may be allowed is a matter for the experts. It should be clear, however, that to transgress the limits is definitely sinful. All of this is discussed in detail in the books of rules that deal with the subject. From the ḥadīths above it should be clear that the sort of *samāᶜ*[262] that may be condoned will never go beyond the limits of spiritual diversion, as the two Companions explained (in ḥadīth [170]). Moreover, if the degree of disapproval is disapproval occasioned by prudence (which is the preferred degree, as is evident from the second ḥadīth in which comparison is made to the instruments of Satan), then it is clear that *samāᶜ* is neither a good thing in and of itself, nor a bad thing. This is because pleasure is not necessarily bad or

260 Literally, *min al-lahw*, which is generally understood to be music or the joyful recitation of poetry on special occasions.YTD.

261 *Musnad Ibn al-Jaᶜd*: 1:254, *az-Zuhd li Ibn al-Mubārak*: 1:12

262 See the translator's footnote at ḥadīth [160] for a more precise definition of what is intended by the word, *samāᶜ*.

good, in and of itself.[263] The sort of pleasure that is allowed, however, is indicated in the ḥadīth by means of comparison.

ḤADĪTH 172

عَنْ أَبِيْ هُرَيْرَةَ رَضِيَ اللهُ عَنْهُ قَالَ: قَالَ رَسُوْلُ اللهِ صَلَّى اللهُ عَلَيْهِ وَسَلَّمَ: «مَا يَنْبَغِيْ لِعَبْدٍ أَنْ يَقُوْلَ أَنَا خَيْرٌ مِنْ يُوْنُسَ بْنِ مَتّي». (أخرجه الشيخان وأبوداؤد)

Abū Huraira ﵁ related that Allāh's Prophet ﷺ said, "No servant of Allāh should say [concerning me] that I am better than Yūnūs ibn Mattā." This was related by Bukhārī, Muslim and Abū Dāwūd.[264]

Reform: Glorifying a Master by Detracting from Another

Yūnūs ﵇ was mentioned in this ḥadīth because his story would appear to include a reprimand from the Almighty which, in turn, would indicate that he was somehow ranked lower than other prophets. This assumption is what the ḥadīth sets out to refute. The practice on the part of certain Sufis to celebrate the virtues of their own master, or of their own Sufi order, by criticising others is certainly wrong. This ḥadīth clearly illustrates this point. Certainly, there is nothing wrong in one's holding such beliefs as a personal matter. In instances in which there is no definitive textual evidence, it is lawful to hold an opinion, but unlawful to suppose that opinion to be binding. In instances in which such an opinion is based on no more than one's love (for a particular Sufi master or order), then this is perfectly natural and beyond the scope of legal responsibility. No one can be blamed for holding such an opinion.[265]

ḤADĪTH 173

عَنْ أَبِيْ هُرَيْرَةَ رَضِيَ اللهُ عَنْهُ قَالَ: قَالَ رَسُوْلُ اللهِ صَلَّى اللهُ عَلَيْهِ وَسَلَّمَ فِيْ قِصَّةِ تَحَاكُمِ

---

263 What the author is trying to convey to the reader is that these are relative matters. Thus, under certain circumstances, certain pleasures are lawful and permitted while, under other circumstances, the very same pleasures are unlawful. In regard to *samāʿ* the relative circumstances are thus all-important. The author is attempting here to reconcile two apparently opposite positions on the issue. His approach is a subtle one and should be appreciated as such by the discerning reader. For the aspirant, the most important thing is to follow the rules established by the order and those who have become accomplished in its disciplines. YTD.

264 Bukhārī: 3395, Muslim: 2376, Abū Dāwūd: 4669

265 No blame will attach as long as one remains within the bounds of one's own opinion, and does not suppose the matter to be anything more than personal opinion. YTD.

الْمَرْأَتَيْنِ قَالَ سُلَيْمَانُ عَلَيْهِ السَّلاَمُ: «ائْتُوْنِيْ بِالسِّكِّيْنِ أَشُقُّهُ بَيْنَهُمَا» فَقَالَتِ الصُّغْرى: لاتَفْعَلْ يَرْحَمُكَ اللهُ هُوَ اِبْنُهَا، فَقَضى بِهِ لِلصُّغْرِي. (أخرجه الشيخان والنسائي)

Abū Huraira ﷺ related that Allāh's Prophet ﷺ, told the story of how Sulaimān ﷺ judged between two women by saying, "Divide the child in half." Then the younger of the two women said, "Don't do that! May Allāh have mercy on you. He is hers." So Sulaimān ﷺ judged in favour of the younger woman. This was related by Bukhārī, Muslim and al-Nasā'ī.[266]

Habits: Testing the Intentions of an Aspirant by Radical Means

It has been the practice of many Sufi masters to gauge the intention and faith of aspirants, in situations in which they deem that to do so is necessary, by saying or doing things the outer aspect of which appear to contradict the inner. So, while in fact these actually comply with the Sharīʿa, their appearance might lead one to assume that they do not. For example, Sheikh Ṣādiq Gangohī, may Allāh have mercy on his soul, once said to one of his disciples, "There is no god but Allāh, and truthful (*ṣādiq*) is Allāh's Prophet!' Of course, the intended meaning was that Allāh's Prophet ﷺ was truthful in his claim to prophethood. However, the apparent meaning is one that may give rise to doubts, as if the Sheikh (whose name was Ṣādiq) were claiming to be a prophet! (Ṣādiq is God's Prophet!) If the aspirant was a simple-minded literalist, he might have run away from the Sheikh right then and there. If he possessed a penetrating mind, however, he would have understood that there was a possibility, at least, that he was being tested by these words, and he would have had recourse to their context, and to his past experience with the Sheikh who uttered them. If those experiences had been positive and indicated that the Sheikh was indeed an accomplished and orthodox master, then he would have interpreted the words of the Sheikh, in either a particular or a general way, and then remained steadfast in his attachment to the Sheikh. The ḥadīth above may be understood as a precedent for such an evaluation.

ḤADĪTH 174

عَنْ أَبِيْ هُرَيْرَةَ رَضِيَ اللهُ عَنْهُ قَالَ: قَالَ رَسُوْلُ اللهِ صَلَّى اللهُ عَلَيْهِ وَسَلَّمَ: «بَيْنَمَا أَيُّوْبُ يَغْتَسِلُ عُرَيَاناً خَرَّ عَلَيْهِ رِجْلُ جَرَادٍ مِنْ ذَهَبٍ فَجَعَلَ يَحْثِيْ فِيْ ثَوْبِهِ فَنَادَاهُ رَبُّهُ: يَا أَيُّوْبُ!

266 Bukhārī: 3427, Muslim: 1720, Nasā'ī: 5404

أَلَمْ أَكُنْ أَغْنَيْتُكَ عَمَّا تَرِي؟ قَالَ: بَلَى يَا رَبِّ، وَلَكِنْ لاغِنى لِيْ عَنْ بَرَكَتِكَ». (أخرجه البخاري والنسائي)

Abū Hurairah ﵁ related that Allāh's Messenger ﷺ said, "While Ayyūb ﵇ was bathing naked, a cloud of golden locusts descended upon him [evidently these were bits of gold in the shape of locusts, not live locusts] and he immediately began collecting these in his clothing. Then, the Lord called out to him, saying, 'O Ayyūb! Have I not relieved you of the need for what you see here?' Ayyūb ﵇ replied, 'Certainly, O Lord! But I will never be free of my need for Your blessings.'" This was related by al-Bukhārī and al-Nasā'ī.[267]

Habits: Not Declining to Accept Luxuries
It has been the practice of the spiritually adept when God-given luxuries are made available to them, and there is no apparent reason to fear that they will lead to corruption, to understand these as having originated with the Divine Benefactor (al-Munʿim) and to accept them. The ḥadīth above would appear to indicate the legality of this practice. Even so, the masters would never allow such things to become a preoccupation.[268]

ḤADĪTH 175

عَنْ أَبِي سَعِيْدٍ رَضِيَ اللهُ عَنْهُ قَالَ: قَالَ رَسُوْلُ اللهِ صَلَّى اللهُ عَلَيْهِ وَسَلَّمَ: «لاتُخَيِّرُوْا بَيْنَ الْأَنْبِيَاءِ». (أخرجه أبوداؤد)

Abū Saʿīd ﵁ related that Allāh's Prophet ﷺ said, "Do not choose between the prophets." This was included in the collection of Abū Dāwūd.[269]

Reform:
The meaning here is similar to that in ḥadīth [172].

ḤADĪTH 176

عَنِ ابْنِ مَسْعُوْدٍ رَضِيَ اللهُ عَنْهُ قَالَ: صَلّى رَسُوْلُ اللهِ صَلَّى اللهُ عَلَيْهِ وَسَلَّمَ الْعِشَاءَ، ثُمَّ

267 Bukhārī: 3391, Nasā'ī: 409

268 A well-known legal maxim states that it is lawful, for those who trust themselves to show proper appreciation, *shukr*, to desire the accumulation of lawful wealth. YTD.

269 Abū Dāwūd: 4668

انْصَرَفَ فَأَخَذَ بِيَدِيْ حَتَّى خَرَجَ إِلَى بَطْحَاءِ مَكَّةَ فَأَجْلَسَنِيْ، وَخَطَّ عَلَيَّ خَطًّا، وَقَالَ:

«لَاتَبْرَحَنَّ مِنْ خَطِّكَ فَإِنَّهُ سَيَنْتَهِيْ إِلَيْكَ رِجَالٌ فَلَاتُكَلِّمْهُمْ؛ فَإِنَّهُمْ لَنْ يُكَلِّمُوكَ».

الْحَدِيثَ (أخرجه البخاري)

Ibn Masʿūd ◈ related that Allāh's Prophet ◈ performed his evening
prayers and, when he had finished, he took my hand and went out to the
rocky flood plain of Makka where he sat me down. Then he drew a circle
around me and said, "Do not cross beyond your line. Many people will
come to you. Do not speak to them, and they will not speak to you." This
was related by al-Bukhārī.[270]

Miscellaneous: Taking Measures

At times the masters will take measures themselves, generally to rectify one situation or another, and then prescribe the same for others. For example, they may
tell someone to go and recite something after drawing a circle around the place
where they are to do the reciting. This is called *ḥaṣar* or spiritual confinement.
The effect of *ḥaṣar*, in most cases, is that despite the comings and goings of others, the one so confined will remain oblivious to outside influences. The above
ḥadīth would seem to indicate a precedent for such a practice.

ḤADĪTH 177

عَنْ عَبْدِ اللهِ بْنِ هِشَامٍ رَضِيَ اللهُ عَنْهُ قَالَ: كُنَّا مَعَ النَّبِيِّ صَلَّى اللهُ عَلَيْهِ وَسَلَّمَ وَهُوَ الآخِذُ

بِيَدِ عُمَرَ، فَقَالَ عُمَرُ: يَارَسُوْلَ اللهِ! لَأَنْتَ أَحَبُّ إِلَيَّ مِنْ كُلِّ شَيْءٍ إِلاَّ نَفْسِيْ فَقَالَ صَلَّى

اللهُ عَلَيْهِ وَسَلَّمَ: «لَا، وَالَّذِي نَفْسِيْ بِيَدِهِ حَتَّى أَكُوْنَ أَحَبَّ إِلَيْكَ مِنْ نَفْسِكَ» فَقَالَ

عُمَرُ: فَإِنَّهُ الانَ، لَأَنْتَ أَحَبُّ إِلَيَّ مِنْ نَفْسِيْ فَقَالَ صَلَّى اللهُ عَلَيْهِ وَسَلَّمَ: «الآنَ يَا عُمَرُ».

(أخرجه البخاري)

ʿAbdullāh ibn Hishām ◈ related, "We were with Allāh's Prophet ◈ and
he had taken hold of ʿUmar's ◈ hand. So, ʿUmar ◈ said to him, 'O Allāh's
Prophet! Verily, you are more beloved to me than any other thing, except-
ing my own life." At that the Prophet ◈ remarked, 'No. By the One Who
holds my soul in His hand, not[271] until I am more beloved to you than

---

270 Bukhārī: 7281, Tirmidhī: 2861

271 i.e., you will not attain the degree of perfection that you seek. YTD.

even your life!' So, ʿUmar ﷺ replied, 'Indeed, now you are more beloved to me than even my life!' So Allāh's Prophet ﷺ said, 'At last,[272] O ʿUmar!'"[273] This ḥadīth was related by al-Bukhārī.[274]

Questions: Blind Love as a Condition for Certain Perfections

Certain literalist critics refuse to believe that it is possible to have a relationship with a master that is based on natural, emotional love. The ḥadīth above would appear to refute that position. Also, it seems quite clear from the ḥadīth that this sort of love is actually a condition for the attainment of certain forms of spiritual achievement.

ḤADĪTH 178

عَنْ أَبِيْ هُرَيْرَةَ رَضِيَ اللهُ عَنْهُ قَالَ: قَالَ رَسُوْلُ اللهِ صَلَّى اللهُ عَلَيْهِ وَسَلَّمَ: «لاتَسُبُّوْا أَصْحَابِيْ فَوَالَّذِيْ نَفْسِيْ بِيَدِهِ لَوْ أَنَّ أَحَداً أَنْفَقَ مِثْلَ أُحُدٍ ذَهَباً مَابَلَغَ مُدَّ أَحَدِهِمْ وَلانَصِيْفَهُ». (أخرجه مسلم) كقوله تعالى: ﴿كَمَثَلِ جَنَّةٍ بِرَبْوَةٍ أَصَابَهَا وَابِلٌ فَاتَتْ أُكُلَهَا ضِعْفَيْنِ فَإِنْ لَّمْ يُصِبْهَا وَابِلٌ فَطَلٌّ﴾ وكقوله عَلَيْهِ السَّلاَمُ: «سَبَقَ دِرْهَمٌ مِائَةَ أَلْفِ دِرْهَمٍ» قِيْلَ: وَكَيْفَ ذٰلِكَ يَارَسُوْلَ اللهِ قَالَ: «كَانَ لِرَجُلٍ دِرْهَمَانِ فَتَصَدَّقَ بِأَحَدِهِمَا وَانْطَلَقَ اخَرُ إِلَى عُرْضِ مَالِهِ فَأَخْرَجَ مِنْهُ مِائَةَ أَلْفِ دِرْهَمٍ فَتَصَدَّقَ بِهَا». (أخرجه النسائي)

Abū Huraira ﷺ related that Allāh's Prophet ﷺ said, "Do not speak negatively about my Companions. By the One Who holds my life in His hands! If one of you were to spend the weight of Mount 'Uḥud in gold, it would still not equal one of their bushel-weights, or even the half of that!" This was related by Muslim.[275]

Rewards of Experts in Multiples Compared to those of non-Experts

It is mentioned in the books on the subject of *taṣawwuf* that the deeds of an

---

272 i.e., at last you have attained the degree of perfection that you seek. YTD.

273 When the Prophet ﷺ made this pronouncement, ʿUmar ﷺ immediately attained the degree of perfection that he had sought. Moreover, the love alluded to here is not rational (as opposed to emotional) love because otherwise the exception made by ʿUmar ﷺ would have been meaningless. Thus, it was emotional love and that sort of love is clearly not a condition for faith. Certainly, however, it is a requisite for spiritual development. This sort of love is also referred to as losing oneself in love for the Master, or *fanā' fi 'l-Sheikh*. Mention of this phenomenon was made in the commentary for ḥadīth [163]. YTD.

274 Bukhārī: 6632

275 Muslim: 2540, Nasā'ī: 2529

accomplished master are far more valuable in terms of reward and virtue than those performed by ordinary people. I have heard from my own master that two cycles, *rakʿah*, of prayer performed by a master are better than a hundred thousand cycles performed by those who are not masters. This ḥadīth may be adduced as evidence for the same. Even though it is the Companions that are named specifically, the *ratio legis* or occasioning factor is shared; and that is the superiority of both groups in terms of the sincerity of their devotion, *ikhlāṣ*. Moroever, the validity of this factor as an effective influence on such a categorisation, *ḥukm*,[276] is established by means of other scriptural evidence:

> The parable of those who spend their possessions out of a longing to please Allāh, and out of their own inner certainty, is that of a garden on high, fertile ground; a rainstorm smites it, and thereupon it brings forth its fruit twofold; and if no rainstorm smites it, then soft rain [falls upon it] (al-Qur'ān, 2:265),

and,

> Allāh's Prophet ﷺ said, "A single dirham once out-valued a thousand dirhams." When he was asked how that could be, he replied, "One man had only two dirhams. He gave away the best of the two[277] as a charitable donation; while another man went to his treasury, withdrew a thousand dirhams, and gave them away to charity."[278] This was related by al-Nasā'ī.

No one should entertain the doubt here that perhaps the occasioning factor in

---

276 In other words, both the Companions and the masters share a distinguishing characteristic, the sincerity of their devotion. In both cases, this characteristic of unselfish devotion to the Almighty may be identified as the effective cause, or occasioning factor, of the different categorisation or value accorded their acts of worship. When the occasioning factor can be thus identified, it is a simple matter to apply the categorisation mentioned in the ḥadīth, by extension, to the situation of the accomplished masters of *tasawwuf* whose worship, too, is characterised by unselfish devotion and sincerity. In this manner, it is possible to say that the worship of the masters is likewise of far greater value than the acts of worship, including charitable giving, performed by those less accomplished. YTD.

277 Not all *dirhams* were valued equally, owing to the practice common at the time of making change by paring them down. YTD.

278 ʿAllāma Sindhī, in his commentary on al-Nasā'ī, explained the meaning of the ḥadīth in the following manner: The apparent meaning of this ḥadīth is that rewards are given in proportion to the status of the giver, not in proportion to the amount that is given. Thus, the one who had only two dirhams gave away half of everything that he owned, so that he was rewarded in proportion to his zeal and determination. The wealthy person, on the other hand, did not give away half of his wealth and therefore received a smaller reward. It is also possible, although ʿAllāma Sindhī felt that the text of the ḥadīth really didn't support this, to understand the ḥadīth as saying that when the poor man gave away half of everything that he owned, this so impressed the wealthy person that he was inspired to give away a thousand dirhams. In such a case, the reward of the poor man would be increased because he became the reason for the giving of the thousand dirhams to charity. YTD.

the ḥadīth above (178) was the companionship[279] of the Companions ﷺ which is obviously a quality that others cannot share with them. At the same time, however, there is no doubt that even while the reason for their increased rewards is the sincerity of their devotions, their "companionship" does figure into the equation by establishing the highest possible level for rewards.

ḤADĪTH 179

عَنْ أَبِيْ مُوْسي رَضِيَ اللهُ عَنْهُ فِيْ حَدِيْثٍ طَوِيْلٍ قَالَ رَسُوْلُ الله رَضِيَ اللهُ عَنْهُ: «وَأَصْحَابِيْ أَمَنَةٌ لِأُمَّتِيْ فَإِذَا ذَهَبَ أَصْحَابِيْ أَتى أُمَّتِيْ مُايُوْعَدُوْنَ». (أخرجه مسلم)

Abū Mūsā ﷺ stated, as part of a lengthy ḥadīth, that Allāh's Prophet ﷺ said, "My Companions are the security of my community. When my Companions pass away, to my community there will come that[280] of which they were cautioned." This was related by Muslim.[281]

Questions: The Diffusion of the Blessings of the Godly to Others

Scholars have pointed out that certain of the blessings of the godly may be classified as volitional, like their spiritual teaching and direction. Others of their blessings, however, are non-volitional in the sense that they occur without the godly intending for them to occur. These are things like their presence in the world being a source of mercy, or like their illumination passing on to seekers of the truth. This ḥadīth appears to establish the validity of such non-volitional blessings.

ḤADĪTH 180

عَنْ بُرَيْدَةَ رَضِيَ اللهُ عَنْهُ قَالَ: قَالَ رَسُوْلُ اللهِ صَلَّى اللهُ عَلَيْهِ وَسَلَّمَ «يَا بِلالُ! بِمَ سَبَقْتَنِيْ إِلَي الْجَنَّةِ؟ فَمَا دَخَلْتُ الْجَنَّةَ قَطُّ إِلاَّ سَمِعْتُ خَشْخَشَتَكَ أَمَامِيْ» فَقَالَ: يَارَسُوْلَ اللهِ! مَا أَذَّنْتُ قَطُّ إِلاَّ صَلَّيْتُ رَكْعَتَيْنِ وَمَا أَحْدَثْتُ قَطُّ إِلاَّ وَتَوَضَّأْتُ عِنْدَهُ وَرَأَيْتُ أَنَّ للهِ عَلَيَّ رَكْعَتَيْنِ فَقَالَ رَسُوْلُ اللهِ: «بِهِمَا».(أخرجه الترمذي وصححه)

279 i.e., the fact that they had actually been in the presence of the Prophet ﷺ and were thus deserving of the name Companion, *saḥāba*, and everything that that name entails (as elaborated in the works of theology, *ʿaqīda*). YTD.

280 The apparent meaning here is that once the Companions are no more, the community will be beset by all manner of temptations and corruption. And, indeed, history bears witness to exactly that. YTD.

281 Muslim: 2531

Burayda 🪶 related that Allāh's Prophet 🪶 said, "O Bilāl! By means of what [deeds] have you preceded me[282] to Paradise? For I had barely entered Paradise[283] when I heard your footsteps in front of me!" He [Bilāl 🪶] replied, "O Allāh's Prophet! Never did I make the call to prayer except that I also performed two cycles of prayer. And never did I break ritual purity except that I immediately performed ablutions and then considered myself responsible[284] to Allāh for two cycles of prayer." This was related by Tirmidhī who declared the ḥadīth a sound one.[285]

Questions: Dispelling False Notions Arising from Visions

Certain travellers on the Sufi Way have experienced visions in which they apparently take precedence over the prophets and messengers of Allāh 🪶. If the traveller is ignorant, such visions may lead him to religious ruination. If the traveller is learned, however, he will immediately understand that what he has witnessed is theologically impossible and will accordingly attempt to interpret his vision. In the ḥadīth above, Bilāl's 🪶 precedence represents the most advanced degree of a servile relationship with Allāh's Prophet 🪶. From all of this, the importance of an education in the Sharīʿa sciences should be obvious. It was perhaps for this reason that Saʿdī wrote the following verses:

> Now, an ignoramus musing in seclusion,
>> Later, a victim stricken by his own delusion.

ḤADĪTH 181

عَنْ أَنَسٍ رَضِيَ اللهُ عَنْهُ قَالَ: كَانَ أُسَيْدُ بْنُ حُضَيْرٍ وَعَبَّادُ بْنُ بِشْرٍ رَضِيَ الله عَنْهُمَا عِنْدَ رَسُوْلِ اللهِ صَلَّى اللهُ عَلَيْهِ وَسَلَّمَ فِي لَيْلَةٍ مُظْلِمَةٍ، فَخَرَجَ مِنْ عِنْدِهِ، فَإِذَا بِنُوْرَيْنِ بَيْنَ أَيْدِيْهِمَا، فَلَمَّا افْتَرَقَا صَارَ مَعَ كُلِّ وَاحِدٍ مِنْهُمَا نُوْرٌ. (أخرجه البخاري)

---

282 The "preceding" spoken of in this ḥadīth is of the nature of a servant's preceding his master. Of course, to be the servant of the Prophet 🪶 is in itself one of the greatest of honours. YTD.

283 Clearly, Allah's Prophet, Allah bless him and give him peace, was not speaking literally as entrance to Paradise will occur after the Day of Judgement. Even so, the Prophet, from time to time, was granted glimpses into the Afterworld by the Almighty so that he could then tell his followers about the glories of the world to come. YTD.

284 The author explains here that Bilāl's 🪶 use of the expression "considered myself responsible. . ." was actually an idiomatic expression for his constancy in this practice. He did not mean to say that these two extra cycles were in any way binding or *wajib*, as that would imply that Bilāl 🪶 had the ability to legislate for himself; and that is clearly the prerogative of the Almighty alone! YTD.

285 Tirmidhī: 3689

Anas ❧ related that Usayd ibn Ḥuḍayr and ʿAbbād ibn Bishr were with Allāh's Prophet ❧ on a dark night. When they left him and went outside two lights were there directly in front of them. When the two men parted company, a light went with each one of them. This was related by Bukhārī.[286]

States: Miracles

The miracle that occurred in relation to both of these Companions ❧ is recorded in this ḥadīth. Since there is consensus that miracles are not the exclusive domain of the Companions, this ḥadīth may be adduced as evidence in support of the occurrence of miracles in general.

ḤADĪTH 182

عَنْ عَائِشَةَ رَضِيَ الله تَعَالَى عَنْهَا قَالَتْ: دَخَلَ أَبُوْبَكْرٍ رَضِيَ اللهُ عَنْهُ عَلَى رَسُوْلِ اللهِ صَلَّى اللهُ عَلَيْهِ وَسَلَّمَ فَقَالَ لَهُ صَلَّى اللهُ عَلَيْهِ وَسَلَّمَ: «أَبْشِرْ فَأَنْتَ عَتِيْقُ اللهِ مِنَ النَّارِ» قَالَتْ: فَمِنْ يَوْمَئِذٍ سُمِّيَ عَتِيْقاً. (أخرجه الترمذي)

ʿĀʾisha ❧ reported, "Abū Bakr ❧ came to see Allāh's Prophet ❧ and when he did, the Prophet ❧ said to him, 'Rejoice! For Allāh has set you free from the Fire!'" She added, "Thereafter, Abū Bakr ❧ was called *ʿAtīq*, or freed." This was related by Bukhārī.[287]

Behaviour: Giving Good Tidings to Aspirants

It is the habit of most masters, when their students attain a spiritual objective, or acquire a praiseworthy state, to inform them of the same. This ḥadīth indicates that to do so is in accordance with the Sunna. There are many benefits in doing this, including the easing of worry, strengthening resolve to do good deeds, and increasing the aspirant's love for the Almighty Benefactor and the one who facilitated[288] those benefits.

Customs: Giving Names to Aspirants

It has been recorded and witnessed that spiritual masters will sometimes begin calling an aspirant by a name that is appropriate to the aspirant's specific cir-

---

286 Bukhārī: 3805
287 Tirmidhī: 3679
288 i.e. the aspirant's spiritual guide or master. YTD.

cumstances. Sometimes, then, he may call him king, for instance, or something else. The ḥadīth above, in which Abū Bakr ☙ is called ʿAtīq, clearly advocates this custom.

ḤADĪTH 183

عَنْ أَبِيْ هُرَيْرَةَ رَضِيَ اللهُ عَنْهُ قَالَ: قَالَ رَسُوْلُ اللهِ صَلَّى اللهُ عَلَيْهِ وَسَلَّمَ فِيْ حَدِيْثٍ طَوِيْلٍ: «وَمَاعَرَضْتُ الإِسْلامَ عَلى أَحَدٍ إِلاَّ كَانَتْ لَهُ كَبْوَةٌ إِلاَّ أَبَابَكرٍ رَضِيَ اللهُ عَنْهُ فَإِنَّهُ لَمْ يَتَلَعْثَمْ». (أخرجه الترمذي)

Abū Huraira ☙ reported that Allāh's Prophet ☙ said [as part of a lengthy ḥadīth], "I have never known Islam to go to anyone except that the person stumbled, other than Abū Bakr. For he never once wavered." Tirmidhī related this ḥadīth.[289]

Questions: The Reality of True Friendship

The scholars who have explained the reality of true friendship[290], those who have developed a thorough understanding of this state through their familiarity with Islamic theological theory, have found themselves so influenced by this state that the performance of their devotions automatically improved. This ḥadīth would appear to indicate the same. In regard to people who have experienced the reality of true friendship, theory becomes self-evident and devotions become habitual. The first of these transformations is actually the result of Divine power, while the second is the result of the perfection of character. It is only the second of these that spells true spiritual perfection.[291]

---

289 This report is not found in Tirmidhī. *Kanz al-ʿUmmāl*: 32609

290 Abū Bakr ☙ was best known as *al-Ṣiddīq* or the True Friend. The reality of true friendship or *Ṣiddīqiyyah*, then, is a reference to the spiritual station that Abū Bakr ☙ had attained through his friendship with the Prophet ☙. As such, Abū Bakr ☙ has come to represent the ideal for this particular spiritual state. Abū Bakr ☙ was not only one of the Prophet's oldest friends, but he was also the friend who stood beside him throughout every trial and every hardship of his mission to humankind. The root of the word, *s-d-q*, in the Arabic language is an infinitive that means to keep faith with, to be truthful, and to be sincere. Thus, the spiritual state known as *ṣiddīqiyyah*, or "true friendship" is one of exceeding perfection in which its possessor combines the elements of truth, faith and sincerity. YTD.

291 Here, the author explains that while Allah may grant a degree of *Ṣiddīqiyah* to someone, perfection may only come about through the efforts of the individual. Obviously, while Abū Bakr ☙ was endowed by Allāh with many of the qualities that constitute "true friendship", it was through his own toil and perseverance that he attained the highest degree of that particular spiritual station. YTD.

ḤADĪTH 184

عَنْ أَبِيْ الدَّرْدَاءِ رَضِيَ اللهُ عَنْهُ قَالَ: كُنْتُ جَالِساً عِنْدَ النَّبِيِّ: إِذْ أَقْبَلَ أَبُوْ بَكْرٍ رَضِيَ اللهُ عَنْهُ . الحديث . وَفِيْهِ : فَقَالَ النَّبِيُّ صَلَّى اللهُ عَلَيْهِ وَسَلَّمَ : «إِنَّ اللهَ بَعَثَنِيْ إِلَيْكُمْ فَقُلْتُمْ : كَذَبْتَ ، وَقَالَ أَبُوْبَكْرٍ: صَدَقَ ، وَوَاسَانِيْ بِنَفْسِهِ وَمَالِهِ ، فَهَلْ أَنْتُمْ تَارِكُوْا لِيْ صَاحِبِيْ؟» مَرَّتَيْنِ أَوْ ثَلثاً. قَالَ: فَمَا أُوْذِيْ بَعْدَهَا. (أخرجه البخاري)

Abū 'l-Dardā' said, "I was sitting with Allāh's Prophet when Abū Bakr approached. . ." In the same ḥadīth, he said, "So the Prophet said [to a Companion who had spoken disrespectfully of Abū Bakr], 'Verily, Allāh sent me to you and you [at first] said, "You lie!" while ʿAbū Bakr said, "You tell the truth!" and he made me his equal with regard to his life and his wealth. So, will you please refrain from tormenting my friend!'" [Abū 'l-Dardā' said,] He repeated this two or three times. Thereafter, he [Abū Bakr] was not picked upon. This was related by al-Bukhārī.[292]

Behaviour: Showing Greater Respect for the Successor of a Master

It has always been a matter of course among the Sufis, and one that accords with human nature, to show a greater degree of respect for the spiritual successors (*khulafā'*) and senior-most aspirants of their masters. The above ḥadīth clearly indicates the same. It also shows that disrespect toward such people, or abuse, or causing them any sort of discomfort must be denounced as matters of envy and pride.

ḤADĪTH 185

عَن ابْنِ عُمَرَ رَضِيَ اللهُ عَنْهُ قَالَ: قَالَ رَسُوْلُ اللهِ صَلَّى اللهُ عَلَيْهِ وَسَلَّمَ: «إِنَّ اللهَ تَعَالَى جَعَلَ الْحَقَّ عَلَى لِسَانِ عُمَرَ وَقَلْبِهِ» وَقَالَ ابْنُ عُمَرَ رَضِيَ اللهُ عَنْهُ: مَا نَزَلَ بِالنَّاسِ أَمْرٌ قَطُّ فَقَالُوْا فِيْهِ وَقَالَ فِيْهِ عُمَرُ رَضِيَ اللهُ عَنْهُ إِلاَّ نَزَلَ الْقُرْآنُ فِيْهِ عَلَى نَحْوِ مَا قَالَ عُمَرُ رَضِيَ اللهُ عَنْهُ . (أخرجه الترمذي وصححه)

Ibn ʿUmar said that Allāh's Prophet said, "Verily, Allāh Almighty has put the truth on the tongue of ʿUmar , and in his heart." Ibn ʿUmar said, "Never did a matter occur to the people in which they voiced their

292 Bukhārī: 3661

opinions and ʿUmar ﵁ voiced his except that revelation came through the Qur'ān confirming the opinion of ʿUmar!" This was related by Tirmidhī.[293]

States: Inspiration and Spiritual Intuition
Both of these states are indicated by the ḥadīth above and, in reality, are categories of spiritual vision, *kashf*.

ḤADĪTH 186

عَنِ ابْنِ عُمَرَ رَضِيَ اللهُ عَنْهُ فِيْ جَوَابِهِ لِلْمِصْرِيْ عَنْ طَعْنِهِ فِيْ عُثْمَانَ قَوْلُهُ: وَأَمَّا غَيْبَتُهُ عَنْ بَيْعَةِ الرِّضْوَانِ فَلَوْكَانَ أَحَدٌ أَعَزَّ بِبَطْنِ مَكَّةَ مِنْ عُثْمَانَ لَبَعَثَهُ، فَبَعَثَ صَلَّى اللهُ عَلَيْهِ وَسَلَّمَ عُثْمَانَ رَضِيَ اللهُ عَنْهُ إِلى مَكَّةَ وَكَانَتْ بَيْعَةُ الرِّضْوَانِ بَعْدَ مَاذَهَبَ عُثْمَانُ، فَجَعَلَ صَلَّى اللهُ عَلَيْهِ وَسَلَّمَ بِيَدِهِ الْيُمْنى عَلَيَ الْيُسْرى وَقَالَ: «هذِهِ لِعُثْمَانَ» وَكَانَتْ لِيُسْرى رَسُوْلِ اللهِ صَلَّى اللهُ عَلَيْهِ وَسَلَّمَ لِعُثْمَانَ خَيْراً مِنْ أَيْمَانِهِمْ. الحديث. (أخرجه البخاري والترمذي)

Ibn ʿUmar ﵁, in answer to the insinuations of a certain Egyptian concerning ʿUthmān ﵁, said [among other things in a lengthy ḥadīth], "As to his not being present at the Pledge of al-Riḍwān,[294] if there was anyone more revered by the people of Makka, that person would have been sent.[295] But the Pledge of al-Riḍwān took place after ʿUthmān ﵁ had left [to go on his mission to Makka]. Allāh's Prophet ﷺ while holding his left hand in his right, said[296] of his left hand, "This is the hand of ʿUthmān!" In this manner, the left hand of the Prophet ﷺ that was for ʿUthmān ﵁ was

293 Tirmidhī: 3682

294 There was, at the time, a need for someone to go and negotiate with the Makkan idolators, someone who was himself a respected and important Makkan and thus not likely to be killed by the Makkans, someone like ʿUthmān.

295 The message that ʿUthmān ﵁ carried from the Prophet, Allah bless him and give him peace, was that the Muslims had come as pilgrims in peace for the purpose of performing the Ḥajj, and not as an army determined to attack Makka and take it by force. The Pledge of al-Ridwan that is alluded to here was the pledge of obedience given by the Companions who had set out from Madīna for the purpose of performing the Ḥajj. The significance of the pledge was that it bore witness to the faith of the Companions whose faith was tested when the Prophet, Allah bless him and give him peace, agreed to the terms of the Makkans by postponing their visit to Makka for another year, thereby greatly disappointing the Muslims. YTD.

296 This is what the Prophet ﷺ said to those gathered for the Pledge. YTD.

better[297] than all of the right hands [of those present]. This was related by Bukhārī and Tirmidhī.[298]

Behaviour: Pledging in absentia

Many masters observe the practice of accepting pledges, *bayʿah*, from aspirants who are not physically present. All of this was discussed previously in my commentary on ḥadīth [68].

Customs: Placing the Master's Hand over the Aspirant's while Pledging

It is the practice of some Sufi masters to place their own hand above the hand of the aspirant while taking the pledge of their allegiance to him. The words in the ḥadīth above would seem to indicate the validity of this practice. Likewise, the verse in the Qur'ān: *The hand of Allāh is over their hands*[299] (48:10) would appear to indicate the same. Doubts may arise from the words of the ḥadīth indicating that it was the left hand of the aspirant that was used, when the practice among Sufis is that the aspirant places his right hand in the right hand of the master. These may be dispelled when we see that the holding of the left hand was by necessity only. Otherwise, the words of the ḥadīth, "... better than all of the right hands," clearly indicate the right hands of both parties are to be used for the pledge. Whatever the case, the physical arrangement is not the important thing here. In fact, even if there is no hand-clasp at all, the pledge may still take place, as in the case of the pledge of a woman aspirant, or one that takes place in absentia. The essential element is the verbal expression of allegiance. Otherwise, in many cases, rather than the master's hand, aspirants will be asked to grasp his clothing, or his turban, or the like.

ḤADĪTH 187

عَنِ ابْنِ عُمَرَ رَضِيَ اللهُ عَنْهُ قَالَ: قَالَ رَسُوْلُ اللهِ صَلَّى اللهُ عَلَيْهِ وَسَلَّمَ حِيْنَ جَهَّزَ جَيْشَ

297 Even though ʿUthmān was not physically present, the Prophet ﷺ used his own hand to represent ʿUthmān's hand. In this manner, ʿUthmān took the pledge even though he was not present. YTD.

298 Bukhārī: 4066, Tirmidhī: 3706

299 This verse was revealed on the occasion of the *Bayʿat al-Riḍwān*, and begins with the words: "Behold, all who pledge their allegiance to you pledge their allegiance to Allah." Thus, the simple hand-clasp takes on the further significance of pledging one's allegiance, or committing one's self, body and soul, firstly to the master, or to the Prophet, Allah bless him and give him peace, and then, by extension, to the Almighty Himself. Those who ridicule the Sufi way would do well to reflect on the symbolic nature of these practices, and on how that symbolism was a part of the practices of the Prophet ﷺ and his Companions. YTD.

الْعُسْرَةِ: «مَا عَلَى عُثْمَانَ مَا عَمِلَ بَعْدَ هذِهِ، مَا عَلَى عُثْمَانَ مَا عَمِلَ بَعْدَ هذِهِ». (أخرجه الترمذي)

Ibn ʿUmar ﵁ stated that Allāh's Prophet ﷺ said at the time preparations[300] for the campaign known as *al-ʿusrah*[301] were being made: "Regardless of what he does after this, ʿUthmān ﵁ has nothing to worry about! Regardless of what he does after this, ʿUthmān ﵁ has nothing to worry about!" This was related by Tirmidhī.[302]

Questions: Perfect Masters who Abandon Spiritual Disciplines

Since Sufi masters who have attained spiritual perfection are constantly involved in devotions, whether openly or otherwise, which are of the highest degree and thus bring them very close to the Almighty, if they no longer practise the basic sorts of spiritual disciplines[303] this will not cause them any difficulties. The ḥadīth above would seem to indicate this.

ḤADĪTH 188

عَنْ جَابِرٍ رَضِيَ اللهُ عَنْهُ قَالَ: دَعَا رَسُوْلُ اللهِ صَلَّى اللهُ عَلَيْهِ وَسَلَّمَ عَلِياً رَضِيَ اللهُ عَنْهُ يَوْمَ الطَّائِفِ فَانْتَجَاهُ فَقَالَ النَّاسُ: لَقَدْ طَالَ نَجْوَاهُ مَعَ ابْنِ عَمِّهِ فَقَالَ: «مَا انْتَجَيْتُهُ وَلكِنَّ اللهَ انْتَجَاهُ». (أخرجه الترمذي)

Jābir ﵁ said, "Allāh's Prophet ﷺ called for ʿAlī ﵁ at the Battle of Ṭā'if and then had a whispered conversation with him. People began talking among themselves about how long the conversation with his nephew had become. At that, the Prophet ﷺ declared, 'I have not whispered to him. Allāh whispered to him!'" This was related by Tirmidhī.[304]

Questions: Unicity in Praxis

In the writings of the Sufis one may find the deeds of both the most accom-

---

300 These preparations included major contributions of money and supplies donated by ʿUthmān ﵁, may Allah be pleased with him.

301 This campaign, leading to the Battle of Tabūk, was known as *al-ʿusrah* owing to the difficulties and hardships endured by those who took part in it. YTD.

302 Tirmidhī: 3700

303 It should be obvious the disciplines referred to here are not required or even recommended acts of worship but rather the extra spiritual disciplines prescribed for apirants by the Order or the Sheikh. YTD.

304 Tirmidhī: 3726

plished worshippers and the deeds of ordinary worshippers ascribed to the Almighty. Such deeds are termed *tawḥīd-e-afʿālī* or unicity in praxis. These are also indicated by the phrase: 'There is no Doer other than Allāh.' In the ḥadīth above, the statement, 'I am not whispering to him. Allāh is whispering to him!' clearly indicates the first sort of unicity in praxis. The effective cause here is occurrence by means of the Divine will. In the same way that an effective cause may be identified for a legal matter, the same may also be done for a natural matter. Then, by analogy, the second sort of unicity in praxis may be explained. In the Qur'ān it is written: "It was not you who slew the enemy, but it was Allāh Who slew them" (8:17) and "It was not you who shot [the arrows], but it was Allāh Who shot them" (8:17).

In these verses, a natural matter would appear to be the nexus of the effective cause. However, from a theological perspective, the belief that what is essential and what is merely possible are one and the same[305] is heretical in the same way that denial of the will of the individual[306] is heretical. It is for this reason that Junayd of Baghdād made his well-known statement; "If I had the power, then any person who said (in an attempt to excuse his unlawful behaviour) that there is no Doer other than Allāh, would have his head cut off!" The reason for such an extreme punishment in that instance is that the person using that excuse is actually undermining the Sharīʿa.[307]

---

305 There are a number of issues here for the consideration of the reader. Obviously, at many levels, tasawwuf and theology converge; and it is for this reason that the author always dealt with his aspirants and their spiritual development in accordance with the level of their knowledge of Shariʿa, by which he meant the classical Shariʿa sciences and disciplines, including theology. The question of free will from an Islamic theological perspective is not an easy matter to understand. However, in essence, Islam teaches that humans are endowed with free will and that they will be judged on the basis of the deeds they choose to do in their lifetimes. At the same time, however, the source of all deeds, of all that happens on earth and in heaven, is the Almighty. What the ḥadīth indicates, and what the author is speaking of in his commentary, is that at times the will of the servant and the will of the Almighty become as one, such that there is a unicity of wills; and then the deeds, or praxis, of the servant become one with the deeds of the Almighty. The author is careful to point out, however, that such a unicity does not mean that the servant and the Almighty are, or become, one in their persons. To hold such a belief is clearly heretical. This also explains why the author has quoted Junayd here. YTD.

306 i.e., that he acts of his own volition. YTD.

307 It may further be pointed out here that it is ignorance of the Sharīʿa sciences that has led so many Sufi aspirants, regardless of how good their intentions might have been, to go astray and, in doing so, to give *taṣwwuf* a bad name. As questions of theology are often so complex, even Sufis who have not gone astray have appeared that way to the general public and, in some cases, to rulers and judges with disastrous results. Generally speaking, it is best to leave theology to the theologians. Those who equate theology with religion do themselves, and their religion, a great disservice. YTD.

ḤADĪTH 189

عَنْ عَائِشَةَ رَضِيَ اللهُ تَعَالَى عَنْهَا قَالَتْ: قَالَ رَسُوْلُ اللهِ صَلَّى اللهُ عَلَيْهِ وَسَلَّمَ لِنِسَاءِهِ: «إِنَّ أَمْرَكُنَّ لَمِمَّا يُهِمُّنِي مِنْ بَعْدِيْ، وَلَيْسَ يَصْبِرُ عَلَيْكُنَّ إِلاَّ الصَّابِرُوْنَ الصِّدِّيْقُوْنَ» ثُمَّ قَالَتْ لِأَبِيْ سَلَمَةَ بْنِ عَبْدِ الرَّحْمنِ رَضِيَ اللهُ عَنْهُ: سَقَى اللهُ أَبَاكَ مِنْ سَلْسَبِيْلِ الْجَنَّةِ، وَكَانَ ابْنُ عَوْفٍ قَدْ تَصَدَّقَ عَلى أُمَّهَاتِ الْمُؤْمِنِيْنَ بِأَرْضٍ بِيْعَتْ بِأَرْبَعِيْنَ أَلْفاً، وَقَالَ أَبُوْسَلَمَةَ بْنُ عَبْدِ الرَّحْمنِ بْنِ عَوْفٍ أَوْصى عَبْدُ الرَّحْمنِ بِحَدِيْقَةٍ لِأُمَّهَاتِ الْمُؤْمِنِيْنَ بِيْعَتْ بِأَرْبَعِ مِائَةِ أَلْفٍ. (أخرجه الترمذي)

ʿĀ'isha ﵂ stated that Allāh's Prophet ﷺ said to his wives, "What happens to you after I am gone is a matter of concern to me. Only those who are highly devoted and accomplished will be able to serve you." Later, ʿĀ'isha ﵂ said to Abū Salama ﵁ ibn ʿAbd al-Raḥmān ibn ʿAwf ﵁, "May Allāh grant[308] your father his fill from the spring of Salsabīl in Paradise!" ʿAbd al-Raḥmān ibn ʿAwf ﵁ gifted land to the Mothers of the Faithful which had been sold for forty thousand. Abū Salama ﵁ said, "ʿAbd al-Raḥmān ibn ʿAwf ﵁ gifted a garden to the Mothers of the Faithful that had sold for four hundred thousand." This was related by Tirmidhī.[309]

Questions: Concern for the Welfare of Family[310]
Certain ignorant people, observing that a master is concerned about his family, suppose that the master is less than completely accomplished. The ḥadīth above indicates clearly that such concern is in fact a part of the Sunna. At the same time, it should be obvious that excess in this regard, like excess in most matters, is indicative of a degree of spiritual inadequacy.

Miscellaneous: Service to the Family of a Master is Service to the Master Himself
In the ḥadīth above, those who cared for the Mothers of the Faithful were referred to as highly devoted and accomplished. Such a characterisation is indicative of how service to a master's family shows the degree of a person's relationship with the master. Service of this kind is very nearly a matter of second nature among the true Sufis.

---

308 i.e., for the way that he had cared for the wives of the Prophet ﷺ.

309 Tirmidhī: 3749

310 This is the abbreviated form of the title. The entire title reads as follows: Concern for the Welfare of Family does not Negate Spiritual Perfection on Condition that it Remain within the Bounds of Equity and Kindness. YTD.

ḤADĪTH 190

عَنْ سَلْمى امْرَأةٍ مِنَ الْأَنْصارِ قَالَتْ: دَخَلْتُ عَلى أُمِّ سَلَمَةَ رَضِيَ اللهُ تَعَالى عَنْهَا وَهِيَ تَبْكِيْ فَقُلْتُ: مَا يُبْكِيْكِ؟ قَالَتْ: رَأَيْتُ الْآنَ رَسُوْلَ اللهِ صَلَّى اللهُ عَلَيْهِ وَسَلَّمَ فِيْ الْمَنَامِ وَعَلى رَأْسِهِ وَلِحْيَتِهِ التُّرَابُ، وَهُوَ يَبْكِيْ فَقُلْتُ: مَايُبْكِيكَ يَارَسُوْلَ اللهِ؟ قَالَ: «شَهِدْتُّ قَتْلَ الْحُسَيْنِ آنِفاً». (أخرجه الترمذي)

Salmā ﵂, a woman of the Anṣār, stated, "I went to see Umm Salama ﵂ and discovered her crying, so I asked, 'Why are you crying?' She replied that she had just then seen Allāh's Prophet ﷺ in a dream, with dirt on his head and beard, and he was crying. When she asked him why he was crying, he replied, 'I have just now witnessed the martyrdom of al-Ḥusayn ﵁.'" This was related by Tirmidhī.[311]

States: Dreams That Come True
Seeing in dreams events that later come true is a praiseworthy spiritual state. The ḥadīth attests to this because the event witnessed in the dream occurred at the same time as Umm Salama ﵂ dreamt about it.

Questions: The Presence of the Spirit
After the soul leaves the physical world, when its original place is elsewhere, then if by Allāh's leave it should be allowed to return to the physical world, then this is possible. For example, the blessed soul of the Prophet ﷺ was witnessed on the field of battle after his death. Moreover, as there is no evidence to indicate otherwise, there is no need to interpret such reports or to suppose them to be metaphorical. Rather, these may be understood literally.

ḤADĪTH 191

عَنْ عَبْدِ الرَّحْمنِ بْنِ زَيْدٍ قَالَ: سَأَلْتُ حُذَيْفَةَ رَضِيَ اللهُ عَنْهُ عَنْ رَجُلٍ قَرِيْبِ السَّمْتِ وَالدَّلِّ وَالْهَدْيِ مِنْ رَسُوْلِ اللهِ صَلَّى اللهُ عَلَيْهِ وَسَلَّمَ حَتّى نَأْخُذَ عَنْهُ، فَقَالَ: مَا نَعْلَمُ أَحَداً أَقْرَبَ سَمْتاً وَلاَ هَدْياً وَلاَ دَلاًّ مِنَ النَّبِيِّ صَلَّى اللهُ عَلَيْهِ وَسَلَّمَ مِنِ ابْنِ أُمِّ عَبْدٍ حَتّى يَتَوَارى بِجِدَارِ بَيْتِهِ. (أخرجه البخاري والترمذي)

311 Tirmidhī: 3771

ʿAbd al-Raḥmān ibn Zayd ﵁ stated, "I asked Ḥudhayfah ﵁ if he knew someone who resembled the Prophet ﷺ in terms of his manner, his ways, and his conduct; someone from whom we may learn. He replied, 'I know of no one who more resembled the Prophet ﷺ in terms of his manner, his ways, and his conduct, than Ibn Umm ʿAbd ﵁, as long as[312] he stands in the shade of his house.'" This was related by Bukhārī and Tirmidhī.[313]

Behaviour: Taking on the Aspect of the Master

In certain of the stories told about Sufis it is mentioned how aspirants, far from confining themselves to emulating their masters in matters of worship, have also sought to be like their masters in their dress, in their dining habits, and even in the ways that they walk and talk. For many Sufis such emulation becomes second nature and habitual, so that they do it without even intending to do so. The connection between aspirant and master often becomes so strong that it may be described by the following verses of poetry:

I become you, then, you become me, just so.
  I become body and you become soul. And so,
After this than me none will say you're other
  Or that I am other than you, you know.

The ḥadīth above clearly indicates this sort of behaviour. Whether or not ʿAbdullāh ibn Masʿūd ﵁ intended to resemble the Prophet ﷺ his doing so was praiseworthy as is evident from the ḥadīth. On the other hand, if he did intend to do so, then that was clearly a good thing.

ḤADĪTH 192

عَنْ أَبِيْ ذَرٍّ رَضِيَ اللهُ عَنْهُ فِيْ حَدِيْثِ إِسْلامِهِ: وَلَقَدْ لَبِثْتُ ثَلثِيْنَ مَا بَيْنَ لَيْلَةٍ وَيَوْمٍ وَمَاكَانَ لِيْ طَعَامٌ إِلاَّ مَاءُ زَمْزَمَ، فَسَمِنْتُ حَتّى تَكَسَّرَتْ عُكَنُ بَطْنِيْ وَمَا وَجَدْتُّ عَلى كَبِدِيْ سُخْفَةَ جُوْعٍ. الحديث (أخرجه مسلم)

In his narration of the story of how he converted to Islam, Abū Dharr ﵁ stated, "I lingered thirty days and nights without sustenance other than the

---

312 This last part of Hudhayfah's ﵁ statement is indicative of the prudence exhibited by the Companions in giving witness. In other words, Hudhayfah ﵁ was saying that he could attest to the resemblance only in terms of what was apparent to him in regard to Ibn Masʿūd ﵁, as he was not privy to knowledge of what went on inside.

313 Bukhārī: 3763, Tirmidhī: 3807

water of Zamzam. But I grew fat from it, so that my belly button protruded and I could sense no traces of hunger." This was related by Muslim.[314]

Miscellaneous: Remaining without Nourishment
Certain ascetic Sufis have claimed the ability to fast for forty days, or to so limit their intake of nourishment for days and weeks on end at levels that under normal circumstances would hardly be expected to sustain life. Hearing such claims, shortsighted critics of Sufism have responded with scepticism. The ḥadīth above, in which Abū Dharr ♦ speaks of his own experience, counters all such attempts at doubt and denial. If one were to counter by saying that it was Zamzam water he drank, it may be pointed out that even if it was Zamzam water, what Abū Dharr ♦ described is not natural. Water simply does not have the nutrients required for this.[315] What Zamzam does possess, however, are blessings; then, if someone who remembers Allāh often drinks Zamzam and brings blessings to himself, then what is so strange about that?

ḤADĪTH 193

عَنْ جَابِرٍ رَضِيَ اللهُ عَنْهُ قَالَ: قَالَ رَسُولُ اللهِ صَلَّى اللهُ عَلَيْهِ وَسَلَّمَ: «اهْتَزَّ الْعَرْشُ» وَفِي رِوَايَةٍ: «اهْتَزَّ عَرْشُ الرَّحْمنِ لِمَوْتِ سَعْدِ بْنِ مُعَاذٍ رَضِيَ اللهُ عَنْهُ». (أخرجه الشيخان والترمذي)

Jābir ♦ stated that Allāh's Prophet ♦ said, "The Throne was shaken," and in another version, he said, "The Throne of the Merciful was shaken . . . at the death of Saʿd ibn Muʿādh." This was related by Bukhārī, Muslim and Tirmidhī.[316]

States: Miracle
This ḥadīth attributes what was clearly a miracle to one of the Companions of the Prophet ♦.

ḤADĪTH 194

عَنْ أَنَسٍ رَضِيَ اللهُ عَنْهُ قَالَ: لَمَّا حُمِلَتْ جَنَازَةُ سَعْدِ بْنِ مُعَاذٍ رَضِيَ اللهُ عَنْهُ قَالَ

---

314 Muslim: 2437
315 That is to produce fat in the body. YTD.
316 Bukhārī: 3802, Muslim: 2466, Tirmidhī: 3848, Ibn Mājah: 158

الْمُنَافِقُوْنَ: مَا أَخَفَّ جَنَازَتُهُ؟ يَعْنُوْنَ لِحُكْمِهِ فِيْ بَنِيْ قُرَيْظَةَ. فَبَلَغَ ذٰلِكَ رَسُوْلُ اللهِ صَلَّى اللهُ عَلَيْهِ وَسَلَّمَ فَقَالَ: «إِنَّ الْمَلَاءِكَةَ كَانَتْ تَحْمِلُهُ». (أخرجه الترمذي)

Anas ﷺ stated, "When the funeral bier of Saʿd ibn Muʿādh ﷺ was lifted, the hypocrites remarked, 'How light is his funeral bier!' referring to his ruling in regard to the Qurayzah tribe.[317] When this [disparaging comment] reached Allāh's Prophet ﷺ he said, 'That's because there were angels to carry it.'" This was related by Tirmidhī.[318]

States: Miracle
This ḥadīth, too, records a significant miracle.

ḤADĪTH 195

عَنْ أَبِيْ مُوْسى رَضِيَ اللهُ عَنْهُ قَالَ: قَالَ لِيْ رَسُوْلُ اللهِ صَلَّى اللهُ عَلَيْهِ وَسَلَّمَ: «لَوْرَأَيْتَنِيْ الْبَارِحَةَ وَأَنَا أَسْتَمِعُ لِقِرَائَتِكَ لَقَدْ أُعْطِيْتَ مِزْمَاراً مِنْ مَزَامِيْرِ الِ دَاوُدَ». (أخرجه الشيخان والترمذي) وَزَادَ فِيْ رِوَايَةِ الْبُرْقَانِيْ عَنْ مُسْلِمٍ: لَوْعَلِمْتُ وَاللهِ يَارَسُوْلَ اللهِ إِنَّكَ تَسْتَمِعُ لِقِرَاءَتِيْ لَحَبَّرْتُهُ لَكَ تَحْبِيْراً.

Abū Mūsā ﷺ stated, "Allāh's Prophet ﷺ said to me, 'If only you had seen me this morning as I listened to your recitation [of the Qur'ān]! Surely, you have been granted a musical instrument from among the musical instruments of the family of Dāwūd!'"[319] This was related by Bukhārī, Muslim and Tirmidhī.[320] In the version related from al-Burqānī by Muslim, the following words are included: "By Allāh! Had I known that you were listening to my recitation, I would have inked it[321] for you in bold letters!"[322]

---

317 See ḥadīth [162] for details of his decision.

318 Tirmidhī: 3849

319 The Prophet Dāwūd ﷺ was famed as a lyricist and was the author of the *Zabūr*, or the Psalms of the Bible. YTD.

320 Bukhārī: 5048, Muslim: 793, Tirmidhī: 3855

321 The meaning here is that Abū Mūsā told the Prophet ﷺ that he would have beautified and embellished his recitation had he known that the Prophet ﷺ himself was listening to him. The verb used in Muslim's version is *h-b-r*, which means to beautify, to adorn, or to embellish language, speech, recitation, and even meaning. The word for ink, *hibr*, is derived from this root because the written word embellishes speech. While there is no reason for me to revert to this meaning in my translation, I have done so in recognition of the ink of the scholars and the blood of the martyrs. YTD.

322 Al-Burqānī's addition has been narrated by Abū Yaʿlā in his *Musnad*, as quoted in *Fatḥ al-Bārī*: 9:114

Questions: Perfecting Performance for Another

In order[323] to please a pious person or an elder, one's extra exertions may appear at first glance to be no more than posturing and hypocrisy. However, since the effort to please the pious or, for that matter, any believer is actually in itself an act of worship, then when this is coupled with another act of worship this can in no way be considered posturing when it is done with sincerity. The ḥadīth above clearly indicates approval for this. For some time, this uninformed one held the suspicion that perhaps it was not a good thing when people went to extra lengths to recite the Qur'ān beautifully when requested by others to recite it. Thank Allāh, the subtleties of this ḥadīth have found their way into my heart and put that suspicion to rest! Upon deeper consideration of this ḥadīth, another virtue of the pious may be ascertained. For, indeed, to seek their pleasure is like seeking the pleasure of the Almighty. The reason for this is that their pleasure is actually a means to the pleasure of the Almighty. In other words, what is really being sought by the aspirant is the pleasure of the Almighty. The relevant maxim here is: Effort expended along the way is effort expended toward achieving the objective.

ḤADĪTH 196

عَنْ أَنَسِ بْنِ مَالِكٍ رَضِيَ اللهُ عَنْهُ قَالَ: قَالَ رَسُوْلُ اللهِ صَلَّى اللهُ عَلَيْهِ وَسَلَّمَ: «كَمْ مِنْ أَشْعَثَ أَغْبَرَ ذِيْ طِمْرَيْنِ لَا يُؤْبَهُ لَهُ، لَوْ أَقْسَمَ عَلَى اللهِ لَأَبَرَّهُ، مِنْهُمُ الْبَرَاءُ بْنُ مَالِكٍ».

(أخرجه الترمذي)

Anas ibn Mālik ﷺ stated that Allāh's Prophet ﷺ said, "How many people are there with dishevelled hair, and covered in dust, who possess no more than the clothes on their backs so that no one takes notice of them; yet if they swear something by Allāh, the Almighty will bring it to pass. Among such people is al-Barā' ibn Mālik ﷺ." This was related by Tirmidhī.[324]

Virtues: Allāh's Acceptance of the Pious

This ḥadīth clearly points to Allāh's ﷻ acceptance of those who dedicate their lives to the pleasure of the Almighty. The initial description, dusty and dishevelled, should not be understood as conditional, as certain ignorant ones would have us believe. Rather, what the ḥadīth expresses is that appearance has nothing

---

323 I have abbreviated this heading. The original Persian reads: How Perfecting the Performance of an Act (of Devotion) in Order to Please the Pious is not posturing. YTD.

324 Tirmidhī: 3854

to do with spiritual perfection. It is the wealthy and the prideful who would have us believe that the poor are somehow less than we are.

ḤADĪTH 197

عَنْ أَبِي هُرَيْرَةَ رَضِيَ اللهُ عَنْهُ قَالَ: قُلْتُ: يَا رَسُوْلَ اللهِ! أَسْمَعُ مِنْكَ أَشْيَاءَ فَلاَ أَحْفَظُهَا فَقَالَ: «ابْسُطْ رِدَاءَكَ» فَبَسَطتُّهُ فَحَدَّثَنِيْ حَدِيْثاً كَثِيْراً فَمَا نَسِيْتُ شَيْئاً حَدَّثَنِيْ بِهِ. (أخرجه الشيخان والترمذي وهذا لفظه)

Abū Huraira ﷺ stated, "I said, 'O Allāh's Prophet! I hear you say many things, but I do not remember them.' He replied, 'Spread your cloak.' So I spread it open. Then he related many things to me and I forgot none of them!" This was related by Bukhārī and Muslim. It was also related by Tirmidhī, and these are the words of his version.[325]

ḤADĪTH 198

عَنْ عَامِرِ بْنِ سَعْدٍ عَنْ أَبِيْهِ رَضِيَ اللهُ عَنْهُ قَالَ: دَخَلَ رَسُوْلُ اللهِ صَلَّى اللهُ عَلَيْهِ وَسَلَّمَ مَسْجِدَ بَنِيْ مُعَاوِيَةَ، فَرَكَعَ فِيْهِ رَكْعَتَيْنِ وَصَلَّيْنَا مَعَهُ، وَدَعَا رَبَّهُ طَوِيْلاً، ثُمَّ انْصَرَفَ إِلَيْنَا فَقَالَ: «سَأَلْتُ رَبِّيْ ثَلثاً فَأَعْطَانِيْ اثْنَتَيْنِ وَمَنَعَنِيْ وَاحِدَةً، سَأَلْتُهُ أَنْ لاَيَهْلِكَ أُمَّتِيْ بِسَنَةٍ عَامَّةٍ فَأَعْطَانِيْهَا، وَسَأَلْتُهُ أَنْ لاَيَهْلِكَ أُمَّتِيْ بِالْغَرْقِ فَأَعْطَانِيْهَا، وَسَأَلْتُهُ أَنْ لا يَجْعَلَ بِأَسَهُم بَيْنَهُمْ فَمَنَعَنِيْهَا». (أخرجه مسلم)

ʿĀmir ibn Saʿd ﷺ related from his father who said, "The Prophet of Allāh ﷺ entered the masjid of Banū Muʿāwiyah and prayed two cycles, while we prayed with him. Then he a supplicated his Lord for a long time before getting up and coming over to us. He ﷺ then said, 'I asked my Lord for three things, and He granted me two of them and refused one. I asked Him not to destroy my *ummah* all at once in a general famine, and He granted me that. Then I asked Him not to destroy my *ummah* in a flood, and He granted me that. Then I asked Him not to set my *ummah* against itself,[326] and He refused to grant me that.'" This ḥadīth was related by Muslim.[327]

---

325 Bukhārī: 3648, Muslim: 2492, Tirmidhī: 3835

326 That is to say, in internal warfare and rebellion. YTD.

327 Muslim: 2890

Reform: The Possibility that the Prayers of the Spiritually Adept May Go Unanswered
This ḥadīth lays bare the folly of the belief that the prayers of the spiritually adept will always be answered. Such a conviction inevitably leads to excesses in practice and belief.

ḤADĪTH 199

عَنْ سَلْمَانَ الْفَارِسِيِّ رَضِيَ اللهُ عَنْهُ قَالَ: قَالَ رَسُوْلُ اللهِ صَلَّى اللهُ عَلَيْهِ وَسَلَّمَ: «لا تُبْغِضْنِيْ فَتُفَارِقَ دِيْنَكَ» فَقُلْتُ: وَكَيْفَ أُبْغِضُكَ يَارَسُوْلَ اللهِ! وَبِكَ هَدَانِيَ اللهُ، قَالَ: «تُبْغِضُ الْعَرَبَ فَتُبْغِضُنِيْ». (أخرجه الترمذي)

Salmān al-Fārisī ﷺ related that the Prophet of Allāh ﷺ said: "Do not hate me, for that will take you from your religion." So I [Salman] asked, "How could I hate you, O Prophet of God, when it was through you that God guided me?" He replied, "Hate the Arabs, and you will hate me." This was related by al-Tirmidhī.[328]

Miscellaneous: Showing Respect for the People of a Master's Homeland
Among the common customs of the Sufis is that they develop natural feelings of affection and respect for the people of their master's homeland, and that they treat them accordingly. This ḥadīth is indicative of the same fact. How well the poet expressed this:

People and places engage my affections but,
Lovers will love whatever they will, you see.

ḤADĪTH 200

عَنْ عُمَرَ رَضِيَ اللهُ عَنْهُ قَالَ: سَمِعْتُ رَسُوْلَ اللهِ صَلَّى اللهُ عَلَيْهِ وَسَلَّمَ: «يَأْتِي عَلَيْكُمْ أُوَيْسُ بْنُ عَامِرٍ» الحديث. وَفِيْهِ: «فَإِنْ اسْتَطَعْتَ أَنْ يَسْتَغْفِرَ لَكَ فَافْعَلْ». (أخرجه مسلم)

ʿUmar ﷺ stated that the Prophet of Allāh a said: "There will come to you one Uways ibn ʿĀmir. . ." In the same ḥadīth, he said, "If you can ask him to seek forgiveness for you, then do so." This was related by Muslim.[329]

328 Tirmidhī: 3927
329 Muslim: 2542

Questions: A Master's Deriving Benefit from One Less Accomplished

In the same way that the less accomplished may benefit from those more accomplished than themselves, the more accomplished may benefit from those less accomplished than themselves. In this ḥadīth, 'Umar ☙, who was a Companion of high standing was advised to seek to benefit in a particular way from Uways, who was of the successor generation. Similarly, a master will sometimes benefit from an aspirant, in terms of knowledge, or spiritual states, or character, or supplication. Therefore, no master should ever suppose himself superior in every respect to those around him.

ḤADĪTH 201

عَنِ الْمُسَيَّبِ بْنِ حُزْنٍ رَضِيَ اللهُ عَنْهُ وَأُنْزِلَ فِي أَبِيْ طَالِبٍ: ﴿إِنَّكَ لاَتَهْدِيْ مَنْ أَحْبَبْتَ وَلَكِنَّ الله يَهْدِيْ مَنْ يَّشَاءُ﴾ (أخرجه الشيخان والنسائي)

Al-Musayyab ibn Ḥazan ☙ stated that it was in regard to Abū Ṭālib that the verse was revealed: 'Verily, you guide not whom you love; but it is Allāh who guides whomsoever He wills.'[330] This ḥadīth was related by Bukhārī, Muslim and Nasā'ī.[331]

Reform: The Masters Cannot Necessarily Dispose of Affairs as they Choose

Many people mistakenly suppose that the masters are capable of disposing of their affairs in whatever way they wish. Some of these people go as far as supplicating the masters, both living and dead, in the same way that they supplicate the Almighty. This ḥadīth and the verse it mentions clearly refute such a notion.[332]

ḤADĪTH 202

عَنْ أَنَسٍ رَضِيَ اللهُ عَنْهُ قَالَ: قَالَ رَسُوْلُ اللهِ صَلَّى اللهُ عَلَيْهِ وَسَلَّمَ: «إِنَّ أُحُداً جَبَلٌ يُحِبُّنَا وَنُحِبُّهُ». (أخرجه الثلثة والترمذي)

Anas ☙ stated that the Prophet of Allāh ☙ said, "Verily, 'Uḥud is a mountain that loves us; and we love it!" This was related by Abū Dāwūd, Nasa'ī, Ibn Mājah and Tirmidhī.[333]

---

330 Al-Qur'an, 28:56

331 Bukhārī: 4772, Muslim: 24, Nasā'ī: 2037

332 Obviously, such supplication is akin to according to others attributes that reside exclusively with the Divine. This is also known as *shirk*, and is the most overt kind of disbelief possible. YTD.

333 Bukhārī: 4083, Muslim: 1393, Tirmidhī: 3922, Ibn Mājah: 3115. A report with these words could not

Question: Sense Perception on the Part of Inanimate Objects

As there is nothing in the text to indicate that other than the literal meaning is intended here, the words "that loves us" should be understood as meaning just that. As an issue related to spiritual perception, we may deduce that inanimate objects can sense things since love is based on sensing, in the same way that, "and we love it," is by consensus to be understood literally. Finally, this is an issue for conjecture and not to be taken as a core belief or an article of faith.

ḤADĪTH 203

عَنْ أَبِي هُرَيْرَةَ رَضِيَ اللهُ عَنْهُ قَالَ: قَالَ رَسُوْلُ اللهِ صَلَّى اللهُ عَلَيْهِ وَسَلَّمَ: «قال الله تعالى: مَنْ عَادَى لِي وَلِيًّا فَقَدْ اذَنْتُهُ بِالْحَرْبِ، وَمَا تَقَرَّبَ إِلَيَّ عَبْدِيْ بِشَيْءٍ أَحَبَّ إِلَيَّ مِنْ أَدَاءِ مَا افْتَرَضْتُ عَلَيْهِ، وَلاَيَزَالُ عَبْدِيْ يَتَقَرَّبُ إِلَيَّ بِالنَّوَافِلِ حَتَّى أُحِبَّهُ، فَإِذَا أَحْبَبْتُهُ كُنْتُ سَمْعَهُ الَّذِيْ يَسْمَعُ بِهِ، وَبَصَرَهُ الَّذِيْ يُبْصِرُ بِهِ، وَيَدَهُ الَّتِيْ يَبْطُشُ بِهَا، وَرِجْلُهُ الَّتِيْ يَمْشِيْ بِهَا» الحديث. (أخرجه البخاري)

Abū Huraira ☙ related that the Prophet of Allāh a said that God Almighty u stated, "Whosoever acts with enmity toward those who are close to Me, I will declare war upon that person! Nothing that My servant does to gain proximity to Me is more loved by Me than his performing the things I have commanded [him to perform]. Indeed, as he continues to seek My favour through the performance of supererogatory acts of worship, I will eventually come to love him. Then, when I love him, I become the ears with which he hears, the eyes with which he sees, the hand with which he strikes, and the feet with which he walks." This ḥadīth was related by Bukhārī.[334]

Virtues: The Rank of the Sufi

This ḥadīth clearly indicates the rank of the Sufis.

Questions: Protection from Sin

It is a well-known article of faith that the prophets are free of sin while the saints [those most devoted to God] are protected from the same. The words of the ḥadīth, even in translation, are meant to convey this meaning.

---

be found in Abū Dāwūd.

334 Bukhārī: 6502

ḤADĪTH 204

عَنِ ابْنِ عَبَّاسٍ رَضِيَ اللهُ عَنْهُ قَالَ: قَالَ رَسُوْلُ اللهِ صَلَّى اللهُ عَلَيْهِ وَسَلَّمَ: «أَتَانِيْ اللَّيْلَةَ اتٍ مِنْ رَبِّيْ» وَفِيْ رِوَايَةٍ: «أَتَانِيْ رَبِّيْ فِيْ أَحْسَنِ صُوْرَةٍ». الحديث. (أخرجه الترمذي)

Ibn ʿAbbās g related that the Prophet of Allāh a said, "One night, a presence from my Lord presented itself. . ." In another version of the ḥadīth, he said, "My Lord presented Himself. . . in the most excellent form." This was related by Tirmidhī.[335]

Explanations: The Appearance of the Almighty in Creation without Indwelling and the Meaning of Unification

In Sufi literature the two expressions in the (above) title indicate special terminology. The reality of the first term is that the form and characteristics of the Almighty ﷻ will sometimes appear in creation without actually being present, in the same way that a writer may be present in his writings, or a speaker in his speeches. In this manner, creation may be thought of as the manifestation and the Almighty ﷻ may be thought of as the Manifestor. The reality of the second term is that there is such a powerful connection between the Manifestor and the manifestation that it is impossible to differentiate between the two. Both of these terms (and the issues that surround them) are based on reason (as opposed to revelation). Even so, the expressions (used to allude to these terms) are disconcerting to a degree. After the meaning of the terms has been explained, however, it should become clear following careful consideration that the ḥadīth may indeed indicate the same. Therefore, "a presence from my Lord" may be understood to correspond with the first term, while "My Lord presented Himself" may be understood to correspond with the second. Also, if the preposition "from" is understood to be exclusive,[336] then the words "in the most excellent form" may likewise be understood as indicative of the second term because in the confusion over the separated form[337] it becomes necessary to call the unmanifested a manifestation. In this manner, a syntactical connection comes about between the unmanifested and the manifestation. Furthermore, if the two versions of the ḥadīth are to be understood as two different events, it is still possible[338] to deduce the same meaning from "in the most excellent form". It must be noted, however,

335 Tirmidhī: 3233

336 أي من تجريدية i.e. such that the presence could only have come from the Lord. YTD.

337 The separated form is the presence of the Lord presenting itself, whereas the direct form is that of the Lord presenting Himself. YTD.

338 i.e. owing to the strength of the connection. YTD.

that it is not correct to assign the words "manifestation" and "unification" literal meanings, in the way that many of the ignorant public insist on doing, thus corrupting their beliefs. I have written on these matters in detail in my *Kalīd-i-Mathnawī* (commentary on Rūmī's Mathnawī).

ḤADĪTH 205

عَنْ أَبِيْ هُرَيْرَةَ رَضِيَ اللهُ عَنْهُ قَالَ: قَالَ رَسُوْلُ اللهِ صَلَّى اللهُ عَلَيْهِ وَسَلَّمَ: «يَقُوْلُ اللهُ عَزَّوَجَلَّ يَوْمَ الْقِيمَةِ مَرِضْتُ فَلَمْ تَعُدْنِيْ، فَيَقُوْلُ: يَارَبِّ! كَيْفَ أَعُوْدُكَ وَأَنْتَ رَبُّ الْعلَمِيْنَ؟ قَالَ: أَمَا عَلِمْتَ أَنَّ عَبْدِيْ فُلاناً مَرِضَ فَلَمْ تَعُدْهُ، أَمَا عَلِمْتَ أَنَّكَ لَوْ عُدْتَّهُ لَوَجَدْتَنِيْ عِنْدَهُ، ثُمَّ ذَكَرَ الاسْتِطْعَامَ وَالاسْتِسْقَاءَ كَذلِكَ وَفِيْهِمَا: «لَوَجَدْتُ ذلِكَ عِنْدَيْ». (أخرجه مسلم)

Abū Huraira رضي الله عنه related that the Prophet of Allāh ﷺ said that on the Day of Judgment, the Almighty ﷻ will say to certain people, "I was ill and you did not come to visit Me." When the people reply, "But, O Lord! How could I visit You, when You are the Lord of the Worlds?" The Lord will say, "Did you not know that My servant, so-and-so, was ill? Yet you did not visit him. Had you gone to visit him, you might have found Me with him." Then the same questions will be asked in relation to food and drink.[339] This was related by Muslim.[340]

Explanations: "Unification" with the Aforementioned Meaning

In the previous ḥadīth an explanation of (the term linked to) this expression was given. In this ḥadīth, when the Lord refers to His servant's illness as His own, "I was ill. . ." the meaning of that term is clarified even further. Moreover, if the sick person is understood to be a particularly favoured servant of the Lord, then the meaning of the ḥadīth supports the well known teaching of the Sufis that sometimes this sort of unification is afforded to certain of the Almighty's special servants and devotees. The words in the ḥadīth, ". . .you might have found Me with him," are also recorded in other versions of the ḥadīth to say: ". . .you might have found the same with Me." Actually, the second version is an explanation of the first, in that it offers a warning that such expressions are metaphorical

339 The Lord will say that the person did not feed Him, and so on, and that the person did not give Him anything to drink, with the same explanation of how this could be possible. YTD.

340 Muslim: 2569

in nature and should not be taken literally because a literal interpretation will lead to faulty beliefs. I have alluded to the same thing in my commentary on the previous ḥadīth [204].

ḤADĪTH 206

عَنْ أَبِي هُرَيْرَةَ رَضِيَ اللهُ عَنْهُ فِيْ حَدِيْثِ: سَبْعَةٌ يُظِلُّهُمُ اللهُ قَالَ رَسُوْلُ اللهِ صَلَّى اللهُ عَلَيْهِ وَسَلَّمَ: «وَرَجُلانِ تَحَابَّا فِيْ اللهِ اجْتَمَعَا عَلَى ذلِكَ وَتَفَرَّقَا عَلَيْهِ». (أخرجه الستة إلا أبا داؤد)

Abū Huraira ﷺ related, in the ḥadīth about the seven people who would be shaded by the Almighty ﷻ on the Day of Judgment, that the Prophet of Allāh ﷺ said, ". . . and two people who love one another for the sake of Allāh, who came together because of Him and who depart because of Him." This was related in each of the Six Most Authentic collections, save that of Abū Dāwūd.[341]

Virtues: Brothers on the Way

While the love between a master and an aspirant may certainly be of this nature, the love between two aspirants is an even better fit for this ḥadīth.

ḤADĪTH 207

عَنْ عَاصِمِ الْأَحْوَلِ قَالَ: رَأَيْتُ قَدَحَ رَسُوْلِ اللهِ صَلَّى اللهُ عَلَيْهِ وَسَلَّمَ عِنْدَ أَنَسِ بْنِ مَالِكٍ رَضِيَ اللهُ عَنْهُ، وَكَانَ قَدِ انْصَدَعَ فَسَلْسَلَهُ بِفِضَّةٍ، قَالَ ابْنُ سِيْرِيْنَ؟: وَقَدْ رَأَيْتُ ذلِكَ الْقَدَحَ وَكَانَ فِيْهِ حَلْقَةٌ مِنْ حَدِيْدٍ فَأَرَادَ أَنَسٌ أَنْ يَجْعَلَ مَكَانَهَا حَلْقَةً مِنْ فِضَّةٍ أَوْ ذَهَبٍ، فَقَالَ لَهُ أَبُوْطَلْحَةَ: لا تُغَيِّرَنَّ شَيْئًا صَنَعَهُ رَسُوْلُ اللهِ صَلَّى اللهُ عَلَيْهِ وَسَلَّمَ، فَتَرَكَهُ. (أخرجه البخاري)

ʿĀṣim al-Aḥwal stated: "I saw the drinking-cup of the Prophet ﷺ with Anas ibn Mālik ﷺ. It had rusted, so he plated it with silver." Ibn Sīrīn said, "I saw that drinking-cup, and it had a rim of iron.[342] So Anas ﷺ wanted to replace the rim with one of silver or gold. Abū Ṭalḥah ﷺ said, 'Do not

341 Bukhārī: 1423, Muslim: 1031, Tirmidhī: 2391, Nasā'ī: 5382, *Muwaṭṭa'*: pg. 377

342 Note here that the rim, the part that touches the lips, was not silver. YTD.

change anything that the Prophet of Allāh 🕮 did, and then left behind.'"
This was related by Bukhārī.[343]

Customs: Preserving Blessed Objects and Not Subjecting them to Alteration
Most Sufis observe this practice by preserving in their original state, to the extent
possible, whatever blessed objects they may possess. The showing of respect in
this manner is considered a matter of etiquette by the Sufis.

ḤADĪTH 208

عَنْ أَبِي سَعِيدٍ رَضِيَ اللهُ عَنْهُ قَالَ: قَالَ رَسُوْلُ اللهِ صَلَّى اللهُ عَلَيْهِ وَسَلَّمَ: «يُوْشِكُ أَنْ

يَكُوْنَ خَيْرَ مَالِ الْمُسْلِمِ غَنَمٌ يَتْبَعُ بِهَا شَعَفَ الْجِبَالِ، وَمَوَاقِعَ الْقَطْرِ، يَفِرُّ بِدِيْنِهِ مِنَ

الْفِتَنِ». (أخرجه البخاري ومالك وأبوداؤد والنسائي)

Abū Saʿīd 🕮 related that the Prophet of Allāh 🕮 said, "Soon [a time will
come when] the best wealth owned by a Muslim will be a herd of goats
with which he may dwell on the highest peaks of a mountain or the lowest
of river beds [so that he may] flee with his religion [intact] from contro-
versies." This was related by Bukhārī, Mālik, Abū Dāwūd and Nasāʾī.[344]

Usages: Benefits of Seclusion
Certain Sufis, when their circumstances require, will seek seclusion. The ḥadīth
above appears to give permission for such isolation, and even to encourage it
when society poses a threat to one's religion.[345]

Earning a Living and Seeking Spiritual Advancement are Not Mutually Exclusive
It should be clear that a herd of goats represents a means of living. Therefore, the
intended meaning of the ḥadīth should also be clear, even if many people suppose wealth and religion to be exclusive of each other.

ḤADĪTH 209

عَنِ ابْنِ عُمَرَ رَضِيَ اللهُ عَنْهُ قَالَ: كَانَ رَسُوْلُ اللهِ صَلَّى اللهُ عَلَيْهِ وَسَلَّمَ يُعْطِيْنِيْ الْعَطَاءَ

---

343 Bukhārī: 5637
344 Bukhārī: 19, Abū Dāwūd: 4267, Nasāʾī: 5039, Ibn Mājah: 3980, *Muwaṭṭaʾ*: pg. 382
345 The noted scholar of *taṣwwuf*, Abū Ḥāmid al-Ghazzālī, wrote a treatise on the *Virtues of Seclusion*.

فَأَقُوْلُ: أَعْطِهِ مَنْ هُوَ أَفْقَرَ إِلَيْهِ مِنِّيْ، فَيَقُوْلُ: «خُذْهُ وَمَا جَاءَكَ مِنْ هذَا الْمَالِ- وَأَنْتَ غَيْرُ مُشْرِفٍ وَلاسَائِلٍ - فَخُذْهُ فَتَمَوَّلَهُ، فَإِنْ شِئْتَ فَكُلْهُ وَإِنْ شِئْتَ فَتَصَدَّقْ بِهِ، وَمَا لا فَلا تُتْبِعْهُ نَفْسَكَ» قَالَ سَالِمٌ: فَلأَجْلِ ذٰلِكَ كَانَ عَبْدُ اللهِ رَضِيَ اللهُ عَنْهُ لايَسْأَلُ أَحَداً شَيْئًا وَلا يَرُدُّ شَيْأً أُعْطِيْهِ.(أخرجه البخاري ومسلم والنسائي)

Ibn ʿUmar ‌ said, "The Prophet of Allāh ‌ used to give me gifts, and I would say, 'Give this to someone who is in greater need of it than I.' But then the Prophet ‌ would reply, 'Take it, and whatever comes to you [as earnings] from it, so that you never covet [another's wealth] and you never ask [for financial help from another]. Take it and invest it. Then, if you like, eat from it and, if you like, give it away as charity. And never set your heart on what will not come your way.'" Then Sālim ‌ said, "It was for this reason that ʿAbdullāh [Ibn ʿUmar] never asked anyone for anything, and never returned any gift that was given to him." This ḥadīth was related by Bukhārī, Muslim and Nasāʾī.[346]

ḤADĪTH 210

عَنْ أَبِيْ سَعِيْدٍ الْخُدْرِيِّ رَضِيَ اللهُ عَنْهُ قَالَ: قَالَ رَسُوْلُ اللهِ صَلَّى اللهُ عَلَيْهِ وَسَلَّمَ: «يَأْتِيْ الدَّجَّالُ» الحديث. وَفِيْهِ: «فَيَقُوْلُ الدَّجَّالُ، أَرَأَيْتُمْ إِنْ قَتَلْتُ هذَا ثُمَّ أَحْيَيْتُهُ هَلْ تَشُكُوْنَ فِيْ الأَمْرِ فَيَقُوْلُوْنَ، لاَ، فَيَقْتُلُهُ ثُمَّ يُحْيِيْهِ» الحديث (أخرجه الشيخان)

Abū Saʿīd al-Khuḍrī ‌ related that the Prophet of Allāh ‌ said, "The Dajjāl will come. . ." And later in that ḥadīth, "The Dajjāl will say, 'Don't you see? If I kill this person and then revive him, will you still doubt me? And the people will say, "No." So he will kill someone and then revive him." This ḥadīth was related by Bukhārī and Muslim.[347]

Reform: Not Being Deceived by Seeming Miracles

Most people suppose seeming miracles to be signs of the godliness of those who perform them. This, however, is a serious mistake. Who could possibly be more lost than the Dajjāl? And what seeming miracle could be greater than reviving the dead? Yet, even though he will perform such a seeming miracle, no believer doubts that the Dajjāl has lost his way.

---

346 Bukhārī: 7164, Muslim: 1045

347 Bukhārī: 7132, Muslim: 2938

ḤADĪTH 211

عَنْ ابْنِ عُمَرَ رَضِيَ اللهُ عَنْهُ فِيْ قِصَّةِ ابْنِ صَيَّادٍ قَالَ رَسُوْلُ الله صَلَّى اللهُ عَلَيْهِ وَسَلَّمَ لَهُ: «مَاذَا تَرَي»؟ قَالَ: يَأْتِيْنِيْ صَادِقٌ وَكَاذِبٌ فَقَالَ صَلَّى اللهُ عَلَيْهِ وَسَلَّمَ: «خُلِّطَ عَلَيْكَ الأَمْرُ» ثُمَّ قَالَ لَهُ صَلَّى اللهُ عَلَيْهِ وَسَلَّمَ: «إِنِّيْ قَدْ خَبَأْتُ لَكَ خَبِيْئاً» فَقَالَ ابْنُ صَيَّادٍ: هُوَ الدُّخُّ فَقَالَ لَهُ رَسُوْلُ اللهِ صَلَّى اللهُ عَلَيْهِ وَسَلَّمَ: «اخْسَأْ، فَلَنْ تَعْدُوَ قَدْرَكَ». الحديث.

(أخرجه الخمسة إلا النسائي)

In telling the story of Ibn Ṣayyād[348], Ibn ʿUmar ﷺ related that the Prophet of Allāh ﷺ said to him [to Ibn Ṣayyād], "What do you see?" Then Ibn Ṣayyād replied, "Truthful ones come to me and liars." So the Prophet ﷺ said, "You are confused by the matter." Then the Prophet ﷺ said, "Can you tell me what I am thinking?"[349] So Ibn Ṣayyād replied, "It is smo. . ."[350] Then the Prophet ﷺ replied, "Away with you! You'll not surpass your station." This was related by Bukhārī, Muslim, Abū Dāwūd and Tirmidhī.[351]

Reform: Even the Deluded may Experience Visions and Insights

Like the preceding ḥadīth, the meaning to be deduced from this ḥadīth is that sometimes even the most deluded and disoriented of individuals may have spiritual insights and visions. Therefore, these must not be supposed to be signs of godliness. Instead, they may serve to mislead the naïve and trusting.

ḤADĪTH 212

عَنْ أَبِيْ هُرَيْرَةَ رَضِيَ اللهُ عَنْهُ قَالَ: قَالَ رَسُوْلُ اللهِ صَلَّى اللهُ عَلَيْهِ وَسَلَّمَ: «هَلْ سَمِعْتُمْ بِمَدِيْنَةٍ جَانِبٌ مِنْهَا فِيْ الْبَرِّ وَجَانِبٌ مِنْهَا فِيْ الْبَحْرِ»؟ قَالُوْا: نَعَمْ. قَالَ: «لاتَقُوْمُ السَّاعَةُ حَتّى يَغْزُوْهَا سَبْعُوْنَ أَلْفاً مِنْ بَنِيْ إِسْحَق، فَإِذَا جَائُوْهَا نَزَلُوْا، فَلَمْ يُقَاتِلُوْا بِسِلاحٍ وَلَمْ

348 Ibn Ṣayyād was well-known among the Arabs of the times as something of a mystic. According to the reports, he was rarely lucid. Even so, his occasional insights had brought him a degree of popularity among the commoners. YTD.

349 What he said, literally, was: "I have hidden something for you," challenging Ibn Ṣayyād to guess what it might be. Most commentators explain that the Prophet ﷺ was thinking of a verse from the Qur'ān: So await the day on which the skies will bring forth a pall of smoke. . . (44:10).

350 I have translated the half word, *dukh*, as smo, as *dukh* is a part of *dukhān* and smo is a part of smoke. YTD.

351 Bukhārī: 1354, Muslim: 2924, Abū Dāwūd: 4329, Tirmidhī: 2246

يَرْمُوْا بِسَهْمٍ، قَالُوْا: لا إِلَهَ إِلاَّ الله وَالله أَكبَرُ فَيَسْقُطُ أَحَدُ جَانِبَيْهَا الَّذِيْ فِي الْبَحْرِ، ثُمَّ يَقُوْلُوْنَ الثَّانِيَةَ لا إِلَهَ إِلاَّ الله وَالله أَكبَرُ فَيَسْقُطُ جَانِبُهَا الآخَرُ». الحديث (أخرجه مسلم)

Abū Huraira ﷺ related that the Prophet of Allāh ﷺ said, "Have you heard of a city, a part of which is on land and a part of which is on the sea?" They replied, "Yes." Then he ﷺ said, "The Day of Judgment will not come until that city has been attacked by seventy thousand warriors from the tribe of Isḥāq who, when they approach it, will neither fight with their weapons nor shoot their arrows. Rather, when they recite, 'There is no god but Allāh, and Allāh is the Greatest' the part of the city over the water will collapse; and when they again recite, 'There is no god but Allāh, and Allāh is the Greatest,' the part of the city on land will collapse." This was related by Muslim.[352]

Questions: The Occurrence of Miracles

Certain scholars with rationalist leanings deny the occurrence of miracles at the hands of God's special devotees. This ḥadīth tells of a patently evident miracle that is to occur at the hands of the tribe of Isḥāq.

ḤADĪTH 213

عَنْ عَلِيٍّ رَضِيَ اللهُ عَنْهُ قَالَ: قَالَ رَسُوْلُ اللهِ صَلَّى اللهُ عَلَيْهِ وَسَلَّمَ: «إِذَا فَعَلَتْ أُمَّتِيْ خَمْسَ عَشَرَةَ خَصْلَةً حَلَّ بِهَا الْبَلاَءُ»، وَفِيْهِ: «وَاتُّخِذَتِ الْقِيَانُ وَالْمَعَازِفُ» الحديث. (رواه الترمذي)

ʿAlī ﷺ related that the Prophet of Allāh ﷺ said, "When my community has committed fifteen kinds of sins, it will be subjected to calamity. . ." Among the sins mentioned were those related to, "singing girls and musical instruments." This was related by Tirmidhī.[353]

Reform: The Prohibition of Popular Singing and Dancing

Certain ignorant Sufis have gone so far in their love of music as to frequent sessions in which both women and instruments are employed. The ḥadīth clearly points to the prohibition of such things.

---

352 Muslim: 2920

353 Tirmidhī: 2210

ḤADĪTH 214

عَنِ النُّعْمَانِ بْنِ بَشِيْرٍ رَضِيَ اللهُ عَنْهُ قَالَ: قَالَ رَسُوْلُ اللهِ صَلَّى اللهُ عَلَيْهِ وَسَلَّمَ: «أَلاَ وَإِنَّ فِيْ الْجَسَدِ مُضْغَةً إِذَا صَلُحَتْ صَلُحَ الْجَسَدُ كُلُّهُ، وَإِذَا فَسَدَتْ فَسَدَ الْجَسَدُ كُلُّهُ، أَلاَ وَهِيَ الْقَلْبُ». (أخرجه الخمسة)

Nuʿmān ibn Bashīr related that the Prophet of Allāh said, "Verily, there is an organ within the body such that when it is sound, the entire body is sound; and when it is corrupt the entire body is corrupt. Verily, that organ is the heart." This was related by Bukhārī, Muslim, Tirmidhī, Nasā'ī and Abū Dāwūd.[354]

Miscellaneous: The Core of the Sufi Way

Success on the Sufi way is linked to rectification of the aspirant's heart. This ḥadīth explains why so much emphasis is given to this matter.

ḤADĪTH 215

عَنْ أَبِيْ مَسْعُوْدٍ الْبَدْرِيِّ رَضِيَ اللهُ عَنْهُ قَالَ: نَهى رَسُوْلُ اللهِ صَلَّى اللهُ عَلَيْهِ وَسَلَّمَ عَنْ ثَمَنِ الْكَلْبِ، وَمَهْرِ الْبَغْيِ، وَحُلْوَانِ الْكَاهِنِ. (أخرجه الستة)

Abū Masʿūd al-Badrī related that the Prophet of Allāh prohibited the proceeds from the sale of a dog, the bride price of an adultress, and the offerings made to a soothsayer. This was related by Bukhārī, Muslim, Abū Dāwūd, Nasā'ī, Tirmidhī and Ibn Mājah.[355]

Reform: Earning Money from Selling Charms

At the present time, many so-called Sufis are involved in these things. For example, they are lax about accepting offerings, even from women from the *bazaar*s (of questionable occupation), and they earn money by selling talismans and charms. This ḥadīth clearly states that these are blameworthy practices.

---

354 Bukhārī: 52, Muslim: 1599, Abū Dāwūd: 3329, Tirmidhi: 1205, Nasā'ī: 4458, Ibn Mājah: 3984

355 Bukhārī: 5761, Muslim: 1567, Abū Dāwūd: 3481, Tirmidhī: 1276, Nasā'ī: 4670, Ibn Mājah: 2159, *Muwaṭṭa'*: pg. 377

ḤADĪTH 216

عَنْ مَالِكٍ أَنَّهُ بَلَغَهُ أَنَّ ابْنَ مَسْعُوْدٍ رَضِيَ اللهُ عَنْهُ قَال : لايَزَالُ الْعَبْدُ يَكْذِبُ وَيَتَحَرَّى الْكَذِبَ فَيَنْكُتُ فِيْ قَلْبِهِ نُكْتَةٌ سَوْدَاءُ حَتَّى يَسْوَدَّ قَلْبُهُ. الحديث.(أخرجه مالك)

Mālik related that he had heard that Ibn Masʿūd ﷺ said, "The servant of God may lie or attempt to lie so that [every time he does so] a black mark is made on his heart; until finally his whole heart is blackened." This was related by Mālik.[356]

Sayings: Blackness of the Heart

Very often one may find in the works of the Sufi masters references to certain practices or other matters that will result in "blackening the heart." This ḥadīth may be taken as evidence for this sort of thing.

ḤADĪTH 217

عَنْ أَسْمَاءَ رَضِيَ الله عَنْهَا قَالَتْ: قَالَ رَسُوْلُ اللهِ صَلَّى اللهُ عَلَيْهِ وَسَلَّمَ: «الْمُتَشَبِّعُ بِمَا لَمْ يُعْطَ كَلابِسِ ثَوْبَيْ زُوْرٍ». (أخرجه الخمسة إلا الترمذي)

Asmā' ﷺ related that the Prophet of Allāh ﷺ said, "One who attempts to show oneself in possession of what one does not really possess is like one who wears two[357] false garments." This was related by Bukhārī, Muslim, Abū Dāwūd, Nasā'ī, and Tirmidhī.[358]

Reform: Pretending to be a Master by Appearing to be a Master

Since the words of the ḥadīth ". . .what one does not really possess" are general[359] they may be understood to include spiritual accomplishments. For this reason, the ḥadīth may be understood as critical of those who, despite their lack of spirit-

356 *Muwaṭṭa'*: pg. 388

357 The classical commentators point out that the reason for the dual here, i.e., "two false garments", may be to point out that the person is falsifying two circumstances; firstly that he has nothing (is bereft of spiritual accomplishments) and secondly that he is incapable of giving to others (is incapable of instructing others in the way of the spirit). Other commentators are more literal in their explanations, saying that the reference is to the two customary garments worn by Arabs at the time, the upper and the lower garments; signifying that such a person was false from head to toe. YTD.

358 Bukhārī: 5219, Muslim: 2129, Abū Dāwūd: 4997, Nasā'ī: 8921

359 The rule here, from theoretical jurisprudence (*uṣūl al-fiqh*), is that the words are general and therefore inclusive. Whereas, if they had been specific they would therefore be exclusive. In such instances, qualified commentators may include whatever they consider reasonable. YTD.

ual ability, persist in appearing to others by means of their speech or their actions as if they were the most accomplished of all spiritual masters. This is especially blameworthy when such people pretend that they are able to instruct others.

ḤADĪTH 218

عَنْ مُعَاذِ بْنِ أَنَسٍ رَضِيَ اللهُ عَنْهُ قَالَ: قَالَ رَسُوْلُ اللهِ صَلَّى اللهُ عَلَيْهِ وَسَلَّمَ: «مَنْ تَرَكَ اللِّبَاسَ تَوَاضُعاً وَهُوَ يَقْدِرُ عَلَيْهِ، دَعَاهُ اللهُ تَعَالَى يَوْمَ الْقِيمَةِ عَلَى رُؤُوْسِ الْخَلائِقِ حَتّى يُخَيِّرَهُ مِنْ أَيِّ حُلَلِ الإِيْمَانِ شَاءَ يَلْبَسُهَا». (أخرجه الترمذي)

Muʿādh ibn Anas ﷺ related that the Prophet of Allāh ﷺ said, "Anyone who, out of humility, shuns fine clothing when they have the ability to wear it will be called by the Almighty on the Day of Judgment before all of creation and given the opportunity to choose whatever garments of faith[360] they would like to wear." This ḥadīth was related by Tirmidhī.[361]

Usages: Intentional Lack of Attention to One's Appearance

The practice of the Sufi masters in this regard differs. Some paid no attention either way, neither to their appearance nor to their disregard of the same. On the other hand, the attention or disregard of some Sufi masters was clearly intentional. In all cases, the matter hinges on their intentions for, after all, "actions are but by intentions".

ḤADĪTH 219

عَنْ أَبِيْ زَمِيْلٍ قَالَ: حَدَّثَنِيْ ابْنُ عَبَّاسٍ رَضِيَ اللهُ عَنْهُ قَالَ: لَمَّا خَرَجَتِ الْحَرُوْرِيَّةُ أَتَيْتُ عَلِيًّا فَقَالَ: اِئْتِ هؤلاءِ الْقَوْمِ، فَلَبِسْتُ أَحْسَنَ مَايَكُوْنُ ثِيَابِيْ مِنْ حُلَلِ الْيَمَنِ فَلَقِيْتُهُمْ، فَقَالُوْا: مَرْحَباً بِكَ يَا ابْنَ عَبَّاسٍ! مَاهذِهِ الْحُلَّةُ؟ قُلْتُ: مَا تَعِيْبُوْنَ عَلَيَّ؟ لَقَدْ رَأَيْتُ عَلَى رَسُوْلِ اللهِ صَلَّى اللهُ عَلَيْهِ وَسَلَّمَ أَحْسَنَ مَايَكُوْنُ مِنَ الْحُلَلِ. (أخرجه أبوداؤد)

---

360 The "garments of faith" mentioned here are those that will be given in recompense for the degree of one's faith. Then, in the same way that faith differs in terms of how it is practised, likewise the garments of faith will also differ in quality. The person in the ḥadīth may not necessarily be deserving of the finest of these garments, owing to the quality of his faith. However, owing to his humility in regard to dress, he will be given the choice of the very best garments of faith in the next world. YTD.

361 Tirmidhī: 2481

Abū Zumayl related that Ibn ʿAbbās ﵁ said to him, "When the Harūrī tribe revolted, I went to ʿAlī ﵁ and he told me to go to them. So I dressed in the best of my Yemenite clothing and, when we met they said, 'Welcome, O son of ʿAbbās! What clothes are these?' So I replied, 'Don't find fault with me. For, verily, I have seen the Prophet of Allāh ﷺ wearing clothes even finer than these.'" This was related by Abū Dāwūd.[362]

Usages: Lack of Attention to One's Appearance

The explanation of this ḥadīth may be found in the explanation of the previous ḥadīth [218]. This ḥadīth is evidence for the usage mentioned there. No one should entertain the doubt that this ḥadīth supports the position that constant attention must be paid to one's appearance. This is because such attention would mean that a habit would have to be made of attending to one's appearance, and that is clearly not a good thing. If, however, a special occasion requires that a master pay special attention to his appearance then there is no harm in that. The actual practice of the Prophet ﷺ and his Companions was a lack of attention to their personal appearance; therefore the ḥadīth should be understood as indicating not disregard for their appearance but a lack of attention to such disregard.

ḤADĪTH 220

عَنْ أَبِيْ رِمْثَةَ رَضِيَ اللهُ عَنْهُ قَالَ: رَأَيْتُ عَلَى رَسُوْلِ اللهِ صَلَّى اللهُ عَلَيْهِ وَسَلَّمَ ثَوْبَيْنِ أَخْضَرَيْنِ. (أخرجه أصحاب السنن)

Abū Rimthah ﵁ related that he saw two green garments on the Prophet of Allāh ﷺ. This was related by Abū Dāwūd, Nasā'ī, Ibn Mājah and Tirmidhī.[363]

Usages: Wearing Clothing of the Same Colour

It is the regular practice of some Sufis to be dressed from head to toe in clothing of the same colour. Now, obviously, if they do this in order to show off, then it is blameworthy. On the other hand, if they do so out of some practical consideration, like if they find that clothing of one color or another shows less dirt and wears longer, then there is no problem with that.

362 Abū Dāwūd: 4037

363 Abū Dāwūd: 4065, Tirmidhī: 2812, Nasā'ī: 5321

ḤADĪTH 221

عَنْ أَبِيْ بُرْدَةَ رَضِيَ اللهُ عَنْهُ قَالَ: دَخَلْتُ عَلَى عَائِشَةَ رَضِيَ اللهُ تَعَالَى عَنْهَا فَأَخْرَجَتْ إِلَيْنَا كِسَاءً مُلَبَّداً وَإِزَاراً غَلِيْظاً، فَقَالَتْ: قُبِضَ رَسُوْلُ اللهِ صَلَّى اللهُ عَلَيْهِ وَسَلَّمَ فِيْ هذَيْنِ.

(أخرجه الخمسة إلا النسائي)

Abū Burda ﷺ said, "I went to see ʿA'ishah ﷺ, and she took out for us a rough blanket and a thick *izār*, saying, 'These are what the Prophet of Allāh ﷺ was wearing when he was taken.'" This was related by Bukhārī, Muslim, Tirmidhī and Abū Dāwūd.[364]

Usages: Wearing Wool

Some Sufis regularly wear woollen blankets. Indeed, it comes as no surprise to this insignificant one that some people say the name Sufi is derived from the word for wool, or *ṣūf*. Then, as long as this is done for reasons other than hypocrisy, this ḥadīth may be said to be the source for such a practice.

ḤADĪTH 222

عَنِ ابْنِ مَسْعُوْدٍ رَضِيَ اللهُ عَنْهُ قَالَ: قَالَ رَسُوْلُ اللهِ صَلَّى اللهُ عَلَيْهِ وَسَلَّمَ: «كَانَ عَلَى مُوْسى عَلَيْهِ السَّلَامُ يَوْمَ كَلَّمَهُ رَبُّهُ تَعَالى سَرَاوِيْلُ صُوْفٍ وَجُبَّةُ صُوْفٍ وَكِسَاءُ صُوْفٍ وَكُمَّةُ صُوْفٍ». الحديث (أخرجه الترمذي)

Ibn Masʿūd related that the Prophet of Allāh ﷺ said, "On the day that the Almighty spoke to Mūsā ﷺ he was wearing woollen trousers, a woollen *jubbah* [floor-length shirt], a woollen blanket and woollen sleeves." This was related by Tirmidhī.[365]

Usages: Wool

This ḥadīth, too, points in an ever more complete manner to what was mentioned in the commentary on the previous ḥadīth [121].

---

364 Bukhārī: 3108, Muslim: 2080, Abū Dāwūd: 4036, Tirmidhī: 1733

365 Tirmidhī: 1734

ḤADĪTH 223

عَنْ سَهْلِ بْنِ سَعْدٍ رَضِيَ اللهُ عَنْهُ أَنَّ عَلِيَّ بْنَ أَبِيْ طَالِبٍ رَضِيَ اللهُ عَنْهُ دَخَلَ عَلَى فَاطِمَةَ رَضِيَ اللهُ تَعَالَى عَنْهَا الحديث. وَفِيْهِ: وَقَالَتْ اِذْهَبْ إِلَى فُلانٍ الْيَهُوْدِيِّ فَاشْتَرِ بِهِ دَقِيْقاً، فَجَاءَهُ فَأَخَذَهُ الدَّقِيْقَ فَقَالَ لَهُ الْيَهُوْدِيُّ: أَنْتَ خَتَنُ هذَا الَّذِيْ يَزْعُمُ أَنَّهُ رَسُوْلُ اللهِ؟ قَالَ: نَعَمْ. قَالَ: فَخُذْ دِيْنَارَكَ وَلَكَ الدَّقِيْقُ. (أخرجه أبو داوٗد)

Sahl ibn Saʿd ﵁ related that ʿAlī ﵁ ibn Abī Ṭālib went to Fāṭima ﵂. . . In this ḥadīth, Fatima ﵂ told ʿAlī ﵁ to go to a certain Jewish merchant and buy flour from him. When ʿAlī ﵁ was buying the flour, the Jewish merchant asked him, "Are you not the son-in-law of the one who claims to be God's Prophet?" ʿAlī ﵁ replied, "Yes." Then the merchant said, "Then take your money. The flour is yours [for free]." This was related by Abū Dāwūd.[366]

Usages: Accepting Gifts and Favours from Disbelievers

Some of those critical of Sufism have objected that the masters are known to have accepted gifts and favours from non-Muslims. This ḥadīth shows that such objections are baseless. However, if such acceptance is linked to a corrupting factor, or if non-acceptance is linked to a good reason, then it will be better not to accept. Another point made clear by the ḥadīth is that if someone's reputation (as a master, for example) or someone's relationship with someone who has such a reputation leads to another's sincerely offering them a service or a favour, then there is no harm in their accepting because this will not place them in the position of "selling" their religion. However, if someone supposes that, owing to their own reputation or to their relationship with someone with such a reputation, they are deserving of favours, then that person is clearly guilty of hypocrisy and self-delusion.

ḤADĪTH 224

عَنْ عَائِشَةَ رَضِيَ اللهُ تَعَالَى عَنْهَا فِيْ قِصَّةِ عَهْدِ عُتْبَةَ إِلَى أَخِيْهِ سَعْدِ بْنِ أَبِيْ وَقَّاصٍ فِيْ ابْنِ وَلِيْدَةِ زَمْعَةَ فَنَظَرَ رَسُوْلُ اللهِ صَلَّى اللهُ عَلَيْهِ وَسَلَّمَ إِلَى شَبَهِهِ فَرَأَى شَبَهاً بَيِّناً بِعُتْبَةَ فَقَالَ: «هُوَ لَكَ يَا عَبْدَ بْنَ زَمْعَةَ، الْوَلَدُ لِلْفِرَاشِ وَلِلْعَاهِرِ الْحَجَرُ» ثُمَّ قَالَ لِسَوْدَةَ بِنْتِ زَمْعَةَ: «احْتَجِبِيْ مِنْهُ». الحديث (أخرجه الستة إلا الترمذي)

366 Abū Dāwūd: 1716

ʿĀ'isha 🙵 related an incident in which ʿUtbah [owing to his having had a son from an adulterous relationship with Zamʿah's slave girl] instructed his brother, Saʿd ibn Abī Waqqāṣ 🙵 to consider the child [in accordance with the pre-Islamic Arab custom] his nephew. [When Saʿd came to claim the child, Zamʿah's son, ʿAbd ibn Zamʿah, objected, saying that the boy was his brother and his father's son by the slave girl. When the matter was referred to the Prophet of Allāh 🙵 he noticed the strong resemblance between the boy and ʿUtbah. [Despite this circumstance, however,] he 🙵 said, "The boy is yours [i.e., your father's son and your brother], O ʿAbd ibn Zamʿah! For verily, a child belongs to its legitimate[367] parents." Thereafter, the Prophet 🙵 ordered Sawdah bint Zamʿah [his wife and the daughter of Zamʿah] to cover herself when the boy was present [even though, in accordance with the Prophet's 🙵 decision, the boy was technically her brother[368]]. This was related by Bukhārī, Muslim, Abū Dāwūd, Nasā'ī and Mālik.[369]

Usages: Avoiding for the Sake of Prudence What is Permitted
According to the Sharīʿa ruling, Sawdah 🙵 was permitted to appear before this boy without covering. However, as a matter of prudence, the Prophet 🙵 ruled that she cover herself. This clearly establishes the legitimacy of the practice of avoiding the lawful for the sake of prudence.[370] However, to do so without a good reason, or to turn the matter over to one of belief[371], will clearly be a form of religious extremism.

ḤADĪTH 225

عَنْ أَبِيْ هُرَيْرَةَ رَضِيَ اللهُ عَنْهُ قَالَ: رَأَى رَسُوْلُ اللهِ صَلَّى اللهُ عَلَيْهِ وَسَلَّمَ رَجُلاً يَتْبَعُ حَمَامَةً يَلْعَبُ بِهَا، فَقَالَ: «شَيْطَانٌ يَتْبَعُ شَيْطَانَةً» (أخرجه أبو داؤد)

---

367 The legitimacy of the relationship between owner and slave was accorded precedence over the adulterous relationship. YTD.

368 If the boy was in fact her brother, then it would not have been necessary for Sawdah to cover herself in his presence. However, despite the Prophet's ruling that Zamʿah was the boy's legal father, and that the boy was therefore Sawdah's legal brother, it was obvious that ʿUtbah was the boy's birth father. This is why the Prophet 🙵 took the precaution to ask Sawdah to cover herself in his presence. YTD.

369 Bukhārī: 2053, Muslim: 1457, Abū Dāwūd: 2273, Nasā'ī: 3514, Ibn Mājah: 2004, *Muwaṭṭa'*: pg. 309

370 Indeed, one of the better known Islamic legal axioms is *sadd al-dharāiʿ* or obstruction of ostensibly legitimate means for illegitimate ends. YTD.

371 In other words, to make covering under those circumstances into a matter of faith is extremism. To cover, however, simply as a matter of prudence is a different matter entirely. It is the lack of appreciation for such subtleties that leads people into error. YTD.

Abū Huraira ﵁ related that the Prophet of Allāh ﷺ saw a man chasing after a pigeon and said, "There goes a devil, chasing after another devil." This was related by Abū Dāwūd.[372]

Sayings: Whatever Takes You from Remembrance of the Almighty is Your Devil

Among the Sufis, this is a well-known teaching. In this ḥadīth, the pigeon is referred to as a devil only because the man chasing it had forgotten about everything else, including the Almighty ﷻ.[373]

ḤADĪTH 226

عَنْ أَبِي هُرَيْرَةَ رَضِيَ اللهُ عَنْهُ قَالَ: قَالَ رَسُوْلُ اللهِ صَلَّى اللهُ عَلَيْهِ وَسَلَّمَ: «قَالَ الله تَعَالى: يُؤْذِيْنِي ابْنُ آدَمَ يَسُبُّ الدَّهْرَ وَأَنَا الدَّهْرُ، بِيَدِيَ الْأَمْرُ أُقَلِّبُ اللَّيْلَ وَالنَّهَارَ». (أخرجه الثلثة وأبو داؤد)

Abū Huraira ﵁ related that the Prophet of Allāh ﷺ stated that the Almighty ﷻ says: "The sons of Adam distress Me! They curse fortune, but I am fortune! In My hands I hold the command [for all that happens]; I turn night into day."[374] This was related by Bukhārī, Muslim, Mālik and Abū Dāwūd.[375]

Interpretations: All is He

Obviously, the Almighty and time are not the same thing. Despite this lack of unity, however, according to the explanation given in this ḥadīth and its transla-

372 Abū Dāwūd: 4940. Ibn Mājah: 3765

373 Forgetting the Almighty ﷻ includes forgetting all of one's religious duties and responsibilities, whether toward one's Lord, or one's family, or one's community. Obviously, there is a difference between recreation and obsession; and this man was clearly an example of the latter. It is sad to note, however, that there is a popular notion that somehow pigeons and pigeon-keeping are incompatible with Islam. Much the same misconception exists in regard to dogs, owing to other ḥadīths. Clearly, if anything is to be learned from this account, it is in regard to how people sometimes lose their sense of perspective, and then ignore their responsibilities. To suppose, however, that the purpose of the ḥadīth is to point out that pigeons are evil is absurd. For an even-handed account of how the Prophet ﷺ viewed dogs, and valued their forms and characteristics, see Ibn Marzubān's *Tafḍīl al-Kilāb ʿalā kathīr min man labisa ath-thiyāb* (Preferring Canines Over Many of Those Who Wear Clothing). YTD.

374 Thus, when people curse fate, or fortune, they are actually cursing the Almighty ﷻ because it is the Almighty ﷻ Who determines the fate of everything in the universe. The Arabic word here, *dahr*, is used to mean fortune and fate because these things come with time and the original significance of the word is a long or indeterminate period of time or, in other words, an age. YTD.

375 Bukhārī: 7491, Muslim: 2246, Abū Dāwūd: 5274, *Muwaṭṭa'*: pg. 386

tion, a literal, superficial connection can be made between the two. According to experts, this explains how (in the popular Sufi saying that "All is He") "all" may be connected to "He". The meaning of "all" encompasses all things in addition to their deeds and the effects of those deeds, all of which is controlled by the Almighty. Thus, the One Who actually and in reality does the disposing, as an independent entity, is the Almighty and the Almighty Alone. So, "All" is really nothing at all (and "He" is everything). Thus, the ḥadīth may be offered as support for the popular Sufi saying that, "All is He." In other words, in the same way that the ḥadīth seeks to establish the Almighty as the determinant, and to negate any notion of fortune as a determinant, the Sufi saying establishes the independence of the Creator and negates the independence of the created, or creation.

ḤADĪTH 227

عَنْ أَبِي الطُّفَيْلِ رَضِيَ اللهُ عَنْهُ قَالَ: أَتى رَجُلٌ عَلِيَّ بْنَ أَبِيْ طَالِبٍ رَضِيَ اللهُ عَنْهُ فَقَالَ: مَاكَانَ رَسُوْلُ اللهِ صَلَّى اللهُ عَلَيْهِ وَسَلَّمَ يُسِرُّ إِلَيْكَ؟ فَغَضِبَ، وَقَالَ: مَاكَانَ يُسِرُّ إِلَيَّ شَيْئًا يَكْتُمُهُ النَّاسَ، غَيْرَ أَنَّهُ حَدَّثَنِيْ بِأَرْبَعِ كَلِمَاتٍ. قَالَ: مَا هُنَّ؟ قَالَ: لَعَنَ اللهُ تَعَالى مَنْ ذَبَحَ لِغَيْرِ اللهِ. الحديث (أخرجه مسلم والنسائي) وزاد رزين عن ابن عباس رَضِيَ اللهُ عَنْهُ: مَلْعُوْنٌ مَنْ صَدَّ أَعْمى عَنِ الطَّرِيْقِ.

Abū Ṭufayl related that a man went to ʿAlī ibn Abī Ṭālib and asked, "What secret matters did the Prophet of Allāh ﷺ tell you?" ʿAlī grew annoyed and replied, "The Prophet ﷺ never told me anything that he kept hidden from others. Even so, he did tell me four things." When the man asked what those were, ʿAlī replied, "Allāh will curse those who sacrifice animals to other than Him. . ." This was related by Muslim and Nasā'ī. At the end, Razīn added, in his version of the same ḥadīth, "Ibn ʿAbbās added, in his version, ". . .and cursed is the one who prevents the blind from finding their way."[376]

Reform: The Claim that the Knowledge of Sufism is Passed from Chest to Chest

Many ignorant folk seem to want to perpetuate the notion that knowledge of *taṣawwuf* was secretly passed to the Caliph ʿAlī and that the same has been

376 Muslim: 1978, Nasā'ī: 4427. Ibn ʿAbbās's addition is reported by Ibn ʿAdī in his *al-Kāmil*, under the entry of Zumayl ibn ʿAbbās.

passed on by similar means even until the present. The ḥadīth above clearly explains that this claim is baseless and without merit. The purpose of those who strive to establish this claim is to prove that there are certain matters that, although contrary to the Sharīʿa, are nonetheless permitted. Such an assertion is not only incorrect, but it borders on disbelief as well. The whispered conversation mentioned in ḥadīth [188] of this collection had to do with some practical matter, as there is nothing to indicate that it was related to *taṣawwuf*. The sort of thing that is passed from chest to chest is a spiritual relationship of the kind explained in ḥadīth [149]. Finally, it should be clear that the instructions passed to aspirants in confidence by Sufi masters are in no way contrary to the Sharīʿa. The confidential nature of such teachings is rather owing to the personalised approach taken by the master as explained in ḥadīth [4].

Reform: Sacrificing in the Name of Other than God

Among ignorant Sufis and their followers the practice of consecrating a pledge by sacrificing an animal is widespread. The prohibition against sacrificing animals in the name of other than Allāh ﷻ explains that such pledges are also prohibited because the prohibition of the first is general in meaning and therefore inclusive of the second. In addition, such pledges, though made in the name of Allāh, are actually performed to placate or influence others, as explained by the author of *ad-Durr al-Mukhtār* and other jurists. This is why the practice of consecrating pledges by sacrificing animals is clearly both blameworthy and akin to *shirk* or associating others with the Almighty.

Reform: Censure of Those Unqualified to be Masters

The ḥadīth openly states that those who prevent the blind from finding their way are accursed. It is also obvious that the way to the afterlife is more important than the highways and byways of the present life. Therefore, those blind to the way to the afterlife are in more need of guidance than those who are blind to the ways of the world.

The Almighty says: It is not their eyes that are blinded but blinded are the hearts in their chests.[377]

So, if people who prevent the blind from finding their way in the world are accursed, people who prevent others from finding their way to the afterlife are even more deserving of such a curse. Those whose claims to be spiritual guides or masters are false, or are made out of ignorance, or in order to deceive others, are clearly the subject of this curse. For such people, it is necessary that they repent.

---

377 Al-Qur'ān, 22:46

ḤADĪTH 228

عَنْ أَبِيْ هُرَيْرَةَ رَضِيَ اللهُ عَنْهُ قَالَ: قَالَ رَسُوْلُ اللهِ صَلَّى اللهُ عَلَيْهِ وَسَلَّمَ: «يَقُوْلُ اللهُ تَعَالَى يَا ابْنَ آدَمَ! تَفَرَّغْ لِعِبَادَتِيْ أَمْلأْ صَدْرَكَ غِنًى وَأَسُدَّ فَقْرَكَ، وَإِنْ لاتَفْعَلْ مَلأْتُ يَدَيْكَ شُغْلاً وَلَمْ أَسُدَّ فَقْرَكَ». (أخرجه الترمذي)

Abū Huraira ﷺ related that the Prophet of Allāh ﷺ stated that the Almighty ﷻ says, "O son of Adam! If you devote yourself to worshipping Me, I will fill your chest [to overflowing with wealth and virtue], and I will render you free from want. But if you do not do this I will fill your two hands to overflowing with toil, and I will not render you free from want." This was related by Tirmidhī.[378]

Usages: Abandoning Worldly Toil

It has ever been the way of the Sufis to eschew concern with worldly affairs, and it has ever been the complaint of their critics to label them unproductive and a burden on society. The above ḥadīth appears to indicate the virtue of what they do, though it should be pointed out that there are conditions to be satisfied, including ability, patience and the absence of subtle leaning of the heart [towards the world].

ḤADĪTH 229

عَنْ أَنَسٍ رَضِيَ اللهُ عَنْهُ قَالَ: قَالَ رَسُوْلُ اللهِ صَلَّى اللهُ عَلَيْهِ وَسَلَّمَ فِيْ حَدِيْثٍ طَوِيْلٍ: «وَمَا أَقْبَلَ عَبْدٌ عَلَى اللهِ بِقَلْبِهِ إِلاَّ جَعَلَ اللهُ قُلُوْبَ الْمُؤْمِنِيْنَ تَنْقَادُ إِلَيْهِ بِالْوُدِّ وَالرَّحْمَةِ، وَكَانَ اللهُ تَعَالَى بِكُلِّ خَيْرٍ إِلَيْهِ أَسْرَعَ». (أخرجه الترمذي)

Anas ﷺ related that the Prophet of Allāh ﷺ stated as part of a lengthy discourse, "No servant ever approaches the Almighty ﷻ in complete sincerity except that the Almighty ﷻ makes the hearts of the believers incline toward that person with love and caring; while Allāh ﷻ is the first to bring that person every manner of goodness." This was related by Tirmidhī.[379]

Miscellaneous: The Truth of Inner Relationships

There are two essential factors for the heart to become attached to Allāh ﷻ: con-

378 Tirmidhī: 2466, Ibn Mājah: 4107

379 Al-Haythamī has recorded this in his *Majmaʿ az-Zawāʾid*: 10/247

stant remembrance and constant obedience. Under most conditions, this may be said to be the essence of internal affinity (*nisbat-e-bāṭinī*). The ḥadīth above alludes to this affinity.

Virtues: In Praise of those Concerned with Internal Purification
This ḥadīth makes obvious reference to this phenomenon; and its effects are witnessed regularly.

ḤADĪTH 230

عَنْ عَلِيٍّ رَضِيَ اللهُ عَنْهُ أَنَّهُ قَالَ: لاخَيْرَ فِيْ قِرَاءَةٍ لَيْسَ فِيْهَا تَدَبُّرٌ وَلا عِبَادَةٍ لَيْسَ فِيْهَا فِقْهٌ. الحديث . (أخرجه رزين)

ʿAlī ﷺ related that: "There is no [real] benefit in recitation of the Qur'ān in which there is no reflection, nor in any act of worship in which there is no cognition."[380]

Commentary: The Need for Reflection and Cognition
The major focus of the path of Sufis is this very reflection and cognition. The need for this shows how necessary the path of the Sufis is.

ḤADĪTH 231

عَنْ مَالِكٍ أَنَّهُ بَلَغَهُ أَنَّ عِيسىَ بْنَ مَرْيَمَ عَلَيْهِ السَّلاَمُ قَالَ: لاتُكْثِرُوْا الْكَلامَ بِغَيْرِ ذِكْرِ اللهِ تَعَالى فَتَقْسُوَ قُلُوْبُكُمْ وَإِنَّ الْقَلْبَ الْقَاسِيْ بَعِيْدٌ مِنَ اللهِ تَعَالى وَلكِنْ لاتَعْلَمُوْنَ، وَلاتَنْظُرُوْا فِيْ ذُنُوْبِ النَّاسِ، وَانْظُرُوْا فِيْ ذُنُوْبِكُمْ كَأَنَّكُمْ عَبِيْدٌ، فَإِنَّمَا النَّاسُ مُبْتَلِيً وَمُعَافى فَارْحَمُوْا أَهْلَ الْبَلاءِ وَاحْمَدُوْا اللهَ تَعَالى عَلَيَ الْعَافِيَةِ. (أخرجه مالك)

Mālik related that ʿĪsā ibn Maryam ﷺ said: "Do not engage in excessive speech apart from the remembrance of Allāh or else your hearts will become hard [in other words, no humility will remain in them and this has been clearly experienced]. The heart that is hard is far from Allāh but you do not know this [that your hearts are gone far from Allāh. The reality of this will dawn upon you in the Hereafter. You may witness the effects of this in this world, but you do not perceive it because of inattention].

380 Ad-Daylamī has recorded this in his *al-Firdaws*: 1/135

Do not look at the sins of people as though you are masters, but look at your own sins as though you are slaves [in other words, it is the duty of the masters to look at the faults of their slaves, to put them right and to punish them. You are not masters, but slaves. And it is the duty of slaves to look at their own faults so that they can make up for them and set them right]. People are of two types: those who are put through trials and tribulations, and those who enjoy well-being. You should show mercy to those who are in trials and tribulations, and praise Allāh for the well-being. [Sin is a trial; you should therefore not despise or criticise a person who is sinning. You should advise him with affection or pray for him. To be protected from sin is a form of well-being. You should therefore not be proud and haughty over this. Rather, you should express your gratitude to Him after considering it to be a bounty of Allāh, which you received without being eligible for it.] This was related by Mālik.[381]

Commentary: Speaking Less and Humility
It is obvious that this ḥadīth makes reference to these characteristics which are praiseworthy. The merit of the path of the *ahl bāṭin* is also gauged from this because it is really their *modus operandi*.

ḤADĪTH 232

عَنْ أَنَسٍ رَضِيَ اللهُ عَنْهُ قَالَ: صَلَّى بِنَا رَسُوْلُ اللهِ صَلَّى اللهُ عَلَيْهِ وَسَلَّمَ يَوْماً، ثُمَّ رَقِيَ الْمِنْبَرَ وَأَشَارَ بِيَدِهِ قِبَلَ الْقِبْلَةِ، وَقَالَ: رَأَيْتُ الْآنَ مُنْذُ صَلَّيْتُ لَكُمُ الصَّلٰوةَ الْجَنَّةَ وَالنَّارَ مُمَثَّلَتَيْنِ فِيْ قِبَلِ هٰذَا الْجِدَارِ فَلَمْ أَرَ كَالْيَوْمِ فِي الْخَيْرِ وَالشَّرِّ. (أخرجه البخاري)

Anas ﷺ related that the Messenger of Allāh ﷺ led us in *ṣalāh* one day. He then climbed the pulpit, pointed with his hand towards the *qiblah*, and said: "While I was leading you in *ṣalah*, I was shown Paradise and the Hellfire, both projected before me on this wall. Never have I seen good and evil like today [because Paradise is the best of all good, and the Hellfire is the worst of all evil]. This was related by Bukhārī.[382]

Commentary: Affirmation of the World of Similitude
This is clearly affirmed from the apparent words of this ḥadīth. The essence of this world [of similitude] is mentioned in the *Mathnawī*.

381 *Muwaṭṭā'*: pg. 386
382 Bukhārī: 6468

ḤADITH 233

عَنْ أَبِيْ عَبْدِ اللهِ بْنِ أَبِيْ بَكْرٍ رَضِيَ اللهُ عَنْهُ أَنَّ أَبَا طَلْحَةَ الْأَنْصَارِيِّ رَضِيَ اللهُ عَنْهُ كَانَ
يُصَلِّيْ فِيْ حَائِطٍ لَهُ، فَطَارَ دِبْسِيٌّ فَطَفِقَ يَتَرَدَّدُ وَيَلْتَمِسُ مَخْرَجاً، فَأَعْجَبَ أَبَاطَلْحَةَ ذٰلِكَ،
فَتَبِعَهُ بَصَرُهُ سَاعَةً، ثُمَّ رَجَعَ إِلَى صَلاتِهِ فَإِذَا هُوَ لا يَدْرِيْ كَمْ صَلّي، فَقَالَ: لَقَدْ أَصَابَنِيْ
فِيْ مَالِيْ هٰذَا فِتْنَةٌ، فَجَاءَ إِلَى رَسُوْلِ اللهِ صَلَّى اللهُ عَلَيْهِ وَسَلَّمَ فَذَكَرَلَهُ الَّذِيْ أَصَابَهُ فِيْ
صَلاتِهِ فَقَالَ: يَا رَسُوْلَ اللهِ! هُوَ صَدَقَةٌ فَضَعْهُ حَيْثُ شِئْتَ. (أخرجه مالك)

Abū ʿAbdullāh ibn ʿAbī Bakr ؓ related that Abū Ṭalḥah al-Anṣārī ؓ was offering *ṣalah* in his orchard when a bird flew into the orchard. It began flying around looking for an exit but could not find one. Abū Ṭalḥah ؓ was pleased with this [fact that his orchard was so dense that a bird was finding it difficult to find a way out]. He followed it with his eyes for some time and then turned his attention back to his *ṣalah*. But he [had become so distracted that he] could not remember how many rakats he had offered. He thought to himself, saying: "This property of mine has put me into a great tribulation [for I could not concentrate in my *ṣalah*]." He went to the Messenger of Allāh ﷺ and informed him of what he experienced in his *ṣalah*. He said: "O Messenger of Allāh! I am giving this orchard away for the sake of Allāh. You may dispose of it as you like." This was related by Mālik.[383]

Commentary: The Practice of Surveillance of the Heart

Among the practices of the Sufis is to maintain constant vigilance over the heart, keeping it under surveillance to see what condition it is in. When they discern changes in its condition, they make appropriate adujstments. Gauged on the action of this Companion ؓ and the Messenger ﷺ considering it to be permissible, the acceptability of this practice becomes clear because his coming back to attention [in *ṣalah*] resulted from his vigilance (*murāqabah*).[384]

The Condition of Self-respect

To detest something which makes a person heedless of Allāh ﷻ is a commendable condition. This is known as *ghayrah* (self-respect). This ḥadīth affirms this condition.

---

383 *Muwaṭṭa'*: pg. 34

384 Also refered to as vigilance and contemplation, *muraqabah* is mentioned in ḥadīths 11, 37, and 52 of this translation. YTD.

Removing from One's Ownership Something which Distracts One from the Truth
Many well known stories are told of the pious who, when they saw a *ṭālib* (one who is in quest of Allāh) greatly attached to something, ordered him to divest himself of it. The present ḥadīth is the source of this treatment. This Companion ؓ thought of this treatment [for himself] and the Messenger of Allāh ﷺ affirmed it. The science of ḥadīth refers to this as a *taqrīr* (an affirmation made by the Messenger of Allāh ﷺ).

ḤADĪTH 234

عَنْ أَبِيْ الْعَبَّاسِ رَضِيَ اللهُ عَنْهُ قَالَ: سَمِعْتُ عُمَرَ رَضِيَ اللهُ عَنْهُ يَقُوْلُ: سَمِعْتُ رَسُوْلَ اللهِ صَلَّى اللهُ عَلَيْهِ وَسَلَّمَ يَقُوْلُ: «لاتَطْرُوْنِيْ كَمَا أَطَرَتِ النَّصَارى ابْنَ مَرْيَمَ؛ فَإِنَّمَا أَنَا عَبْدٌ، فَقُوْلُوْا: عَبْدُ اللهِ وَرَسُوْلُهُ». (أخرجه البخاري)

Ibn ʿAbbās ؓ related that he heard ʿUmar ؓ say: I heard the Messenger of Allāh ﷺ saying: "Do not elevate me as the Christians elevated the son of Maryam [by claiming that he is a god or the son of God]. I am merely a servant. So refer to me as the servant and Messenger of Allāh. [Because all of my virtues and merits are included in this. When enumerating my virtues and merits, it is necessary to confine yourselves to these qualities. Anything beyond this belongs to the rank of divinity, and that is not lawful for me]." Bukhārī reported it.[385]

Commentary: Abstaining from Excesses in Praising One's Sheikh
It is learnt from this ḥadīth that one should not go to excesses in praising one's sheikh or any other pious personality to the extent that one reaches the limit of lies or polytheism. If such excesses are prohibited vis-à-vis a prophet, how can they be permitted for a (close friend of Allāh)?

ḤADĪTH 235

عَنْ أَبِيْ بَكْرٍ رَضِيَ اللهُ عَنْهُ قَالَ: قَالَ رَسُوْلُ اللهِ صَلَّى اللهُ عَلَيْهِ وَسَلَّمَ: «مَنْ كَانَ مَادِحاً أَخَاهُ لامَحَالَةَ فَلْيَقُلْ: أَحْسِبُ فُلاناً وَاللهُ حَسِيْبُهُ، وَلايُزَكِّيْ عَلَى اللهِ أَحَداً أَحْسِبُ فُلاناً كَذَا وَكَذَا إِنْ كَانَ يَعْلَمُ مِنْهُ ذلِكَ». (أخرجه الشيخان وأبو داؤد)

385 Bukhārī: 3445

Abū Bakr ﷺ related that the Messenger of Allāh ﷺ said: "If it is essential for a person to praise his brother, he should say: 'I think that such and such person is like this. Apart from this, Allāh knows best.' He should not unduly praise anyone with Allāh. Even if he has to say: 'I think that such and such person is like this', the pre-condition is for the person to be really like that in his knowledge [or else, he cannot even praise him in this manner]." This was related by Bukhārī, Muslim and Abū Dāwūd.[386]

Commentary: Abstaining from Labelling Someone as a Walī without Certainty
It is gauged from the general nature of this ḥadīth that it is absolutely forbidden to refer to a person as a *walī* without any proof, based merely on assumption. Most people are not cautious in this regard. However, there is nothing wrong if it is said by way of thinking the person to be so. It is better for the person to expressly state his thoughts. But even if he does not expressly state them on the basis of the circumstances or the context of his speech, there is nothing wrong in this. Yes, to refer to a person as a sheikh is permissible even if said with certainty. The reason for this is that it is a matter which is witnessed. In other words, his knowledge of training and educating. On the contrary, referring to someone as a *walī*—that is, being accepted in the sight of Allāh ﷻ—this is related to the Unseen.

ḤADĪTH 236

عَنْ أُسَيْدِ بْنِ حُضَيْرٍ رَضِيَ اللهُ عَنْهُ أَنَّ رَجُلاً مِنَ الْأَنْصَارِ كَانَ فِيْهِ مِزَاحٌ، فَبَيْنَمَا هُوَ يُحَدِّثُ الْقَوْمَ وَيُضْحِكُهُمْ إِذْ طَعَنَهُ النَّبِيُّ صَلَّى اللهُ عَلَيْهِ وَسَلَّمَ فِيْ خَاصِرَتِهِ بِعُوْدٍ كَانَ فِيْ يَدِهِ، فَقَالَ: أَصْبِرْنِيْ يَا رَسُوْلَ اللهِ! قَالَ: اصْطَبِرْ، فَقَالَ: إِنَّ عَلَيْكَ قَمِيْصاً وَلَيْسَ عَلَيَّ قَمِيْصٌ فَرَفَعَ النَّبِيُّ صَلَّى اللهُ عَلَيْهِ وَسَلَّمَ قَمِيْصَهُ فَاحْتَضَنَهُ وَجَعَلَ يُقَبِّلُ كَشْحَهُ وَقَالَ: إِنَّمَا أَرَدْتُ هذَا يَارَسُوْلَ اللهِ. (أخرجه أبو داؤد)

Usayd ibn Ḥuḍayr ﷺ related that a man from the Anṣār had a jovial temperament. One day, he was talking to some people and making them laugh. The Messenger of Allāh ﷺ jabbed him lightly with a stick which he had in his hand. The man said: "O Messenger of Allāh! You have to let me avenge this." He said: "You may take revenge." The man said: "You are wearing a shirt while I was not wearing a shirt [when you jabbed me]." The Messenger of Allāh ﷺ raised his shirt and the man embraced him

386 Bukhārī: 6061, Muslim: 3000, Abū Dāwūd: 4805, Ibn Mājah: 3744

and began kissing his waist. He said: "This is what I really wanted to do." This was related by Abū Dāwūd.[387]

Commentary: Joking does not Negate Perfection

Some people are under the mistaken impression that to attain *wilāyah* and *kamāl* (perfection) it is necessary for a person to have an absolutely emotionless heart and that he should have no human traits in him. It is clear from this ḥadīth that a balanced and cheerful disposition in speech or in action whereby the person does not belittle anyone nor hurt him does not negate perfection and piety. This is especially so when the purpose is to cheer someone up or, more than this, to make the person feel at ease so that he may be able to ask something about Islam openly [and without hesitation]. In such a situation, it [this joking and light-heartedness] will become an act of worship.

In a dream, I gave this reply to a European queen with whom I saw myself riding in a vehicle. The queen voiced an objection to the Prophet's prophethood ﷺ on the basis that he used to joke [with people] whereas joking negates dignity, and dignity is one of the intrinsic requisites of prophethood. She said: "There is no doubt about the authenticity of Islam apart from this [quality of joking of his]." When I shared the [above-mentioned] wisdom with her, she remained silent and accepted [what I said]. Thereafter, when I awoke, I learned through certain indications that the queen had probably embraced Islam in her heart.

We also learn from this ḥadīth that although it is necessary for the aspirant *murīd* to be extremely respectful of his sheikh, if he sees that the sheikh himself is in a jovial mood, he should emulate him because this is what respect demands at such a time.

Kissing the Body of the Sheikh

It is also obvious from this ḥadīth that there is nothing wrong with a person kissing the hands, feet, forehead, etc. of one's sheikh. However, one should not transgress the limits of the Sharīʿa in this regard.

ḤADĪTH 237

عَنْ عَائِشَةَ رَضِيَ اللهُ تَعَالَى عَنْهَا قَالَتْ: لَمَّا أَرَادُوْا غُسْلَ النَّبِيِّ صَلَّى اللهُ عَلَيْهِ وَسَلَّمَ قَالُوْا: وَ اللهِ لا نَدْرِيْ أَنُجَرِّدُ رَسُوْلَ اللهِ صَلَّى اللهُ عَلَيْهِ وَسَلَّمَ مِنْ ثِيَابِهِ كَمَا نُجَرِّدُ مَوْتَانَا أَوْ نَغْسِلُهُ وَعَلَيْهِ ثِيَابُهُ، فَلَمَّا اخْتَلَفُوْا أَلْقَى اللهُ تَعَالَى عَلَيْهِمُ النَّوْمَ حَتَّى مَا مِنْهُمْ رَجُلٌ إِلاَّ

387 Abū Dāwūd: 5224

وَذَقَنُهُ فِيْ صَدْرِهِ فَكَلَّمَهُمْ مُكَلِّمٌ مِنْ نَاحِيَةِ الْبَيْتِ لَايَدْرُوْنَ مَنْ هُوَ أَنِ: اغْسِلُوْا رَسُوْلَ اللهِ صَلَّى اللهُ عَلَيْهِ وَسَلَّمَ وَعَلَيْهِ ثِيَابُهُ، فَقَامُوْا فَغَسَلُوْهُ وَعَلَيْهِ قَمِيْصُهُ يَصُبُّوْنَ الْمَاءَ فَوْقَ الْقَمِيْصِ وَيَدْلُكُوْنَهُ بِالْقَمِيْصِ دُوْنَ أَيْدِيْهِمْ. (أخرجه أبو داؤد)

ʿĀ'isha ﵂ related that: When the people intended bathing the Messenger of Allāh ﷺ [after his demise], they said: "By Allāh, we do not know whether we should remove the clothes of the Messenger of Allāh ﷺ as we remove the clothes of our deceased or should we bathe him with his clothes on?" When they differed in this matter, Allāh caused them to fall asleep such that every single one of them had his chin touching his chest [because he was overcome by sleep]. Someone from the corner of the house addressed them—none knew who he was—saying: "Bathe the Messenger of Allāh ﷺ with his clothes on him." They got up and bathed him with his shirt on. They poured water over the shirt and rubbed his body together with the shirt, without their hands touching his actual body. This was related by Abū Dāwūd.[388]

Commentary: Unseen Speech

For an unseen voice to speak to a pious personality is also a praiseworthy condition. This is confirmed from this ḥadīth.

Acting on the Indication of an Unseen Voice Provided it is not Against the Sharīʿa

There is widespread agreement among the masters that it is lawful to act on the indication of an unseen voice provided it says or asks nothing contrary to the Sharīʿa. This is what was done in this incident: there was nothing to indicate that it is impermissible to bathe the deceased with his shirt on. [The Companions] therefore acted on the advice of the unseen voice. What if someone were to ask if it made any special difference if this order was obtained even before this inspiration and unseen voice? The reply is that it is learnt from the guidelines of the pious that through this inspiration or unseen voice, this specific order becomes a bit more emphasised for the person who was inspired. It does not mean that if they act against it, it will be harmful in the Hereafter. If any legal proof is attached to further emphasise the act, then the legal emphasis is obvious. By pondering over this incident we can say that through this [unseen] speech, the difference of opinion was removed. Moreover, since the consensus (*ijmāʿ*) of the Companions is a legal proof in itself, it may be said that no other opinion in this case is lawful.

388 Abū Dāwūd: 3141

ḤADĪTH 238

عَنْ أَسْمَاءَ بِنْتِ يَزِيْدَ رَضِيَ اللهُ تَعَالَى عَنْهَا قَالَتْ: قَالَتِ امْرَأَةٌ مِنَ النِّسْوَةِ: مَا هٰذَا الْمَعْرُوْفُ الَّذِيْ لا يَنْبَغِيْ لَنَا أَنْ نَعْصِيَكَ فِيْهِ يَا رَسُوْلَ اللهِ؟ فَقَالَ: لا تَنُحْنَ قَالَتْ: يَا رَسُوْلَ اللهِ! إِنَّ بَنِيْ فُلانٍ كَانُوْا قَدْ أَسْعَدُوْنِيْ عَلَى عَمِّيْ فَلا بُدَّ مِنْ قَضَاءِهِنَّ، فَأَبَى عَلَيْهَا فَعَاوَدَتْهُ مِرَاراً، قَالَتْ: فَأَذِنَ لِيْ فِيْ قَضَاءِهِنَّ فَلَمْ أَنُحْ بَعْدَ قَضَاءِهِنَّ وَلا فِيْ غَيْرِهِ حَتّى السَّاعَةِ. (أخرجه الترمذي)

Asmā' bint Yazīd ﷺ related that a woman asked: "O Messenger of Allāh! What is the good deed regarding which it is not permissible for us to disobey you?" He replied: "You must abstain from wailing [over the deceased]." She said: "O Messenger of Allāh! A certain family came and helped me [and wailed with me] when my uncle passed away. Now I have to pay them back [so permit me to perform this wailing one more time and I will not do it anymore]." But he refused. She made this request several times. The woman said: "He eventually permitted me to pay them back. Even so, I have not performed this wailing in repayment nor have I performed it for anyone else since then." This was related by Tirmidhī.[389]

Commentary:

The point established by ḥadīth [166] is established here as well. The most probable reason for the Messenger of Allāh ﷺ granting permission to "wail" just once is so that, once over, the person may not ever have to go back on his or her determination to repent. It may be noticed that the masters will sometimes give permission for impermissible employment or something similar when in actual fact permission is not their objective. Rather, by doing so, they intend to spare the person from a greater evil. As the wise men said:

مَنِ ابْتُلِيَ بِبَلِيَّتَيْنِ فَلْيَخْتَرْ أَهْوَنَهُمَا

The person who is compelled into making a choice between two evils should choose the lighter of the two.

This is especially so when some temperaments are such that when they are prohibited, they display weakness. And when they abstain, they lose courage and feel constricted. But when they are permitted, they feel energetic and free, and their temperament develops the strength and courage to give up evil. In such a situation permission becomes a matter of externals, while prohibition is an internal matter.

389 Tirmidhī: 3307

ḤADĪTH 239

عَنِ ابْنِ عُمَرَ رَضِيَ اللهُ عَنْهُ أَنَّهُ رَأَى فُسْطَاطاً عَلَى قَبْرِ عَبْدِ الرَّحْمنِ فَقَالَ: يَا غُلامُ انْزِعْهُ إِنَّمَا يُظِلُّهُ عَمَلُهُ. (أخرجه البخاري)

Ibn ʿUmar ﷺ saw a tent over the grave of ʿAbd ar-Raḥmān ﷺ. He said [to his attendant]: "Remove it, young man! For verily he is shaded by his deeds." This was related by Bukhārī.[390]

Commentary: Abstaining from Erecting Tents and Buildings over Graves

Some of those who claim internal purity have got into the custom of erecting tents and buildings over the graves of the pious *awliyā'*. This ḥadīth exposes the uselessness and futility of this practice. If it leads to the corruption of beliefs, then this practice is far more evil.

ḤADĪTH 240

عَنْ جَابِرٍ رَضِيَ اللهُ عَنْهُ قَالَ: نَهى رَسُوْلُ اللهِ صَلَّى اللهُ عَلَيْهِ وَسَلَّمَ أَنْ يُّجَصَّصَ الْقَبْرُ وَأَنْ يُبْنى عَلَيْهِ وَأَنْ يُقْعَدَ عَلَيْهِ وَأَنْ يُكْتَبَ وَأَنْ يُوْطَأَ. (أخرجه الخمسة إلا البخاري)

Jābir ﷺ related that the Messenger of Allāh ﷺ prohibited that a grave be plastered, that a building be constructed over it, that anyone sit on it, that anything be written on it, and that anyone walk over it. This was related by Muslim, Abū Dāwūd, Tirmidhī, Nasā'ī.[391]

Commentary: Matters Related to Graves

The essence of this ḥadīth is to teach the balanced manner in which people should treat graves. Graves should not be shown excessive respect, nor should they be held in contempt. Those who transgress these simple rules engage in evil; those who solidify the graves, build edifices over them and write inscriptions on them. On the other extreme are those who are so strict as to ignore graves. If a grave is very old, and not on another's private property, then if there is a need to do so, it is permissible to remove all signs that it is a grave, to sit on it, and to walk over it.

---

390 Bukhārī: An unnumbered remark under the chapter-heading '[Placing a] wet branch on the grave' in the Book of Funerals.

391 Muslim: 970, Abū Dāwūd: 3225, Tirmidhī: 1052, Nasā'ī: 2030, Ibn Mājah: 1562, 1563

ḤADĪTH 241

عَنِ الْمُطَّلِبِ بْنِ أَبِي وَدَاعَةَ رَضِيَ اللهُ عَنْهُ قَالَ: لَمَّا مَاتَ عُثْمَانُ بْنُ مَظْعُوْنٍ رَضِيَ اللهُ

عَنْهُ وَهُوَ أَوَّلُ مَنْ مَاتَ بِالْمَدِيْنَةِ مِنَ الْمُهَاجِرِيْنَ فَلَمَّا دُفِنَ أَمَرَ رَسُوْلُ اللهِ صَلَّى اللهُ عَلَيْهِ

وَسَلَّمَ رَجُلاً أَنْ يَأْتِيَهُ بِحَجَرٍ، فَيُعْلِمَ قَبْرَهُ بِهِ فَأَخَذَ حَجَراً ضَعُفَ عَنْ حَمْلِهِ، فَقَامَ رَسُوْلُ

اللهِ صَلَّى اللهُ عَلَيْهِ وَسَلَّمَ فَحَسَرَ عَنْ ذِرَاعَيْهِ، ثُمَّ حَمَلَهُ فَوَضَعَهُ عِنْدَ رَأْسِهِ، وَقَالَ: «أَتَعَلَّمُ

بِهَا قَبْرَ أَخِي وَأُدْفِنُ عِنْدَهُ مَنْ مَاتَ مِنْ أَهْلِي». (أخرجه أبو داؤد)

Al-Muṭṭalib ibn Abī Wadāʿah ☞ said: When ʿUthmān ibn Mazʿūn passed away—and he was the first of the Emigrants to pass away in Madīna—and he was buried, the Messenger of Allāh ☞ ordered a person to bring a rock to him so that the grave could be identified by this rock. The man chose a rock but could not carry it. The Messenger of Allāh ☞ stood up, folded his sleeves, lifted the rock and placed it at the head of the grave. He ☞ said: "I will recognise the grave of my brother [ʿUthmān] through this rock, and bury whoever passes away from my family near his grave." This was related by Abū Dāwūd.[392]

To Place a Rock or Plant a Tree Near a Grave as a Means of Identification
Some people place these objects near graves merely to serve as a means of identification when they visit the grave or come to read something over it. If this is done with simplicity, and with the above-mentioned purpose [i.e. of identification], there is no harm in these practices. However, if it is a rock, no attention should be paid to making it well-shaped. Likewise, there should be no engraving on it, and nothing should be written on it. If someone goes to such extremes, however, these will suffice as proof that the person is not truthful in his claim to be doing this for a good reason; and the person is therefore prohibited from doing so.

ḤADĪTH 242

عَنْ بُرَيْدَةَ رَضِيَ اللهُ عَنْهُ أَوْصَى أَنْ تُجْعَلَ عَلَى قَبْرِهِ جَرِيْدَتَانِ. (أخرجه البخاري في

ترجمة الباب)

Buraydah ☞ related that his will provided that two branches of a date

---

palm be placed at his grave. This was related by al-Bukhārī in a chapter-heading.[393]

Commentary: The Custom of Planting a Tree Near a Grave

Some people plant a tree near a grave with the intention of the deceased deriving benefit from the *tasbīḥ* (glorification) of the tree and enjoying the companionship of the tree. The basis for this is derived from this ḥadīth. The bequest of this Companion ﷺ is probably based on the act of the Messenger of Allāh ﷺ when he ﷺ saw the inhabitants of two graves being punished. He ﷺ placed two fresh date branches on each and said: "There is hope that the punishment may be lightened at least until these branches become dry." The Companion ﷺ, like many scholars after him, considered this act to be the *ratio legis* for the above-mentioned practice. Therefore, there is precedent for the practice if this is one's intention.

Others are of the opinion that this lightening of the punishment was due only to the Prophet's ﷺ supplication, that the acceptance of the supplication was time-bound, and that the period of time was till the branches become dry.

Based on this, this custom has no connection whatsoever with this ḥadīth. But the majority of scholars prefer the first explanation. However, this does not prove the permissibility of laying flowers or a bed of flowers because the purpose of this is solely adornment or gaining proximity to the one in the grave. This practice or this belief is an absolute innovation (*bidʿah*). If this was not their purpose, why would they have first of all resorted to these formalities? Secondly, the graves of ordinary, sinful servants of Allāh were more eligible for this and not the graves of the *awliyāʾ* (the pious servants of Allāh). There is greater need for this where there is the possibility of punishment.

ḤADĪTH 243

عَنْ أَنَسٍ رَضِيَ اللهُ عَنْهُ قَالَ: قَالَ رَسُوْلُ اللهِ صَلَّى اللهُ عَلَيْهِ وَسَلَّمَ: «إِنَّ الْعَبْدَ إِذَا وُضِعَ فِيْ قَبْرِهِ وَتَوَلَّى عَنْهُ أَصْحَابُهُ أَنَّهُ لَيَسْمَعُ قَرْعَ نِعَالِهِمْ إِذَا انْصَرَفُوْا». (أخرجه الخمسة إلا الترمذي)

Anas ﷺ related that the Messenger of Allāh ﷺ said: "When a person is buried in his grave and his companions turn away to depart, he [the per-

393 Bukhārī: Under the chapter-heading '[Placing a] wet branch on the grave' in the Book of Funerals.

son in the grave] hears their footsteps." This was related by Bukhārī, Muslim, Abū Dāwūd and Nasā'ī.[394]

Commentary: The Issue of the Deceased's Ability to Hear

This is a contentious issue. Some scholars affirm this on the basis of this ḥadīth while others reject it on the basis of the Qur'ānic verse: "Surely you cannot make the deceased hear"[395]. Those who affirm the ability of the dead to hear say that the verse makes a figurative reference to the unbelievers as being "dead" and therefore has no connection with this issue. Those who reject the ability of the dead to hear reply that although the verse contains a figurative expression, the intrinsic meaning is essential in the thing which is used figuratively. Therefore, the inability to hear is established for the deceased in its real meaning. In turn, the reply of those who affirm the ability of the dead to hear is that this principle establishes only that the meaning of the "deceased" is the intrinsic meaning of deceased; while having nothing to do with the meaning of "you cannot make the deceased hear". In this case there is a figurative giving of an unrestricted meaning to a restricted circumstance; and the ability to hear refers to hearing that is beneficial. This therefore means that the deceased, in the true meaning of being deceased, are unable to hear anything that is beneficial. In this case, the need to turn to a figurative interpretation is in order to reconcile the meanings of the two apparently contradictory texts. Evidence for the same is that it is obvious that while the unbelievers have the ability to hear, they are nonetheless unable to hear what is beneficial. In short, both sides of this debate go into lengthy discussions in this regard and there is leeway on both sides. However, the belief of the masses who consider the deceased to be omni-present, watching, possessing absolute powers over matters, etc. is an absolute deviation. If their belief cannot be rectified without rejection of the deceased's ability to hear, it becomes obligatory to unilaterally reject the deceased's ability to hear.

ḤADĪTH 244

عَنْ أَبِيْ هُرَيْرَةَ رَضِيَ اللهُ عَنْهُ قَالَ: قَالَ رَسُوْلُ اللهِ صَلَّى اللهُ عَلَيْهِ وَسَلَّمَ: «إِنَّ الْحَصَاةَ لَتُنَاشِدُ اللهَ الَّذِيْ يُخْرِجُهَا مِنَ الْمَسْجِدِ لِيَدَعَهَا». (أخرجه أبو داؤد)

Abū Huraira ﷺ related that the Messenger of Allāh ﷺ said: "The remaining pebbles in the masjid take the name of Allāh and beseech the person

394 Bukhārī: 1374, Muslim: 2870, Abū Dāwūd: 4751, Nasā'ī: 2052

395 Al-Qur'ān, 27:80

who wants to throw them out of the masjid to leave them in the masjid." This was related by Abū Dāwūd.[396]

Commentary: The Issue of Inanimate Objects Having the Power of Perception
The perception and speech of inanimate objects which are exposed to the people of *kashf* (unveiling) is obviously supported by this ḥadīth. The pebble has such perception that it knows that it is being taken outside. It also has this power of speech whereby it resorts to the name of Allāh as an intermediary. There is no justification for turning away from the plain meaning [of this ḥadīth]. The other ḥadīth, which makes reference to the pillars [of the masjid crying], is even more explicit in this regard.

ḤADĪTH 245

عَنْ طَلْقِ بْنِ عَلِيٍّ رَضِيَ اللهُ عَنْهُ قَالَ: خَرَجْنَا وَفْداً إِلَى رَسُوْلِ اللهِ صَلَّى اللهُ عَلَيْهِ وَسَلَّمَ فَبَايَعْنَاهُ وَصَلَّيْنَا مَعَهُ وَأَخْبَرْنَاهُ أَنَّ بِأَرْضِنَا بِيْعَةً لَنَا، وَاسْتَوْهَبْنَاهُ مِنْ فَضْلِ طَهُوْرِهِ فَدَعَا بِمَاءٍ فَتَوَضَّأَ وَتَمَضْمَضَ ثُمَّ صَبَّهُ لَنَا فِيْ إِدَاوَةٍ وَقَالَ: «إِذَا أَتَيْتُمْ أَرْضَكُمْ فَاكْسِرُوْا بِيْعَتَكُمْ وَانْضَحُوْا مَكَانَهَا بِهٰذَا الْمَاءِ وَاتَّخِذُوْهَا مَسْجِداً» فَقُلْنَا: إِنَّ الْبَلَدَ بَعِيْدٌ وَالْحَرَّ شَدِيْدٌ وَالْمَاءَ يَنْشِفُ، فَقَالَ: «مُدُّوْهُ مِنَ الْمَاءِ فَإِنَّهُ لا يَزْدَادُ إِلاَّ طَيِّباً». الحديث (أخرجه النسائي)

Ṭalq ibn ʿAlī ﷺ related that: "We went as a delegation to the Messenger of Allāh ﷺ and pledged allegiance to him and offered *ṣalāh* with him. We informed him ﷺ that there was a Christian place of worship in our land [and we wished to convert it into a masjid]. We asked him ﷺ for some of his left over ablution water [which we would sprinkle at that place for blessings]. He ﷺ asked for some water, performed ablution, gargled with it, and then poured it into a small water skin. He ﷺ then said: "When you go to your land, raze the place of worship, sprinkle this water over it, and build a masjid at the spot." We said: "Our land is far, and the heat is intense. The water will evaporate." He ﷺ said: "Add more water [to the water which I gave you] and its blessings will also increase." This was related by Nasā'ī.[397]

396 Abū Dāwūd: 459
397 Nasā'ī: 702

ḤADĪTH 246

عَنْ أَنَسٍ رَضِيَ اللهُ عَنْهُ قَالَ: رَأَيْتُ رَسُوْلَ اللهِ صَلَّى اللهُ عَلَيْهِ وَسَلَّمَ وَالْحَلاَّقُ يَحْلِقُهُ، وَقَدْ أَطَافَ بِهِ أَصْحَابُهُ، فَمَا يُرِيْدُوْنَ أَنْ تَقَعَ شَعْرَةٌ إِلاَّ فِيْ يَدِ رَجُلٍ. (أخرجه مسلم)

Anas related, "I saw the Messenger of Allāh when the barber was shaving his head. His Companions were standing around him, not allowing his hair to fall anywhere but into the hands of one of them [i.e. every hair of his fell into the hand of someone or the other]." This has been reported by Muslim.[398]

ḤADĪTH 247

عَنْ أَنَسٍ رَضِيَ اللهُ عَنْهُ قَالَ: كَانَتْ أُمُّ سُلَيْمٍ تَبْسُطُ لِرَسُوْلِ اللهِ صَلَّى اللهُ عَلَيْهِ وَسَلَّمَ نِطَعاً، فَيَقِيْلُ عِنْدَهَا، فَإِذَا قَامَ أَخَذَتْ مِنْ عَرَقِهِ وَشَعْرِهِ فَجَمَعَتْهُ فِيْ قَارُوْرَةٍ، ثُمَّ جَعَلَتْهُ فِيْ مِسْك، فَلَمَّا حَضَرَ أَنَسٌ رَضِيَ اللهُ عَنْهُ أَوْصى أَنْ يُجْعَلَ فِيْ حَنُوْطِهِ مِنْ ذٰلِكَ المسك.

(أخرجه الشيخان والنسائي)

Anas related that Umm Sulaym used to lay out a leather mat for the Messenger of Allāh [when he used to go to her house]. He used to take a siesta there [she was a close relative of his]. When he got up, she used to gather his perspiration and hair [which had fallen off his body] and place it in a bottle. She would then mix it with another perfume. When Anas [who was the son of Umm Sulaym] approached death, he made a request for this mixture to be added to his burial shroud." This was related by Bukhārī, Muslim and Nasā'ī.[399]

Commentary: The Practice of Acquiring Blessings

Having a desire and showing reverence for the items belonging to the pious masters, as well as seeking to acquire blessings from them, both when they are alive and dead, are established as acceptable practices from the above three ḥadīths.

ḤADĪTH 248

عَنْ أَبِيْ مُوْسي رَضِيَ اللهُ عَنْهُ قَالَ: سَمِعْتُ النَّجَاشِيَّ صَاحِبَ الْحَبَشَةِ رَحِمَهُ اللهُ تَعَالٰى

398 Muslim: 2325

399 Bukhārī: 6281, Muslim: 2332, Nasā'ī: 5373

يَقُوْلُ: أَشْهَدُ أَنَّ مُحَمَّداً رَسُوْلُ اللهِ، وَأَنَّهُ الَّذِيْ بَشَّرَ بِهِ عِيْسى عَلَيْهِ السَّلَامُ، وَلَوْلَا مَا أَنَا فِيْهِ مِنَ الْمُلْكِ، وَمَاتَحَمَّلْتُ مِنْ أُمُوْرِ النَّاسِ لَأَتَيْتُهُ حَتّى أَحْمِلَ نَعْلَيْهِ. (أخرجه أبو داؤد)

Abū Mūsā ﷺ related, "I heard an-Najāshī, the ruler of Abyssinia, saying: 'I testify that Muḥammad is the Messenger of Allāh and he is the one whose glad tidings ʿĪsā conveyed. Were it not for this kingdom and the affairs of the people for which I am responsible, I would have gone to him and carried his shoes.'" This was related by Abū Dāwūd.[400]

Commentary: The Practice of Attending to the Pious

It is considered to be an honour to carry the shoes of the spiritual masters. The desirability of this practice is obvious from this ḥadīth. However, if the spiritual master personally prohibits this, obedience to his order is given preference over this service. To unnecessarily insist on carrying out this service entails causing discomfort to him and is a very detestable act.

ḤADĪTH 249

عَنِ ابْنِ عَبَّاسٍ رَضِيَ اللهُ عَنْهُ فِيْ حَدِيْثِ مُكَالَمَةِ هِرَقْل أَبَاسُفْيَان (وَلَمْ يُنْكِرْ عَلَيْهِ) وَسَأَلْتُكَ هَلْ يَرْتَدُّ أَحَدٌ مِنْهُمْ عَنْ دِيْنِهِ بَعْدَ أَنْ يَدْخُلَ فِيْهِ سَخْطَةً لَهُ فَزَعَمْتَ أَنْ لا، وَكَذلِكَ الإِيْمَانُ إِذَا خَالَطَ بَشَاشَةَ الْقُلُوْبِ. الحديث (أخرجه الشيخان)

Ibn ʿAbbās ﷺ related the conversation between Heraclius and Abū Sufyān [these statements of Heraclius were not refuted by the Companions, thus establishing their authenticity]. [Heraclius said]: "I asked you: 'After embracing the religion of Muḥammad, does anyone renounce it out of displeasure with it?' You replied: 'No.' This describes the state of true faith when its freshness is absorbed in the believers' hearts." This was related by Bukhārī and Muslim.[401]

Commentary: There is One Thing [Imān] which Never Subsides

This theme is well known by another statement: "When something achieves its goal and is perfected, it does not subside and it does not reject what it has achieved." This is clearly supported by this ḥadīth. Although this statement is attributed to Heraclius, it can be accepted as authentic since it was accepted by

400 Abū Dāwūd: 3205

401 Bukhārī: 7, Muslim: 1773

the scholars of the early generations. Seekers (*sālikīn*) who go astray should be understood as never having achieved their goal even though they may appear, and are understood, to have done so.

ḤADĪTH 250

عَنْ عَائِشَةَ رَضِيَ اللهُ تَعَالَى عَنْهَا قَالَتْ: أَوَّلُ مَابُدِئَ بِهِ رَسُوْلُ اللهِ صَلَّى اللهُ عَلَيْهِ وَسَلَّمَ مِنَ الْوَحْيِ الرُّؤْيَا الصَّالِحَةُ فِيْ النَّوْمِ، وَكَانَ لايَرى رُؤْيَا إِلَّا جَائَتْ مِثْلَ فَلَقِ الصُّبْحِ وَحُبِّبَ إِلَيْهِ الْخَلاءُ، فَكَانَ يَخْلُوْ بِغَارِ حِرَاءٍ فَيَتَحَنَّثُ فِيْهِ، وَهُوَ التَّعَبُّدُ اللَّيَالِيْ ذَوَاتِ الْعَدَدِ قَبْلَ أَنْ يَنْزِعَ إِلى أَهْلِهِ، وَيَتَزَوَّدُ لِذلِكَ ثُمَّ يَرْجِعُ إِلى خَدِيْجَةَ فَيَتَزَوَّدُ لِمِثْلِهَا حَتّى جَاءَ الْحَقُّ، وَهُوَ فِيْ غَارِ حِرَاءٍ فَجَاءَهُ الْمَلَكُ، فَقَالَ: اقْرَأْ، فَقَالَ: مَا أَنَا بِقَارِئٍ قَالَ: فَأَخَذَنِيْ فَغَطَّنِيْ حَتّى بَلَغَ مِنِّيْ الْجُهْدَ ثُمَّ أَرْسَلَنِيْ، فَقَالَ: اقْرَأْ، فَقُلْتُ: مَا أَنَا بِقَارِئٍ، فَأَخَذَنِيْ فَغَطَّنِيْ الثَّالِثَةَ حَتّى بَلَغَ مِنِّيْ الْجُهْدَ، ثُمَّ أَرْسَلَنِيْ فَقَالَ: ﴿اِقْرَأْ بِاسْمِ رَبِّكَ الَّذِيْ خَلَقَ، خَلَقَ الإنْسَانَ مِنْ عَلَقٍ، اِقْرَأْ وَرَبُّكَ الاَكْرَمُ الَّذِيْ عَلَّمَ بِالْقَلَمِ، عَلَّمَ الاِنْسَانَ مَالَمْ يَعْلَمْ﴾ فَرَجَعَ بِهَارَسُوْلُ اللهِ صَلَّى اللهُ عَلَيْهِ وَسَلَّمَ يَرْجُفُ فُؤَادُهُ فَدَخَلَ عَلى خَدِيْجَةَ، فَقَالَ: زَمِّلُوْنِيْ، زَمِّلُوْنِيْ. الحديث. (أخرجه البخاري)

ʿĀʾisha ؓ related that, "Revelation to the Messenger of Allāh ﷺ commenced with dreams that came true whatever dream he saw, he ﷺ would see the realisation thereof as clear as the morning light. He then became attached to solitude and would go into seclusion in the cave of Ḥirā and engage in worship for several nights in succession without going back to his family. He used to carry provisions [food, drink, etc.] for this stay. He would then return to Khadījah and again take provisions for a further period. This continued until the truth came to him while he was in the cave of Ḥirā. The Angel [of revelation] came to him and said: 'Read!' He replied: 'I cannot read.' The Messenger of Allāh ﷺ then said: 'He seized me and squeezed me till I reached the limit of my strength [i.e. till I had no strength left]. Then he released me and said: 'Read!' I replied: 'I cannot read.' He again seized me and squeezed me till I reached the limit of my strength. Again he released me and said: 'Read!' I replied: 'I cannot read.' He seized me a third time and squeezed me till I reached the limit of my strength. He then released me and said: 'Read!' I replied: 'I cannot read.' He said: 'Read in the name of your Lord Who created: He created man from a clot. Read! And your Lord is the Most Noble, The One Who taught by the pen; Who taught man that which he knew not.' With his heart trembling, the Messenger of Allāh returned home with these verses. He went to Khadījah and said: 'Cover me, cover me.'" This was related by Bukhārī.[402]

Commentary: True Dreams
This ḥadīth makes obvious reference to this.

The Practice of Remaining in Solitude and Carrying Provisions for this Solitude
These practices are clearly mentioned in this ḥadīth.

The Practice of Directing One's Attention and Conditioning
The angel of revelation was Jibra'īl ﷺ. The command to read was not given in the way that someone is asked to read something that he or she already knew how to read. Rather, the command was similar to a teacher placing the letters of the alphabet before a child and asking him or her to read. In other words, the command was to "Read what I read to you." The reply of the Messenger of Allāh ﷺ "I cannot read" was probably made on the basis that he did not consider this particular meaning of the command "Read" [i.e. reading after a person], or because he thought the angel would have him read something which required the ability to read and write. Then, if the Prophet ﷺ was to be able to receive and accept the commanded recitation, it was necessary to fortify and perfect his abilities. This is why the angel squeezed him several times, thus endowing his heart with attentiveness and courage. The spiritual practice of embracing is thus clearly established through this ḥadīth.

The Limbs are Affected by Unseen Bestowals
Since the heart is affected by unseen bestowals and the limbs are subservient to the heart, if the bestowal is strong, its effect is felt by the limbs as well. At times, the mere unseen takes place. This ḥadīth mentions that the Prophet wrapped himself in his clothes because the effects of trembling were on his body. This [fact that the limbs are affected by unseen bestowals] is established from this.

ḤADĪTH 251

عَنْ عُمَرَ رَضِيَ اللهُ عَنْهُ قَالَ: قَالَ رَسُوْلُ اللهِ صَلَّى اللهُ عَلَيْهِ وَسَلَّمَ إِذَا نَزَلَ عَلَيْهِ الْوَحْيُ يُسْمَعُ عِنْدَ وَجْهِهِ كَدَوِيِّ النَّحْلِ. الحديث (أخرجه الترمذي)

402 Bukhārī: 3

ʿUmar ؓ related that when revelation came over the Messenger of Allāh ﷺ, an unintelligible sound like that of the buzzing of a bee could be heard near his face. This was related by Tirmidhī.[403]

Commentary: The Enunciation of a Voice from the Unseen
At times, a voice from the Unseen is enunciated as a consequence of a certain practice, due to blessings from the proximity of a pious personality or for some other reason. This ḥadīth makes mention of such an enunciation. However, not every enunciation resulting from a practice (*shughl*) is a voice from the Unseen. In most cases, it is the spiritual aspirant's (*shāghil*) breath that stops and moves in his mind and which consequently causes the perception of an enunciation.

ḤADĪTH 252

عَنْ أَنَسٍ رَضِيَ اللهُ عَنْهُ فِيْ حَدِيْثِ الإِسْرَاءِ لِقَاءَهُ صَلَّى اللهُ عَلَيْهِ وَسَلَّمَ مَعَ مُوْسى عَلَيْهِ السَّلَامُ فِيْ آخَرِيْنَ مِنَ الأَنْبِيَاءِ عَلَيْهِمُ السَّلامُ مَعَ مَارُوِيَ عَنْ أَنَسٍ رَضِيَ اللهُ عَنْهُ قَالَ: قَالَ رَسُوْلُ اللهِ صَلَّى اللهُ عَلَيْهِ وَسَلَّمَ: أَتَيْتُ لَيْلَةَ أُسْرِيَ بِيْ عَلى مُوْسى عَلَيْهِ السَّلَامُ قَائِماً يُصَلِّيْ فِيْ قَبْرِهِ عِنْدَ الْكَثِيْبِ الأَحْمَرِ. (أخرجه مسلم والنسائي)

Anas ؓ related in the ḥadīth of al-Isrā' (the night journey) wherein the Messenger of Allāh ﷺ met Mūsā ؑ in a group of other Prophets. He also related that the Messenger of Allāh ﷺ said: "On the night of the ascension, I passed by Mūsā ؑ standing and offering *ṣalāh* at his grave which is near the red hill." This was related by Muslim and Nasā'ī.[404]

Commentary: The Possibility of the Souls of Perfect Servants Taking a Physical Form
It is established from both these narrations that although Mūsā ؑ was already in his grave, he and the other Prophets met the Messenger of Allāh ﷺ outside the grave. All the Prophets were certainly outside their graves. It may be deduced from this narration that it is possible for the souls of pious personalities to take a physical form, to occupy space, and to be visible. However, understand well that this condition is not permanent, nor is it within their control.

---

403 Tirmidhī: 3173

404 Muslim: 2375, Nasā'ī: 1632

ḤADĪTH 253

عَنْ أَبِيْ هُرَيْرَةَ رَضِيَ اللهُ عَنْهُ قَالَ: لَمَّا فُتِحَتْ خَيْبَرُ أُهْدِيَتْ لِرَسُوْلِ اللهِ صَلَّى اللهُ عَلَيْهِ وَسَلَّمَ شَاةٌ فِيْهَا سُمٌّ. الحديث. (أخرجه البخاري)

Abū Huraira ؓ related that when Khaybar was conquered the Messenger of Allāh ﷺ was presented with a grilled sheep that was poisoned. This is reported by Bukhārī.[405]

Commentary: Exposure of the Unseen is not Continuous

The latter part of this ḥadīth states that the Messenger of Allāh ﷺ actually ate some of it. But when he learned [that it was poisoned], his hand retracted [and he refrained from eating more of it]. However, the effect of this poison lasted till the end of his life. Two lessons may be learned from this: (1) knowledge of the Unseen is not granted on a permanent basis. Indeed, if that had been so, the poisonous nature of the meat would not have been concealed from him when he began eating. (2) Supernatural abilities are not permanent. If not, this poison would not have had an effect on him. When the paranormal knowledge and supernatural abilities of a Prophet are not permanent, what can be said of these things in relation to others?

ḤADĪTH 254

عَنْ أَبِيْ هُرَيْرَةَ رَضِيَ اللهُ عَنْهُ قَالَ: أَتَيْتُ رَسُوْلَ اللهِ صَلَّى اللهُ عَلَيْهِ وَسَلَّمَ يَوْماً بِتَمَرَاتٍ، فَقُلْتُ: يَا رَسُوْلَ اللهِ! ادْعُ فِيْهِنَّ بِالْبَرَكَةِ فَضَمَّهُنَّ ثُمَّ دَعَا لِيْ فِيْهِنَّ بِالْبَرَكَةِ، ثُمَّ قَالَ: «خُذْهُنَّ فَاجْعَلْهُنَّ فِيْ مِزْوَدِكَ هذَا كُلَّمَا أَرَدْتَّ أَنْ تَأْخُذَ مِنْهُ شَيْأً أَدْخِلْ يَدَكَ فِيْهِ وَخُذْهُ وَلاتَنْثُرْهُ نَثْراً» فَفَعَلْتُ، فَلَقَدْ حَمَلْتُ مِنْهُ كَذَا وَكَذَا وَسْقاً فِيْ سَبِيْلِ اللهِ فَكُنَّا نَأْكُلُ مِنْهُ وَنُطْعِمُ، وَكَانَ لايُفَارِقُ حَقْوِيْ حَتّى كَانَ يَوْمُ قَتْلِ عُثْمَانَ انْقَطَعَ. زاد رزين: فَسَقَطَ فَحَزِنْتُ عَلَيْهِ. (أخرجه الترمذي)

Abū Huraira ؓ related, "I went to the Messenger of Allāh ﷺ one day with some dates and said: 'O Messenger of Allāh! Pray for blessings in these dates.' He gathered them together, prayed for blessings in them, and said: 'Take them and place them in this bag of yours. Whenever you wish

---

405 Bukhārī: 3169

to take dates from there, place your hand inside the bag and take out as many as you want, but do not empty the bag.' This is what I did and I took out so many *wasaqs* (a dry measure) from it while in the cause of Allāh. I continued eating from it and gave others to eat as well. This bag never left my side until the day when ʿUthmān ﷺ was martyred, the bag burst and fell to the ground. I was greatly saddened by this." This was related by Tirmidhī.[406]

Commentary: The Realīty of the Unseen Hand

Apart from the normal ways of earning one's livelihood, there are three other categories: (1) By way of a supernatural act as related in this ḥadīth. (2) A person reads a certain supplication and without seeing anyone openly giving him, he finds something daily in his pocket or under his pillow, etc. (3) The servants of Allāh serve and attend to him. The third category is known as *futūḥāt* (openings). The masses refer to the second category as the "unseen hand". It is known that provision of the second category may be delivered by jinn irrespective of whether it comes from the wealth of others by illegal means, or from one's own wealth. Such wealth may also be obtained under compulsion. Clearly, these categories are unlawful. However, the first category of the "unseen hand" is lawful and is essentially a miracle attributable to a Prophet or a pious personality.

ḤADĪTH 255

عَنِ الْمِسْوَرِ بْنِ مَخْرَمَةَ حِيْنَ خَطَبَ عَلِيٌّ رَضِيَ اللهُ عَنْهُ بِنْتَ أَبِيْ جَهْلٍ قَالَ: سَمِعْتُ رَسُوْلَ اللهِ صَلَّى اللهُ عَلَيْهِ وَسَلَّمَ يَقُوْلُ وَهُوَ عَلَى الْمِنْبَرِ: «إِنَّ بَنِيْ هِشَامِ بْنِ الْمُغِيْرَةَ اسْتَأْذَنُوْنِيْ أَنْ يُنْكِحُوْا ابْنَتَهُمْ عَلِيَّ بْنَ أَبِيْ طَالِبٍ فَلا آذَنُ ثُمَّ لا آذَنُ ثُمَّ لا آذَنُ، إِلاَّ أَنْ يُرِيْدَ ابْنُ أَبِيْ طَالِبٍ أَنْ يُطَلِّقَ ابْنَتِيْ وَيُنْكِحَ ابْنَتَهُمْ؛ فَإِنَّمَا هِيَ بَضْعَةٌ مِنِّيْ يَرِيْبُنِيْ مَارَابَهَا وَيُؤْذِيْنِيْ مَاآذَاهَا». (أخرجه الخمسة إلا النسائي)

Al-Miswar ibn Makhramah ﷺ related the incident when ʿAlī ﷺ proposed to the daughter of Abū Jahl. He [al-Miswar] said: "I heard the Messenager of Allāh ﷺ saying while on the pulpit: 'Banū Hāshim ibn Mughīrah sought my permission to marry their daughter to ʿAlī ibn Abī Ṭālib. I will not permit this. I will not permit this. I will not permit this unless Ibn Abī Ṭālib wants to divorce my daughter first and then marry their daughter.

---

406 Tirmidhī: 3839

Faṭimah is a part of me, and whatever causes uneasiness to her causes uneasiness to me, and whatever hurts her hurts me.'" This was related by Bukhārī, Muslim, Abū Dāwūd and Tirmidhī.[407]

Commentary: Expressing Anger Over Certain Lawful but Unpleasant Matters
Such a marriage was permissible and lawful, as is obvious from the teachings of the Shariʿa. In fact, there are express statements by the Messenger of Allāh ﷺ to support the lawfulness of marriage to multiple women. Nonetheless, this particular marriage was one that the Prophet ﷺ disliked. It may be inferred from this ḥadīth that under special circumstances, if unhappiness is expressed over a lawful matter, and others refrain from it in consideration of that displeasure, then refraining from that lawful act will not be considered an attempt to make the lawful unlawful. Such incidents are also witnessed with regard to spiritual masters.

ḤADĪTH 256

عَنْ ثَابِتِ بن الضَّحَّاكِ رَضِيَ اللهُ عَنْهُ قَالَ رَجُلٌ لِرَسُوْلِ اللهِ صَلَّى اللهُ عَلَيْهِ وَسَلَّمَ: إِنِّيْ نَذَرْتُ أَنْ أَذْبَحَ بِمَكَانٍ كَذَا وَكَذَا مَكَانٌ يَذْبَحُ فِيْهِ أَهْلُ الْجَاهِلِيَّةِ فَقَالَ: «هَلْ كَانَ بِذلِكَ الْمَكَانِ وَثَنٌ مِنْ أَوْثَانِ الْجَاهِلِيَّةِ يُعْبَدُ»؟ قَالَ: لا، قَالَ: «فَهَلْ كَانَ فِيْهِ عِيْدٌ مِنْ أَعْيَادِهِمْ»؟ قَالَ: لا، قَالَ: «أَوْفِ بِنَذْرِكَ». (أخرجه أبو داؤد)

Thābit ibn aḍ-Ḍaḥḥāk related that a man said to the Messenger of Allāh ﷺ: "I vowed to slaughter an animal at a certain place—a place where people in the times before Islam (*jāhiliyyah*) used to slaughter their animals." He asked: "Was that a place where animals were slaughtered to idols?" He replied: "No." He asked: "Were any pagan festivals celebrated at that place?" He replied: "No." He said: "You may fulfil your vow." This was related by Abū Dāwūd.[408]

Commentary: An Incorrect Intention has an Effect on the Slaughtered Animal
It is certain that this person would have slaughtered the animal in the name of Allāh because he was a Muslim. Despite this, the Messenger of Allāh ﷺ made inquiries about the description of the place in order to gauge the intention of the person who took this vow. It is clear from this ḥadīth that even if a person slaughters an animal in the name of Allāh but has an evil intention; the evil

407 Bukhārī: 5230, Muslim: 2449, Abū Dāwūd: 2071, Tirmidhī: 3867, Ibn Mājah: 1998
408 Abū Dāwūd: 3313

intention will have an effect on the slaughtered animal. The ruling with regard to slaughtering animals in the name of saints or pious personalities should be inferred from this ḥadīth. Certain Sufis and like-minded people have been known to commit errors in this regard.

ḤADĪTH 257

عَنِ ابْنِ عَبَّاسٍ رَضِيَ اللهُ عَنْهُ قَالَ: قَالَ رَسُوْلُ اللهِ صَلَّى اللهُ عَلَيْهِ وَسَلَّمَ: «مَنْ أَخْلَصَ لله أَرْبَعِيْنَ صَبَاحاً ظَهَرَتْ يَنَابِيْعُ الْحِكْمَةِ مِنْ قَلْبِهِ عَلَى لِسَانِهِ». (أخرجه رزين)

Ibn ʿAbbās ﵁ related that the Messenger of Allāh ﷺ said: "Whoever worships Allāh for forty days with sincerity, fountains of wisdom shall gush forth from his heart and issue from his tongue." This has been reported by Razīn.[409]

Commentary: The Practice of Forty Days

Many spiritual masters have adopted the practice of remaining in seclusion for forty days for the purpose of worship. This ḥadīth is the basis for this practice.

Affirmation of Knowledge of Mysteries

It is related in the statements of the spiritual masters that certain special servants of Allāh are bestowed with certain knowledge that is neither related [handed down from person to person] nor acquired [learnt]. This knowledge is sometimes referred to as *ʿilm wahbī* (bestowed knowledge) and also as *ʿilm asrār* (knowledge of mysteries). At times, esoteric knowledge and spiritual truths are spoken by the spiritual masters even though these were never uttered by anyone before them. This ḥadīth is the basis for the affirmation and consideration of such knowledge.

ḤADĪTH 258

عَنِ الْأَسْوَدِ قَالَ: كُنَّا فِيْ حَلْقَةِ عَبْدِاللهِ رَضِيَ اللهُ عَنْهُ فَجَاءَ حُذَيْفَةُ رَضِيَ اللهُ عَنْهُ حَتّى قَامَ عَلَيْنَا فَسَلَّمَ، ثُمَّ قَالَ: لَقَدْ أُنْزِلَ النِّفَاقُ عَلى قَوْمٍ خَيْرٍ مِنْكُمْ، فَقُلْنَا: سُبْحَانَ اللهِ! إِنَّ اللهَ عَزَّوَجَلَّ يَقُوْلُ: ﴿إِنَّ الْمُنَافِقِيْنَ فِي الدَّرْكِ الأَسْفَلِ مِنَ النَّارِ﴾ فَتَبَسَّمَ عَبْدُ اللهِ

409 *Musnad ash-Shihāb*: 1:285, *al-Maqāṣid al-Ḥasanah*: pg. 395. It has also been reported by Abū Nuʿaym in his *al-Ḥilyah*.

وَجَلَسَ حُذَيْفَةُ رَضِيَ اللهُ عَنْهُ فِيْ نَاحِيَةِ الْمَسْجِدِ، فَلَمَّا قَامَ عَبْدُ اللهِ وَتَفَرَّقَ أَصْحَابُهُ رَمَانِيْ بِالْحَصْبَاءِ، فَأَتَيْتُهُ فَقَالَ: عَجِبْتُ مِنْ ضَحِكِهِ وَقَدْ عَرَفَ مَاقُلْتُ، لَقَدْ أُنْزِلَ النِّفَاقُ عَلَى قَوْمٍ خَيْرٍ مِنْكُمْ ثُمَّ تَابُوْا، فَتَابَ اللهُ عَلَيْهِمْ. (أخرجه البخاري)

Al-Aswad related, "We were seated in the assembly of ʿAbdullāh Ibn Masʿūd ﵁ when Ḥudhayfah ﵁ came and stood over us. He offered the *salām* and said: 'Hypocrisy overcame a people some of whom were better even than you.' We said [in surprise]: 'Glory be to Allāh! Allāh says that the hypocrites shall be in the lowest level of the Hellfire, [so how can those people be better than we Muslims]?' Then ʿAbdullāh ﵁ smiled while Ḥudhayfah ﵁ sat down in one corner of the masjid. When ʿAbdullāh ﵁ stood up and his companions dispersed, Ḥudhayfah ﵁ threw some pebbles at me and called me. I went to him and he said: 'I am astonished at his [ʿAbdullāh's] laughter, even though he understood what I said. [He ought to have clearly affirmed what I said. Those who were present could have misconstrued his laughter and assumed that he did not agree with my statement].' Then Ḥudhayfah ﵁ explained his statement, saying: 'Hypocrisy did overcome some people who were better than you. But they repented and Allāh accepted their repentance.'" This was related by Bukhārī.[410]

This means that those who repented from hypocrisy were actually some of the Companions [of the Messenger of Allāh ﷺ]. It is an accepted article of faith that the Companions ﵃ were superior [in terms of their spiritual ranking] to the Successors, Tābiʿūn [those who came after the Companions ﵃]. Since the Tābiʿūn made up the majority in this particular assembly of people, the statement: "They were better than you and hypocrisy overcame them", therefore, applies to the Companions ﵃. Both conditions [of hypocrisy and absence of hypocrisy], however, did not obtain at the same time. Those who heard this statement [in that assembly] took the obvious meaning of this statement, considered the period of both conditions to be one, and therefore expressed their surprise.

Commentary: Speaking in Veiled Terms

Some statements of certain spiritual masters appear to transgress the bounds of the Sharīʿa. The purpose of the masters in making these statements is either to conceal something from those who are not capable of understanding it or to suggest a possible excuse. The following verse is an example of the first purpose:

---

410 Bukhārī: 4602

Do not share the secrets of love and its ecstasy with the vainglorious
Keep it from him so he can perish in the torment of self-conceit

And the following is an example of the second reason:

The talk of the lovers in matters of Divinity
Is a mere rapture of love, and never insolence

This ḥadīth is the basis for all of this provided, of course, that the intention of the person making the statement is a good one. While the statement of this Companion appeared to be incorrect, it was in reality perfectly right. The most probable reason for his making this statement was to test his listeners and to demonstrate to them that the Almighty ﷻ controls peoples' hearts and that they should therefore abstain from being conceited and thinking ill of others.

ḤADĪTH 259

عَنْ أَبِيْ مُلَيْكَةَ قَالَ: أَدْرَكْتُ ثَلٰثِيْنَ مِنْ أَصْحَابِ رَسُوْلِ اللهِ صَلَّى اللهُ عَلَيْهِ وَسَلَّمَ مَنْ شَهِدَ بَدْراً، كُلُّهُمْ يَخَافُ النِّفَاقَ عَلٰى نَفْسِهِ وَلَا يَأْمَنُ الْمَكْرَ عَلٰى دِيْنِهِ. الحديث (أخرجه البخاري)

Abū Mulaykah ؓ related, "I met thirty Companions of the Messenger of Allāh ﷺ who participated in the battle of Badr [and thus earned special merit]. All of them feared hypocrisy for themselves and feared changes in their spiritual states." This was related by Bukhārī.[411]

Commentary: Considering Oneself to be Irreligious

Such statements are often found in the speech and writings of the spiritual masters. The reason for this is that they are overpowered by fear. This ḥadīth affirms the same condition with regard to the Companions. If this fear is with regard to the Hereafter, hypocrisy is taken in its obvious sense. If this fear is with regard to the present, hypocrisy refers to certain traces or acts of hypocrisy that represent to one degree or another a stage of hypocrisy.

ḤADĪTH 260

عَنْ ابْنِ عَبَّاسٍ رَضِيَ اللهُ عَنْهُ قَالَ: كُنْتُ رَدِيْفَ رَسُوْلِ اللهِ صَلَّى اللهُ عَلَيْهِ وَسَلَّمَ فَقَالَ:

411 Bukhārī: Under the chapter-heading 'Fear of a believer that his deeds are obliterated without his realisation' in the Book of Faith.

«يَا غُلامُ احْفَظِ اللهَ تَجِدْهُ تُجَاهَكَ» وَفِيْ الْحَدِيْثِ: «فَإِنْ اسْتَطَعْتَ أَنْ تَعْمَلَ للهِ تَعَالَى بِالرِّضَاءِ فِيْ الْيَقِيْنِ فَافْعَلْ، فَإِنْ لَمْ تَسْتَطِعْ فَإِنَّ فِيْ الصَّبْرِ عَلَى مَا تَكْرَهُ خَيْراً كَثِيْراً».

(أخرجه رزين بهذا اللفظ)

Ibn ʿAbbās related, "I was sitting behind the Messenger of Allāh on the same animal when he said: 'O son! Remain constantly aware of Allāh and you will find Him before you.'" This same ḥadīth also states: "If you can act for the pleasure of Allāh with conviction, then do so. If you cannot, then there is also a lot of good in exercising patience over distasteful matters." This is reported by Razīn with these words.[412]

Commentary: The Practice of Murāqabah

The meaning of the words "Remain constantly aware of Allāh" is the essence of *murāqabah* which is from among the essential practices of the *ahl Ṭarīq* (aspirants treading the path of Sufism). As for the special posture that is to be adopted when engaging in *murāqabah*, this is merely to reinforce the practice of *murāqabah* and is not the objective in itself. There is therefore no need for textual evidence to establish the legitimacy of this particular practice.

Closeness and Proximity

The fruits of *murāqabah* are closeness and proximity [to Allāh]. The words "you will find Him before you" are the consequence of "Remain constantly aware of Allāh".

The Superiority of an ʿĀrif [Gnostic] over an ʿĀbid [Worshipper]

According superiority to seeking the Almighty's pleasure and to true conviction—both of which are among the practices of the spiritually adept, *ahl bāṭin*—over exercising patience with distasteful matters—which is among the practices of the worshippers (*ʿabidīn*)—is clear proof of the superiority of the spiritually adept over those who practise outward deeds.

ḤADĪTH 261

عَنْ زَيْدِ الْخَيْرِ رَضِيَ اللهُ عَنْهُ قَالَ: قُلْتُ: يَا رَسُوْلَ اللهِ! تُخْبِرُنِيْ مَاعَلامَةُ اللهِ فِيْمَنْ يُرِيْدُهُ وَمَاعَلامَتُهُ فِيْ مَنْ لا يُرِيْدُهُ فَقَالَ: «كَيْفَ أَصْبَحْتَ يَا زَيْدُ»؟ قُلْتُ: أُحِبُّ الْخَيْرَ وَأَهْلَهُ

412 Recorded in Hannād ibn al-Sarīy's *Kitāb az-Zuhd*: 1:304

وَإِنْ قَدَرْتُ عَلَيْهِ بَادَرْتُ إِلَيْهِ، وَإِنْ فَاتَنِيْ حَزِنْتُ عَلَيْهِ وَحَنَنْتُ إِلَيْهِ فَقَالَ صَلَّى اللهُ عَلَيْهِ وَسَلَّمَ: «فَتِلْكَ عَلامَةُ اللهِ تَعَالى فِيْمَنْ يُرِيْدُهُ وَلَوْ أَرَادَكَ لِغَيْرِهَا لَهَيَّأَكَ لَهَا». (أخرجه الترمذي)

Zayd al-Khayr ﵁ related: I asked, "O Messenger of Allāh! Tell me the signs that differentiate between a person for whom Allāh wills good and one for whom He does not will good." He asked: "O Zayd! Tell me how did you get up this morning?" I replied: "I love good and those who do good. If I find the ability to do good, I hasten towards it. If I lose such an opportunity, I become grieved and I become desirous of it." The Messenger of Allāh ﷺ said: "That is the sign of a person for whom Allāh wills good. Had He willed something contrary to this for you, He would have prepared you for it." This was related by Tirmidhī.[413]

Commentary: The Sign of Acceptance
This is clearly indicated in this ḥadīth.

ḤADĪTH 262

عَنِ ابْنِ عَبَّاسٍ رَضِيَ اللهُ عَنْهُ قَالَ: قِيْلَ: يَا رَسُوْلَ اللهِ! إِنَّ أَحَدَنَا يَجِدُ فِيْ نَفْسِهِ وَيُعَرِّضُ بِشَيْءٍ لَأَنْ يَكُوْنَ حُمَمَةً أَحَبُّ إِلَيْهِ مِنْ أَنْ يَتَكَلَّمَ بِهِ فَقَالَ: «اللهُ أَكْبَرُ، اَلْحَمْدُ لِلهِ الَّذِيْ رَدَّ كَيْدَهُ إِلَى الْوَسْوَسَةِ». (أخرجه أبو داؤد)

Ibn ʿAbbās ﵁ related that someone said: "O Messenger of Allāh! We occasionally have such thoughts in our hearts and experience such things that we would rather burn and become coal than express them verbally." The Messenger of Allāh ﷺ [became pleased and said]: "Allāh is Greatest! All thanks are due to Allāh Who turned Satan's trap into nothing more than whisperings [and did not permit them to go beyond that]." This was related by Abū Dāwūd.[414]

Commentary: The Way to Ward off Whisperings
The masters teach that the way to deal with whisperings is by means of the treat-

413 This is how the source of this *ḥadīth* has been given in the original. However, in *Jāmiʿ al-ʿUṣūl*, it is referenced to Razin, which seems to be correct. It is also found in *al-Iṣābah*, 1:572, under the entry for Zayd al-Khayr.

414 Abū Dāwūd: 5112

ment described in this ḥadīth. The essence of this treatment is that a person should not be troubled by whisperings. Instead, one should be pleased with them in the sense that Allāh spared one the sort of tribulations that are worse than whisperings. One benefit of this happiness is that Satan is unhappy when a believer is pleased. When Satan sees a person deriving pleasure from whisperings, Satan will cease whispering to that person. Whisperings may also play a role in saving a person from greater tribulations. This is because when the soul obsessively turns its attention to these whisperings, then at such times, it does not find the opportunity to occupy itself with other more serious external or internal acts of disobedience. It thus safeguards itself [from those acts of disobedience]. The Persian poet therefore said:

> This is an affliction to kill off many other afflictions.

We used the words "obsessively turns its attention" because one should not wittingly turn one's attention to those whisperings. Although this is not sinful, it is harmful. A ḥadīth of Bukhārī and Muslim contains an explicit order in this regard: "One must abstain". The happiness alluded to in the commentary above also refers to this situation. It should be obvious that when a person is preoccupied by happiness, the attention he or she gives to such whisperings will be negligible.

ḤADĪTH 263

عَنْ وَاثِلَةَ بْنِ الأَسْقَعِ رَضِيَ اللهُ عَنْهُ قَالَ: قَالَ رَسُوْلُ اللهِ صَلَّى اللهُ عَلَيْهِ وَسَلَّمَ: «إِنَّ مِنْ أَعْظَمِ الْفِرى أَنْ يَدَّعِيَ الرَّجُلُ إِلى غَيْرِ أَبِيْهِ أَوْ يُرِيَ عَيْنَيْهِ مَا لَمْ تَرَ، أَوْ يَقُوْلَ عَلى رَسُوْلِ اللهِ صَلَّى اللهُ عَلَيْهِ وَسَلَّمَ شَيْئًا لَمْ يَقُلْ». (أخرجه البخاري)

Wāthilah ibn al-Asqaʿ ﵁ related that the Messenger of Allāh ﷺ said: "One of the greatest fabrications is for a person to attribute himself to someone other than his own father [in other words, he/she is the son/daughter of someone, but claims to be that of someone else. For example, it is the habit of some people to claim that they are *sayyids*—from the family of the Messenger of Allāh, Allāh bless him and give him peace,—when in actual fact they are not]. Or he claims to have seen something which he did not really see [this includes false dreams and false visions]. Or he attributes something to the Messenger of Allāh, Allāh bless him and give him peace, which he did not say." This was related by Bukhārī.[415]

415 Bukhārī: 3509

Commentary: False Claims to Unveilings

This ḥadīth makes obvious reference to this being a sin. Unfortunately, many of those who make such claims are actually [doing so falsely and are guilty of] committing a sin.

Carelessness in Narrating Ḥadīth

One may be excused if, when quoting a ḥadīth, one assumes that the narrator (from whom the ḥadīth was related) was not mistaken (even though the narrator was mistaken). In their letters and writings, certain spiritual masters have used this license to include, whether intentionally or not, baseless ḥadīths. If, however, after being informed by legitimate scholars of ḥadīth that the ḥadīths they have quoted are spurious, the masters persist in quoting such narrations, as is the way of many an ignorant Sufi, there can be no excuses.

ḤADĪTH 264

عَنْ عِيسَى بْنِ وَاقِدٍ قَالَ : قَالَ رَسُولُ اللهِ صَلَّى اللهُ عَلَيْهِ وَسَلَّمَ: «إِذَا كَانَتْ سَنَةُ ثَمَانِينَ وَمِائَةٍ فَقَدْ أَحْلَلْتُ الْعُزْبَةَ وَالتَّرَهُّبَ فِي رُؤُوسِ الْجِبَالِ». (أخرجه رزين)

ʿĪsa ibn Wāqid ☙ related that the Messenger of Allāh ☙ said: "When the year 180 arrives, I permit my *ummah* to abstain from marriage and to resort to living a solitary life on the mountain tops." This was narrated by Razīn.[416]

Commentary: Abstaining from Marriage and Living in Solitude

Some spiritual masters opted for this in order to avoid internal and external temptation are known to have adopted these means. The ḥadīth here clearly permits this in such circumstances. The year is named in order to make reference to this very situation [of temptation] because it was a time of many temptations.[417]

---

416 ʿAlī al-Kanānī has recorded this in his *Tanzīh ash-Sharīʿa al-Marfūʿa*: 2:346

417 It may seem incongruous to find a ḥadīth of questionable authenticity coming immediately after the author has cautioned against the circulation of such ḥadīths by Sufi masters. The only explanation that comes to mind is that the author regarded the collection (*Taysīr al-Wuṣūl* by al-Shaybānī) from which he drew all the ḥadīths in this book, as reliable. However, while this is generally true, *Taysīr* does include some dubious narrations and this, perhaps, is one of them. YTD.

ḤADĪTH 265

عَنْ أَنَسٍ رَضِيَ اللهُ عَنْهُ قَالَ: قَالَ رَجُلٌ لِرَسُوْلِ اللهِ صَلَّى اللهُ عَلَيْهِ وَسَلَّمَ: أَعْقِلُهَا وَأَتَوَكَّلُ أَوْ أُطَلِّقُهَا وَأَتَوَكَّلُ قَالَ: «اعْقِلْهَا وَتَوَكَّلْ». (أخرجه الترمذي)

Anas ؓ related that a man said to the Messenger of Allāh ﷺ: "Should I tie my camel and place my trust in Allāh, or untie it and place my trust in Allāh?" He replied: "Tie it and place your trust in Allāh." This was related by Tirmidhī.[418]

Commentary: Resorting to Means does not Negate Placing One's Trust in Allāh

Abandoning the means is not necessary for *tawakkul* (placing one's trust in Allāh). This ḥadīth is clear in this regard. It is not permitted to abandon certain means for all people. While certain means may not be abandoned by the weak-hearted. This ḥadīth can be explained in both ways.

ḤADĪTH 266

عَنِ ابْنِ أَبِيْ كَثِيْرٍ قَالَ: قَالَ أَبُوْ سَهْمٍ رَضِيَ اللهُ عَنْهُ مَرَّتْ بِيْ امْرَأَةٌ فَأَخَذْتُ كَشْحَهَا ثُمَّ أَطْلَقْتُهَا، فَأَصْبَحَ رَسُوْلُ اللهِ صَلَّى اللهُ عَلَيْهِ وَسَلَّمَ يُبَايِعُ النَّاسَ، فَأَتَيْتُهُ فَقَالَ: «أَلَسْتَ بِصَاحِبِ الْجَذْبَةِ بِالأَمْسِ»؟ قُلْتُ: بَلَى، وَإِنِّي لا أَعُوْدُ يَا رَسُوْلَ اللهِ فَبَايَعَنِي. (أخرجه رزين)

Ibn ʿAbī Kathīr related that Abū Sahm ؓ said: "A woman passed by me [in the street] and I brushed against her [being overcome by lust]. However, I immediately took my hand away [out of fear for Allāh]. The next day, the Messenger of Allāh ﷺ was accepting pledges of allegiance, *bayʿah*, from people and I, too, went [to him for the same purpose]. He said to me: 'Are you not the one who touched [that woman] yesterday?'[419] I replied:

418 Tirmidhī: 2517

419 The error alluded to in this ḥadīth actually included a third party. The assumption must be made here that the woman in question was unaware of what transpired. Otherwise, had harm been caused, the matter would not have been dealt with lightly. In this instance, the lady neither reported the matter nor presented evidence to support a claim of wrongdoing. Interfering with women is clearly a prohibited and reprehensible act. Generally speaking, the Sharīʿa prohibits all acts, however negligible in their own right that may lead to prohibited acts. Thus, even following women about (when there is no good reason to do so) is prohibited. In this case, when the Prophet ﷺ had extrasensory knowledge of the act, it is clear that he understood as well that the woman had not been aware of the touch and had therefore not been alarmed. Most importantly, the Prophet ﷺ was satisfied that the guilty party had caused harm only to himself; and that the man had truly repented and would never commit such an act again. Finally, in the absence of either a complaint or evidence, no ruling could be made against the offender. It should also be noted that

Indeed, O Messenger of Allāh! But I will never do that again.' He ﷺ then took the pledge of allegiance from me." This was reported by Razīn.[420]

Commentary: Apprising an Aspirant of an Error Committed in Privacy

It is the practise of some spiritual masters when they learn, either through a spiritual vision, *kashf*, or through evidence or information, of an improper act commited by an aspirant, that they apprise the aspirant of the same for purposes of reprimanding and correcting. If they apprise the aspirant in the presence of others, they do so in vague terms so that the aspirant may not be publicly embarrassed. This ḥadīth makes reference to all of this. However, spiritual visions are not to be used [or accepted] as legal evidence. Therefore, punishing the person or thinking ill of him or her on the basis of such visions is not permissible. At times a spiritual master may be aware of a wrong committed by an aspirant, and yet the master will not apprise him of it owing to some underlying reason such as the fear that it might make the aspirant more audacious, and so on.

ḤADĪTH 267

عَنْ عُمَرَ بْنِ الْخَطَّابِ رَضِيَ اللهُ عَنْهُ فِيْ حَدِيْثِ سُوَالِ جِبْرِيْلَ عَلَيْهِ السَّلَامُ عَنِ النَّبِيِّ صَلَّى اللهُ عَلَيْهِ وَسَلَّمَ قَالَ جِبْرِيْلُ: فَأَخْبِرْنِيْ عَنِ الْإِحْسَانِ قَالَ: «أَنْ تَعْبُدَ اللهَ كَأَنَّكَ تَرَاهُ، فَإِنْ لَمْ تَكُنْ تَرَاهُ فَإِنَّهُ يَرَاكَ». الحديث (رواه مسلم)

ʿUmar ibn al-Khaṭṭāb ؓ related the ḥadīth in which Jibra'īl ؑ posed certain questions to the Messenger of Allāh ﷺ. [One of the questions was this]: "Tell me. What is *iḥsān*?" [The literal meaning of this word is to worship in the best possible manner. In other words, in a way that is devoid of ostentation and inattention. In short, such worship must have the qualities of sincerity and presence of mind]. He replied: "It refers to worshipping Allāh as though you are seeing Him. [In other words, if you were to see Allāh at such a time, how would you worship Him? That is how you should worship Allāh. It is inevitable that worship under such circumstances will be performed with the utmost sincerity and presence of mind. That is how you are supposed to worship Allāh. If you do not see Him, the need to worship Him like that is still present because] if you do

---

extrasensory evidence, even when presented by the Prophet ﷺ himself, cannot be considered admissible in a court of law. And Allāh knows best. YTD.

420 This is reported in *al-Istīʿāb* under the entry of Abū Sahm. Its chain is strong as Ḥāfiẓ Ibn Ḥajar has commented in *al-Iṣābah*: 4:103.

not see Him, He certainly sees you [and this is sufficient reason to worship Him in this way]." This was related by Muslim.[421]

Commentary: The Essential Sufi Way
This question was posed after the Messenger of Allāh ﷺ was asked about the essence of *iman* and Islam. It may be inferred from this that, apart from beliefs and outward deeds, there is something else worthy of acquiring. This is referred to as *iḥsān*. *Iḥsān*, as explained in this ḥadīth, is the essence of the Sufi way. This ḥadīth therefore affirms the correctness of the Sufi way.

ḤADĪTH 268

عَنْ عُبَادَةَ بْنِ الصَّامِتِ رَضِيَ اللهُ عَنْهُ قَالَ: قَالَ رَسُوْلُ اللهِ صَلَّى اللهُ عَلَيْهِ وَسَلَّمَ وَحَوْلَهُ عِصَابَةٌ مِنْ أَصْحَابِهِ: «بَايِعُوْنِيْ عَلى أَنْ لا تُشْرِكُوْا بِاللهِ وَلا تُسْرِقُوْا» . الحديث. (متفق عليه)

ʿUbādah ibn aṣ-Ṣāmit ؓ related that while a group of his Companions were around him, the Messenger of Allāh ﷺ said: "Give me your pledge that you will not ascribe partners to Allāh and that you will not steal." This was related by Bukhārī and Muslim.[422]

Commentary: Pledging Allegiance (bayʿah)
This ḥadīth clearly states that the people whose pledge he sought were Companions. Thus, it may be established that apart from pledging allegiance on embracing Islam and before waging jihād, a pledge to abstain from acts of disobedience and to adhere to acts of obedience and worship also used to be taken. Such a pledge is the same pledge which is practised by the Sufis. Rejection of this practice is therefore tantamount to ignorance.

ḤADĪTH 269

عَنْ فُضَالَةَ الْكَامِلِ رَضِيَ اللهُ عَنْهُ قَالَ: قَالَ رَسُوْلُ اللهِ صَلَّى اللهُ عَلَيْهِ وَسَلَّمَ: «الْمُجَاهِدُ مَنْ جَاهَدَ بِنَفْسِهِ فِيْ طَاعَةِ اللهِ». الحديث (رواه البيهقي في شعب الإيمان)

Fuḍālah al-Kāmil ؓ related that the Messenger of Allāh ﷺ said: "A

421 Muslim: 8

422 Bukhārī: 18, Muslim: 1709, Tirmidhī: 1439, Nasā'ī: 4215

mujāhid is one who strives against his desires in order to obey Allāh." This was related by Bayhaqī.[423]

Commentary: Jihād Against Desire is Referred to as the Greater Jihād

Striving against one's desires is referred to as the greater jihād in many of the sayings of the spiritual masters. This is established from the ḥadīth above because the grammar in this expression "A *mujāhid* is one who" indicates that the speaker intends to restrict the reference to a certain kind of *mujāhid* and, when there is nothing to indicate otherwise, the assumption is that the kind of *mujāhid* intended is the perfect *mujāhid*. This sort of expression is well known to scholars of Arabic. The ḥadīth therefore means that a perfect *mujāhid* is a *mujāhid* who struggles with his or her desires. It should be obvious from the foregoing that the most perfect form of jihād is jihād against desires. Here, the words "perfect" and "greater" have the same meaning.

ḤADĪTH 270

عَنْ عُثْمَانَ رَضِيَ اللهُ عَنْهُ قَالَ: إِنَّ رِجَالاً مِنْ أَصْحَابِ النَّبِيِّ صَلَّى اللهُ عَلَيْهِ وَسَلَّمَ حِيْنَ تُوُفِّيَ حَزِنُوْا عَلَيْهِ حَتّى كَادَ بَعْضُهُمْ يُوَسْوِسُ، قَالَ عُثْمَانُ: وَكُنْتُ مِنْهُمْ فَبَيْنَمَا أَنَا جَالِسٌ مَرَّ عَلَيَّ عُمَرُ رَضِيَ اللهُ عَنْهُ وَسَلَّمَ فَلَمْ أَشْعُرْ بِهِ، فَاشْتَكى عُمَرُ رَضِيَ اللهُ عَنْهُ عَلى أَبِيْ بَكْرٍ رَضِيَ اللهُ عَنْهُ، ثُمَّ أَقْبَلاَ حَتّى سَلَّمَا عَلَيَّ جَمِيْعاً وَقَالَ أَبُوْبَكْرٍ رَضِيَ اللهُ عَنْهُ: مَا حَمَلَكَ أَنْ لاتَرُدَّ عَلى أَخِيْكَ عُمَرَ سَلامَهُ؟ قُلْتُ: مَافَعَلْتُ، فَقَالَ عُمَرُ رَضِيَ اللهُ عَنْهُ: بَلى وَ اللهِ لَقَدْ فَعَلْتَ، قَالَ: قُلْتُ: وَ اللهِ مَاشَعُرْتُ أَنَّكَ مَرَرْتَ وَسَلَّمْتَ ، قَالَ أَبُوْ بَكْرٍ رَضِيَ اللهُ عَنْهُ: صَدَقَ عُثْمَانُ، قَدْ شَغَلَكَ عَنْ ذلِكَ أَمْرٌ، فَقُلْتُ: أَجَلْ، قَالَ: مَا هُوَ؟ قُلْتُ: تَوَفَّى اللهُ تَعَالى نَبِيَّهُ صَلَّى اللهُ عَلَيْهِ وَسَلَّمَ قَبْلَ أَنْ نَسْأَلَهُ عَنْ نَجَاةِ هذَا الأَمْرِ. الحديث (رواه أحمد)

ʿUthmān ؓ related: Many people from among the Companions of the Messenger of Allāh ﷺ became quite grieved when he passed away, to the extent that some of them began experiencing whisperings. ʿUthmān ؓ said: "I was also from among these people. While I was sitting down one day, ʿUmar ؓ passed by me and offered *salām* to me but I did not even perceive his presence. ʿUmar ؓ went and complained to Abū Bakr ؓ. They both came to me and offered *salām* to me together. Abū Bakr ؓ

423 Al-Bayhaqī has reported this in his *Shuʿab al-Īmān*: 11123 [7:499]

then said: 'Why is it that you did not reply to the *salām* of your brother, 'Umar 🙵?' I replied: 'I did not do that.' 'Umar 🙵 said: 'I take an oath by Allāh that you did that.' I said: 'By Allāh, I did not even realise that you passed by me; nor did I know that you offered *salām* to me.' Abū Bakr 🙵 said: "Uthmān is speaking the truth. It seems that some serious matter has kept you preoccupied.' I said: 'Indeed.' He asked: 'What is the matter?' I said: 'Allāh took away His Messenger 🙵 and we did not even have the opportunity to ask him the actual basis for salvation in this religion [of Islam].'" (In other words, the Sharī'a specifies numerous injunctions, but what is the fundamental principle of all this?) The ḥadīth further states that Abū Bakr 🙵 consoled 'Uthmān 🙵 by informing him that he had posed this question to the Messenger of Allāh 🙵 and that the Prophet 🙵 replied that it is belief in unicity and prophecy (that Allāh is One and that Muhammad 🙵 is His Messenger). This was related by Aḥmad.[424]

Commentary: *Whisperings do not Negate Perfection in the Path*
Can anyone have doubts about the perfection of 'Uthmān 🙵? Yet he experienced whisperings. It should be clear from this incident that whisperings neither negate perfection nor are they harmful to one's internal self.

Absence
To be lost in thought about something related to religion is something that occasionally happens to people. The intensity of this experience caused 'Uthmān 🙵 to ignore his surroundings. This state is known as absence and obliviousness. This ḥadīth affirms the same.

ḤADĪTH 271

عَنْ أَبِيْ هُرَيْرَةَ رَضِيَ اللهُ عَنْهُ قَالَ: قَالَ رَسُوْلُ اللهِ صَلَّى اللهُ عَلَيْهِ وَسَلَّمَ: «يَأْتِيْ الشَّيْطَانُ أَحَدَكُمْ فَيَقُوْلُ، مَنْ خَلَقَ كَذَا مَنْ خَلَقَ كَذَا حَتَّى يَقُوْلَ مَنْ خَلَقَ رَبَّكَ فَإِذَا بَلَغَهُ فَلْيَسْتَعِذْ بِاللهِ وِلْيَنْتَهِ». (متفق عليه)

Abū Huraira 🙵 related that the Messenger of Allāh 🙵 said: "Satan comes to a person and asks: 'Who created this? Who created that?' He eventually asks: 'Who created your Lord?' If he reaches such a stage, the person

---

424 *Musnad Aḥmad*: 1:6

should seek refuge in Allāh and abstain [from having such thoughts]." This was related by Bukhārī and Muslim.[425]

Commentary: The Means to Repel Whisperings

This was explained previously in ḥadīth [262]. The present ḥadīth provides another method, viz. to say: "I seek refuge in Allāh". Apart from the blessedness of this supplication, it has another secret, viz. when the person turns his attention towards Allāh by seeking of refuge, this will draw his attention away from the whispering. This is because the soul cannot turn its attention to two things at the same time. The essence of this method is thus to become occupied in the remembrance of Allāh. Thereafter, there will be no need to focus specific attention on repelling the whisperings.

ḤADĪTH 272

عَنِ الْقَاسِمِ بْنِ مُحَمَّدٍ أَنَّ رَجُلاً سَأَلَهُ فَقَالَ: إِنِّيْ أَهِمُ فِيْ صَلاتِيْ فَيَكْثُرُ ذٰلِكَ عَلَيَّ فَقَالَ لَهُ: امْضِ فِيْ صَلوتِكَ فَإِنَّهُ لَنْ يَذْهَبَ ذٰلِكَ عَنْكَ حَتّيٰ تَنْصَرِفَ وَأَنْتَ تَقُوْلُ مَا أَتْمَمْتُ صَلوتِيْ. (رواه مالك)

Al-Qāsim ibn Muḥammad ﷺ related that a person asked him saying: "I experience a lot of doubts when offering my *ṣalāh*." He said to him: "[Pay no attention to them] and continue offering your *ṣalāh* [in this way] because even if you try to avoid such thoughts, they will never be repelled. Even when you complete your *ṣalāh*, you will continue thinking to yourself that you did not complete your *ṣalāh* [thinking that you have certainly left something out. You will therefore repeat your *ṣalāh* and still have the same doubts upon completing this second *ṣalāh* as well. So how many times are you going to repeat your *ṣalāh*? It is therefore better not to even bother about such thoughts]." This was related by Mālik.[426]

Commentary: The Means to Repel Whisperings

This narration provides another method, viz. the person should not bother about these whisperings, not act upon them, and not turn his attention to them. This treatment has proven to be the greatest cure.

This is explained in another way in *Lamaʿāt* and *Mirqāt*: This whispering will

425 Bukhārī: 3276, Muslim: 134

426 *Muwaṭṭa'*: pg. 35

not be warded off unless you complete your *ṣalāh* and say [to Satan]: "Even if I were to accept that my *ṣalāh* is incomplete, Allāh is Merciful—He will either accept it [as it is] or forgive me. I am not in need of your advice. This is between me and my Allāh."

ḤADĪTH 273

عَنْ عُثْمَانَ رَضِيَ اللهُ عَنْهُ قَالَ: قَالَ رَسُوْلُ اللهِ صَلَّى اللهُ عَلَيْهِ وَسَلَّمَ: «مَنْ تَوَضَّأَ وُضُوْئِي هٰذَا ثُمَّ يُصَلِّيْ رَكْعَتَيْنِ لاَيُحَدِّثُ نَفْسَهُ فِيْهِمَا بِشَيْءٍ غُفِرَ لَهُ مَاتَقَدَّمَ مِنْ ذَنْبِهِ». (متفق عليه ولفظه للبخاري)

ʿUthmān ﷺ related that the Messenger of Allāh ﷺ said: "Whoever performs an ablution as I performed this ablution and then offers two *rakʿāt*s of *ṣalāh* without talking to himself about anything in these two *rakʿāt*s, his past sins [minor sins] are forgiven." This was related by Bukhārī and Muslim.[427]

Commentary: Unintentional Thoughts in Ṣalāh are not Harmful

Most people are under the assumption that stray thoughts in *ṣalāh* are harmful to one's concentration. Since the concentration is considered beyond one's control, most people ignore the matter entirely. The ḥadīth above uses the verb talking, *yuhaddithu*, which is an act within one's control. It may be inferred from this that thoughts which are knowingly brought to mind are harmful to one's concentration. Giving this up is within one's control. As for thoughts that come unintentionally and unwittingly, they are not harmful. Paying attention to concentration in prayer is therefore necessary and also attainable.

ḤADĪTH 274

عَنْ عُقْبَةَ بْنِ عَامِرٍ رَضِيَ اللهُ عَنْهُ قَالَ: قَالَ رَسُوْلُ اللهِ صَلَّى اللهُ عَلَيْهِ وَسَلَّمَ: «مَا مِنْ مُسْلِمٍ يَتَوَضَّأُ فَيُحْسِنُ وُضُوْءَهُ ثُمَّ يَقُوْمُ فَيُصَلِّيْ رَكْعَتَيْنِ مُقْبِلاً عَلَيْهِمَا بِقَلْبِهِ وَوَجْهِهِ إِلاَّ وَجَبَتْ لَهُ الْجَنَّةُ». (رواه مسلم)

ʿUqbah ibn ʿĀmir ﷺ related that the Messenger of Allāh ﷺ said: "When a person performs a perfect ablution and offers two cycles, *rakʿatayn* of

427 Bukhārī: 159, Muslim: 229

ṣalāh in such a manner that his heart and face [internal and external self] are totally devoted to them, Paradise most certainly awaits [becomes obligatory for] him." This was related by Muslim.[428]

Commentary: concentration in Ṣalāh

This method is gauged by pondering over the words: "that his heart and face are totally devoted to them". The words "to them" refer to the two cycles. A cycle is made up of several words and actions. Being devoted to a cycle therefore entails devotion to the components of the cycle [i.e. to the words and actions of that cycle]. Therefore, the method of attaining a state of concentration in prayer is that the words and actions which are executed in the *ṣalāh* should be done with attention and intent. They should not be performed merely by rote. For example, when a person verbally says: "*subḥānaka Allāhumma*", he should turn his attention to the fact that he is saying this with his tongue. When he says: "*bi ḥamdika*", he must likewise turn his attention and intention to this. He must continue in this way till the end of the *ṣalāh*. In this way, all his time in *ṣalāh* will be devoted to the act of worship. When one's attention is turned towards a particular thing, it cannot turn to something else. It is therefore inevitable that one's attention will not be directed to anything apart from *ṣalāh*. In so doing, one will have achieved complete presence of heart.

The word "face" [in this ḥadīth] makes reference to the fact that preoccupation with the limbs has the effect of keeping the heart preoccupied. Controlling the limbs is therefore necessary for perfection in concentration. If not, by turning the face around, one's thoughts will also stray through the straying of the eyes.

ḤADĪTH 275

عَنْ أَنَسٍ رَضِيَ اللهُ عَنْهُ أَنَّ النَّبِيَّ صَلَّى اللهُ عَلَيْهِ وَسَلَّمَ قَالَ: «يَا أَنَسُ! اجْعَلْ بَصَرَكَ حَيْثُ تَسْجُدُ». (رواه البيهقي)

Anas ﷺ related that the Messenger of Allāh ﷺ said: "O Anas! Direct your eyes to the point of prostration." This was related by Bayhaqī.[429]

Commentary: Confining One's Eyes

It is established through experience that one is able to acquire concentration by

---

428 Muslim: 234, Abū Dāwūd: 906

429 Al-Bayhaqī in his *Sunan*: 2:284

confining one's eyes [to one spot]. This is the object of several different spiritual practices or *ashghāl*. This ḥadīth is thus a basis for these practices.

ḤADĪTH 276

عَنْ مَطَرِّفِ بْنِ عَبْدِ اللهِ بْنِ الشِّخِّيرِ عَنْ أَبِيْهِ رَضِيَ اللهُ عَنْهُ قَالَ: أَتَيْتُ النَّبِيَّ صَلَّى اللهُ عَلَيْهِ وَسَلَّمَ وَهُوَ يُصَلِّيْ وَلِجَوْفِهِ أَزِيْزٌ كَأَزِيْزِ الْمِرْجَلِ يَعْنِيْ يَبْكِيْ، وَفِيْ رِوَايَةٍ قَالَ: رَأَيْتُ النَّبِيَّ صَلَّى اللهُ عَلَيْهِ وَسَلَّمَ يُصَلِّيْ وَفِيْ صَدْرِهِ أَزِيْزٌ كَأَزِيْزِ الرَّحى مِنَ الْبُكَاءِ. (رواه أحمد وروى النسائي الرواية الأولى وأبوداؤد الثانية)

Muṭarrif ibn ʿAbdullāh ibn ash-Shikhkhīr related from his father who said: "I went to the Messenger of Allāh ﷺ while he was offering *ṣalāh*. There was a sound in his chest like something boiling in a cauldron." In other words, he was crying. Another narration states: "I saw the Messenger of Allāh ﷺ offering *ṣalāh* and in his chest was a sound like that of a grinding stone because he was crying." Both narrations were related by Aḥmad, the first by Nasā'ī, and the second by Abū Dāwūd.[430]

Commentary: Wajd (ecstasy)

To be overcome by a strange yet praiseworthy condition is known as *wajd*. This condition of the Messenger of Allāh ﷺ [described in these narrations] was of this type. The *wajd* of the close servants of Allāh is in most cases intricate and subtle like this. It does not entail screaming, tearing of one's clothes, etc. Those who unintentionally experience such things, however, [screaming, etc.] may be excused.

ḤADĪTH 277

عَنْ أُمِّ الدَّرْدَاءِ رَضِيَ الله عَنْهَا قَالَتْ: سَمِعْتُ أَبَا الدَّرْدَاءِ رَضِيَ اللهُ عَنْهُ يَقُوْلُ: سَمِعْتُ أَبَاالقَاسِمِ صَلَّى اللهُ عَلَيْهِ وَسَلَّمَ يَقُوْلُ: «إِنَّ الله تَبَارَكَ وَتَعَالى قَالَ: يَا عِيْسى! إِنِّيْ بَاعِثٌ مِنْ بَعْدِكَ أُمَّةً». الحديث وَفِيْهِ: «قَالَ الله تَعَالى: أُعْطِيْهِمْ مِنْ حِلْمِيْ وَعِلْمِيْ». (رواه البيهقي)

Umm al-Dardā' ﷺ related: I heard Abū al-Dardā' ﷺ saying: I heard Abū al-Qāsim ﷺ saying: "Allāh said: 'O ʿĪsā! I am going to send a nation after

430 *Musnad Aḥmad*: 4:26, Abū Dāwūd: 904, Nasā'ī: 1215

you [referring to the nation of Muhammad ﷺ].'" This ḥadīth also states: "Allāh said: 'I will give them of My forbearance and knowledge.'" This was related by Bayhaqī.[431]

Commentary: Manifestation

It is stated in the explanations of most monotheist theologians that certain attributes of the Almighty, which are both obligatory and possible, are manifested in certain of His creations. For example, the attribute of giving life is found in water, the quality of retracting (or withholding) is found in fire, and many other attributes are found in man. In short, only certain appropriate attributes have been identified in this sort of manifestation. However, some overly strict people are under the misconception that the spiritual master—Allāh forbid—believe in the transferral of these very attributes (to humans) or that they are equally possible and obligatory (for humans). The words "I will give them of My forbearance and knowledge" in this ḥadīth obviously support this belief (of the monotheists). The explanation given by the masters is the very same which is provided by this ḥadīth. At times, the entirety of creation is considered to be a unilateral manifestation of these appropriate and shared attributes. When such is the case, there can be no doubt about this matter; nor does it require further explanation.

ḤADĪTH 278

عَنْ عَائِشَةَ رَضِيَ اللهُ تَعَالَى عَنْهَا قَالَتْ: كُنْتُ أَدْخُلُ بَيْتِيْ إِلَى قَوْلِهَا فَلَمَّا دُفِنَ عُمَرُ مَعَهُمْ فَوَاللهِ مَا دَخَلْتُهُ إِلاَّ وَأَنَا مَشْدُوْدَةٌ عَلَى ثِيَابِيْ حَيَاءً مِنْ عُمَرَ. (رواه أحمد)

ʿĀ'isha ؓ related: "I used to go into my house [in which the Messenger of Allāh ﷺ and Abū Bakr ؓ were buried]. But when ʿUmar ؓ was buried with them, by Allāh, I never entered that room without first covering myself properly out of modesty for ʿUmar ؓ." This was related by Aḥmad.[432]

Commentary: According Respect to the Dead as it is Accorded to the Living

The spiritual masters state that one may go to the grave of the deceased and accord as much respect to that person as one used to when the person was alive. This is on condition that one does not transgress the limits of the Sharīʿa such that one, for example, sits the same distance from the grave as one used to sit

431 Al-Bayhaqī has narrated it in *Shuʿab al-Īmān*: 4482 [4:114]

432 *Musnad Aḥmad*: 6:202

from the deceased when he or she was alive, etc. This is established from this ḥadīth. When 'Ā'isha 🙎 used to go to 'Umar 🙎 for any work when the latter was alive, she would thoroughly cover herself and go. She adopted the same practice when going to his grave and this was the reason for going in this way. This is the meaning of "out of modesty for 'Umar 🙎". As for using this as proof that the deceased have perception and knowledge [while in their graves], the heart definitely does not accept this.

ḤADĪTH 279

عَنِ ابْنِ عَبَّاسٍ رَضِيَ اللهُ عَنْهُ قَالَ: ضَرَبَ بَعْضُ أَصْحَابِ النَّبِيِّ صَلَّى اللهُ عَلَيْهِ وَسَلَّمَ خِبَاءَهُ عَلَى قَبْرٍ، وَهُوَ لَا يَحْسَبُ أَنَّهُ قَبْرٌ، فَإِذَا فِيهِ إِنْسَانٌ يَقْرَأُ ﴿تَبَارَكَ الَّذِي بِيَدِهِ الْمُلْكُ﴾ حَتَّى خَتَمَهَا، فَأَتَى النَّبِيَّ صَلَّى اللهُ عَلَيْهِ وَسَلَّمَ فَأَخْبَرَهُ فَقَالَ النَّبِيُّ صَلَّى اللهُ عَلَيْهِ وَسَلَّمَ: «هِيَ الْمَانِعَةُ هِيَ الْمُنْجِيَةُ تُنْجِيهِ مِنْ عَذَابِ اللهِ». (رواه الترمذي)

Ibn 'Abbās 🙎 related: "One of the Companions of the Messenger of Allāh 🙎 pitched his tent over a grave without knowing that it was a grave. He then heard someone [apparently from the grave] reciting the Chapter of Dominion [from the Qur'ān], till he completed its recitation. The Companion 🙎 went to the Messenger of Allāh 🙎 and informed him of what he heard. The Messenger of Allāh 🙎 said: 'This chapter is a protector. It is a saviour—it saves its reader from the punishment of Allāh [that is meted out in the grave].'" This was related by Tirmidhī.[433]

Commentary: Spiritual Vision from Graves
Spiritual visions from graves sometimes occur unintentionally and without effort, as was the case with this Companion 🙎. Sometimes these occur as a result of one's spiritual exertions and disciplines. Nevertheless, that such visions may occur is established from this ḥadīth.

Spiritual Benefit from Grave Dwellers
There is no doubt whatsoever that listening to the Qur'ān bestows a spiritual benefit. The Companion mentioned in the ḥadīth above obtained this benefit through the person who was buried in the grave. This proves that blessings may in fact be bestowed upon the living by those who dwell in their graves.

---

433 Tirmidhī: 2890

ḤADĪTH 280

عَنِ ابْنِ عُمَرَ رَضِيَ اللهُ عَنْهُ قَالَ: قَالَ رَسُوْلُ اللهِ صَلَّى اللهُ عَلَيْهِ وَسَلَّمَ: «إِنَّ هٰذِهِ الْقُلُوْبَ تَصْدَأُ كَمَا يَصْدَأُ الْحَدِيْدَ إِذَا أَصَابَهُ الْمَاءُ» قِيْلَ: يَارَسُوْلَ اللهِ وَمَا جَلاءُهَا؟ قَالَ: «كَثْرَةُ ذِكْرِ الْمَوْتِ وَتِلاوَةِ الْقُرْآنِ». (رواه البيهقي)

Ibn ʿUmar ﷺ related that the Messenger of Allāh ﷺ said: "These hearts become rusty just as steel becomes rusty when water falls onto it." He ﷺ was asked: "O Messenger of Allāh! How can they be polished?" He ﷺ replied: "Profuse remembrance of death and recitation of the Qur'ān." This was related by Bayhaqī.[434]

Commentary: Proof that the Heart Becomes Light or Dark

The statements of the spiritual masters often mention lightness and darkness of peoples' hearts. This ḥadīth clearly affirms this.

ḤADĪTH 281

عَنْ طَاوٗسٍ مُرْسَلاً قَالَ: سُئِلَ النَّبِيُّ صَلَّى اللهُ عَلَيْهِ وَسَلَّمَ: أَيُّ النَّاسِ أَحْسَنُ صَوْتاً لِلْقُرْآنِ وَأَحْسَنُ قِرَائَةً، قَالَ: مَنْ إِذَا سَمِعْتَهُ يَقْرَأُ رَأَيْتَ أَنَّهُ يَخْشَى اللهَ تَعَالَى، قَالَ طَاوٗسٌ: وَكَانَ طَلْقٌ كَذٰلِكَ. (رواه الدارمي)

Ṭāwūs related that the Messenger of Allāh ﷺ was asked: "Who has the best voice and best recitation of the Qur'ān?" He ﷺ replied: "The person whose recitation makes you feel he fears Allāh." Ṭāwūs said: "Ṭalq ﷺ was [a person who recited] in this way." This was related by Dārimī.[435]

Commentary: The Way of Reciting the Qur'ān

Since humility is not experienced without imagining that one is presenting oneself before Allāh, this ḥadīth makes reference to the fact that when one is reciting the Qur'ān, one should imagine that one is sitting before Allāh, reciting to Him, and that He is listening. This is a good way of reciting the Qur'ān and is also taught by the spiritual masters.

---

434 Al-Bayhaqī has reported it in his *Shuʿab al-Īmān*: 2:353

435 Dārimī: 3489

ḤADĪTH 282

عَنْ أُبَيِّ بْنِ كَعْبٍ رَضِيَ اللهُ عَنْهُ قَالَ: كُنْتُ فِيْ الْمَسْجِدِ فَدَخَلَ رَجُلٌ يُصَلِّيْ فَقَرَأَ قِرَائَةً أَنْكَرْتُهَا عَلَيْهِ، ثُمَّ دَخَلَ آخَرُ فَقَرَأَ قِرَائَةً سِوى قِرَائَةِ صَاحِبِهِ، فَلَمَّا قَضَيْنَا الصَّلوةَ دَخَلْنَا جَمِيْعاً عَلى رَسُوْلِ اللهِ صَلَّى اللهُ عَلَيْهِ وَسَلَّمَ فَقُلْتُ: إِنَّ هذَا قَرَأَ قِرَائَةً أَنْكَرْتُهَا عَلَيْهِ، وَدَخَلَ آخَرُ فَقَرَءَ سِوى قِرَائَةِ صَاحِبِهِ، فَأَمَرَهُمَا النَّبِيُّ صَلَّى اللهُ عَلَيْهِ وَسَلَّمَ فَقَرآ، فَحَسَّنَ شَأْنَهُمَا، فَسُقِطَ فِيْ نَفْسِيْ مِنَ التَّكْذِيْبِ، وَلا إِذْ كُنْتُ فِيْ الْجَاهِلِيَّةِ، فَلَمَّا رَأى رَسُوْلُ اللهِ صَلَّى اللهُ عَلَيْهِ وَسَلَّمَ مَا قَدْ غَشِيَنِيْ ضَرَبَ فِيْ صَدْرِيْ فَفِضْتُ عَرَقاً وَكَأَنَّمَا أَنْظُرُ إِلَى اللهِ فَرَقًا.الحديث (رواه مسلم)

Ubayy ibn Kaʿb ؓ related: "I was in the masjid when a person came and offered *ṣalāh*. He recited in a manner I considered wrong [because some of the words which he read were different from what I remembered]. Another person entered the masjid and his recitation was different from that of the first person. When we completed our *ṣalāh*, we all went to the Messenger of Allāh ﷺ and I said to him: 'This person read the Qur'ān in a way which I considered wrong. This second person entered and recited the Qur'ān differently from the first person.' He ﷺ asked both of them to recite and, when they recited, he ﷺ said that both their recitations were correct. My heart experienced a state of disbelief [to the extent of a whispering], but this state was not like that of *jāhiliyyah* [but even more]. When the Messenger of Allāh ﷺ saw this state which had overcome me, he ﷺ struck me on my chest. I began perspiring profusely and was overcome by such fear as if I was seeing Allāh. He then gave the reason for considering their recitations to be correct by saying that it is permissible to recite in all these ways." This was related by Muslim.[436]

Commentary: The Practice of Taṣarruf

Striking a person and causing him to experience this condition is known as *taṣarruf* (conditioning or imposing).

The Condition of Ecstasy and Enthralment

The condition experienced by 'Ubayy ؓ after he was struck by the Prophet's ﷺ hand is known as ecstasy, *wajd*. Being overcome in this manner is an extreme

436 Muslim: 820

state of enthralment, *istighrāq*. We learn that it was an extreme state because the person compared it to seeing Allāh. It is obvious that if it were really possible to see Allāh in this world, Ubayy 🙏 would certainly not have remained conscious.

ḤADĪTH 283

عَنْ عُمَرَ بْنِ الْخَطَّابِ رَضِيَ اللهُ عَنْهُ قَالَ: اسْتَأْذَنْتُ النَّبِيَّ صَلَّى اللهُ عَلَيْهِ وَسَلَّمَ فِي الْعُمْرَةِ فَأَذِنَ لِيْ، وَقَالَ: «أَشْرِكْنَا يَا أَخِيْ فِيْ دُعَائِكَ وَلاَتَنْسَنَا» فَقَالَ كَلِمَةً مَايَسُرُّنِيْ أَنْ لِيْ بِهَا الدُّنْيَا. (رواه أبوداؤد)

ʿUmar ibn al-Khaṭṭāb 🙏 related: "I sought permission from the Messenger of Allāh 🙏 to perform ʿumrah. He 🙏 gave me permission and said: 'O my brother! Include us in your supplications and do not forget us.' This [request for supplication] was such that I would not agree to exchanging it for the entire world." This was related by Abū Dāwūd.[437]

Commentary: Benefiting from Those Below You
It is learnt from this ḥadīth that the people of perfection can obtain certain benefits from those below them. Therefore no one has the right to consider himself absolutely independent.

ḤADĪTH 284

عَنْ عَبْدِ اللهِ بْنِ عُمَرَ رَضِيَ اللهُ عَنْهُ عَنِ النَّبِيِّ صَلَّى اللهُ عَلَيْهِ وَسَلَّمَ أَنَّهُ كَانَ يَقُوْلُ: «لِكُلِّ شَيْءٍ صَقَالَةٌ وَصَقَالَةُ الْقُلُوْبِ ذِكْرُاللهِ». (رواه البيهقي)

ʿAbdullāh ibn ʿUmar 🙏 related that the Messenger of Allāh 🙏 used to say: "There is a polish for everything, and the polish for hearts is the remembrance of Allāh." This was related by Bayhaqī.[438]

Commentary: Proof for the Polishing of the Heart
The spiritual masters make frequent mention of the polishing of the heart. This ḥadīth clearly proves this.

---

437 Abū Dāwūd: 1498, Tirmidhī: 3562, Ibn Mājah: 2894
438 Al-Mundhirī has recorded it in *at-Targhīb wa 't-Tarhīb* from Ibn Abī'd-Dunyā and al-Bayhaqī: 2:254

ḤADĪTH 285

عَنِ ابْنِ مَسْعُوْدٍ رَضِيَ اللهُ عَنْهُ قَالَ: تَلا رَسُوْلُ اللهِ صَلَّى اللهُ عَلَيْهِ وَسَلَّمَ: ﴿فَمَن يُرِدِ اللهُ أَنْ يَّهْدِيَهُ يَشْرَحْ صَدْرَهُ لِلإِسْلاَمِ﴾ فَقَالَ رَسُوْلُ اللهِ صَلَّى اللهُ عَلَيْهِ وَسَلَّمَ: «إِنَّ النُّوْرَ إِذَا دَخَلَ الصَّدْرَ تَفَسَّحَ» فَقِيْلَ: يَارَسُوْلَ اللهِ! هَلْ لِتِلْكَ مِنْ عَلَمٍ يُعْرَفُ بِهِ؟ قَالَ: «نَعَمْ، التَّجَافِى مِنْ دَارِ الْغُرُوْرِ، وَالإِنَابَةُ إِلَى دَارِالْخُلُوْدِ، وَالاسْتِعْدَادُ لِلْمَوْتِ قَبْلَ نُزُوْلِهِ».

(رواه البيهقي)

Ibn Masᶜūd ﷺ related that the Messenger of Allāh ﷺ recited the verse: "Whomsover Allāh wills to guide, He expands his breast for Islam," he commented: "When light enters the breast, it expands." He ﷺ was asked: "O Messenger of Allāh! Is there any way of identifying this?" He ﷺ replied: "Yes, avoidance of the abode of deception [this world], attention to the abode of eternity, and preparation for death before its descent." This was related by Bayhaqī.[439]

Commentary: The Sign of Internal Affinity

Internal affinity for the Almighty is also known as enlightenment and expansion of the heart (*sharḥ aṣ-ṣadr*). The signs of this state are mentioned in the ḥadīth above. These signs may aid a person in his or her search for a spiritual guide. Other qualities are also necessary for a person to be eligible for the office of spiritual guide. But these qualities are also dependent (upon the presence of other qualifications). As such they should be understood as prerequisites and not reasons for eligibility as a spiritual guide.

ḤADĪTH 286

عَنْ أَبِيْ هُرَيْرَةَ رَضِيَ اللهُ عَنْهُ وَأَبِيْ خَلاَّدٍ رَضِيَ اللهُ عَنْهُ أَنَّ رَسُوْلَ اللهِ صَلَّى اللهُ عَلَيْهِ وَسَلَّمَ قَالَ: «إِذَا رَأَيْتُمُ الْعَبْدَ يُعْطى زُهْداً فِيْ الدُّنْيَا وَقِلَّةَ مَنْطِقٍ، فَاقْتَرِبُوْا مِنْهُ فَإِنَّهُ يُلْقَى الْحِكْمَةَ». (رواه البيهقي في شعب الإيمان)

Abū Huraira ﷺ and Abū Khallād ﷺ relate that the Messenger of Allāh ﷺ said: "If you see a person endowed with abstinence in this world and the

439 Al-Bayhaqī has recorded this in his *Shuᶜab al-Īmān*: 10552

trait of speaking less, stay close to him for he is bestowed with wisdom [from Allāh]." This was related by Bayhaqī.[440]

Commentary: Esoteric Knowledge
The sort of knowledge alluded to in the ḥadīth above is also known as esoteric, *ʿilm ladunnī* and bestowed knowledge, *ʿilm wahbī* (as opposed to acquired knowledge). Such knowledge may be gifted to the closest servants of the Almighty ﷻ. Indeed, many of the writings of these servants contain such knowledge and have been compiled and preserved. The literalists, owing to their lack of understanding, reject all this and may be understood to be those described in the following poem:

> How many people find fault with a correct statement,
> when their trouble is only that they suffer from poor understanding.

ḤADĪTH 287

عَنْ أُمَيَّةَ بْنِ خَالِدِ بْنِ عَبْدِ اللهِ بْنِ أُسَيْدٍ عَنِ النَّبِيِّ صَلَّى اللهُ عَلَيْهِ وَسَلَّمَ أَنَّهُ كَانَ يَسْتَفْتِحُ بِصَعَالِيْكِ الْمُهَاجِرِيْنَ. (رواه في شرح السنة)

Umayyah ibn Khālid ibn ʿAbdullāh ibn Usayd ؓ related that the Messenger of Allāh ﷺ used to supplicate for victory through the poor Emigrants. This is related in the *Sharḥ as-Sunnah*.[441]

Commentary: The Practice of Using an Intermediary
It is common practice, known as *tawassul*, for Sufis to supplicate the Almighty ﷻ through the offices of an intermediary among the accepted servants of Allāh ﷻ. The legitimacy of such a practice is established from the ḥadīth above. This practice also explains the essence and purpose of reciting the aspirant's spiritual family tree, *shajarah* (the names of spiritual masters in a continuous chain) which is popular among Sufis.

ḤADĪTH 288

عَنْ أَنَسٍ رَضِيَ اللهُ عَنْهُ أَنَّ عُمَرَ بْنَ الْخَطَّابِ رَضِيَ اللهُ عَنْهُ كَانَ إِذَا قَحَطُوْا اسْتَسْقَى

---

440 Al-Bayhaqī has recorded this in his *Shuʿab al-Īmān*: 4985 [4:254]
441 Al-Baghawī has reported this in his *Sharḥ as-Sunnah*: 7:303

بِالْعَبَّاسِ بْنِ عَبْدِ الْمُطَّلِبِ فَقَالَ: اللّٰهُمَّ إِنَّا كُنَّا نَتَوَسَّلُ إِلَيْكَ بِنَبِيِّنَا فَتَسْقِيْنَا، وَإِنَّا نَتَوَسَّلُ إِلَيْكَ بِعَمِّ نَبِيِّنَا فَاسْقِنَا ، فَيُسْقَوْنَ. (رواه البخاري)

Anas ﷺ related that "When they experienced a drought, ʿUmar ibn al-Khaṭṭāb ﷺ used to supplicate for rain through ʿAbbas ibn ʿAbd al-Muṭṭalib ﷺ saying: 'O Allāh! We used to supplicate for rain through our Prophet ﷺ and You used to send rain to us. We are now supplicating You through the uncle of the Prophet ﷺ, so send rain to us.' Rain would then come down to them." This was related by Bukhārī.[442]

Commentary
Like the previous ḥadīth, this ḥadīth also proves the permissibility of *tawassul.* The permissibility of *tawassul* through the Messenger of Allāh ﷺ was obvious. This statement of ʿUmar ﷺ was to show that *tawassul* is permissible through people other than Prophets as well. Therefore, the assertion that there is a difference in the ruling for *tawassul* with regard to those who are alive and those who are deceased is a baseless assertion. First of all, the Messenger of Allāh ﷺ is alive in his grave, as expressly stated in an authentic ḥadīth. Secondly, since the basis for permissibility is found in both cases, why should the ruling not be the same for both?

ḤADĪTH 289

عَنْ أَبِيْ الدَّرْدَاءِ رَضِيَ اللهُ عَنْهُ عَنِ النَّبِيِّ صَلَّى اللهُ عَلَيْهِ وَسَلَّمَ قَالَ: «أَبْغُوْنِيْ فِيْ ضُعَفَاءِكُمْ فَإِنَّمَا تُرْزَقُوْنَ أَوْ تُنْصَرُوْنَ بِضُعَفَاءِكُمْ». (رواه أبو داؤد)

Abū ad-Dardā' ﷺ related that the Messenger of Allāh ﷺ said: "Search for me [on the day of Resurrection] among your poor because [they enjoy such a status whereby] you receive sustenance or victory by virtue of your poor." This was related by Abū Dāwūd.[443]

Commentary
Like the previous two ḥadīths, this ḥadīth also proves the permissibility of *tawassul.* In fact, this ḥadīth establishes *tawassul* merely on the basis of Islam. This is because non-Muslims are certainly not intended in the ḥadīth. The precondition is the person must have some basis for acceptance [in the sight of Allāh] such as poverty, as mentioned in this ḥadīth.

442 Bukhārī: 1010
443 Abū Dāwūd: 2594, Tirmidhī: 1702, Nasā'ī: 3181

ḤADĪTH 290

عَنْ أَبِيْ هُرَيْرَةَ رَضِيَ اللهُ عَنْهُ قَالَ: دَخَلَ رَجُلٌ عَلى أَهْلِهِ، فَلَمَّا رَأى مَالَهُمْ مِنَ الْحَاجَةِ خَرَجَ إِلَى الْبَرِيَّةِ، فَلَمَّا رَأَتْ امْرَأَتُهُ قَامَتْ إِلَى الرَّحَى فَوَضَعَتْهَا، وَإِلَى التَّنُّوْرِ فَسَجَّرَتْهُ، ثُمَّ قَالَتْ: اللّٰهُمَّ ارْزُقْنَا، فَنَظَرَتْ فَإِذَا الْجَفْنَةُ قَدْ امْتَلأَتْ، قَالَ: وَذَهَبَتْ إِلَى التَّنُّوْرِ فَوَجَدَتْهُ مُمْتَلِئاً، قَالَ: فَرَجَعَ الزَّوْجُ قَالَ: أَصَبْتُمْ بَعْدِيْ شَيْئًا؟ قَالَتِ امْرَأَتُهُ: نَعَمْ مِنْ رَبِّنَا، وَقَامَ إِلَى الرَّحَى فَذَكَرَ ذٰلِكَ لِلنَّبِيِّ صَلَّى اللهُ عَلَيْهِ وَسَلَّمَ فَقَالَ: «أَمَا إِنَّهُ لَوْلَمْ يَرْفَعْهَا لَمْ تَزَلْ تَدُوْرُ إِلى يَوْمِ الْقِيمَةِ». (رواه أحمد)

Abū Huraira related that a man entered his home and, seeing the needs of his family, went out to earn something for them. When his wife saw this, she went to the mill-stone and placed the upper stone onto the lower stone. Then she went to the oven and ignited it, making the following supplication: "O Allāh! Provide us with sustenance." When she looked, she saw that the circle of the mill-stone was filled [with flour]. She went to the oven and saw that it was filled [with bread]. When her husband returned home, he asked: "Did you receive anything in my absence?" She replied: "Yes. We received it from our Sustainer." The man went to the mill-stone [and lifted its stone]. This incident was related to the Messenger of Allāh who said: "Had he not lifted the stone, it would have continued milling till the day of Resurrection [and flour would have continued coming out of it]." This was related by Aḥmad.[444]

Commentary
See the commentary for ḥadīth [254].

ḤADĪTH 291

عَنِ ابْنِ مَسْعُوْدٍ رَضِيَ اللهُ عَنْهُ قَالَ: كَأَنِّيْ أَنْظُرُ إِلى رَسُوْلِ اللهِ صَلَّى اللهُ عَلَيْهِ وَسَلَّمَ يَحْكِيْ نَبِيًّا مِنَ الْأَنْبِيَاءِ ضَرَبَهُ قَوْمُهُ فَأَدْمَوْهُ وَهُوَ يَمْسَحُ الدَّمَ عَنْ وَجْهِهِ وَيَقُوْلُ: «اللّٰهُمَّ اغْفِرْ لِقَوْمِيْ فَإِنَّهُمْ لَايَعْلَمُوْنَ. (متفق عليه)

Ibn Masʿūd related: "It is as though I can picture the Messenger of

---

444 *Musnad Aḥmad*: 2:513

Allāh ﷻ relating the story of one of the previous Prophets ﷺ whose people had beat him and caused blood to flow from his body. He was wiping the blood off his face and saying: 'O Allāh! Forgive my people because they know not what they do.'" This was related by Bukhārī and Muslim.[445]

Commentary: Picturing One's Spiritual Master

Among the many benefits of envisioning one's spiritual master, though the vision is not real, and though the purpose of the exercise is not mentioned in the ḥadīth above, is to draw one's attention toward the absent in the same way one's attention is drawn toward the present. Such a practice is clearly indicated in the ḥadīth above. Even so, owing to a preponderence of ignorance among people today, the practice has become subject to abuse and, in view of these factors, most scholars lean toward its prohibition.

ḤADĪTH 292

عَنْ أَبِيْ هُرَيْرَةَ رَضِيَ اللهُ عَنْهُ قَالَ: قَالَ رَسُوْلُ اللهِ صَلَّى اللهُ عَلَيْهِ وَسَلَّمَ: «يَخْرُجُ فِيْ آخِرِ الزَّمَانِ رِجَالٌ يَخْتِلُوْنَ الدُّنْيَا بِالدِّيْنِ يَلْبَسُوْنَ لِلنَّاسِ جُلُوْدَ الضَّأْنِ مِنَ اللِّيْنِ، أَلْسِنَتُهُمْ أَحْلى مِنَ السُّكَّرِ، وَقُلُوْبُهُمْ قُلُوْبُ الذِّئَابِ يَقُوْلُ اللهُ: أَبِيَ يَغْتَرُّوْنَ أَمْ عَلَيَّ يَجْتَرِئُوْنَ؟ فَبِيْ حَلَفْتُ لأَبْعَثَنَّ عَلى أولِئَكَ مِنْهُمْ فِتْنَةً تَدَعُ الْحَلِيْمَ مِنْهُمْ حَيْرَاناً». (رواه الترمذي)

Abū Huraira رضي الله عنه related that the Messenger of Allāh ﷺ said: "In the latter days people will emerge who will deceptively acquire the world in exchange for their religion. They will wear the skins of sheep and their tongues will be sweeter than sugar, while in their hearts they will be wolves. Allāh ﷻ says: 'Are these people deluded by Me? Or are they displaying their audacity against Me? I take an oath on Myself. I will subject them to a tribulation which will leave even the most forebearing among them in trauma.'" This was related by Tirmidhī.[446]

Commentary: Fake Sufis

This ḥadīth is clear in its condemnation of spiritual pretenders and false Sufis.

445 Bukhārī: 3477, Muslim: 1792

446 Tirmidhī: 2404

ḤADĪTH 293

عَنْ أَبِيْ هُرَيْرَةَ رَضِيَ اللهُ عَنْهُ قَالَ: قَالَ النَّبِيُّ صَلَّى اللهُ عَلَيْهِ وَسَلَّمَ: «إِنَّ لِكُلِّ شَيْءٍ شِرَّةً وَلِكُلِّ شِرَّةِ فَتْرَةً، فَإِنْ صَاحِبُهَا سَدَّدَ وَقَارَبَ فَارْجُوْهُ وَإِنْ أُشِيْرَ إِلَيْهِ بِالأَصَابِع فَلا تَعُدُّوْهُ». (رواه الترمذي)

Abū Huraira related that the Messenger of Allāh said: "There is a novelty to everything, and after every novelty there is boredom. If a person remains steadfast and balanced, there is hope for that person (in the sense that you may expect to continue to see good things from this person). But if he continues to attract attention from people (for no more than his novelty), do not think too much of him (as he is probably not worthy of consideration)." This was related by Tirmidhī.[447]

Commentary: Moderation in Striving
The spiritual masters prohibit excess in an aspirant's striving, *mujāhadah* through spiritual disciplines. This is clearly taught in this ḥadīth. When a person commits excesses in this regard, the novelty wears off, he becomes fed up, and his health deteriorates. This also leads to his abandonment of good deeds and striving. It may also lead to lunacy at times.

ḤADĪTH 294

عَنْ أَبِيْ هُرَيْرَةَ رَضِيَ اللهُ عَنْهُ قَالَ: لَمَّا نَزَلَتْ: ﴿وَأَنْذِرْ عَشِيْرَتَكَ الأَقْرَبِيْنَ﴾ دَعَا النَّبِيُّ صَلَّى اللهُ عَلَيْهِ وَسَلَّمَ قُرَيْشاً. الحديث. وَفِيْه: «يَا فَاطِمَةُ! أَنْقِذِيْ نَفْسَكِ مِنَ النَّارِ فَإِنِّيْ لا أَمْلِكُ لَكِ مِنَ اللهِ شَيْئاً. (رواه مسلم)

Abū Huraira related that when this verse was revealed: "And warn your close relatives", the Messenger of Allāh summoned the Quraysh and gathered them. This ḥadīth also states that he said [to Fatimah]: "O Fatimah! Save yourself from the Hellfire because I do not have the power to save you from Allāh." This was related by Muslim.[448]

Commentary: There is no Basis for Boasting of One's Lineage
Some people proudly boast that they are the offspring of such and such a pious

---

447 Tirmidhī: 2453
448 Muslim: 204, Tirmidhī: 3185, Nasāʾī: 3674

personality, or that they pledged their allegiance (bay'ah) to such and such a family or Sufi order. Consequently, they neglect their beliefs and actions. This ḥadīth cuts the roots off of all such claims and boasting.

ḤADĪTH 295

عَنْ صَالِحِ بْنِ دِرْهَمٍ يَقُوْلُ: انْطَلَقْنَا حَاجِّيْنَ فَإِذَا رَجُلٌ فَقَالَ لَنَا: إِلَى جَنْبِكُمْ قَرْيَةٌ يُقَالُ لَهَا الْأُبُلَّةُ؟ قُلْنَا: نَعَمْ، قَالَ: مَنْ يَضْمَنُ لِيْ مِنْكُمْ أَنْ يُصَلِّيَ لِيْ فِيْ مَسْجِدِ الْعَشَّارِ رَكْعَتَيْنِ أَوْ أَرْبَعاً وَيَقُوْلُ هذِهِ لِأَبِيْ هُرَيْرَةَ؟ سَمِعْتُ خَلِيْلِيْ أَبَا الْقَاسِمِ صَلَّى اللهُ عَلَيْهِ وَسَلَّمَ يَقُوْلُ: «إِنَّ اللهَ عَزَّ وَجَلَّ يَبْعَثُ مِنْ مَسْجِدِ الْعَشَّارِ يَوْمَ الْقِيَمَةِ شُهَدَاءَ، لَا يَقُوْمُ مَعَ شُهَدَاءِ بَدْرٍ غَيْرُهُمْ». (رواه أبو داؤد)

Ṣāliḥ ibn Dirham ؓ related: "We departed for the Ḥajj and met a person on the way who asked us: 'Is there any village near you by the name of al-Ubullah?' We replied: 'Yes.' He asked: 'Is there anyone among you who can take the responsibility of offering two or four cycles of prayer in the Masjid al-'Ashshār [which is in this village] and say that these cycles are on behalf of Abū Huraira ؓ? I heard my bosom-friend Abū al-Qāsim ﷺ saying: 'On the day of Resurrection Allāh ﷻ will raise from the Masjid al-'Ashshār such martyrs who will rise with the martyrs of Badr. No other martyrs will rise with them.'" This was related by Abū Dāwūd.[449]

Commentary: Conveying Rewards to Others
It is obvious that asking someone to offer [this ṣalāh] on behalf of Abū Huraira ؓ is solely for the purpose of conveying this reward to Abū Huraira ؓ. Two issues with regard to conveying spiritual rewards, īṣāl thawāb are established from this ḥadīth: (1) Just as the rewards for worship by expenditure [such as charity] reach [the person in whose name it is carried out], in like manner, the rewards for physical worship reach [the person in whose name it is carried out]. (2) Just as the rewards reach the deceased, they also reach those who are alive. This is because the person who made this request was Abū Huraira ؓ himself, and he was obviously alive at the time.

Fulfilling Acts of Worship in Blessed Places
It is noticed that some of those who love their spiritual masters pay particular

---

449 Abū Dāwūd: 4308

attention to engaging in remembrance and other acts of worship at the places where their spiritual master lives or at the places where he performs his acts of worship. They do this because they consider these places to be blessed. The blessed nature of such places is obvious; and the ḥadīth establishes the benefit of carrying out acts of worship in blessed places.

ḤADĪTH 296

عَنْ أَبِيْ سَعِيْدٍ رَضِيَ اللهُ عَنْهُ قَالَ: لَقِيَ رَسُوْلُ اللهِ صَلَّى اللهُ عَلَيْهِ وَسَلَّمَ ابْنَ صَيَّادٍ فِيْ بَعْضِ طُرُقِ الْمَدِيْنَةِ، فَقَالَ لَهُ رَسُوْلُ اللهِ صَلَّى اللهُ عَلَيْهِ وَسَلَّمَ: «أَتَشْهَدُ أَنِّيْ رَسُوْلُ اللهِ» فَقَالَ هُوَ: أَتَشْهَدُ أَنِّيْ رَسُوْلُ اللهِ؟ فَقَالَ رَسُوْلُ اللهِ صَلَّى اللهُ عَلَيْهِ وَسَلَّمَ: «اٰمَنْتُ بِاللهِ وَمَلَائِكَتِهِ وَكُتُبِهِ وَرُسُلِهِ، مَاذَا تَرَي؟» قَالَ: أَرى عَرْشاً عَلَيَ الْمَاءِ، فَقَالَ رَسُوْلُ اللهِ صَلَّى اللهُ عَلَيْهِ وَسَلَّمَ: «تَرى عَرْشَ إِبْلِيْسَ عَلَيَ الْبَحْرِ». الحديث (رواه مسلم)

Abū Saʿīd ﵁ related that the Messenger of Allāh ﷺ met Ibn Ṣayyād[450] on one of the roads of Madīna. The Messenger of Allāh ﷺ asked him: "Do you testify that I am the Messenger of Allāh?" He replied: "Do you testify that I am the Messenger of Allāh?" The Messenger of Allāh ﷺ said: "I believe in Allāh, His angels, His Books and His Messengers." [That is, "I do not testify to the prophethood of one who is not a prophet." However, in order to avoid conflict, the Messenger of Allāh ﷺ did not state this outwardly.] "Very well, now you tell me. What do you see?" Ibn Ṣayyād replied: "I see a throne on the water." The Messenger of Allāh ﷺ said: "You see the throne of Satan over an ocean." This was related by Muslim.[451]

Commentary: Resorting to Ambiguity When Fearing Tribulation

In order to safeguard themselves from the excesses of corrupt rulers or ignorant people in general, some spiritual masters will use ambiguous language to express themselves. People who consider everything literally are therefore under the illusion that the spiritual master is concealing the truth. However, if the reason for concealing is based on an underlying reason which is acceptable in the Sharīʿa, then it is in total accordance with this ḥadīth.

---

450 See the notes regarding Ibn Ṣayyād at Ḥadīth 211.

451 Muslim: 2925

Deceptive Spiritual Visions

It may be inferred from this ḥadīth that even people who are deluded may also experience spiritual visions, *kashf*. The ḥadīth also explains that not every spiritual vision is either acceptable or commendable. Consequently, the vision of Satan's throne experienced by this person, Ibn Ṣayyād, is referred to in critical terms [by the Messenger of Allāh ﷺ]. Therefore, those who consider a spiritual vision to be a sign of a close relationship with the Almighty, *wilāyah*, or who give credence to and rely upon every spiritual vision (without differentiating between what is true and what is false) must examine their beliefs in this regard after considering this ḥadīth.

ḤADĪTH 297

عَنِ ابْنِ عَبَّاسٍ رَضِيَ اللهُ عَنْهُ قَالَ: سِرْنَا مَعَ رَسُوْلِ اللهِ صَلَّى اللهُ عَلَيْهِ وَسَلَّمَ بَيْنَ مَكَّةَ وَالْمَدِيْنَةِ فَمَرَرْنَا بِوَادٍ فَقَالَ: «أَيُّ وَادٍ هذَا؟» فَقَالُوْا: وَادِيْ الْأَزْرَقِ قَالَ: «كَأَنِّيْ أَنْظُرُ إِلى مُوْسى عَلَيْهِ السَّلاَمُ - فَذَكَرَ مِنْ لَوْنِهِ وَشَعْرِهِ شَيْئاً - وَاضِعاً إِصْبَعَيْهِ فِيْ أُذُنَيْهِ، لَهُ جُؤَارٌ إِلَيَ اللهِ بِالتَّلْبِيَةِ مَاراًّ بِهذَا الْوَادِيْ» قَالَ: ثُمَّ سِرْنَا حَتّى أَتَيْنَا عَلى ثَنِيَّةٍ، فَقَالَ: «أَيُّ ثَنِيَّةٍ هذِهِ؟» قَالُوْا: هَرْشى أَوْ لَفْتٌ. فَقَالَ: «كَأَنِّيْ أَنْظُرُ إِلى يُوْنُسَ عَلَيْهِ السَّلاَمُ عَلى نَاقَةٍ حَمْرَاءَ، عَلَيْهِ جُبَّةٌ صُوْفٍ، خِطَامُ نَاقَتِهِ لِيْفٌ خُلْبَةٌ، مَارًّا بِهذَا الْوَادِيْ مُلَبِّيًا». (رواه مسلم)

Ibn ʿAbbās ﷺ related: "We were travelling with the Messenger of Allāh ﷺ between Makka and Madīna when we passed by a valley. He ﷺ asked: 'What valley is this?' The people replied: 'This is the Azraq valley.' He ﷺ said: 'I can see Mūsā here as if he were present.' He then described the complexion of his skin and something about his hair, adding that his fingers were in his ears and that he was chanting the pilgrims' chant, *talbiyah* (i.e. saying *Labbayk*) to Allāh as he passed through the valley." Ibn ʿAbbās ﷺ said: "We then proceeded until we reached a pass. The Messenger of Allāh ﷺ asked: 'Which pass is this?' The people replied: 'It is the Harshay or Laft pass.' He ﷺ said: 'I can see Yūnūs here as if he were present, riding a red camel and wearing a woollen cloak. The halter of his camel is made of the bark of the date palm. He is passing by this valley saying the *talbiyah*.'" This was related by Muslim.[452]

---

452 Muslim: 166

Commentary: The Appearance of the Soul at a Place after Death
This ḥadīth shows that Mūsā ﷺ and Yūnūs ﷺ were seen by the Messenger of Allāh ﷺ. This was a spiritual manifestation because at the time both of their bodies were in their graves.

ḤADĪTH 298

عَنْ جُبَيْرِ بْنِ مُطْعِمٍ رَضِيَ اللهُ عَنْهُ قَالَ أَتَى رَسُوْلَ اللهِ صَلَّى اللهُ عَلَيْهِ وَسَلَّمَ أَعْرَابِيٌّ فَقَالَ: جُهِدَتِ الْأَنْفُسُ وَجَاعَتِ الْعِيَالُ وَنُهِكَتِ الْأَمْوَالُ وَهَلَكَتِ الْأَنْعَامُ فَاسْتَسْقِ اللهَ لَنَا فَإِنَّا نَسْتَشْفِعُ بِكَ عَلَى اللهِ وَنَسْتَشْفِعُ بِاللهِ عَلَيْكَ . فَقَالَ النَّبِيُّ صَلَّى اللهُ عَلَيْهِ وَسَلَّمَ: «سُبْحَانَ اللهِ سُبْحَانَ اللهِ» فَمَا زَالَ يُسَبِّحُ حَتَّى عُرِفَ ذٰلِكَ فِيْ وُجُوْهِ أَصْحَابِهِ ثُمَّ قَالَ: «وَيْحَكَ إِنَّهُ لَايُسْتَشْفَعُ بِاللهِ عَلَى أَحَدٍ، شَأْنُ اللهِ أَعْظَمُ مِنْ ذٰلِكَ». الحديث (رواه أبوداؤد)

Jubayr ibn Mutʿim ﷺ related that a Bedouin came to the Messenger of Allāh ﷺ and said: "People have done everything they could do, but families are hungry, fortunes (orchards and plantations) have been destroyed, and cattle are dying. Pray to Allāh ﷻ for us and ask Him to send down rain. We petition you as an intercessor before Allāh ﷻ, and we petition Allāh ﷻ as an intercessor before you." The Messenger of Allāh ﷺ (became distressed by these words: "we petition Allāh ﷻ as an intercessor before you" and) began saying, "Glory be to Allāh, glory be to Allāh, *subḥānAllāh, subḥānAllāh*." He ﷺ repeated these words with such intensity that their effects were seen on the faces of his Companions. Finally he ﷺ said: "Woe unto you! Allāh is not to be considered an intercessor before anyone. Allāh's status is far beyond that." (In other words, an intercession entails a supplication and a need. Allāh does not supplicate anyone, nor is He in need of anyone. This statement supposes Allāh to have need, and is therefore repulsive). This ḥadīth was related by Abū Dāwūd.[453]

Commentary: Etiquette and the Status of the Almighty
Some Sufis are overly audacious when supplicating Allāh ﷻ. This ḥadīth should provide guidance to such people. When the Messenger of Allāh ﷺ so emphatically distanced himself from the supplication made by this ordinary person, how much more reprehensible will it be for a person who seeks a relationship with Allāh to say such things?! Some people are not audacious but make inappropri-

453 Abū Dāwūd: 4726

ate statements out of ignorance, as was the case with this Bedouin. It is essential, even in such situations, to avoid all impropriety. However, in such cases (in which things are said out of ignorance), the one saying these things will not be declared an unbeliever, as the Messenger of Allāh ﷺ did not declare this Bedouin to be guilty of disbelief. It is nevertheless obligatory to bring the matter to the attention of the offender and to reject it to the clearest degree possible. Yes, those who are overcome by their spiritual condition may be excused for their enthusiasm and pardoned. Once they recover from their condition, however, the matter should be explained to them gently.

ḤADĪTH 299

عَنْ أَبِيْ هُرَيْرَةَ رَضِيَ اللهُ عَنْهُ قَالَ رَسُوْلُ اللهِ صَلَّى اللهُ عَلَيْهِ وَسَلَّمَ: «وَالَّذِيْ نَفْسُ مُحَمَّدٍ بِيَدِهِ لَوْ أَنَّكُمْ دَلَّيْتُمْ بِحَبْلٍ إِلَيَ الْأَرْضِ السُّفْلَى لَهَبَطَ عَلَيَ اللهِ». الحديث (رواه أحمد والترمذي)

Abū Huraira ﷺ related that the Messenger of Allāh ﷺ said: "I swear by the One Whose hands hold the life of Muḥammad! If you were to lower a rope to the lowest level on earth, it will fall on Allāh." (In other words, Allāh ﷻ is present there as well). This was related by Aḥmad and Tirmidhī.[454]

Commentary: Allāh is Everywhere

In explaining the omnipresent attribute of the Almighty, the speech of many Sufis portrays His all-encompassing Being in physical form. To begin with, the issue of omnipresence is a subject of debate among the theologians; and likewise the issue of how this is manifested. The only certain way to avoid error in this regard is to maintain that the Almighty is above all earthly, material, corporeal and ephemeral phenomena. At the same time, according to scripture (the Qur'ān and authentic ḥadīth literature) the Almighty assumes a position on a throne; and therefore there are literalists who mistakenly suppose the sayings of the Sufis to be contrary to the orthodox theological interpretations. The ḥadīth above, however, upholds the position of the Sufis. To those who hold misgivings with regard to the Sufis we say that whatever explanation they offer for the ḥadīth above is the same explanation the Sufis will give for the statements they make.

454 *Musnad Aḥmad*: 2:370, Tirmidhī: 3298

ḤADĪTH 300

عَنْ عَائِشَةَ رَضِيَ الله تَعَالى عَنْهَا فِيْ حَدِيْثٍ طَوِيْلٍ أَنَّ النَّبِيَّ صَلَّى اللهُ عَلَيْهِ وَسَلَّمَ حَزِنَ حُزْناً غَدَا مِنْهُ مِرَاراً كَيْ يَتَرَدّى مِنْ رُؤُوْسِ شَوَاهِقِ الْجِبَالِ، فَكُلَّمَا أَوْفى بِذِرْوَةِ جَبَلٍ لِكَيْ يُلْقِيَ نَفْسَهُ مِنْهُ تَبَدّى لَهُ جِبْرَئِيْلُ فَقَالَ: يَا مُحَمَّدُ إِنَّكَ رَسُوْلُ اللهِ حَقاً، فَيَسْكُنُ لِذٰلِكَ جَأْشُهُ وَتَقِرُّ نَفْسُهُ. (رواه البخاري)

ʿĀ'isha ﵂ related in a lengthy ḥadīth that (at the beginning of prophethood when there was a pause in revelation), the Messenger of Allāh ﷺ became so distressed that he went out several times to fling himself from the mountain tops and kill himself. Each time he climbed a mountain in order to fling himself from it, Jibra'īl ﵇ would appear before him and say: "O Muḥammad! (Do not be distressed). You are most certainly the Messenger of Allāh." His heart would then experience ease from this and his soul would come to rest." This was related by Bukhārī.[455]

Commentary: The state of Spiritual Contraction
The cessation of spiritual expansion, for whatever reason, is known as contraction, *qabḍ*. That such a condition may occur is confirmed in this ḥadīth.

The person who experiences contraction may be excused from committing suicide. It sometimes happens that people who experience contraction become disheartened and dejected to the extent that they commit suicide. A close reading of the ḥadīth above, however, reveals that it is not unreasonable to assume that such people may be excused in the sight of the Almighty. When the Messenger of Allāh ﷺ himself, despite his well-known powers of self-control, considered doing this, it is not difficult to see how others might fall into such a situation. There is nothing in the ḥadīth or sīrah literature to suggest that he was reprimanded for this intention. The same can be assumed if he actually committed the act.[456]

---

455 Bukhārī: 6982

456 Suicide is a painful and tragic act and must never be encouraged. This may explain why the Prophet ﷺ avoided the funeral prayer for suicides and taught that community leaders and officials should also avoid them. This does not mean, however, that people should scorn or in any other way belittle or malign those who take their own lives. On the contrary, friends and family should join in the funeral proceedings, including the *janāzah* prayer, both to seek blessings for the departed and as a way of giving solace to one another. Suicide is an act of desperation; and only the Almighty ﷻ can know the reasons for its occurrence. Judgment is for Allāh ﷻ alone. For those left behind, there is grief and, in many cases, guilt. The funeral prayer is a way to bring closure to all of that. The author's commentary here is perceptive and, to my knowledge, unique. YTD.

Consolation from the Sheikh When a Person Experiences Contraction
Spiritual masters may also provide consolation to aspirants who are beset by such conditions by telling them that their condition is actually a praiseworthy one, and by explaining to them the underlying reasons and advantages of such a condition. All of this may actually benefit the *murīd*.

ḤADĪTH 301

عَنْ عَائِشَةَ رَضِيَ الله تَعَالى عَنْهَا أَنَّ الْحَارِثَ بْنَ هِشَام سَأَلَ رَسُوْلَ الله صَلَّى اللهُ عَلَيْهِ وَسَلَّمَ، فَقَالَ: يَا رَسُوْلَ الله! كَيْفَ يَأْتِيْكَ الْوَحْيُ؟ فَقَالَ رَسُوْلَ الله صَلَّى اللهُ عَلَيْهِ وَسَلَّمَ: «أَحْيَاناً يَأْتِيْنِيْ مِثْلَ صَلْصَلَةِ الْجَرَسِ». الحديث (متفق عليه)

'Ā'isha ♦ related that al-Ḥārith ibn Hishām ♦ asked the Messenger of Allāh ♦: "O Messenger of Allāh! How does revelation come to you?" The Messenger of Allāh ♦ replied: "At times it comes to me like the ringing of a bell." This was related by Bukhārī and Muslim.[457]

Commentary: The Confirmation of an Unseen Voice
Unseen voices are often mentioned in the works of the spiritual masters. The validity of this is confirmed from this ḥadīth. It is, however, a serious mistake to consider every voice to be an unseen voice when a person is engaged in spiritual exercises like *murāqabah* and *dhikr*. For example, when a person is engaged in certain breathing exercises, the person may experience what he assumes is a voice. So, while some people assume it to be a voice from the Unseen, it is more likely the result of the wave-like movement of air from one's breathing. It was the belief among many Indian Sufis that this is indeed an unseen voice; and it was for this reason that they named it "*unadiy*" which means "ancient". This is a completely false and mistaken belief; firstly for considering it to come from the Unseen, and secondly for considering it to be the voice of truth or of the Almighty Himself. Allāh ♦ is most pure of this. This is the belief of our genuine Sufis.

ḤADĪTH 302

عَنْ عَائِذِ بْنِ عَمْرٍو رَضِيَ اللهُ عَنْهُ فِيْ حَدِيْثٍ طَوِيْلٍ أَنَّ النَّبِيَّ صَلَّى اللهُ عَلَيْهِ وَسَلَّمَ قَالَ:

---

457 Bukhārī: 3, Muslim: 2333, Tirmidhī: 3634, Nasā'ī: 935

«يَا أَبَا بَكْرٍ! لَعَلَّكَ أَغْضَبْتَهُمْ لَقَدْ أَغْضَبْتَ رَبَّكَ»، فَأَتَاهُمْ فَقَالَ يَا إِخْوَتَاهْ أَغْضَبْتُكُمْ قَالُوْا: لا، يَغْفِرُ اللهُ لَكَ يَا أَخِيْ. (رواه مسلم)

ʿĀ'idh ibn ʿAmr ﷺ related in a lengthy ḥadīth (wherein Abū Bakr ﷺ offered advice to Salmān, Ṣuhayb and Bilāl ﷺ in a way which seemed to be siding with a certain tribal leader) that the Messenger of Allāh ﷺ said: "O Abū Bakr! You may have angered them. And if you angered them, you most certainly angered your Lord." Immediately, Abū Bakr ﷺ went to them and said: "My brothers, it seems perhaps that I have angered you." They replied: "No, brother. May Allāh forgive you." This was related by Muslim.[458]

One Who Wishes to Sit with Allāh Should Sit with the People of Tasawwuf

This is a well-known statement of the Sufis. The correctness of this statement is established from this ḥadīth in the following manner. The words of the Messenger of Allāh ﷺ: "If you angered them. . ." demonstrate that Allāh ﷻ is treated in the manner in which the accepted servants of Allāh ﷻ are treated. Based on this, it is also correct to say that sitting in the company of the accepted servants of Allāh ﷻ is similar to sitting in the company of Allāh ﷻ. The words "sitting in the company" is proven from another ḥadīth wherein Allāh ﷻ says: "I am the sitting companion (*jalīs*) of the one who remembers Me."

ḤADĪTH 303

عَنْ شُرَيْحِ بْنِ عُبَيْدٍ قَالَ: ذُكِرَ أَهْلُ الشَّامِ عِنْدَ عَلِيٍّ رَضِيَ اللهُ عَنْهُ وَقِيْلَ: الْعَنْهُمْ يَا أَمِيْرَ الْمُؤْمِنِيْنَ قَالَ: لا، إِنِّيْ سَمِعْتُ رَسُوْلَ اللهِ صَلَّى اللهُ عَلَيْهِ وَسَلَّمَ يَقُوْلُ: «الأَبْدَالُ يَكُوْنُوْنَ بِالشَّامِ وَهُمْ أَرْبَعُوْنَ رَجُلاً كُلَّمَا مَاتَ رَجُلٌ أَبْدَلَ اللهُ مَكَانَهُ رَجُلاً يُسْقَى بِهِمُ الْغَيْثُ وَيَنْتَصِرُ بِهِمْ عَلَى الْأَعْدَاءِ وَيَنْصَرِفُ عَنْ أَهْلِ الشَّامِ بِهِمُ الْعَذَابُ».(رواه أحمد)

Shurayḥ ibn ʿUbayd related that someone made mention of the people of Syria in the presence of ʿAlī ﷺ. Someone [who was present there] said: "O Commander of the Faithful! Curse them." He replied: "No. I heard the Messenger of Allāh ﷺ saying: "The *abdāl* [a category of friends (*awliyā'*) of Allāh] live in Syria. They are forty in number. When any of them passes away, Allāh replaces him with another person. It is through their blessings that the rain falls, it is through them that enemies are vanquished,

458 Muslim: 2504

and it is through them that [worldly] punishment is averted from the people of Syria." This was related by Aḥmad.[459]

Commentary: The Existence of Abdāl and Others

The statements and writings of the Sufis make reference to *abdāl*, *aqṭāb*, *awtād*, *ghawth*, etc. and also speak of their qualities, blessings and actions. Since this ḥadīth makes reference to one category, the existence of other categories is not unreasonable to imagine. The existence of one giving support to the existence of another is an established and well-known fact. The blessings of these spiritual giants is clearly attested to in this ḥadīth. As for their actions in conceptual matters, this is affirmed from the story of Khiḍr in the Qur'ān.

ḤADĪTH 304

عَنْ شُفَيٍّ الْأَصْبَحِيِّ قُلْتُ لِأَبِيْ هُرَيْرَةَ رَضِيَ اللهُ عَنْهُ أَسْأَلُكَ بِحَقٍّ وَبِحَقٍّ لِمَا حَدَّثْتَنِيْ حَدِيْثاً سَمِعْتَهُ مِنْ رَسُوْلِ اللهِ صَلَّى اللهُ عَلَيْهِ وَسَلَّمَ عَقَلْتَهُ وَعَلِمْتَهُ، فَقَالَ أَبُوْ هُرَيْرَةَ رَضِيَ اللهُ عَنْهُ: أَفْعَلُ لَأُحَدِّثَنَّكَ حَدِيْثاً حَدَّثَنِيْهِ رَسُوْلُ اللهِ صَلَّى اللهُ عَلَيْهِ وَسَلَّمَ عَقَلْتُهُ وَعَلِمْتُهُ، ثُمَّ نَشَغَ أَبُوْ هُرَيْرَةَ رَضِيَ اللهُ عَنْهُ نَشْغَةً، فَمَكَثْنَا قَلِيْلاً، ثُمَّ أَفَاقَ فَقَالَ: لَأُحَدِّثَنَّكَ حَدِيْثاً حَدَّثَنِيْهِ رَسُوْلُ اللهِ صَلَّى اللهُ عَلَيْهِ وَسَلَّمَ فِيْ هٰذَا الْبَيْتِ مَا مَعَنَا أَحَدٌ غَيْرِيْ وَغَيْرُهُ، ثُمَّ نَشَغَ أَبُوْ هُرَيْرَةَ رَضِيَ اللهُ عَنْهُ نَشْغَةً شَدِيْدَةً، ثُمَّ أَفَاقَ وَمَسَحَ وَجْهَهُ، وَقَالَ: أَفْعَلُ لَأُحَدِّثَنَّكَ حَدِيْثاً حَدَّثَنِيْهِ رَسُوْلُ اللهِ صَلَّى اللهُ عَلَيْهِ وَسَلَّمَ أَنَا وَهُوَ فِيْ هٰذَا الْبَيْتِ مَا مَعَنَا أَحَدٌ غَيْرِيْ وَغَيْرُهُ، ثُمَّ نَشَغَ أَبُوْ هُرَيْرَةَ رَضِيَ اللهُ عَنْهُ نَشْغَةً شَدِيْدَةً، ثُمَّ مَالَ خَارًّا عَلَى وَجْهِهِ فَأَسْنَدْتُهُ طَوِيْلاً، ثُمَّ أَفَاقَ فَقَالَ: حَدَّثَنِيْ رَسُوْلُ اللهِ صَلَّى اللهُ عَلَيْهِ وَسَلَّمَ. الحديث (رواه الترمذي)

Shufayy al-Aṣbaḥī related: I said to Abū Huraira ﵁: "I am asking you for the sake of the truth, and again, for the sake of the truth, that you should narrate such a ḥadīth of the Messenger of Allāh ﷺ which you fully understood and comprehended." Abū Huraira ﵁ said: "I will do so. I will relate a ḥadīth to you which the Messenger of Allāh ﷺ related to me, and which I fully understand and comprehend." Abū Huraira ﷺ then screamed [either because of restlessness or intense fear because one has to be extremely

459 *Musnad Aḥmad*: 1:112

cautious about narrating a ḥadīth without any omissions or additions. Or this might have been out of intense yearning, in the sense that the close companionship of the Messenger of Allāh ﷺ was right before his eyes]. We waited for a long time until he recovered. He then said: "I will relate a ḥadīth to you which the Messenger of Allāh ﷺ related to me in this very place. There was no one there apart from me and him." Abū Huraira ﵁ screamed loudly. He then recovered, wiped his face, and said: "I will relate a ḥadīth to you which the Messenger of Allāh ﷺ related to me in this very place. There was no one there apart from me and him." Abū Huraira ﵁ then screamed loudly. He leaned forward and fell on his face. I gave him support for a long time. He then recovered and said: "The Messenger of Allāh ﷺ related a ḥadīth to me. . ." This was related by Tirmidhī.[460]

Commentary: The Condition of Ecstasy

The ḥadīth's reference to this spiritual state is obvious. Owing to their ability to control themselves, the past masters rarely allowed themselves to be overcome while experiencing ecstasy of this magnitude. However, it is difficult not to imagine that, at times, even they were overcome.

ḤADĪTH 305

عَنْ أَنَسِ بْنِ مَالِكٍ رَضِيَ اللهُ عَنْهُ قَالَ: قَالَ رَسُوْلُ اللهِ صَلَّى اللهُ عَلَيْهِ وَسَلَّمَ: «اَلْمَرْءُ مَعَ مَنْ أَحَبَّ وَلَهُ مَا اكْتَسَبَ».(رواه الترمذي)

Anas ibn Mālik ﵁ related that the Messenger of Allāh ﷺ said: "[On the day of Resurrection] a person will be with those he loved and will receive the reward for what he did." This was related by Tirmidhī.[461]

Commentary: The Practice of Pledging Allegiance for Admission into a Silsilah

Although it is known that certain individuals will not live up to the promises they made when pledging allegiance, *bayʿah*, or that they will not fulfil their responsibilities with regard to the prescribed spiritual practices, such as *dhikr*, in some cases they will still be admitted into the Sufi order, *silsilah*. This ḥadīth should be understood as the basis for this because the effect of *bayʿah* is that it becomes a cause of love for one's spiritual master. Consequently, there is the hope of acquiring the blessings of this love, which are mentioned in this ḥadīth.

---

460 Tirmidhī: 2382

461 Tirmidhī: 2386

ḤADĪTH 306

عَنْ عَبْدِ اللهِ بْنِ هِشَامٍ رَضِيَ اللهُ عَنْهُ وَكَانَ قَدْ أَدْرَكَ النَّبِيَّ صَلَّى اللهُ عَلَيْهِ وَسَلَّمَ ، وَذَهَبَتْ بِهِ أُمُّهُ زَيْنَبُ بِنْتُ حُمَيْدٍ إِلى رَسُوْلِ اللهِ، فَقَالَتْ: يَا رَسُوْلَ اللهِ! بَايِعْهُ، فَقَالَ النَّبِيُّ صَلَّى اللهُ عَلَيْهِ وَسَلَّمَ: «هُوَ صَغِيْرٌ فَمَسَحَ رَأْسَهُ وَدَعَالَهُ». (رواه البخاري)

ʿAbdullāh ibn Hishām ﵁ related that he was present in the era of the Messenger of Allāh ﷺ and that his mother, Zaynab bint Ḥumayd ﵂, had taken him to meet the Messenger of Allāh ﷺ saying: "O Messenger of Allāh! Take a pledge of allegiance (*bayʿah*) from him." The Messenger of Allāh ﷺ said: "He is a child." He then passed his hand over his head and supplicated for him. This was related by Bukhārī.[462]

Commentary: The Practice of Refusing Allegiance from a Child

It is the practice of the spiritual masters to refuse allegiance from a child. The obvious reason for this is that this allegiance is a pledge to uphold obligatory injunctions, and a child is not required to uphold obligatory injunctions. The essence of this allegiance cannot therefore be realised. When such allegiance is occasionally accepted, it is a nominal allegiance performed merely for the sake of blessings.

ḤADĪTH 307

عَنْ عَلِيِّ بْنِ الْحُسَيْنِ قَالَ: قَالَتْ صَفِيَّةُ رَضِيَ اللهُ تَعَالى عَنْهَا: كَانَ رَسُوْلُ اللهِ صَلَّى اللهُ عَلَيْهِ وَسَلَّمَ مُعْتَكِفاً فَأَتَيْتُهُ أَزُوْرُهُ لَيْلاً فَحَدَّثْتُهُ، ثُمَّ قُمْتُ لِأَنْقَلِبَ فَقَامَ مَعِيْ حَتَّى إِذَا بَلَغَ بَابَ الْمَسْجِدِ مَرَّ رَجُلانِ مِنَ الْأَنْصَارِ، فَلَمَّا رَأَيَا رَسُوْلَ اللهِ صَلَّى اللهُ عَلَيْهِ وَسَلَّمَ أَسْرَعَا، فَقَالَ: «عَلى رِسْلِكُمَا إِنَّهَا صَفِيَّةُ بِنْتُ حُيَيٍّ» فَقَالاَ: سُبْحَانَ اللهِ يَا رَسُوْلَ اللهِ! فَقَالَ: «إِنَّ الشَّيْطَانَ يَجْرِيْ مِنِ ابْنِ ادَمَ مَجْرَى الدَّمِ وَإِنِّيْ خَشِيْتُ أَنْ يَقْذِفَ فِيْ قُلُوْبِكُمَا شَرًّا أَوْ قَالَ شَيْئاً». (أخرجه الشيخان وأبو داؤد)

ʿAlī ibn al-Ḥusayn ﵁ related that Ṣafiyyah ﵂ said: "The Messenger of Allāh ﷺ was in seclusion (*iʿtikāf*) so I went to visit him one night. I spoke to him for some time and then got up to leave. He accompanied me until, when he reached the door of the *masjid*, two men from the Anṣār passed by. When they saw the Messenger of Allāh ﷺ they hastened [so that they

462 Bukhārī: 2501, 2502

may leave the precinct of the masjid quickly because they saw Ṣafiyyah ؓ with him, and etiquette demanded that they do this]. The Messenger of Allāh ﷺ said to them: 'Walk slowly [there is no need to hurry]. This is Ṣafiyyah bint Ḥuyayy [my wife. Do not have any other thoughts].' They said: 'Glory to Allāh, O Messenger of Allāh! [Can we have any evil thoughts about you that some strange woman is in solitude with you?!]' He ﷺ said: 'Satan flows in man as blood flows through his veins. I feared he might cast some evil in your hearts', or he said: 'some evil thoughts in your hearts.'" This was related by Bukhārī, Muslim and Abū Dāwūd.[463]

Commentary: Avoiding Whatever Gives Rise to Suspicion
Some Sufis are extremely imprudent. Despite their adherence to the Sharīʿa, they make careless statements or perform acts which cause not only the masses, but also their close associates to have negative thoughts about them. Such Sufis should ponder the lesson of this ḥadīth, how cautious the Messenger of Allāh ﷺ was! As for those Sufis who really do not consider it essential to follow the Shariʿa, what can be said about them?! These days, most aspirants are like this [not bothered about following the Sharīʿa], and so are their masters.

ḤADĪTH 308

عَنْ صَفِيَّةَ رَضِيَ اللهُ تَعَالَى عَنْهَا أَنَّ رَسُوْلَ اللهِ صَلَّى اللهُ عَلَيْهِ وَسَلَّمَ دَخَلَ عَلَيْهَا وَبَيْنَ يَدَيْهَا أَرْبَعَةُ الافِ نَوَاةٍ تُسَبِّحُ بِهِنَّ. الحديث (رواه أبوداؤد والحاكم)

Ṣafiyyah ؓ related that the Messenger of Allāh ﷺ came to her when she had in front of her 4000 date-pits which she was using [as counters] for the glorification of Allāh [i.e. saying *subḥānAllāh*]. This was related by Abū Dāwūd and Ḥākim.[464]

Commentary: The Practice of Using Counters
Most of those who engage in the remembrance of Allāh are in the practice of using counters (*tasbīḥ*) to count the different repetitions of *dhikr*. This ḥadīth is the basis for this because there is no difference between date pits and the beads which they use. The string [which is used for the counter] is merely to keep the beads attached. This ḥadīth shows that those date pits were kept together [and not scattered everywhere]. As for the objection that holding such a counter in

463 Bukhārī: 2035, Muslim: 2175, Abū Dāwūd: 2470, Ibn Mājah: 1779

464 Tirmidhī: 3554, Ḥākim: 1:54

one's hand smacks of ostentation, the reply to this is that it is necessary to abstain from the essence of ostentation and not the form [or outward appearance] of ostentation. Towards the end of this book is a ḥadīth from Ṭabarānī which clearly states that abstention from the outward form of ostentation is not obligatory.

ḤADĪTH 309

عَنْ أَبِيْ سَعِيْدٍ رَضِيَ اللهُ عَنْهُ عَنِ النَّبِيِّ صَلَّى اللهُ عَلَيْهِ وَسَلَّمَ: «لَيَذْكُرُنَّ اللهَ قَوْمٌ فِيْ الدُّنْيَا عَلَيَ الْفُرُشِ الْمُمَهَّدَةِ يُدْخِلُهُمُ الْجَنَّاتِ الْعُلي». (رواه أبو يعلي)

Abū Saʿīd ﷺ related that the Messenger of Allāh ﷺ said: "Many will be the people in this world who engage in the remembrance of Allāh on soft cushions. Allāh shall admit them to lofty gardens." This was related by Abū Yaʿlā.[465]

Commentary: Comfort and Luxury do not Negate Wilāyat

Most of the masses are under the illusion that deprivation is necessary for piety. It should be apparent from the ḥadīth above that if a person remains steadfast in his/her practice of remembrance and obedience, while living in comfort and luxury, he/she can still enjoy the fruits of a close relationship with Allāh. However, there are occasions when it is necessary to avoid the circumstances of luxury, or to avoid the company of certain people for a specified time or, in some cases, altogether. This is prescribed by a spiritual master for the sake of spiritual striving, *mujāhadah*. Such avoidance is prescribed in particular situations and is not in itself a prerequisite for spiritual success.

ḤADĪTH 310

أَخْرَجَ أَبُوْ يَعْلى عَنْ عَائِشَةَ رَضِيَ اللهُ تَعَالى عَنْهَا قَالَتْ: قَالَ رَسُوْلُ اللهِ صَلَّى اللهُ عَلَيْهِ وَسَلَّمَ: «يَفْضُلُ الذِّكْرُ الْخَفِيُّ الَّذِيْ لا يَسْمَعُهُ الْحَفَظَةُ سَبْعُوْنَ ضِعْفاً إِذَا كَانَ يَوْمُ الْقِيمَةِ وَجَمَعَ اللهُ الْخَلْقَ لِحِسَابِهِمْ وَجَائَتِ الْحَفَظَةُ بِمَا حَفِظُوْا وَكَتَبُوْا قَالَ لَهُمْ: انْظُرُوْا هَلْ بَقِيَ لَهُ مِنْ شَيْءٍ فَيَقُوْلُوْنَ: مَاتَرَكْنَا شَيْئاً مِمَّا عَلِمْنَاهُ وَحَفِظْنَاهُ إِلاَّ وَقَدْ أَحْصَيْنَاهُ وَكَتَبْنَاهُ فَيَقُوْلُ اللهُ: إِنَّ لَكَ عِنْدِيْ حَسَناً لا تَعْلَمُهُ وَأَنَا أُجْزِيْكَ بِهِ وَهُوَ الذِّكْرُ الْخَفِيُّ».

(ذكره السيوطي في «البدور السافرة في أحوال الاخرة»)

465 Abū Yaʿlā: 2:1110

Abū Yaʿlā related from ʿĀ'isha ﵂ that the Messenger of Allāh ﷺ said: "The silent *dhikr* which even the angel scribes, *al-kirām al-kātibān*, cannot hear is seventy times superior to [vocal *dhikr*] on the day of Resurrection. Allāh will gather all of creation for the accounting of their deeds and the angel scribes will come forward with whatever they preserved or recorded. Allāh will say to them: '[Apart from the deeds which are recorded], is there anything else that is left?' They will reply: 'As far as we know and what we recorded, there is nothing that has been left out or left unrecorded.' Allāh will say [to the person]: 'I have a good deed of yours which even you are not aware of [at present, although you were aware of it when you were doing it because you did it by intent], and I will reward you for it. The deed is silent *dhikr*.'" This was related by Suyūṭī.[466]

Commentary: The Validity of Mental Dhikr

The spiritual masters sometimes teach verbal remembrance and sometimes remembrance with the heart. Those who are concerned with the outward aspects of Islam are under the illusion that as long as the letters are not uttered by the tongue, such remembrance is not considered valid remembrance. This ḥadīth clearly states the validity and consideration of such *dhikr* because, in order for an utterance to be valid, it is necessary for the angel scribes to hear it. Since their hearing is negated [in this ḥadīth], the verbal utterance is also negated. However, a verbal utterance is unanimously considered to be a prerequisite in certain injunctions, for example, in recitation of the Qur'ān, in *ṣalāh*, in the marriage contract, in divorce, and in many other situations.

As for the objection that although the angelic scribes may not hear, they nonetheless have knowledge of deeds of the heart and therefore most certainly recorded this. Consequently it is mentioned in other ḥadīths that good intentions are recorded by these angels. The answer to this objection is that while it would appear they have knowledge of most deeds of the heart, there are exceptions. Unless, however, there is certainty regarding the particular exceptions, the deeds will be considered to be included with the majority. And Allāh knows best.

ḤADĪTH 311

عَنْ أَبِي الطُّفَيْلِ رَضِيَ اللهُ عَنْهُ أَنَّ رَجُلاً مَرَّ عَلى قَوْمٍ فَسَلَّمَ عَلَيْهِمْ، فَرَدُّوْا عَلَيْهِ السَّلَامُ، فَلَمَّا جَاوَزَ بِهِمْ قَالَ رَجُلٌ مِنْهُمْ: وَ اللهِ إِنِّيْ لَأُبْغِضُ هذَا فِي اللهِ، فَقَالَ أَهْلُ الْمَجْلِسِ:

466 Suyūṭī has recorded this in *al-Budūr as-Sāfirah* and so has Abū Yaʿlā, as in *Majmaʿ az-Zawā'id*: 10:81

بِئْسَ وَ اللهِ مَا قُلْتَ، أَمَا وَاللهِ لَنُنَبِّئَنَّهُ، قُمْ يَا فُلانُ - رَجُلاً مِنْهُمْ - فَأَخْبَرَهُ، قَالَ: فَأَدْرَكَهُ رَسُوْلُهُمْ فَأَخْبَرَهُ بِمَا قَالَ، فَانْصَرَفَ الرَّجُلُ حَتّى أَتى رَسُوْلَ اللهِ صَلَّى اللهُ عَلَيْهِ وَسَلَّمَ، فَقَالَ: يَا رَسُوْلَ اللهِ! مَرَرْتُ بِمَجْلِسٍ مِنَ الْمُسْلِمِيْنَ فِيْهِمْ فُلانٌ، فَسَلَّمْتُ عَلَيْهِمْ، فَرَدُّوْا السَّلامَ، فَلَمَّا جَاوَزْتُهُمْ أَدْرَكَنِي رَجُلٌ مِنْهُمْ، فَأَخْبَرَنِيْ أَنَّ فُلاناً قَالَ: وَ اللهِ إِنِّيْ لَأُبْغِضُ هذَا الرَّجُلَ فِيْ اللهِ، فَادْعُهُ، فَسَلْهُ عَلى مَا يُبْغِضُنِيْ؟ فَدَعَاهُ رَسُوْلُ اللهِ صَلَّى اللهُ عَلَيْهِ وَسَلَّمَ فَسَأَلَهُ عَمَّا أَخْبَرَهُ الرَّجُلُ، فَاعْتَرَفَ بِذلِكَ، وَقَالَ: قَدْ قُلْتُ لَهُ ذلِكَ يَا رَسُوْلَ اللهِ! قَالَ: «فَلِمَ تُبْغِضُهُ؟» فَقَالَ: أَنَا جَارُهُ وَأَنَا بِهِ خَابِرٌ، وَ اللهِ مَا رَأَيْتُهُ يُصَلِّيْ صَلوةً قَطُّ إِلاَّ هذِهِ الصَّلوةَ الْمَكْتُوْبَةَ الَّتِيْ يُصَلِّيْهَا الْبَرُّ وَالْفَاجِرُ، فَقَالَ الرَّجُلُ: سَلْهُ يَا رَسُوْلَ اللهِ! هَلْ رَآنِيْ قَطُّ أَخَّرْتُهَا عَنْ وَقْتِهَا؟ أَوْ أَسَأْتُ الْوُضُوْءَ لَهَا؟ أَوْ أَسَأْتُ الرُّكُوْعَ وَالسُّجُوْدَ فِيْهَا؟ فَسَأَلَهُ رَسُوْلُ اللهِ صَلَّى اللهُ عَلَيْهِ وَسَلَّمَ عَنْ ذلِكَ، فَقَالَ: لا، ثُمَّ قَالَ: وَ اللهِ مَا رَأَيْتُهُ يَصُوْمُ قَطُّ إِلاَّ هذَا الشَّهْرَ الَّذِيْ يَصُوْمُهُ الْبَرُّ وَالْفَاجِرُ، قَالَ: فَسَلْهُ يَا رَسُوْلَ اللهِ! هَلْ رَآنِيْ قَطُّ فَرَّطْتُ فِيْهِ؟ أَوْ انْتَقَصْتُ مِنْ حَقِّهِ شَيْئاً؟ فَسَأَلَهُ رَسُوْلُ اللهِ ا، فَقَالَ: لا، ثُمَّ قَالَ: وَ اللهِ مَا رَأَيْتُهُ يُعْطِيْ سَائِلاً قَطُّ، وَلا رَأَيْتُهُ يُنْفِقُ مِنْ مَالِهِ شَيْئاً فِيْ سَبِيْلِ اللهِ إِلاَّ هذِهِ الصَّدَقَةَ الَّتِيْ يُؤَدِّيْهَا الْبَرُّ وَالْفَاجِرُ، قَالَ: فَسَلْهُ يَا رَسُوْلَ اللهِ! هَلْ كَتَمْتُ ذلِكَ؟ قَالَ: لا، فَقَالَ رَسُوْلُ اللهِ صَلَّى اللهُ عَلَيْهِ وَسَلَّمَ: «قُمْ، إِنْ أَدْرِيْ لَعَلَّهُ خَيْرٌ مِنْكَ». (رواه أحمد)

Abū Ṭufayl ﷺ related that when a man passed by some people and greeted them, they replied to his greeting. When he passed beyond them, one of them said [to the others]: "By Allāh, I detest this person for the sake of Allāh." Those present in the assembly objected, saying: "You said an evil thing. By Allāh, we will inform him. O such and such person, get up and go inform him." Their messenger caught up with the man and informed him of what the man had said. The passerby turned and went immediately to the Messenger of Allāh ﷺ exclaiming: "O Messenger of Allāh! I passed by an assembly of Muslims in which a certain person was sitting. I greeted them and they replied to my greeting. When I had passed them by, one of them came running to inform me that such and such person amongst them had said: 'By Allāh, I detest this person for the sake of Allāh.' So, please call him and ask him why he detests me so?" The Messenger of Allāh ﷺ called for the person and asked him in regard to what had transpired with the passerby. The person acknowledged everything by saying: "O Messenger of Allāh! I did make this statement." He asked: "Why do you detest him?" The person replied: "I am his neighbour and I know all about him. By Allāh, I never saw him performing any prayer, *ṣalāh*, except for the compulsory prayers which everyone, good and bad, offers." The passerby replied: "O Messenger of Allāh! Ask him if he ever saw me delaying in performing these prayers, not performing a proper ablution for them, or not performing the bowing and prostrating postures correctly for these prayers?" The Messenger of Allāh ﷺ asked him about all this and he replied: "No." The person then said: "By Allāh, I never saw him fasting except in this month [of Ramaḍān] in which everyone, good and bad, keeps fast." The passerby replied: "O Messenger of Allāh! Ask him if he ever saw me commit errors in the fasts or if I was otherwise neglectful about them?" The Messenger of Allāh ﷺ asked him about this and he replied: "No." Then the person said: "By Allāh, I have never seen him give anything to a beggar, nor have I ever seen him spending his wealth in the cause of Allāh except for this *zakāh* which everyone, good and bad, gives." The passerby replied: "O Messenger of Allāh! Ask him if I ever concealed this *zakāh* [from the *zakāh* collector or did not publicly give all my *zakāh*]?" The person said: "No." The Messenger of Allāh ﷺ said to the person [who made all these allegations]: "Go now. I do not know for sure, but he is probably better than you." This was related by Aḥmad.[467]

Commentary: The Practice of Sufficing with the Essentials of Islam

From among the physical acts of worship, the person who suffices himself with performing no more than what is obligatory and who occupies himself the rest of the time with remembrance [of Allāh] and contemplation is referred to as a qalandar in the terminology of Sufism. This ḥadīth confirms this because sufficing with the essentials is mentioned here in the text, and the Companions' remaining in constant remembrance [of Allāh] and contemplation is inferred from the verse: "Men whom neither commerce nor buying diverts from the remembrance of Allāh." The Companions ﵃ are at the head of the list of such men. As the passerby was a Companion ﵁, he is included in this group. As an aside, there is a Sufi order which is known as the Malāmatiyya (those who seek rebuke). Members of this order are very particular about concealing their extra deeds of devotion. Their methodology is established from ḥadīth [48]. All of this is explained there.

467 *Musnad Aḥmad*: 5:455

ḤADĪTH 312

فِيْ الْمُسْنَدِ لِلدَّيْلَمِيْ عَنْ أَنَسٍ رَضِيَ اللهُ عَنْهُ مَرْفُوْعاً: «لاتَكُوْنُ الحِدَّةُ إِلاَّ فِيْ صَالِحِيْ أُمَّتِيْ أَوْ أَبْرَارِهَا» وَبِهٰذَا السَّنَدِ بِلَفْظِ: «لَيْسَ أَحَدٌ أَوْلى بِالْحِدَّةِ مِنْ صَاحِبِ الْقُرْآنِ لِعِزِّ الْقُرْآنِ فِيْ جَوْفِهِ».

It is related in the *Musnad* of Daylamī from Anas ﷺ that the Messenger of Allāh ﷺ said: "Severity is found only in the righteous and obedient servants of My community, *ummah*." In another version of the ḥadīth, with the same chain of narrators, the words used are: "None is as worthy of a short temper as a person who has memorised the Qur'ān, owing to the honour he accords the Qur'ān in his heart."[468]

Commentary: Short Temper

Some spiritual masters have a very delicate temperament and it is this subtlety that causes them to become annoyed by improprieties. This annoyance of theirs may be discerned on their face or by their speech. At times, this change in their temperament reaches the level of anger. Consequently, some narrow-minded people accuse them of ill-mannerliness. Ill-mannerliness is that which transgresses the limit of the Sharīʿa. A short temper, in itself, is not impious, as illustrated by this ḥadīth. There are certain authentic traditions wherein it is related that the Messenger of Allāh ﷺ was even angered by ill-timed questions. One should therefore not hasten in raising objections of this nature against the spiritual masters.

ḤADĪTH 313

عَنْ عَبْدِ اللهِ بْنِ مَسْعُوْدٍ رَضِيَ اللهُ عَنْهُ قَالَ: قَالَ رَسُوْلُ اللهِ صَلَّى اللهُ عَلَيْهِ وَسَلَّمَ: «إِذْنُكَ عَلَيَّ أَنْ تَرْفَعَ الْحِجَابَ وَأَنْ تَسْمَعَ سَوَادِيْ حَتّى أَنْهَاكَ». (رواه ابن ماجة)

ʿAbdullāh ibn Masʿūd ﷺ related: "The Messenger of Allāh said to me: 'You have the permission to raise the curtain and listen to my secrets until I prohibit you from doing this." This was related by Ibn Mājah.[469]

468 *Kashf al-Khifā'*: 1:423

469 Ibn Mājah has reported this in the Virtues of ʿAbdullāh ibn Masʿūd ﷺ.

ḤADĪTH 314

عَنِ الْحُسَيْنِ بْنِ عَلِيٍّ رَضِيَ اللهُ عَنْهُ قَالَ: سَأَلْتُ أَبِي عَنْ دُخُوْلِ رَسُوْلِ اللهِ صَلَّى اللهُ عَلَيْهِ وَسَلَّمَ فَقَالَ: كَانَ إِذَا اوى إِلى مَنْزِلِهِ جَزَّءَ دُخُوْلَهُ ثَلٰثَةَ أَجْزَاءٍ: جُزْءً لله عَزَّوَجَلَّ، وَجُزْءً لِأَهْلِهِ، وَجُزْءً لِنَفْسِهِ، ثُمَّ جَزَّءَ جُزْءَهُ بَيْنَهُ وَبَيْنَ النَّاسِ، فَيَرُدُّ ذٰلِكَ بِالْخَاصَّةِ عَلَى الْعَامَّةِ وَلَايَدَّخِرُ عَنْهُمْ شَيْئًا، وَكَانَ مِنْ سِيْرَتِهِ فِيْ جُزْءِ الْأُمَّةِ إِيْثَارُ أَهْلِ الْفَضْلِ. الحديث. (رواه الترمذي في الشمائل)

Al-Ḥusayn ibn ʿAlī ﷺ related: "I asked my father about what the Messenger of Allāh ﷺ used to do when he entered his house. He replied: 'When he went to his house, he would divide his time in three: one part for Allāh [e.g. engaging in optional acts of worship], one part for his family [speaking and conversing with them], and one part for himself [personal relaxation]. He would then divide his personal time between necessary work and work for the benefit of the people. [In other words, some time for his own work and some time for the people]. This portion [which he set aside for the people] was spent by conveying to his close associates [who would then convey this] to the masses. He would not withhold anything from them. As for the portion which he set aside for the *ummah* [outside his house], it was his habit to give preference to the people of virtue.'" This was related by Tirmidhī.[470]

ḤADĪTH 315

عَنْ أَبِيْ مُوْسى الْأَشْعَرِيِّ رَضِيَ اللهُ عَنْهُ قَالَ: كُنْتُ مَعَ النَّبِيِّ صَلَّى اللهُ عَلَيْهِ وَسَلَّمَ فِيْ حَائِطٍ مِنْ حِيْطَانِ الْمَدِيْنَةِ، فَجَاءَ رَجُلٌ فَاسْتَفْتَحَ، فَقَالَ النَّبِيُّ صَلَّى اللهُ عَلَيْهِ وَسَلَّمَ: «افْتَحْ لَهُ وَبَشِّرْهُ بِالْجَنَّةِ» فَفَتَحْتُ لَهُ فَإِذَا أَبُوْ بَكْرٍ فَبَشَّرْتُهُ بِمَا قَالَ رَسُوْلُ اللهِ صَلَّى اللهُ عَلَيْهِ وَسَلَّمَ فَحَمِدَ اللهَ. الحديث. وَفِيْهِ: مَجِيْءُ عُمَرَ رَضِيَ اللهُ عَنْهُ وَعُثْمَانَ رَضِيَ اللهُ عَنْهُ كَذٰلِكَ. (متفق عليه)

Abū Mūsā al-Ashʿarī ﷺ related: "I was with the Messenger of Allāh ﷺ in

470 Tirmidhī has recorded this in his *ash-Shamāʾil* in the 'Chapter of what has been reported about the Humility of the Noble Messenger of Allāh ﷺ'.

one of the orchards of Madīna when a man came and asked for the door to be opened. The Messenger of Allāh ﷺ said: 'Go open the door and give him the glad tidings of Paradise.' I opened the door and saw Abū Bakr ؓ. I conveyed to him the glad tidings mentioned by the Messenger of Allāh ﷺ and he praised Allāh [over these glad tidings]." The ḥadīth also mentions the arrival of ʿUmar and ʿUthmān. This was related by Bukhārī and Muslim.[471]

The Practice of Scheduling, Visits During Times of Solitude and Attendants at the Door

It is generally the practice of the spiritual masters to have their time scheduled so that they may enjoy certain periods of time in solitude. During these times, they do not meet the general public. At times they even appoint an attendant to remain outside and to prevent the rush of visitors. At other times, they give their special associates permission to come to them. Some people have raised a number of objections to these practices. They harbour misgivings of selfishness, favouritism and other feelings against the pious personalities. Some people see the attendant going in to the master and so they creep in behind him, attempting to use the permission which is granted to the attendant as license for their own entry. The above ḥadīths clearly provide answers to these objections. Ḥadīth [314] establishes scheduling, having a time set aside for solitude and privacy, and giving permission to close associates only. ḥadīth [313] is proof that if the attendant is given permission to enter, others do not necessarily enjoy the same permission. Ḥadīth [315] clearly proves the appointment of someone to sit at the door. However, it is not good to refuse permission to meet if a person has a severe and immediate need. Apart from these ḥadīths, the Qur'ānic verse: "If you are asked to go away, then go away"[472] permits this, i.e. it is also permissible to refuse to meet someone at a certain time. Similarly, the ḥadīth: "Treat people in accordance with their standing" proves the permissibility of giving preference to one's special associates over the masses. All of these objections are based on ignorance.

ḤADĪTH 316

عَنِ ابْنِ عَبَّاسٍ رَضِيَ اللهُ عَنْهُ قَالَ: إِنَّ رَفْعَ الصَّوْتِ بِالذِّكْرِ حِيْنَ يَنْصَرِفُ النَّاسُ مِنَ الْمَكْتُوْبَةِ كَانَ عَلَى عَهْدِ النَّبِيِّ صَلَّى اللهُ عَلَيْهِ وَسَلَّمَ. (رواه البخاري)

Ibn ʿAbbās ؓ related: "Engaging in *dhikr* in a loud voice when the con-

471 Bukhārī: 6216, Muslim: 2403, Tirmidhī: 3710

472 Al-Qur'ān, 24:28

gregation had completed the compulsory *ṣalāh* was prevalent in the era of the Messenger of Allāh ﷺ." This was reported by Bukhārī.[473]

Commentary: The Practice of Reciting Dhikr Aloud
Some people object to the Chishtiyyah Sufi order by saying that the practice of vocalised *dhikr* is unsubstantiated. This practice is clearly mentioned in this ḥadīth. However, it is related from Imam Shafiʿī that the meaning of this ḥadīth is not that this sort of *dhikr* should always be practised after the *ṣalāh*.

ḤADĪTH 317

عَنْ أَسْمَاءَ بِنْتِ يَزِيْدَ رَضِيَ الله تَعَالى عَنْهَا فِيْ حَدِيْثِ الدَّجَّالِ قَالَتْ: قُلْتُ: يَا رَسُوْلَ الله! وَ الله إِنَّا لَنَعْجِنُ عَجِيْنَتَنَا فَمَا نُخْبِزُهُ حَتّى نَجُوْعَ فَكَيْفَ بِالْمُؤْمِنِيْنَ يَوْمَئِذٍ؟ قَالَ: «يُجْزِيْهِمْ مَا يُجْزِيْ أَهْلُ السَّمَاءِ مِنَ التَّسْبِيْحِ وَالتَّقْدِيْسِ. (رواه أحمد)

Asmā' bint Yazīd ﷺ related in the ḥadīth of the Dajjāl [in which the Messenger of Allāh ﷺ spoke about his tribulation and the famine which will be experienced during his time]. I said: "O Messenger of Allāh! By Allāh, at times we make the dough and have not yet made the bread when we already feel hungry [and thereby become restless]. What will happen to the believers on that day [when their adversaries will be experiencing such severe famine]?" He ﷺ replied: "The glorification and extolling the greatness of Allāh which suffices the inhabitants of the heavens [the angels] will suffice them [in place of food]." This was related by Aḥmad.[474]

Commentary: Remaining Without One's Usual Sustenance
It is related with regard to certain spiritual masters that they did not eat food for lengthy periods during their times of solitude. Those who are only concerned with the outward aspects of Islam reject such practices. It is clearly demonstrated, however, by the ḥadīth above that there are times when mere remembrance and glorification [of Allāh] can take the place of food.

ḤADĪTH 318

عَنْ عِمْرَانَ بْنِ حُصَيْنٍ رَضِيَ اللهُ عَنْهُ قَالَ: قَالَ رَسُوْلُ اللهِ صَلَّى اللهُ عَلَيْهِ وَسَلَّمَ: «مَنْ

473 Bukhārī: 841
474 *Musnad Aḥmad*: 6:456

سَمِعَ بِالدَّجَّالِ فَلْيَنْأَ مِنْهُ، فَوَ اللهِ إِنَّ الرَّجُلَ لَيَأْتِيهِ وَهُوَ يَحْسِبُ أَنَّهُ مُؤْمِنٌ فَيَتْبَعُهُ مِمَّا يَبْعَثُ بِهِ مِنَ الشُّبُهَاتِ». (رواه أبوداؤد)

ʿImrān ibn Ḥuṣayn ﷺ related that the Messenger of Allāh ﷺ said: "Whoever hears of the Dajjāl should keep as far away from him as possible. By Allāh, even a person who considers himself a true believer will go to the Dajjāl [for no other reason than to look at what he is doing or to debate with him] and end up beset by doubts, until he starts following him." This was related by Abū Dāwūd.[475]

Commentary: Remaining Aloof from Tribulation

The spiritual masters teach that if there is a pretender to spiritual accomplishment through *taṣawwuf*, no one other than a master should even consider meeting with the person for the purpose of debating with him or otherwise refuting his claims. Such a pretender's words and actions might easily lead a person to confusion and tribulation. This teaching is expressed explicitly in this ḥadīth. The "big" Dajjāl and the "small" Dajjāl are equal in this regard.

ḤADĪTH 319

عَنِ النَّوَّاسِ بْنِ سَمْعَانَ رَضِيَ اللهُ عَنْهُ فِيْ ذِكْرِ الدَّجَّالِ قُلْنَا: يَا رَسُوْلَ اللهِ! وَمَا لُبْثُهُ فِيْ الأَرْضِ؟ قَالَ: «أَرْبَعُوْنَ يَوْماً، يَوْمٌ كَسَنَةٍ وَيَوْمٌ كَشَهْرٍ وَيَوْمٌ كَجُمُعَةٍ وَسَائِرُ أَيَّامِهِ كَأَيَّامِكُمْ». (رواه مسلم)

An-Nawwās ibn Samʿān ﷺ related with regard to the Dajjāl: We asked: "O Messenger of Allāh! How long will he remain on Earth?" He ﷺ replied: "Forty days. One day like a year, one day like a month, one day like a week, and the rest of the days will be like your normal days." This was related by Muslim.[476]

ḤADĪTH 320

عَنْ أَسْمَاءَ بِنْتِ يَزِيْدَ بْنِ السَّكَنِ رَضِيَ اللهُ تَعَالَى عَنْهَا قَالَتْ: قَالَ النَّبِيُّ صَلَّى اللهُ عَلَيْهِ

475 Abū Dāwūd: 4319
476 Muslim: 2937

وَسَلَّمَ: «يَمْكُثُ الدَّجَّالُ فِيْ الْأَرْضِ أَرْبَعِيْنَ سَنَةً، السَّنَةُ كَالشَّهْرِ وَالشَّهْرُ كَالْجُمُعَةِ وَالْجُمُعَةُ كَالْيَوْمِ وَالْيَوْمُ كَاضْطِرَامِ السَّعْفَةِ فِيْ النَّارِ». (رواه في شرح السنة)

Asmā' bint Yazīd ibn as-Sakan ﷺ related that the Messenger of Allāh ﷺ said: "Dajjāl will remain on earth for forty years. A year will be like the month, a month will be like a week, a week will be like a day, and a day will be like wood burning in a fire." This is related in *Sharḥ as-Sunnah*.[477]

Commentary: The Expansion and Contraction of Time

One of the ways to reconcile the contradictions in the above two ḥadīths is to say that for some people the passage of time will be tedious while for others it will be quick. In actual fact, however, this entire period will have a specific duration. So, by means of the explanation above, the expansion and contraction of time mentioned in the two ḥadīths may be understood. As regards the first ḥadīth, it is stated in other versions of the same narration that the prayers of one year will be obligatory on the day which will be equal to one year. It may therefore be understood that the day will in reality also be of one year's duration. The reply to this is that it is possible that that one particular day will be of one year's duration and that the above explanation will apply to the rest of the days [i.e. to some the days will seem long while to others they will seem short]. Nevertheless, these ḥadīths express possibility. The following ḥadīth explicitly mentions the expansion of time.

ḤADĪTH 321

عَنْ أَبِيْ سَعِيْدٍ الْخُدْرِيِّ رَضِيَ اللهُ عَنْهُ قَالَ: سُئِلَ رَسُوْلُ اللهِ صَلَّى اللهُ عَلَيْهِ وَسَلَّمَ عَنْ يَوْمٍ كَانَ مِقْدَارُهُ أَلْفَ سَنَةٍ، مَا طُوْلُ هذَا الْيَوْمِ؟ فَقَالَ: «وَالَّذِيْ نَفْسِيْ بِيَدِهِ إِنَّهُ لَيُخَفَّفُ عَلَى الْمُؤْمِنِيْنَ حَتّى يَكُوْنَ أَهْوَنَ عَلَيْهِ مِنَ الصَّلوةِ الْمَكْتُوْبَةِ يُصَلِّيْهَا فِيْ الدُّنْيَا». (رواه البيهقي في كتاب البعث والنشور)

Abū Saʿīd al-Khudrī ﷺ related that the Messenger of Allāh ﷺ was asked about the length of the day which will be equal to 50,000 years [i.e. about the day of Resurrection]. He ﷺ said: "I swear in the name of the One Who holds my life in His hands! It will be so light on the believers that it will be lighter than even the compulsory *ṣalāh* which they used to offer in the world." This was related by Bayhaqī.[478]

---

477 Musnad Aḥmad: 6:454. Al-Baghawī has recorded this in his *Sharḥ as-Sunnah*: 4159.

478 *Musnad Aḥmad*: 3:75. Al-Bayhaqī has recorded it in *al-Baʿth wa an-Nushūr*.

Commentary: The Contraction of Time

This ḥadīth makes obvious reference to this. There is no difference in the possibility of the contraction and expansion of time. Expansion can also take place in this way.

ḤADĪTH 322

عَنِ ابْنِ عَبَّاسٍ رَضِيَ اللهُ عَنْهُ قَالَ: قَالَ رَسُوْلُ اللهِ صَلَّى اللهُ عَلَيْهِ وَسَلَّمَ: «مَنْ سَمِعَ الْمُنَادِيْ فَلَمْ يَمْنَعْهُ مِنِ اتِّبَاعِهِ عُذْرٌ»، قَالُوْا: وَمَا الْعُذْرُ؟ قَالَ: «خَوْفٌ أَوْ مَرَضٌ لَمْ تُقْبَلْ مِنْهُ الصَّلٰوةُ الَّتِيْ صَلَّى». (رواه أبو داؤد والدار قطني)

Ibn ʿAbbās ؉ related that the Messenger of Allāh ؉ said: "If a person hears the call to prayer and has no excuse for not responding to the call, [i.e. from attending the congregation], then the prayers he performs [on his own] will not be accepted." The Companions ؉ asked: "What is a [valid] excuse?" He ؉ replied: "Fear or illness." This is reported by Abū Dāwūd.[479]

Commentary: The Importance of Congregational Prayer

These days, most "superficial" Sufis do not bother themselves with prayer in a congregation. In the light of this ḥadīth, it would appear that their prayers on their own are not accepted. Obviously, if a person's prayers are not accepted, how can that person be thought worthy of being a spiritual master?!

ḤADĪTH 323

عَنِ الْمُغِيْرَةِ بْنِ شُعْبَةَ رَضِيَ اللهُ عَنْهُ أَنَّهُ غَزَا مَعَ رَسُوْلِ اللهِ صَلَّى اللهُ عَلَيْهِ وَسَلَّمَ قَالَ الْمُغِيْرَةُ: فَتَبَرَّزَ رَسُوْلُ اللهِ صَلَّى اللهُ عَلَيْهِ وَسَلَّمَ قِبَلَ الْغَائِطِ، فَحَمَلْتُ مَعَهُ إِدَاوَةً قَبْلَ الْفَجْرِ، فَلَمَّا رَجَعَ أَخَذْتُ أُهْرِيْقُ عَلَى يَدَيْهِ، فَغَسَلَ يَدَيْهِ وَوَجْهَهُ، وَغَسَلَ ذِرَاعَيْهِ، ثُمَّ مَسَحَ بِنَاصِيَتِهِ ثُمَّ أَهْوَيْتُ لِأُنْزِعَ خُفَّيْهِ. الْحَدِيثُ مختصراً. (رواه مسلم)

Al-Mughīrah ibn Shuʿbah ؉ related that he accompanied the Messenger of Allāh ؉ on the expedition to Tabūk. He said: "The Messenger of Allāh ؉ went out into the field before the dawn prayer in order to relieve

---

479   Abū Dāwūd: 551, Ibn Mājah: 793, Dāraquṭnī: 1542

himself. I carried a utensil of water and accompanied him. When he returned, I poured water for him [so that he may perform his ablution] on his hands. He washed his hands, his face, his arms, and then passed wet hands over the front part of his head [this narration also states that he passed his wet hands over the area that is covered by the turban, i.e. over his entire head]. I then bent down to remove his leather socks." This was related by Muslim.[480]

The Practice of Accepting Help from an Attendant for Performing Ablution
Spiritual masters occasionally take the assistance of their attendants for performing ablution. Some short-sighted people consider this to be a sign of pride. Such an assumption amounts to harbouring evil thoughts [about the spiritual master]. This ḥadīth establishes the permissibility of this practice without any reprehensibility.

ḤADĪTH 324

عَنِ ابْنِ عَبَّاسٍ رَضِيَ اللهُ عَنْهُ قَالَ: قَالَ رَسُوْلُ اللهِ صَلَّى اللهُ عَلَيْهِ وَسَلَّمَ: «إِنَّ الْوُضُوْءَ عَلَى مَنْ نَامَ مُضْطَجِعاً فَإِنَّهُ إِذَا اضْطَجَعَ اسْتَرَخَتْ مَفَاصِلُهُ». (رواه الترمذي وأبو داؤد)

Ibn ʿAbbās ﷺ related that the Messenger of Allāh ﷺ said: "Ablution is obligatory on the person who lies down and falls asleep because when he lies down, his joints become loose [and there is the possibility of his passing wind]." This was related by Tirmidhī and Abū Dāwūd.[481]

Commentary: Ablution Breaks When One Falls After Experiencing Ecstasy
Most Sufis are unaware of the ruling that if they become unconscious and fall while in a state of ecstasy, *wajd*, or otherwise fall down and become unconscious, it becomes obligatory on them to renew their ablution. The reason for this is that the joints become loose in the same way they loosen when one falls asleep. The jurists clearly state that ablution breaks when one falls unconscious.

ḤADĪTH 325

عَنْ أَنَسٍ رَضِيَ اللهُ عَنْهُ قَالَ: لَمْ يَكُنْ شَخْصٌ أَحَبَّ إِلَيْهِمْ مِنْ رَسُوْلِ اللهِ صَلَّى اللهُ عَلَيْهِ

480 Muslim: 274
481 Abū Dāwūd: 201, Tirmidhī: 77

وَسَلَّمَ، وَكَانُوْا إِذَا رَأَوْهُ لَمْ يَقُوْمُوْا لِمَا يَعْلَمُوْنَ مِنْ كَرَاهِيَتِهِ لِذلِكَ. (رواه الترمذي وقال: هذا حديث حسن صحيح)

Anas ﷺ related that: "There was none who was more beloved to the Companions ﷺ than the Messenger of Allāh ﷺ. Despite this, when they saw him, they did not stand up because they knew he disliked this." This was related by Tirmidhī.[482]

Commentary: Abstaining from According Respect that is Disliked

It is clear from this ḥadīth that any act of respect, honour or service which is disliked by one's spiritual master should be studiously avoided. These days, people are so accustomed to following popular practices that they fail to take into consideration the comfort of their spiritual masters. Oftentimes, people will simply adopt the formalities of non-Muslims, going to extremes in according respect, and insisting on attending to them as a means of attaining proximity and good fortune. Such acts include massaging his body, carrying his shoes and sitting behind him. Many ignorant Sufis mistakenly believe that one's remembrance and prayer, *dhikr wa ṣalāh*, are more likely to be accepted if performed in the direction of the spiritual master's back. This practice is absolutely the same as idol-worship. Such evils are very much in vogue these days.

ḤADĪTH 326

عَنْ أَبِيْ هُرَيْرَةَ رَضِيَ اللهُ عَنْهُ قَالَ: قَالُوْا: يَا رَسُوْلَ اللهِ! إِنَّكَ تُدَاعِبُنَا قَالَ: «إِنِّيْ لا أَقُوْلُ إِلاَّ حَقًّا». (رواه الترمذي)

Abū Huraira ﷺ related that the Companions ﷺ said: "O Messenger of Allāh! You joke with us?!" He said: "I say nothing but the truth [in other words, my joking does not contain any falsehood nor anything impermissible such as lies or causing harm to a Muslim]." This was related by Tirmidhī.[483]

Commentary: Joking does not Negate Perfection

Some people of dry temperament look down upon the humour of the spiritual masters. If the precondition which is mentioned in this ḥadīth is fulfilled, such humour is a practice established by the Sunna. If this precondition is not ful-

482 Tirmidhī: 2754

483 Tirmidhī: 1990, 1995

filled, its prohibition is mentioned in another ḥadīth: "Do not show off to your brother, nor joke[484] with him."

ḤADĪTH 327

عَنْ أَبِيْ شُرَيْحِ الْكَعْبِيِّ أَنَّ رَسُوْلَ اللهِ صَلَّى اللهُ عَلَيْهِ وَسَلَّمَ قَالَ فِيْ حَدِيْثٍ طَوِيْلٍ: «وَلَا يَحِلُّ لَهُ أَنْ يَثْوِيَ عِنْدَهُ حَتّٰى يُحْرِجَهُ». (متفق عليه)

Abū Shurayḥ al-Kaʿbī ﷺ related that the Messenger of Allāh ﷺ said in a lengthy ḥadīth: "It is not lawful for a guest to remain so long with a host to the extent that he causes him hardship." This was related by Bukhārī and Muslim.[485]

Commentary: Abstaining from Imposing on a Disciple's (murīd's) Hospitality

These days, many spiritual masters consider themselves in such control over the lives and wealth of their aspirants, *murīds*, that they ask them for whatever they want without hesitation. Thus, they will continue living in their houses for as long as they like and continue eating delicious meals. They will take as many people as they like to that poor person's house regardless of whether the person likes it or not, and regardless of whether or not he is inconvenienced. Such a spiritual master is included in the general ruling of the ḥadīth above. The basis for this prohibition is the causing of discomfort to others. When a person becomes bothered by something, and this something is not his responsibility, then it is unlawful, *ḥarām* to demand the same of him. Another ḥadīth is more clear on this point: When the Messenger of Allāh ﷺ was invited to someone's house, the Messenger ﷺ would always seek permission to bring along people who were not invited by name. When this was the case with regard to the Messenger of Allāh ﷺ, what can be said of others?!

ḤADĪTH 328

عَنْ مُحَمَّدِ بْنِ سِيْرِيْنَ قَالَ: الرُّؤْيَا ثَلٰثٌ: حَدِيْثُ النَّفْسِ، وَتَخْوِيْفُ الشَّيْطَانِ، وَبُشْرٰى مِنَ اللهِ. (متفق عليه) وَعَنْ جَابِرٍ رَضِيَ اللهُ عَنْهُ قَالَ رَسُوْلُ اللهِ صَلَّى اللهُ عَلَيْهِ وَسَلَّمَ:

484 Here, the context of the ḥadīth suggests that the meaning is: "Do not joke with him in a way that demeans or otherwise shows disrespect to him, or her." YTD.

485 Bukhārī: 6135, Muslim: 48, Abū Dāwūd: 3748, Tirmidhī: 1968

«إِذَا رَأَى أَحَدُكُمُ الرُّؤْيَا يَكْرَهُهَا فَلْيَبْصُقْ عَنْ يَسَارِهِ ثَلَاثاً، وَلْيَسْتَعِذْ مِنَ الشَّيْطَانِ ثَلَاثاً، وَلْيَتَحَوَّلْ عَنْ جَنْبِهِ الَّذِيْ كَانَ عَلَيْهِ». (رواه مسلم)

Muḥammad ibn Sīrīn related: "Dreams are of three types: thoughts, fear instilled by Satan [in other words, because of his enmity towards man, Satan causes him to dream evil things in order to worry him], and glad tidings from Allāh." This was related by Bukhārī and Muslim.[486]

Jābir ؓ related that the Messenger of Allāh ﷺ said: "When any of you sees a bad dream, he should spit to his left three times, seek refuge from Satan three times, and change his sleeping position." This was related by Muslim.[487]

Commentary: Abstain from Paying Excessive Attention to Dreams
Many ignorant Sufis pay too much attention to their dreams. When there is a shortage of good dreams, they consider it to be a sign of distance from Allāh and therefore become disheartened and distressed. When they see good dreams, they consider it to be the height of accomplishment and grow proud. When they see an incident in a dream, they rely upon their vision implicitly. When they have a bad dream, they become caught up in its foreboding. This ḥadīth demonstrates the error of all these ideas, and also teaches the way to avoid the negative effects of bad dreams. In short, a dream is not as great as people make it out to be. The essential concern of a person should be to ask himself: When I am awake, am I acting in a way that will bring the pleasure of Allāh or His displeasure?

I like what the Persian poet had to say:

I am neither night nor night-worshipper who speaks of dreams.
 Like a slave of the sun, all I can talk about is the sunshine.

ḤADĪTH 329

عَنِ ابْنِ عَبَّاسٍ رَضِيَ اللهُ عَنْهُ مَرْفُوْعاً: «اذْكُرُوا الله ذِكْراً يَقُوْلُ الْمُنَافِقُوْنَ إِنَّكُمْ تَرَاؤُوْنَ». (رواه الطبراني كذا في الجامع)

Ibn ʿAbbās ؓ related that the Messenger of Allāh ﷺ said: "Be excessive in remembering Allāh to the extent that the hypocrites say you are showing off." This was related by Ṭabarānī.[488]

---

486 Bukhārī: 7017, Muslim: 2263, Tirmidhī: 2270
487 Muslim: 2261
488 At-Ṭabarānī has recorded this in his *al-Muʿjam al-Kabīr*: 12786 [12:131]

Commentary: The Ostentation of the Sheikh is Better than the Sincerity of the Murīd

This ḥadīth means that one should engage in excessive remembrance. It is obvious that one cannot conceal [his *dhikr*] if he engages in it excessively. And when he exposes it, his antagonists will definitely accuse him of ostentation. This ḥadīth commends such public display, and while the ignorant may consider it ostentation, it is not really ostentation. When something is commended, it is necessary for it to be good. Since good has some superiority in it, it also needs something over which it is superior [in other words, something that is inferior to it]. The inferior will be the opposite of the superior thing. In this case, the superior thing is ostentation in the special meaning it takes on in this particular context. The inferior will be the absence of ostentation. This absence of ostentation is also known as sincerity. It is therefore proved that some forms of ostentation are actually better than some forms of sincerity. It is established from external evidence that the display [of the spiritual master's deeds] has certain specific advantages. Based on this generality, it is established that ostentation on the part of the sheikh is better than sincerity on the part of the *murīd*. Understand this well.

ḤADĪTH 330

عَنْ أَبِيْ أُمَامَةَ رَضِيَ اللهُ عَنْهُ قَالَ مَرَّ النَّبِيُّ صَلَّى اللهُ عَلَيْهِ وَسَلَّمَ فِيْ يَوْمٍ شَدِيْدِ الْحَرِّ نَحْوَ بَقِيْعِ الْغَرْقَدِ، فَكَانَ النَّاسُ يَمْشُوْنَ خلفَهُ، فَلَمَّا سَمِعَ صَوْتَ النِّعَالِ وَقَرَ ذلِكَ فِيْ نَفْسِهِ فَجَلَسَ حَتّى قَدَّمَهُمْ أَمَامَهُ لِئَلاَّ يَقَعَ فِيْ نَفْسِهِ شَيْءٌ مِنَ الْكِبْرِ. (رواه ابن ماجة)

Abū Umāmah ﵁ related that the Messenger of Allāh ﷺ passed by Baqīʿ al-Gharqad [the graveyard of Madīna] on an intensely hot day and sensed that people were walking behind him. When he heard their footsteps, this weighed heavily upon him. He therefore sat down until all the people had passed him by. He did this to avoid the effects of pride settling on his heart [in other words, so that he may not feel proud that people chose to walk behind him]." This was related by Ibn Mājah.[489]

The Elders of the Path should Constantly Worry about their Personal Reformation

I end this book on the theme of this ḥadīth because it is appropriate for the end to contain a warning. This is done so that the warning will awaken the reader into emulating and practising the knowledge and deeds which this book con-

489 Ibn Mājah: 245

tains. Moreover, this is also in emulation of the Qur'an because the last verse to be revealed is this: "Fear the Day on which you will be returned to Allāh, and every soul shall be repaid in full for what it has earned, and none shall be wronged."[490]

I would like to say that a close study of this ḥadīth will open the eyes of any aspirant and, indeed, the eyes of any spiritual master as well. What is obvious here is the error of those who assume that they have attained some manner of spiritual perfection and therefore begin to neglect their own condition. It should be clear that when someone is raised to the status of spiritual master, they must not sit back and rest. Like the novice, they should pay particular attention to rectifying their deeds and constantly fear the reversal of their own condition. There is absolute good in this. Allāh ﷻ says: "None feel safe from Allāh's deep devising except the people who are already lost."[491] A Persian poet rightly said:

> Be careful where you step, even when following the caravan of mankind, for the stones in the desert will cut your feet.
> Yet, do not lose hope. A wine-drinking mendicant may without warning suddenly arrive at his destination.

O Allāh! Help us to remain steadfast with acceptance and kindness, in this world as on the day of Resurrection. Peace and blessings on the finest of His creation, Muhammad, and on his family and Companions.

490 Al-Qur'ān, 2:281
491 Al-Qur'ān, 7:99

Conclusion

All praise is due to Allāh ﷻ that this book, *A Sufi Study of Ḥadīth, Ḥaqīqat aṭ-Ṭarīqah*, which comprises ḥadīths dealing with the subject of *taṣawwuf* is now concluded. The subject of this volume is a vast one. However, since the purpose of this book was to convey to the reader the depth of the subject, and this amount should suffice as an example, I have written only this much; though I did write on a few subjects of revelance in a brief supplement to this book entitled: *an-Nukat ad-Daqīqah*.

All praise is due to Allāh at the beginning, in the end, internally and externally. Peace in Abundance to His Messenger, Muhammad ﷺ, his family and Companions ﷺ. This work was completed at the beginning of Rabīʿ al-Awwal 1327 AH (March, 1909).[492]

---

492 The work of translating this book into English, which began at the behest of my teacher, Maulānā Muḥammad Yūsūf Binnorī in 1975, was finally completed in November of 2009, *wa'l-Ḥamdu lillāh Ḥamdan Kathīran*. YTD.

Indices

INDEX OF GENERAL TERMS

S

INDEX OF SUFIC TERMS

INDEX OF NAMES AND PLACES

INDEX OF COMPANIONS AND FOLLOWERS

INDEX OF BOOK TITLES